J. M. Coetzee AND ETHICS

COLUMBIA UNIVERSITY PRESS   NEW YORK

J. M. Coetzee and Ethics

Philosophical Perspectives on Literature

EDITED BY
Anton Leist
& Peter Singer

Columbia University Press
Publishers Since 1893
New York   Chichester, West Sussex
Copyright © 2010 Columbia University Press
All rights reserved

Library of Congress Cataloging-in-Publication Data
J. M. Coetzee and ethics : philosophical perspectives on literature / edited by
Anton Leist and Peter Singer.
p. cm.
Includes bibliographical references and index.
ISBN 978-0-231-14840-5 (cloth : alk. paper)—ISBN 978-0-231-14841-2 (pbk. : alk. paper)—
ISBN 978-0-231-52024-9 (e-book)
1. Coetzee, J. M., 1940- —Criticism and interpretation.
2. Coetzee, J. M., 1940- —Ethics.   3. Coetzee, J. M., 1940- —Philosophy.
4. Philosophy in literature.   5. Literature—Philosophy.   I. Leist, Anton, 1947-
II. Singer, Peter, 1946-   III. Title.

PR9369.3C58Z73   2010
823'.914—dc22
2009043271

∞

Columbia University Press books are printed on permanent and durable acid-free paper.
This book is printed on paper with recycled content.
Printed in the United States of America

c 10 9 8 7 6 5 4 3 2 1
p 10 9 8 7 6 5 4 3 2

References to Internet Web sites (URLs) were accurate at the time of writing. Neither the author nor Columbia University Press is responsible for URLs that may have expired or changed since the manuscript was prepared.

Contents

1   *Introduction: Coetzee and Philosophy*
            Anton Leist and Peter Singer

Part I. People, Human Relationships, and Politics

19   1   The Paradoxes of Power in the Early Novels of J. M. Coetzee
            Robert Pippin
43   2   Disgrace, Desire, and the Dark Side of the New South Africa
            Adriaan van Heerden
65   3   Ethical Thought and the Problem of Communication: A Strategy for Reading *Diary of a Bad Year*
            Jonathan Lear
89   4   Torture and Collective Shame
            Jeff McMahan

Part II. Humans, Animals, and Morality

109   5   Converging Convictions: Coetzee and His Characters on Animals
            Karen Dawn and Peter Singer
119   6   Coetzee and Alternative Animal Ethics
            Elisa Aaltola
145   7   Writing the Lives of Animals
            Ido Geiger
171   8   Sympathy and Scapegoating in J. M. Coetzee
            Andy Lamey

Part III. Rationality and Human Lives

197	9	Against Society, Against History, Against Reason: Coetzee's Archaic Postmodernism
		Anton Leist
223	10	Coetzee's Critique of Reason
		Martin Woessner
249	11	J. M. Coetzee, Moral Thinker
		Alice Crary
269	12	Being True to Fact: Coetzee's Prose of the World
		Pieter Vermeulen

Part IV. Literature, Literary Style, and Philosophy

293	13	Truth and Love Together at Last: Style, Form, and Moral Vision in *Age of Iron*
		Samantha Vice
317	14	*The Lives of Animals* and the Form-Content Connection
		Jennifer Flynn
337	15	Irony and Belief in *Elizabeth Costello*
		Michael Funk Deckard and Ralph Palm
357	16	Coetzee's Hidden Polemic with Nietzsche
		Alena Dvorakova
385		*List of Contributors*
389		*Index*

J. M. Coetzee AND ETHICS

Introduction

Coetzee and Philosophy

Anton Leist and Peter Singer

PHILOSOPHY'S AWKWARD RELATION TO LITERATURE

Why should philosophers and writers, readers of philosophical literature and readers of the belles lettres, be interested in each other? In actual fact, they rarely are, but once in a while a philosopher strikes a chord with the readers of fine literature, and, vice versa, a writer of poetry or novels provokes philosophers to read him. John M. Coetzee is surely a candidate for this second category, and therefore motivates the questions asked in the present selection of essays. The fact that philosophers and writers have to confront each other to come into contact at all is something requiring explanation, however. The best explanation, perhaps, is a historical reminder pointing to the beginning of Western philosophy, as it illustrates the extent to which a certain distance between philosophy and literature is constitutive for philosophy. Plato, we should not forget, suggested banning artists from the ideal state. This distancing move, one among others, not only set philosophy on a path of development different from the writing of narratives about the gods and human lives, but also fixed part of the program that philosophy was meant to follow.

As a founder of Western philosophy, Plato demarcated the epistemological work done by philosophers from what other people do, especially from the work of artists seeking to influence politicians and religious believers. Plato valued philosophical reflection as a kind of pure truth seeking, a striving for pure knowledge. And a first step toward pointing out what pure knowledge could be was to distinguish it from the less pure and reflective thinking of more practically inclined contemporaries. Plato had Socrates—in the name of truth—fight against Protagoras and the other sophists, teachers of would-be politicians, and make clear to Euthyphro that even the gods depend upon the good, rather than the other way round. Under the stubborn probing and tweaking of Socrates, the knowledge to be had from politicians and their strategists, from religious believers and from the artists turned out not to be pure enough to be called knowledge at all. Or so Plato thought.

Against the background of such wide-scale deficiencies, knowledge received a new status and famously became the knowledge relevant to "a life worth living." To make things more complicated, it was not knowledge itself that received this elevated status but a new way of thinking that aimed at this knowledge, a thinking motivated and structured by the idea of this form of knowledge and devoted to the hows and ifs of this knowledge, a way of thinking focused more and more on the knowledge of knowledge, that is, to a new professional method called "philosophy." Throughout its movement into modernity, and to some extent right up to the present, philosophy has identified itself with this search for pure knowledge, even if its distance from religion has fluctuated and its demarcation from art has, since romanticism, shown signs of porosity.

By the time of the Enlightenment, philosophy had won its struggle to distinguish itself from religion by offering "nature" and "reason" as secular substitutes for a non-human God. Religion dropped out of the center of culture, and philosophy sought to take its place. This substitution project was successful, not least because of the ambiguity of "nature" and "reason." Both are humanistic concepts, but they also suggest, at least for formerly religious ears, a status beyond human beings. Socrates' teaching to Euthyphro had succeeded in giving priority to reason and knowledge and in downgrading religion, but to do so it had to upgrade reason and knowledge into something potentially transhuman. In addition, philosophy's situation became more complex during the Enlightenment when it took up two further tasks. On the one hand, it had aligned itself narrowly with the new natural sciences and therefore had to keep up with the rapid development of the scientific disciplines. On the other hand, it had assumed responsibility for organizing society on a rational basis and had to take up the task of translating former utopias into concrete politics.

With the beginning of the nineteenth century, however, three countermovements began to put this culturally dominant role of philosophy into perspective. In modified forms these movements—historicism, romanticism and materialism—still make themselves felt today, even if they are transfigured within more complicated scenarios. Historicists like Herder and Humboldt questioned the universal claims of enlightened knowledge by pointing out the relevance and plural existence of languages and cultures. Romantics like Schiller and Shelley called for individualized aesthetic education instead of a generalizing search for eternal knowledge. Materialists like La Mettrie or Feuerbach shifted attention away from philosophy and toward the empirical sciences, a process accelerated by the breakthrough of Darwin in biology. Each of these movements questions the Platonic program in its own way. Historicism seeks a developmental explanation of human knowledge, thereby ushering in a different model. Knowledge is now not granted by objective external states; instead, its sign is an improvement on earlier states. If Hegel tried to make good on this historicist challenge, romanticism saw in the diversity of ideas and the plurality of traditions forceful reasons to think of human imagination and the passions as being much more powerful than knowledge and reason. Romanticism substituted sensitivity for knowledge. Materialism, of course, contested the importance of both historical diversity and sensitivity, but it, too, voted for a fundamental change, suggesting natural science as the sole means of obtaining the master knowledge traditionally promised by philosophers.

Current philosophical endeavors can best be understood against the background of this scenario laid out in the nineteenth century. Philosophical interests and projects today are deeply impregnated by one of two conflicting attitudes toward philosophy's program of knowledge: should philosophy give more importance to the aim of gaining knowledge or to exploring noncognitive human characteristics? To put this in a simplified way, the group holding to the tradition of knowledge coincides largely with what is still called "analytic philosophy," while the group turning away from it divides into the "pragmatists" and the "postmodernists."

Analytic philosophers in the tradition of the Enlightenment follow a "conceptualist" or "naturalist" strategy to give an objective meaning to central concepts of knowledge, even if in part only in a "deflated" or minimalist manner. These philosophers vary in their relations to the sciences, but many of them sympathize with a naturalist approach and thereby follow a converging path with the natural sciences. What unites all analytic philosophers with natural scientists, surely, is the view that the history of a topic and its knowledge are clearly distinct.

Those philosophers who have given up on the knowledge program altogether are a more motley crew. Pragmatists and postmodernists are unified by the idea that knowledge is a purely social affair and that its normative claims of truth and rationality do not have to be given priority over other claims and aspirations. But they differ in their reasons for cutting back on the claims of knowledge, in their explanatory anthropological frame for knowledge, and, accordingly, in their idea of the tasks to which philosophy should devote itself, instead of pursuing knowledge. Pragmatists like Wittgenstein and Rorty see their function purely negatively: they want to rid philosophy of its traditional burdens and get rid of philosophy itself, more or less directly, making room instead for other practices, especially art and politics. Postmodernists in part share the critique of philosophy and the idea that philosophy and literature are on converging paths. But in addition they make use of further theories, partly philosophical, partly psychological or sociological, both in their argument against traditional philosophy and in their treatment of specific topics. Beginning with Nietzsche, postmodernists have also tried to synthesize historic descriptions and overviews with a new kind of explanation called "genealogy." Genealogies are intended to bring together genetic, historical reconstructions of a social phenomenon with a sociopsychological analysis of its present use. The repressive aspects of pity and compassion are made visible, for example, by reminding us of the minor role both had in ancient virtue ethics and how this role was and is related to the situation of socially weak and strong persons. Only through a strategic change in the meaning of the words "good" and "bad," in Nietzsche's famous explanation, did compassion become something positive. In earlier times, to be the object of compassion was so bad that compassion could not have been a virtue. Such a suggestion offers a new perspective on our present practice, something genealogy thinks to be more important than straight-out rational argument.

If philosophy today is perhaps more difficult to assess than at any previous point in time, this is because of the diversified positions that fall under the umbrella of postmodernism, the pending conflict between the postmodernists and pragmatists, and the even more open and sometimes more hostile conflict between the anti-knowledge camp and the analytic philosophers. Analytic philosophers see their opponents as proponents of skepticism and relativism, at best slightly modified. They regard these as positions that can be refuted simply by reminding their proponents of the meta-knowledge claims they themselves seem happy to make. As a second trump card, the more traditional philosophers also point to the potentially disastrous political consequences of discarding truth. Is not a naked power struggle the only thing left for those who give up on the friendly force of arguments, as illustrated early on by Socrates' adversaries, notably Thrasymachus and Callicles?

As far as the last move is concerned, the postmodernists claim that such conflicts are unavoidable because of powers working beneath civilized discourse. They add that pure truth seekers blind themselves to the illusory consequences of their epistemic obsession. To the reproach that their own claims about knowledge presuppose the possibility of objective truth, they answer that this objection is effective only against those who already accept the priority of knowledge, whereas those reconstructing human actions with different psychologies are not proper addressees of the classical arguments. This is, of course, either a confession that they are relativists about truth or a disavowal of interest in any kind of talk about what we can really know, including whether we can really know that relativism is true. Analytic philosophers are likely to see this as confirming their view that the postmodernist position cannot even be coherently put forward as a view about the way the world is.

Literature, as it may by now be clear, offers different things to different kinds of philosophers. Like philosophy, it comes in different sizes, styles, and positions. As we have just done in the case of philosophy, we can distinguish postmodern literature from what could be called classical and modern literature. In a manner not too far removed from Enlightenment philosophy, classical literature builds on ideas of realism, objective narrative points of view, and closed narratives, whereas modern literature, above all as manifested by Virginia Woolf, James Joyce, and T. S. Eliot, brings in the stream of consciousness and minute personal descriptions. Beside the relentless subjectivization of everything, techniques like parody, playfulness, surrealism, and Dadaistic experimentation turn the ideas of eternal truth, objective reality, and uncontested ideals on their heads.

The differentiation of postmodernism from modernism in literature was caused by a widespread reaction to the most atrocious events of World War II, the impression that no substantial part of Enlightenment optimism was able to withstand such unprecedented events as the Holocaust or the bombing of Hiroshima and Nagasaki. Beginning with such writers as Beckett, Kerouac, and Burroughs (though foreshadowed by Poe and Kafka), postmodern writers minimize the rational foundations that can be built on within a work of literature, though they usually refrain from directly attacking classical philosophical ideas. Beckett, for one, takes away from his figures the ability to discourse, to narrate a story, and to develop a character, or even to live a life that is recognizably human. Not being bound, as philosophers are, by the technical logic of their discipline to appeal to reason even when they criticize the rational itself, literary writers were able to transform the shock of a disrupted civilization much more rapidly and radically into verbal analogues of what had happened and was still happening. Writing therefore both runs ahead of philosophy and behind it; philosophy stays behind and, by following the same path in principle, prepares to perhaps move ahead on another occasion.

To sum this up, the contact between philosophers and writers can manifest itself in different discursive forms and therefore bring about potentially different outcomes. Philosophers who still favor the ideas of the Enlightenment see literature as a supplement to philosophy and the sciences, something to be made use of educationally and politically for an improved way of life. Literature's innovative power, its extension of the imagination, surely has an advantage within the nonrationalized (and nongeneralizable) parts of individual lives, within the nonrational pockets of the private. Aesthetics, for a Kantian like Habermas, has to remain largely private. At best it will indirectly feed its innovative offerings into the public discourse. With Kant, and beginning with the Kantian Schiller, aesthetics becomes pigeonholed alongside the cognitive and the moral as one of the three different layers of the world. Philosophers in this tradition do not think that literature could pull the carpet from under their feet as philosophers because for them literature, even in its most provocative creations, fails to penetrate the hard shell of rational concepts or serious argument. This goes for naturalist philosophers even more than for concept-bound ones, as their infatuation with the sciences fixes their interest more on the material basis of our existence than on the full experience of a human life.

The most readily apparent prospects for lively interaction are, one could think, those between the postmodernists on both sides, philosophy and literature. Thanks to literature's not being bound to a disciplinary matrix, philosophers in this constellation still have potentially more to learn from literature than vice versa. Literary works, on the other hand, may always be in danger of remaining idiosyncratic obsessions of particular writers; their transpersonal experience can easily be lost and remain forever hidden. It is less that philosophers have to translate particular literary texts into theory, whether epistemic, existential, moral, or what have you (something that will often be impossible), and more that they comment on what already fits into the public culture and what still awaits translation or what hopefully will never be so translated, for example, the inner perspective of those whose lives are devoted to terrorism or sadism. Philosophers and writers take upon themselves the task of reformulating the frame of our experiences. In undertaking this task, those optimally aware of what is unsuitable in our present language and ways of thinking, of what no longer fits present experiences or the conflicts of the day, have an edge.

We have said that the most lively contacts between philosophy and literature might be those between postmodern philosophers and writers. But this does not present the full picture of what is going on in philosophy and literature. It is the confrontation between the traditional and postmodern philosophers and, perhaps correspondingly, between modernist and postmodernist writing that is most enlightening for an analysis of our present situation. Progress could be made by a deepened understanding of what this split really means, why there is an urge to make the distinctions. New labels in culture politics are often a sign of hidden changes, the importance of which can only be seen later. Following these changes in literature can be enlightening for philosophers, just as it may be informative for literary writers to come to know of developments in philosophical discourse that are structurally similar to their writing. From this perspective, the work of John Coetzee seems especially promising both because he stands at a transitional point between modern and postmodern literature and because of the philosophical character of his writing. We will first try to be more explicit on the "philosophical" character of Coetzee's novels and then come back to the relationship of the modern and postmodern.

COETZEE'S PARADOXICAL OEUVRE

Which characteristics in Coetzee's novels make them "philosophical"? Three, at least, are prominent in most of his texts. First, an unusual degree of *reflectivity*, meaning thereby a reflective distance to the conventional understanding of everything, which expresses itself, strangely, through a normally rather sparse, sober, precise, restrained selection of words and descriptions. The impression of restraint delivers the message of an additional complexity hidden behind the open sentences. As in standard philosophical discourse, sparse but precise literary language suggests a field of contextual thinking and a selection of words and sentences out of others that were not deemed important enough. Calling Coetzee's texts unusually reflective matches well with the standard linguistic analysis of his texts as "allegorical," "perceptive," or "singularizing." Such an analysis refers to the way in which the texts reject most conventional value reactions. Instead, they move the reader to a level of elementary human experiences while taking away the usual armament of responses to these experiences. Coetzee's typical style of literalness throws the unprepared reader into an uneasy feeling of having been given clues to important meanings but being unable to decipher them.

In a sense this first, largely textual characteristic and technique is the by-product of a second, deeper-layered intellectual attitude of *paradoxical truth seeking*. Truth seeking may unavoidably involve one in paradoxes, but in a radically subjectivized truth orientation, similar to philosophical skepticism, such paradoxes are without end. (Philosophical skepticism is only one version of this truth seeking.) What is meant by "paradox" and "paradoxical truth seeking" can be explained best by two axioms valid for Coetzee: the belief that "truth" most relevantly is the truth of "truth-fullness" and that truth-fullness is the engagement in a never-ending spiral movement that at no point leads to "full" truth. Truth seeking must be, according to this position, paradoxical because there is always a counterargument to an argument, a second story to a first, another description to a given one. Lest total skepticism set in, truth is to be substituted by the subjective attempt to search for truth, the engagement in relevant work, and usage of adequate language.[1] Let it be said at this point that what distinguishes paradoxical literature from philosophical literature is the latter's need to dissolve the paradox and not work with or through it (Hegel being the rare exception to this need). Paradoxical philosophy ends in Pyrrhonic skepticism; paradoxical literature ends in confessions and expressive subjectivization, in living through the attitude of criticism and self-criticism.

The textual trademarks mentioned as a first characteristic of Coetzee's writing, especially allegory or alienation of the well known, are but the flipside of this paradoxical truth seeking. Readers feel uneasy once the authorial normative guidance is drawn away and frequently feel angry at being offered only vague hints of how to begin a treatment of the problem at hand: how to situate oneself in relation to elementary questions of life and living. Michael (*Life and Times of Michael K*) receives an urn with the remains of his mother, delivered to the hospital by him not so long ago. Surely a difficult moment, but we are not given Michael's attitude towards it.

Lucy (*Disgrace*) decides to give in to the degrading offer by Petrus to become his third wife. We are not given her own view on the decision.

Given textual reflectivity and paradoxical truth seeking it goes without saying that topics of existential importance constitute the content of Coetzee's novels. Nevertheless, it is an *ethics of social relationships* that is especially at the thematic center of most of his stories. In contrast to what is understood by this in the work of most contemporary Anglo-Saxon (as distinct from French) moral philosophers, the writer's eye concerning personal relationships is not fixed on "values" or "rights" but is attentive to the social and psychological mechanisms structuring relationships. As Coetzee is observing people under the most socially extreme circumstances of racism and civil war, this approach embraces, albeit unintentionally, the moral philosopher's endeavor to find the most secure grounding of morality or civil society. A basis of morality or civil society that works under conditions of civil war will work in friendlier times as well—as Hobbes knew. This association with Hobbes also suggests a personal explanation as to why ethics lies at the bottom of most of Coetzee's writings. Both men were acquainted with periods of civil war, in Coetzee's case the thirty-five-year history of the Afrikaner Apartheid regime, the imprint of which on his thoughts and feelings as a child is self-critically reconstructed in *Boyhood*. It takes Coetzee most of his writer's life to struggle out of that repressive social culture and to bring its scale and complexity to the fore. To achieve such a thing using the means available to a writer unavoidably seems to go hand in hand with a phenomenological ethics of the other, something Coetzee's novels have been, and still are, working at.

Coetzee's findings from his literary research in the complex field of the normatively unmediated—the "other" stripped free of conventions—are diverse, however, and, as we might expect, conflicted. When the three characteristics of reflectivity, truth seeking, and an ethics of the social come together, questions of priority immediately arise. Reflectivity, as in classical philosophy, can become an outstanding and isolated ideal because the skeptical distance to the commonly accepted verities that it involves may also invite neglect of the practical circumstances of life. Truth seeking can involve a character with his own mind to such an extent that he drops out of the social world altogether. Social immediacy can dissolve the single individual within collectives, or it can lead to a speechless acceptance of social phenomena, the existence and claims of other beings. All three characteristics are typically philosophical ones, including their self-destructive excesses if pushed to such limits. In philosophy, an Aristotelian wisdom of the ordinary or the practical interest in things helps one out of these impasses. In literature, the coherence of stories and the plausibility of characters permits, in principle, a much more differentiated grasp of the same qualities. Literary characters must go to the limit, but not beyond. Like transcendental arguments in philosophy, they must radiate their status of being extreme but at the same time must be able to shed some light on the less extreme and its relation to the extreme. Coetzee's novels are populated with characters of this kind, and they provide ample material for what it means when characters go near to the limit.

Coetzee's treatment of a specific character can be taken as the prime example of such a dialectics of the margin: the character of Coetzee himself. *Boyhood* and *Youth*, the two autobiographical novels, show the author in search of himself through the emotional reconstruction of his former selves. The younger child is seen in his immersion in a repressive South African culture, the young man living as a literary student and computer specialist in London is accompanied on his self-absorbed migration through a series of personal and emotional affairs. In both cases events are narrated without the knowledge of hindsight, or an objective view of either present societal standards or more advanced experience. Episodes of cruelty against, but also caused by the child are narrated without comment and follow only the writer's strategy to narrate intensive occasions for shame. Shame is taken as the most significant index of personal involvement, and Coetzee's self-description follows the imperative of approaches to shameful truths, truths that are authorized by being shameful.[2] Later motives and attitudes develop slowly and on the basis of a nearly imperceptible impetus on the side of the individual. Children and adolescents per se are figures of transition, casting light on the normality of the adult world. Young Coetzee calls into question large parts of this world and, in typical manner, sets the reader on a voyage to find a skyhook point of his own.

If there is a development in Coetzee's work it is most definitely within the third of the three characteristics mentioned, his ethics of social immediacy. This ethics turns into a gradually deeper and more nuanced affair, beginning from, especially, *Age of Iron*. Mrs. Curren, the novel's central figure, narrates the last months of her life in a lengthy letter to be sent to her daughter after her death, meant both as an intensive renewal of their relationship and as a bequest. Given the situation, the homeless and personally impenetrable Mr. Vercueil seems to be the only person at hand to be entrusted with the task of delivering the letter. The choice is a difficult or even impossible one, as the homeless person is also the person to be trusted least, the one most easily shirking trust himself. The novel states a case for the necessity of trust, even toward those who seem beyond trust.

Trust, however constitutive it may be for social life, rests on irrational decision, and Mrs. Curren opts for trust. Coetzee's later novels elaborate on this shaky element of trust or pro-decisions both in the direction of making visible the contingency of our control of such decisions and their outcomes and the contingency of our being on the positive side of such decisions. *Disgrace* sheds some light on the restriction of human intentions and strivings by making use of the quasi-religious idea of "grace," a state of well-being that is not under the control of the actor but has to fall upon him. At the same time and connected with the encompassing terminology, "disgrace," the state of having fallen out of all recognition, asks for more than small corrections and learning steps, it asks for a deep personal purgatory. The novel develops the steps within the process of such a purgation undergone by its main character, David Lurie. Purgation comes, in the end, through the creative reception of music and the awareness of the importance of animal lives, especially through their decent treatment in dying and on the occasion of the disposal of their carcasses. Both attitudes, an awareness of the dependency of luck upon something other, something impersonal, and an awareness of our deep relationship with animals, go hand in hand in the novel.

Elizabeth Costello, the selection of episodic stories of an elderly writer of the same name, expands on this strong importance of human attitudes toward animals, notoriously comparing animal butchery on a mass scale with the Holocaust. Again, in both *Disgrace* and *Elizabeth Costello*, the extension of human awareness to include animals is urged not by rational argument but by immediate acquaintance with animal suffering. The poet's imaginative identification with animals is suggested as sufficient proof for the ethical inclusion of other beings, lifting animals up to eye level with humans. Of course, the implicit and explicit criticism of human "rationalism," by both Costello and Coetzee, as partially interested and morally blind asks for explicit reconstructions, more reasoned defense, or criticism. Is such a notion of grace, and its opposite, disgrace, at all possible on a secular basis? Is Costello's literary pathocentrism different from the more well-known philosophical ones? Is it one that philosophers can follow only by giving up most of their tradition? Has it to remain personal, or is it publicly and politically relevant?

As said earlier, human reflectivity and truth seeking imply some instability of human experiences and truths, and signs of this tendency, openly admitted or even explicitly stated, also surface against the background of Coetzee's deepened ethics. Coetzee's own most explicit gesture toward the possibly deep connection between creativity and amoralism is made at the end of *The Master of Petersburg*. This novel gives us a view of the personally dramatic period of a historical writer, Fyodor Dostoevsky, shortly before his breakthrough to writing a new novel that later became known as *The Possessed*. To create something new, the writer has to surpass his present restrictions and, in the style of a Nietzschean "overcoming," the breakthrough succeeds through the writer's identification with an amoral figure in the novel to be written. Movement into the new narration starts by going through possibly the most evil deed this figure, Stavrogin, is capable of. The point of view from which human creativity sets out, thus the book's overall message, can also be one of merciless neutral contingency, the fully humanly disinterested perspective that reduces the movement of glaciers and the rolling tears of children to the same size. The

Dostoevsky figure in the novel surely comes close to his own limit of imagination, indeed, has to in order to find a way with his new novel. The outlook he brings with him is not one of ethical immediacy but rather one from an ahuman world, even if not fully unreal for humans.

Taking the point of view of the suffering animal and reducing humans to suffering animals, as *Elizabeth Costello* does, is not a stable position, either. First of all, it is only one among several positions illustrated by different people in the book. Costello's siding with the animals against the philosophers and scientists is shown not to rely on "rational argument." Instead, the aptness of rational argument itself is questioned. Granted the appropriateness of argument, a sound argument would be forceful. But to those skeptical toward the premises, an argument is only another human instrument, with the same typical flaws and problematic side effects as other human instruments. Emotional identification with the animals seems as restricted (even if a bit less so) as rational distancing from them, and the first overall effect of Costello's attack is one of general puzzlement. No clear positive ethics underlies the stories involving Costello. In a sense, Coetzee lays all the options before the readers and suggests that they make their own choices. The effect of all the references to animal suffering is relativized by the show of bottomlessness of all the other moral positions involved.

Perhaps not least because of this irritating experience of the experimental openness of some of Coetzee's texts, a number of literary critics and philosophers have searched for something more fundamental and have tried to read him as suggesting a "metaphysics of the other."[3] According to this reading, situations of speechless confrontation with other beings, human or nonhuman, are meant to present a reality of the other that is normally closed up by our conscious intentionality, not to speak of our rational endeavors, which always are, implicitly or explicitly, hostile toward the other being. According to this view, human immediacy would be both the only possible source for a social world and a moral paradigm of noninstrumental relations with the others. Strong skepticism toward human rationality leads to the discovery of social bonds, of both a psychological and a normative nature, that are constitutively important for every individual and often visible only through the destructive nature of their absence. Coetzee, then, is read as working out, by remarks like Costello's about trying to walk "flank to flank, beside the beast that is prodded down the chute to his executioner," phenomenological pieces of a metaphysics of the social. Stripped of all active intentionality and being one with the other, man, animal, or nature, an ethics of care is meant to follow. There is a development in the later novels of Coetzee, some think, toward such a metaphysical position.

This double reading of Coetzee throws some light on the more general problem of where to place him within the modernism/postmodernism schism, and on this distinction itself. "Modernism" and "postmodernism" carry, as we have mentioned, different, even if somehow related meanings in philosophical and literary discourses. Within literary discourse more narrowly conceived, these concepts signal different content if taken at the level of technique or theory, New Criticism and poststructuralism standing for postmodernism. Even if applied on such different levels of concreteness, the modernism/postmodernism distinction still identifies modernism with self-questioning and the replacement of traditional verities by authentic new ones and identifies postmodernism with a worldview that has been further developed. The distinction is, of course, extremely slippery and not very helpful even if terminologically widespread, at least among literary and cultural scholars. What motivates the distinction is the impression that there is a "new worldview," that modernism somehow changed its character through being applied to itself and that its central concepts lost the role they had earlier and thereby lost their meaning. Whether this is the case depends, of course, on what one thinks concepts such as "nature," "reason," and "truth" in philosophy and "subjectivity" or "authenticity" in literary theory are meant to cover essentially. Philosophy being the paradigmatic foundational discipline, this is easier to say for it. The quality of modern philosophy changes significantly if it is accepted that its central epistemic concepts do not carry any specific essential content with them, and the same might perhaps be extended to literary theory and then to literature. If "reason" is to be substituted by "intelligence" understood particularistically and contextually, or if "truth" is to be substituted by "justification," "agreement," or "consensus," then philosophy's claim to rational guidance gives way to a plurality of alternative understandings. The content of philosophy and literature, then, begins making this change and its consequences its central topic. Debates about Nietzsche or Derrida in philosophy are of this sort, but unavoidably they always include also what modernism was or is about and to what extent it can or should be surpassed. The distinction is a slippery one, therefore, because the very situation undermines all attempts to make epochal distinctions.

There are different opinions on what can be changed in our modern worldview and what has to be kept, and the two possible readings of Coetzee correspond with this difference. Some, the pragmatists mentioned earlier, think that nearly everything can be intellectually given up without putting our everyday civilized practices in danger. What was called the experimental reading of Coetzee would harmonize with this position. According to this reading, figures like Michael K, David Lurie, and Elizabeth Costello make an impression on us deep enough to be able to bring their way of seeing things into our own experience. We have, for example, a different sense of animals after listening to Costello's taking the perspective of one of Köhler's intelligent apes. It is, of course, left open what follows practically from this extension of imagination, as the changes of view in part are too extreme to be realized by most readers and also are reflectively weakened by the perspective of opposite characters or the counterpoints that the same figure makes. In contrast to her passion for the animals, Costello in the later stories of the collection displays her loss of belief in the novel ("The Novel in Africa"), claiming even its dangerousness ("The Problem of Evil"), as she already in the first "lesson" had given up hope for realism ("Realism"). Nevertheless, there is the slightly positive answer to the judges in a Kafka-like scenario, when she opts for piecemeal advance: "Her mind, when it is truly itself, appears to pass from one belief to the next, pausing, balancing, then moving on" ("At the Gate"). As with some of Coetzee's other figures, Lucy or Mrs. Curren, this is not much, or hardly anything, but at least more than nothing.

One might begin to admire this minimal offer by Coetzee after a more sober look at the problems of a metaphysical reading of his texts. According to the metaphysical reading of Coetzee, there is not an endless series of possibly deep impressions made by literary figures on us but one specific metaphysical "point of contact" with "reality" that provides for necessary reasons and a forcing into the direction of growing moral sensitivity, moral awareness, empathy with the animals, and so on. Perhaps not Coetzee himself but some of his readers and admirers see a development in the later work toward an ethics of suffering as a kind of metaphysics, evoked by descriptions like the one referred to, in which suffering is an underlying element of reality in which all sentient beings participate. It goes without saying that these critics, being sufficiently critical of traditional metaphysics, would not identify their reading with this term, but nevertheless the terminology they use and the illustrations to which they refer can hardly be categorized otherwise. Criticism of modernism is always in danger of falling back from the positive insights it has achieved, and the linguistic form of our human intelligence is not something to be forgotten in enthusiasm about the more primitive social existence of others.

Whatever position in philosophy one takes, an awareness of how literature responds to the external pressures put on the mental format of our modern Western tradition has an extremely liberating effect on philosophy's internal self-control and, in part, self-restriction. Philosophy tends to involve its students in foundational projects instead of opening their view to more practical problems of the real world—although applied ethics and political philosophy are often exceptions. Literature is frequently a more natural and more human way of expressing oneself. In the hands of great artists, it portrays our most elementary experiences. Other art forms may also do this, but literature is the most verbally explicit of the arts and therefore always the ultimate medium in which to be critical toward something, including philosophy, and to orient ourselves in the world. Ethics, and applied ethics especially, is helped by the literary imagination, if it confronts the conflicting forces visible in different philosophical positions as well as in our everyday culture. Coetzee's literary work is exemplary in this sense, as he himself is driven by the different tendencies and alternatives that are liberated when modernism is put on trial. Not least among these is the attempt to find pieces of transcendental philosophy in literature, which again shows both the problem faced by philosophy and the advantage of literature. To shift the puzzles of philosophical reflection into literature could be at least a first step towards tackling them in a more realistic and practical manner. It could yield insights hard to come by in the usual academic style of philosophical work.

THIS COLLECTION

If we hope that these remarks illuminate our trust in the innovative potential of cooperation and confrontation between philosophy and literature, it is this volume's contributions that in the end have to prove us right. Unsurprisingly, the ethics of animals looms large in this collection, but in fruitful reaction to the intellectual and artistic breadth and depth of Coetzee's work, the essays herein cover a multitude of other topics: the psychological and moral phenomenology of personal relationships; the consequences of human suffering, evildoing, and death for human rationality and reason; and the literary methods invoked to open areas of experience beyond the abstract language of philosophers. Within the four fields of debate introduced here, something new is going on, something at least missing in more traditional philosophical symposia and perhaps also in less reflective immersions into literature. The essays that follow show the folly of Plato's idea that literature has nothing to contribute to philosophical discussion. Instead, they are an invitation to a dialogue that can sharpen the issues that literature raises while making philosophy more imaginative.

Notes

1. Coetzee refers to this via Paul de Man's critical stylistic analysis of J. J. Rousseau's *Confessions*: "Confession and Double Thoughts: Tolstoy, Rousseau, Dostoevsky," in *Doubling the Point: Essays and Interviews*, ed. D. Attwell (Cambridge, Mass.: Harvard University Press, 1992), 251–93.
2. This and other illuminating statements are taken from the excellent study on Coetzee by D. Attridge, *J. M. Coetzee and the Ethics of Reading* (Chicago: University of Chicago Press, 2004), 147. In stressing the ethical side of Coetzee, Attridge's Derrida-inspired and richly detailed discussion of Coetzee's books helped enormously to summarize the books' major thrust, as attempted in this introduction, despite, or perhaps even because of, his slightly metaphysical reading of Coetzee's ethics.

3. Attridge's study belongs in this category, as does M. Marais, "Little Enough, Less Than Little: Nothing: Ethics, Engagement, and Change in the Fiction of J. M. Coetzee," *Modern Fiction Studies* 46, no. 1 (2000): 159–82; Marais, "Death and the Space of the Response to the Other in J. M. Coetzee's *Master of Petersburg*," in *J. M. Coetzee and the Idea of the Public Intellectual*, ed. J. Poyner (Athens: Ohio University Press, 2005), 83–99; "J. M. Coetzee's *Disgrace* and the Task of the Imagination," *Journal of Modern Literature* 29, no. 2 (2006): 75–93; D. Chesney, "Towards an Ethics of Silence: Michael K," *Criticism* 49, no. 3 (2007): 307–25. See also articles in this volume, especially those by Vermeulen and Vice.

Part One

People, Human Relationships, and Politics

1

The Paradoxes of Power in the Early Novels of J. M. Coetzee

Robert Pippin

Quiconque est maître ne peut être libre; et règner, c'est obéir.
—Montaigne, *Lettres*

POLITICAL PHILOSOPHY AND POLITICAL ACTUALITY

Any human social world is obviously finite, limited in resources and space, and it comprises agents whose pursuit of individual ends unavoidably must limit what others would otherwise be able to do, often directly conflicting with such other pursuits. This situation forces the issue of power: who will be subject to whose will, who will subject whom. But these individual agents are finite as well, unable to achieve most of their ends without forms of cooperation and dependence. The biology of human development insures a profound familial dependence throughout childhood, and the variety and breadth of the distribution of human talent and the frailty and vulnerability of human life all insure that various forms of social dependence will be impossible to avoid. So it has long been acknowledged that a human society is both deeply conflictual and competitive, as well as necessarily cooperative and communal.[1] Our nature ensures a constant tension between a self-regarding desire for independence and freedom from subjection to the will of other self-regarding agents, as well as a powerful need to achieve some stable form of dependence and relative trust. The major, though not at all exclusive, arena where solutions to this basic problem are proposed and tried out is commonly known as the political.

Even if we presuppose a great deal of agreement at some time within some community about the proper form of the political (already a great idealization), we cannot ever be sure of the trustworthy compliance of everyone with the basic rules and procedures. So all political life involves the use of violence and the coercive threat of violence by one group of people against another. The claim that there *is* such a thing as political life amounts to the claim that, while there is such violence and coercion, its exercise is legitimate, that power may be justifiably exercised over those who may in fact resist such an exercise. Those, like Marx and Nietzsche, who reject the idea that there really is such a thing as politics, deny this claim and so argue that what some call political power is just a disguised version of the exercise of violence by one group against another or by one "type" against another. According to some versions of such a critique, like Alexandre Kojève's, there never are rulers and subjects, representatives and citizens, never even "human beings" as such. Until the final bloody revolution ensures classlessness, there are always and everywhere only masters and slaves, those who subject the will of others to their own, and those whose will is subject to the will of others.[2]

Those who defend the claim to the legitimacy of politics argue in familiar ways. An ancient claim is that no true human excellence may be achieved without hierarchical relations of power, that without such coercive constraint, the baser instincts of human beings would reign and nothing worthwhile could be collectively achieved. Such baser passions, it is claimed, are not subject to persuasion or argument, and there are some human beings in whom such passions are paramount. These people (sometimes said to be most people) must be constrained "from above" just as any one individual's passions must be ruled, rather than allowed to rule. The appeal to this sort of argument in the project of European colonialism (and the long history of male exercise of power over "naturally inferior" or "emotional" or "irrational" women) has understandably made it difficult for any such possible claim to be entertained now without the suspicion that it must be an apology for the brute exercise of self-interested power, masquerading in the form of such an argument. In "postcolonialism," we are much more suspicious that anyone is ever free of such putatively tyrannical passions, and so "the natural rulers" always present the same danger as the "naturally ruled," or that what looks base and nearly inhuman to one might look perfectly fine to another.

One might argue that everyone would simply be better off under some system of political rule, perhaps better off with respect to necessary common goods that no one could reasonably reject; perhaps better off merely by avoiding a state of such anarchy that no sane person could reasonably prefer it. Those inclined to think this way often think that even if there are a few who are very, very much better off, a coercive use of violence to preserve such an order is acceptable if everyone is at least better off than they would be otherwise. This kind of argument has its colonial echoes too. ("Yes, we got fabulously wealthy, but we 'gave' them the gift of English, or French schools, or developed industrial societies. Think how much better off they are.")[3] Or one might argue that what appears coercion really isn't, that *inuria non fit volenti* and everyone can be presumed to have reasonably consented to such an arrangement or would consent if they were rational agents. On an extension of this approach one could argue that the use of force to protect basic human rights is not only permissible but required, that no claim for the existence of such rights would be coherent unless measures, even violent and coercive measures, could be taken to protect and enforce them. There is no loss of freedom when one is constrained from doing what one may not do or is compelled to do what is a universal and rational obligation.

This is all familiar and proceeds as classical and modern political philosophies always have: by assuming that the question of the legitimacy (or the goodness or value) of some form of rule involves a search for a rationale, an argument, a demonstration by force of the better case in favor of some arrangement of power and against some others, all in the service of resolving the original tension noted at the outset. But I have sketched this set of issues in its abstract form in order to stress that these familiar ways of looking at the issue *are* abstract. In order for philosophy to get a grip on the core problem of dependence and independence, a great abstraction must be made from, let us say, the complex psychological stake that individuals have in achieving and maintaining independence and the ways they come to care about and understand their varieties of mutual dependence. Of course some of this might inevitably have something to do with what can be rationally defended, justified without reliance on particular interest or bias. We can certainly come to care about such a standard a great deal and base a great deal on it. But there is no a priori reason to think that such a consideration always and everywhere trumps other ways of mattering, other stakes and investments, and there is no reason to think that we could ever agree on what counts as the actualization of such a standard. Its persuasive trump power might be illusory, might stem simply from its abstractness. To add to the problem, these different ways of caring and kinds of investments vary a great deal across different communities and across historical epochs.

And all of this makes philosophical abstraction both understandable and problematic. One wants some view of the resolution of this tension or problem that can be *shared*, and there is no reason to believe that one's particular investment or the way things happen to matter to one (or to one's group) will or can be shared. The assumption of a rational standpoint, entertaining considerations that rely on no particular point of view, would appear the only way to proceed.

But this comes at a high price. Since no one actually occupies such a rational standpoint (it is artificial, a fiction for the sake of argument), it is unclear what it can effect for finite, concrete agents. We cannot simply assume that, no matter their particular attachments and investments (parents, children, group, status, the motherland, God) they can be assumed to care *more* about what reason demands: the greatest good for the greatest number, what form of law is consistent with pure practical reason, the supreme importance of avoiding the state of nature, what they must be assumed to have consented to, and so forth. None of these considerations have any obvious or inherent psychological actuality, and it seems absurd to wave away such concerns with actuality as a matter of mere "irrationality" that cannot concern philosophers. That approach threatens to turn political philosophy into a mere game, operating under initial abstraction conditions so extreme that they allow no actual role other than as "ideals" that we might hope to approach asymptotically, if even that. Indeed, an insistence on the putative purity of such ideal considerations—the claim that the philosophical cogency of an argument form is one, wholly distinct thing, its possible application in a colonial project another—is just what inspires suspicions that the argument form itself is mere "ideology."[4] What can be said about such a situation?

THE POLITICAL ACTUALITY OF POWER AND COETZEE'S FIRST THREE NOVELS

Hegel is the most prominent philosopher to argue that "philosophy is its own time comprehended in thought," and he argued for this with an elaborate theory about the necessarily historical and experiential content of normative principles and ideals, especially, in his own historical period, the ideal of a free life. His insistence that philosophy must attend to the actuality of the norms it considers is quite controversial and is often accused of accommodating the status quo, forming a "might makes right" theory of history, and abandoning philosophy's critical and reflective task. This is no place to begin to consider such a theory. I mention it only to introduce one important aspect of Hegel's attempt to understand and come to terms with what a norm or ideal has come to mean, how it has come to matter as experienced by subjects who avow it, that is, his appeal in his 1807 *Phenomenology of Spirit* to Sophocles, Goethe, Jacobi, and Schiller, to the literature of an age, as necessary moments of human self-knowledge about themselves and what they value.[5] He does not treat such literature as examples of an ideal or moral commitment or general norm but as criterial aspects of just *what it could be* to espouse or avow such a value or, more important in his account, for such a value to lose its grip on its adherents (something that rarely happens because of any dawning realization about the force of any better argument).

Although his novels are more informed by philosophy, especially by the work of Hegel and Nietzsche and Buber, and by a wide array of literary theory and criticism than those of anyone now writing, and although is it not clear whether his texts are novels or allegories or fables or parables or more generally just "fictions," J. M. Coetzee is obviously not a political philosopher and novels in general do not in any normal sense express or defend *claims* about modern political life. Characters in novels are aesthetic constructs, and we "get to know them" in a way that is extraordinarily restricted and controlled, all in a context whose main values are aesthetic. And Coetzee's novels are complex modernist objects: verisimilitude is not the point, and the relation between text and psychological person, narrative and event, is complex, dense, and often problematic. But almost all his novels,[6] and certainly the first three, take place in a recognizable historical world charged with explicitly political tension, profound dissension, and violent exercises of power justified by transparently self-serving or self-deceived appeals to reason or fact: the prosecution of the Vietnam war and the eighteenth century "exploration" and colonization of Africa (*Dusklands*); a colonizer's life in the country and the relations of power between whites and blacks, men and women, colonizer and colonized (*In the Heart of the Country*); and a magistrate administering an outpost at the edges of empire and beginning to disintegrate psychologically under the realization of what he represents, with what he is unavoidably complicit, forced into such a realization by his intense relation with a young "barbarian" girl (*Waiting for the Barbarians*). Indeed, his first novels seem deliberately designed as an extended historical series on colonial political power and its psychological meaning, charting something like the experience or, one might say, the psychological truth of the imperial exercise of power in its founding moments: a moment of European moral exhaustion or ending, a Gotterdammerung, a land at dusk in *Dusklands*;[7] in the "heart" of the colonial experience of the eighteenth and nineteenth (and perhaps twentieth) centuries (*In the Heart of the Country*);[8] at the moment of empire's disintegration, potential revolution, and loss of faith in itself (*Waiting for the Barbarians*); and in the historical chaos of civil war in some distant future (*The Life and Times of Michael K*). After this series the novels all have a more determinate historical place and time, although there are obviously mythological and allegorical connections with the first series of books. (There is London in the eighteenth century for *Foe*, Capetown in the 1980s for *Age of Iron*, Petersburg in the nineteenth century for *The Master of Petersburg*, Capetown and its provinces in the late 1990s for *Disgrace*, and contemporary settings all over the world for the Elizabeth Costello stories and those that have followed.)

In the spirit of the above remarks about the importance of finding a way to understand the "actuality"—experiential, psychological, and historical—of various ideals and norms, especially political ones, especially the tension and so the need to find some equipoise between the desire for some sort of independence and the deep dependencies among human beings, and with the somewhat fanciful suggestion of Hegel as a model, I want to suggest that Coetzee's novels represent unique, brilliant attempts at a kind of political self-knowledge. The subject of the exploration is the psychological actuality of power, especially the exercise of power over another and even over nature and oneself, and the question asked is not directly about the legitimacy or overall defensibility of such an exercise, at least in the standard philosophical sense. For one thing, the issue of power is always tied to a deeper one in the novels. In modern philosophy we typically link the question of the possibility of agency or subjectivity itself with the exercise of power, either a causal power of initiating bodily movements ("spontaneity") or the general power to achieve one's ends in a world constrained by others' pursuits.[9] So the issue is not limited to a question of politics (of power exercised in the name of the common, the public, the state), although the core problem is the one discussed in the first section here: the right way to understand the relation between independence in a political or constrained, finite context (and so some sense that the life I lead is *my own*), and dependence, something like the proper acknowledgement of such dependence, without mere strategic compromises and certainly without subjection and conformism. These issues are approached in an unusual and extremely rich way by means of a trope or figure that is common in Coetzee's work.

The early novels are, to a large degree, concerned with forms of physical and psychological disintegration. This disintegration in physical and mental illness is in turn clearly linked with a Hegelian theme that Coetzee, in several interviews and essays, terms "reciprocity" or, more exactly, the failure of reciprocity; in explicitly Hegelian terms, the failure to achieve any mutuality of recognition and so the perpetuation of relations of mastery and servitude in some form (including in relations to nature and to oneself). The exercise of power in situations without reciprocity, situations of gross inequality, is clearly understood to be connected with a kind of illness or suffering that burdens the "master" in Coetzee's presentation of various versions of Hegel's famous "Lord and Bondsman" dialectic. The suggestion, or whatever one wants to call it—what we are clearly supposed to appreciate—is that such an exercise of unequal power is in some way difficult to sustain psychologically, difficult at least with the smallest dawning of some self-consciousness, escapable only with elaborate self-deceit or labored, deliberate ignorance. Eugene Dawn, trying to write a report about psychological warfare in Vietnam, goes mad and even injures his own beloved son. Jacobus Coetzee in the second half of *Dusklands*, even in his ignorance and willful blindness, becomes deathly ill and dependent on "one whom he does not recognize as a recognizer," one could say in Hegelese, his servant, Klawer. Magda in *In the Heart of the Country* begins as the spinster daughter of a brute colonial farmer. She loses that role and must establish a new one with the black servant Hendriks, and, in some way because she cannot establish anything reciprocal (neither can he, for that matter), she disintegrates into delusional madness. And the Magistrate in *Waiting for the Barbarians* loses hold of his own position and role once he is caught between, on the one hand, the dawning realization, provoked by the visiting brutal Colonel Joll, of just what empire he is administering, and, on the other, by his being erotically and, one might say, morally captivated by a tortured barbarian girl. And so he begins to suffer a confusion and disorientation that finally places him well on the other side of the representatives of power he had once been part of, finally suffering as their tortured victim.

Coetzee is often termed a bleak, uncompromisingly dystopian novelist who belongs with Beckett, Musil, Kafka, and other modernist, experimental writers, and in a literary sense, this is obviously the case (although it needs to be immediately qualified). Or he is considered a stern moralist, contemptuous and dismissive of the failings of meat eaters and the compromising, bet-hedging bourgeoisie (far too crude a characterization). But these repeated moments of disintegration suggest something about the internally *self*-defeating exercise of unequal power that is not a moralistic critique but an "internal" one, one that does not presuppose at all a settled moral position brought to bear on the characters from an independent or external point of view. And the suggestion that there is a form of suffering, perhaps (eventually) existentially unsustainable, or that there is a form of self-disintegrating suffering, is a much more complicated view than these characterizations would suggest.[10] This is all certainly linked to similar themes in modernist and postmodernist writing, especially in opposition to the pretense of autonomous subjectivity and authorial independence and related assumptions about the transparency and referentiality of language and the possibility of narrative and so the nature of historical time. In Coetzee, however, these issues are not driven by reflections on language itself, by evocations about the power of the unconscious, or by skepticism about referentiality or even meaning but by a link between a kind of political and a kind of psychological breakdown or failure, a failure that has to imply a possible if limited recovery and success. In some way, it is (in that contemporary modernist and postmodernist context) an unusual expression of hope. At any rate, this is what I would like to understand in what follows.

THE FANTASY OF POWER: *DUSKLANDS*

Dusklands begins with an epigraph, a quotation from Herman Kahn taken from an actual report written in 1968 by the Hudson Institute, a discussion by several authors, including Kahn, called *Can We Win in Vietnam? The American Dilemma*.

Kahn noted the understandable revulsion with which European and American audiences had reacted to scenes of American pilots "exhilarated" by their success in napalm bombing runs, but Kahn then coolly pointed out that "it is unreasonable to expect the U.S. government to obtain pilots who are so appalled by the damage they may be doing that they cannot carry out their missions or become excessively depressed or guilt-ridden." The words "unreasonable" and "excessive" stand out in this attempt to adopt some sort of wholly analytic or objective attitude toward the moral issues involved, as if those issues could be discussed from some wholly third person and exclusively strategic point of view. *Dusklands* itself is a parody of such a stance and related attitudes, a parody of the presumptions of such a scientific analysis, and, in the second half, a parody of the pretensions of documentary history, of the way first-person reportage comes to be incorporated in what pretends to be the objective historical record. (Kahn's "argument" is almost a parody of itself, as if an argument for the need to hire only sociopaths as pilots.) Both pretensions are also clearly intended to be connected with the kind of general stance or attitude that could make possible the project of a modern neocolonial war like Vietnam, or the original British and Dutch subjection and colonization of South Africa. Presenting the two documents together in one book, with no explanation or connection between them, suggests both a kind of mythic, repetitive, or circular time (as opposed to any linear or progressive history) and thereby an underlying, perhaps archetypal psychological pattern implicated in the extreme violence manifest in both accounts.

That stance, to return to the set of issues I have introduced, is the presumption of mastery, self-sufficiency, or autonomy, and the two aspects of this attitude of interest here are the kind of difficulties encountered in sustaining that stance and what such a failure implies about some redemption or reconciliation, and ultimately a world of genuine reciprocity. Eugene Dawn has been assigned to write an assessment of the psychological aspects of the U.S. propaganda campaign in the war, and it is the writing of the report that seems to drive him mad. We read in the first half Eugene Dawn's report itself in numbered sections in part 2, but the majority of what we read are his scattered, disjointed remarks about the act of writing it, his understanding of what it is to try to provide an account of the mythological meaning of the propaganda war, and eventually what led him to give up on such a project. (Given all the self-thematization of writing itself, one understandably sometimes hears Coetzee's fiction characterized as "metafiction.") Dawn's supervisor is a man named Coetzee, a expert in game theory whom Dawn mistrusts, and with reason.[11] We learn later that Coetzee deleted and destroyed Dawn's reflections on mythology. Dawn argues that the "self" embodied in U.S. propaganda has been too much a "Cartesian" self, divided against itself, skeptical and self-doubting, too rational, too distanced from itself. He proposes an approach more in tune with traditional Vietnamese folk society, a division of labor in which our Vietnamese allies adopt a "fraternal" role, and we a "paternal" or sky-god voice, striking fear into the rebellious band of sons according to the basic script provided by the (not named) Freudian account in *Totem and Taboo*.

But Dawn realizes that such a posture is also self-defeating. "For one thing, the myth of rebellion has a no-surrender clause. Punishment for falling into a father's hands is to be eaten alive or penned eternally in a volcano" (25). The myth, that is, hardly encourages surrender or compromise. But, more importantly, Dawn comes to realize that the whole notion of a mythic approach to propaganda presupposes a stance toward the world and others that "history" has already "outdated":

> The myth of rebellion assumes that heaven and earth, father and mother, live in symbiosis. Neither can exist alone. If the father is overthrown, there must be a new father, new rebellion, endless violence, while no matter how deep her treachery toward her mate, the mother may not be annihilated. The scheming of mothers and sons is thus endless. (26)

Dawn goes on to suggest that it is this presumption of symbiosis (or the acknowledgment of any form of deep dependence) that has become outdated, that "we live no longer by tilling the earth but by devouring her and her waste products" (26). Given that this is so, "When the earth conspires incestuously with her sons should our recourse not be to the goddess of *techne* who springs from our brains?" (26). So Dawn loses any sense that his report and the approach it embodies any longer make any sense; his text in part 2 in effect deconstructs itself. It is a useless "Phase IV." The *next* phase is all that matters and we should get on with it, Phase V, total victory, an open and merciless bombing campaign (perhaps what was famously known at the time as Curtis LeMay's plan—that we bomb the Vietnamese "back into the stone age"), defeating at once both the enemy and the pretense that there is or can be any great question of the "meaning" of what is being done.

The suggestion of a voracious, devouring predatory subject, flattening any question about meaning and value into the questions of human survival, comfort, and the power to effect one's will echoes with Horkheimer and Adorno's *Dialectic of Enlightenment* and its charge that the Enlightenment attempt to reject myth has turned into its own unreflective myth of absolute self-sufficient power and the total negation of nature, with Marcuse's analysis in *One-Dimensionsal Man*, and, of course, with Heidegger's attempt to show that the late-modern reliance on technology does not just create technical problems and is not the mere application of a tool but has fundamentally altered our sense of ourselves, our sense of Being itself, so that we have come to live comfortably with a thoughtlessness and forgetfulness so complete it may become final and unredeemable. But as noted throughout, the interesting twist on these issues given by Coetzee is what the embodiment of such a stance comes to mean psychologically for Eugene Dawn.

Dawn comes to understand what the war reveals about "who we have become" as that stance is embodied in three horrific photographs of abuse and violence against Vietnamese people that he carries around with him almost as totems. His realization of his part in it all, even as he (like Kurtz in *The Heart of Darkness*) begins encouraging a war of complete annihilation ("Kill them all!"), drives him mad. His paranoia grows; he kidnaps his own son, and when tracked down and confronted by the authorities, impulsively stabs his boy and is captured and confined to a mental hospital. There Dawn adopts a kind of therapeutic, almost third-personal attitude about what he has done, and, while generally agreeing with his therapists that it wasn't "him" who stabbed his son and rejecting any guilt, he remains baffled by what he has done. He ends by saying "I have high hopes of finding whose fault I am" (49).

Clearly Coetzee is associating the political, national subjection of others both with classical mythological meaning (even as Dawn is coming to reject the relevance of this association) and with modern strategic calculations of self-interest, but he is also suggesting that there is something qualitatively different and potentially more inhumane and blind to itself in modern assertions of imperial power. For one thing, such a modern exercise seems associated with a much broader assertion of absolute mastery over oneself and over nature, a presumption that is wholly unchecked by any modesty or humility; it is associated with a worldview, or a form of life itself. At this level of meaning, the concern is not beliefs or principles but a broad, pervasive, and much deeper prereflective orientation that is difficult to view as a whole. For Dawn and the people he works for, in a postmetaphysical or scientific age all that is "other" than the self and human will is merely stuff, obstacle, material, chaos, and dangerous contingency to be mastered. There is pure will and obstacles to the realization of will, and that is all. Potential patterns of meaning and perhaps purpose arise only as possibly strategically useful illusions in a propaganda war, and even in that sense are pronounced "outdated." The allegorical dimensions of Dawn's fate at the end, as a kind of culmination of such a way of being-in-the-world, embodies our own fate: self-reflection and self-knowledge severely limited to a kind of inquiry into causes, as if *we* don't do anything but are mere elements in a causal series. And even with such a reduction and flattening, we get no real answers. We are "doing" all this over historical time *to ourselves*—destroying or injuring, like Eugene, our own children, in effect, as well as ourselves and the earth—and we have no idea why. Given what we have come to think counts as genuine knowledge—predictability and control—and the unsuitability of such a model for self-knowledge, this is no surprise.[12]

So such independence and autonomy is bought at a high price. We end up with the same sort of stupefied wonder as Eugene in the end, wondering if we can ever discover "whose fault we are." One thinks of Nietzsche's "last men," who have invented happiness and merely "blink" in a similar state of stupefaction.

The question of self-knowledge is foregrounded by a number of literary details that have been much discussed. The document itself is supposed to be the product of Eugene's reflections, his attempt at self-knowledge, and its paranoid, chaotic form is in some way connected with the profoundly monologic character of his voice, a stance that itself embodies the insistence on mastery and control typical of both the prosecution of the war, the larger "metaphysical" (for want of a better word) theme of human subjectivity itself (as, essentially, effective power), and the controlling, unyielding voice of Dawn himself. Dawn recounts few dialogues; nothing "gets through" his own projections and fantasies. His musings about his wife, Marilyn, give us no sense at all of her except as an object of his fantasy and paranoia. The question of who is the "real" author of the document, what role his supervisor "Coetzee" might have played in its current form, what it means for Eugene to worry about "getting it past Coetzee," and the relation of all this to the historical author, J. M. Coetzee, further warn us, at the least, not to take any representation of self-knowledge and self-mastery at face value, even the relation between author and his creations.

This ambiguity is extended in the novel's second half in the flurry of "Coetzee's" we have to disentangle, given the four documents that make up the texts concerning Jacobus Coetzee's so-called explorations in the eighteenth century.[13] Self-opacity or self-blindness is not the only implication of the modern conception of subjectivity; the second half of *Dusklands* deals with another. The main document is the narrative written by Jacobus Coetzee of his trip deep into the "land of the great Namaqua." This recounts Coetzee's "detention" of sorts (as he sees it)[14] by Namaquas he calls "Hottentots"; the desertion of some of his crew; his illness, delirium, and slow recovery, during which he is taken care of by his oldest servant, Klawer; their journey back, during which Klawer is killed; and then a horrific second journey of revenge when Coetzee returns and massacres his former tormentors. The voice that we hear in this narrative is full of arrogance, racism, self-satisfaction, and phony, self-deceived humanistic concern for his servant, and a nearly mad sense of his own significance and fury at perceived slights. And the unreliability of the narrative is again stressed. Coetzee narrates incidents, the death of Klawer, for example, that are then contradicted by others, such as Klawer's reappearance in the narrative only to die again, all of which makes us wonder what, if anything, "really" did happen to Klawer. But there is one point at which another implication of this picture of predatory subjectivity is stressed.

Jacobus Coetzee becomes lyrically articulate about just this issue. He imagines himself a modern, separate, spectatorial master subject, and then by an internal poetic logic, imagines what that means.

> I become a spherical reflecting eye moving through the wilderness and ingesting it. Destroyer of the wilderness, I move through the land cutting a devouring path from horizon to horizon. There is nothing from which my eye turns, I am all that I see. Such loneliness! Not a stone, not a bush, not a wretched provident ant that is not comprehended in this traveling sphere. What is there that is not me? I am a transparent sac with a black core full of images and a gun.
>
> (79)

Coetzee eventually calls this the "metaphysics" of the gun: a subject conceived not as an embodied, desiring, vulnerable, and especially dependent being but a supreme eye, a transparent sac, its world locked away inside it as a core of images, a Cartesian subject locked up inside itself and therefore unable to reassure itself about its claims about the world or its position in the world without a violent assault on nature and others to realize its mere ideas. Colonialism is seen as the extension of this idea of the self-sufficient and masterful self, and its assertion (since the acknowledgement of dependence is rejected) can only count as successful by this test of power. But in the human or, as I am using the word, psychological dimension, this project must result, above all, in a position necessarily and irredeemably *lonely*: trapped by being so successful in denying and negating all dependence-making otherness that the voice of such a subject becomes not just monological but monomaniacal, the modern voice still echoing with Descartes's original promise to make us "masters and possessors of nature," to create technical power that will "enable us to enjoy without any trouble the fruits of the earth,"[15] and so reversing by technical power the fate decreed for human beings in Genesis, that they must forever toil by the sweat of their brow (3:19). The burden of such a project is not just the epistemological skepticism and potential subjective idealism of this Cartesian stance but a cost perhaps only manifest in a novel like Coetzee's, a cost realized by Jacobus in a flash: "Such loneliness!"

A FAILED SELF: *IN THE HEART OF THE COUNTRY*

Extreme loneliness, extreme to the point of being a kind of ontological burden, the burden of a *failed self* (the way we speak now of a failed state), is most prominent in

Magda's suffering in *In the Heart of the Country*. That is, a human subject can continue to exist in some form but only as failed, not what a self or state truly is. In the former case, this is because a self is not on object in the standard sense and cannot be apprehended by observation or introspection. To be a self, I must take myself to be who I am in some determinate way or other. And *I am* who I take myself to be. A self is thus self-constituting. But this also means, in the most obvious sense, that I can take myself to be some subject in a way that is not acknowledged, affirmed, or perhaps even noticed in my social world, and in that sense would have to be counted a failed self, living a mere fantasy of self-identity. Without such reciprocal gestures as acknowledgment, love, esteem, solidarity, and respect, I cannot distinguish between who I really am and who I merely imagine myself to be. And this is the language of failure and reciprocity that Coetzee himself frequently uses in his essays and some speeches.[16]

So Magda says at one point, "Drowning, I drown into myself" (54). And the result: "For I seem to exist more and more intermittently. Whole hours, whole afternoons go missing. I seem to have grown impatient with the sluggish flow of time" (80). The form of the suffering and its meaning are often given a recognizably Hegelian characterization. It is a burden brought on by the lack or reciprocity or any mutuality of recognition. She says, "I was born into a language of hierarchy, of distance and perspective. It was my father tongue. I do not say it is the language my heart wants to speak, I feel too much the pathos of its distances, but it is all we have" (97). The striking phrase, "the pathos of its distance," is from Nietzsche's *On the Genealogy of Morals* and suggests in quite a compressed way something that only arises indirectly in Nietzsche's account of and apparent enthusiasm for "master morality."[17] It is the isolation and loneliness, the complete lack of reassurance and acknowledgment, that results from the master's indifference to those whom his willing affects. (Nietzsche's frequent, though not thematized, expressions of his own loneliness certainly have something to do with such a pathos, whether knowingly or not.) Magda, the only child of a coarse colonial farmer at an isolated farm,[18] says at the beginning, "I create myself in the words that create me, I, who living among the downcast have never beheld myself in the equal regard of another's eye, have never held another in the equal regard of mine" (8). Elsewhere she says, "It is not speech that makes man man, but the speech of others" (126).

The dense dialectical first phrase in the first quotation, "I create myself in the words that create me," poses an ontological problem (what is it to be a self, a subject of one's life, an agent?) that is immediately given a quite modern, romantic meaning ("I create myself") and then a social dimension in the rest of the sentence and the book, as if proposing a social ontology. The self fashions itself and is also itself fashioned in a social world.[19] Such a subject is never the pure or absolute subject dreamt of in much of modernity, autonomously decreeing what its word and actions mean. It is dependent not just on the social conventions of language but on the various ways meaning and significance are always already established and inherited, and all this without mere subjection to the regard of others. (In that case we would lose the first half of the phrase, would lose any grip on the notion of "creating myself." As we shall see, in Magda's world, there is no effective social structure within which this balance can be worked out, and the forms of mastery and even, with Hendriks, her attempts [or imagined attempts] at abject subjection that she acts out are therefore deeply unsatisfying.) Such mutuality would allow me to see myself in the regard of another if and only if I regard that other as an equal. And this kind of language reappears several times. In a frequent image (one we already have seen in Jacobus Coetzee's account) a disembodied eye, *seeing but not being seen*, not allowing oneself to be seen, is often tied to Magda's extreme "solitude and vacancy" (47); her relation to their servants is such that they might as well be on "separate planets" (28). The solitude and sense of isolation is so extreme that it counts as itself a form of insanity. She says at one point, "Too much misery, too much solitude, makes of one an animal. I am losing all human perspective" (53). And the social pathology of what she calls "the psychology of masters" (33) is described in terms that sound like a quotation from Hegel's famous discussion of Lord and Bondsman in his *Phenomenology of Spirit*. Magda writes, supposedly of what she hears spoken by the sky gods in aircraft at the end of the book,

> *It is the slave's consciousness that constitutes the master's certainty of his own truth. But the slave's consciousness is a dependent consciousness. So the master is not sure of the truth of his autonomy. His truth lies in an inessential consciousness and its inessential acts.*[20]

(130; italics in the original)

In the Heart of the Country is also the novel with the most elaborate modernist structure and so the most unreliable and often confusing narration. The diary or journal or whatever we are reading is in numbered paragraphs, emphasizing, Coetzee once noted, what is *missing*, discontinuous, in the narration.[21] The suggestion of gaps, that there is no way to make a narrative out of what we are reading, is only the beginning.[22] I noted earlier that it is difficult to pick an actual historical time for the events, since we seem to range from horse and buggy days to the airplane, perhaps even the jet age. Or at least Magda cannot locate herself. Her sense of her historical time seems dreamy, often fantastic. And the narrative is most untrustworthy. Her father is described bringing home a bride. But there is no bride. Magda describes how she axe-murders her father. Then he shows up again and she kills him again, this time with a rifle, to some extent accidentally. The father dies a slow, agonizing death. Hendrik either rapes her several times or one time imagined different ways or the whole thing is an archetypal colonial fantasy of Magda's. Suddenly Magda reports, "The voices speak to me out of machines that fly in the sky. They speak to me in Spanish" (126). And Magda arranges stones in messages, trying to communicate in Spanish, a language she does not understand but finds "immediately comprehensible" (126). Finally, at the end of the book, in paragraph 161, her father seems to reappear, infirm, blind, and old, cared for by Magda with some tenderness. The reader has no idea if this is some compensatory fantasy, or if it is true and Magda has only imagined the affair between her father and Hendrik's wife, imagined killing her father and the rape by Hendrik.

Such unreliability has sparked a lot of discussion about Coetzee's postmodernism and the relation between postmodernism and postcolonialism. This involves a number of large distinctions and labels. I need here to point out only that the unreliability of the narration is not tied in any obvious way to the unreliability of narration itself, but to *Magda's* position. It is *her* voice that is fractured, discontinuous, increasingly unsure of her own reality or of the distinction between reality and fantasy in what she narrates. Having lost confidence in any master narration, she has lost hold of all the norms for rendering intelligible what is happening to her. There is no alternative known to her to the language of power and domination, although she is suffering from the isolation and loneliness that such a "pathos of distance" creates and knows she is suffering from just that. (She resembles the Magistrate at the end of *Waiting for the Barbarians*, "like a man who lost his way long ago but presses on along a road that may lead nowhere" [152].)

This crisis has occurred because to purport to narrate is to claim some sort of authority for the selection of and emphasis on the details one includes and for the claimed irrelevance of what one slights or ignores. And such implied claims to authority raise the same normative and psychological questions as colonial authority itself and can often be deeply linked with that sort of authority. (Recall Magda's complaint about being born into a *language* of hierarchy and distance.) Authority differs from mere power not simply by virtue of the fact that a philosophical argument can be provided justifying its exercise. It also has to have a psychological legitimacy in the eyes of those who administer and accept it, and the minimum condition for that sort of authority is missing in colonial power: some sort of reciprocity, without which no acknowledgment of genuine authority and so no psychological actuality can be possible. Absent that distinction, the claim to genuine authority is empty (compliance is forced not given, and coerced acknowledgment is not acknowledgment), and the one who exercises power sees himself reflected back to himself as other than what he takes himself to be. One might argue that there has been evidence for a long time in human history that such a situation is hardly "unendurable," that there are plenty who have endured it easily. Dawn's supervisor, Coetzee, Magda's father, and Colonel Joll do not seem racked with doubt about their authority. But one can pay a price without acknowledging it, and the sterility and unacknowledged loneliness of such lives count as a high price indeed.

It would be the start of a broad additional discussion to bring these issues to bear on the question of how the question of putative or claimed authority and its true actualization plays out in the stance of J. M. Coetzee himself, the real historical author of all this, and his audience. But one suggestion would be to see the issue as an extension of this discussion. That is, Coetzee's complex presentation of the problem of his own authorship or even control over the meaning of his creation could be understood outside of what has become a fairly standard "postmodernist" way: as dissolving into mere play, toying with its own impossibility, finally being about only itself, not what it purports to be about, and revealing, if that is the right word, only the impossibility of revelation.[23] That is, the issue could be treated in the same way I have been treating Dawn's and Magda's self-narration. The problem with any form of confident assertions of authorial authority could be viewed much more historically and contextually, as a dilemma forced on us by the fractured and unreciprocal context of the writing itself and not "by writing" itself. (Modernism is a historical fate; not a literary and artistic experiment.) The incompleteness and gaps in the text would then be viewed as merely provisional, and much more like an invitation for completion by the work of the reader, completing what the isolation and loneliness caused by this arrangement of power has left hanging and unresolved. But, as noted, that is a much larger issue.[24]

In this context, Magda has some intimation of what it would be not to rely on such authority, on mere power, but no sense of how to realize that aspiration. (As we shall see in the next section, it is perhaps naïve to think that such a recalibration of the struggle for recognition can be effected by individual moral gestures.) She tells Klein-Anna (Hendrik's young wife and the girl Magda's father compels to be his mistress), "I only wanted to talk, I have never learned to talk with another person. It has always been that the word has come down to me and I have passed it on. I have never known words of true exchange, Anna" (101). And the consequence of this:

> I find her head and press my lips against her forehead. For a moment she struggles, then stiffens and endures me. We lie together, at odds, I waiting for her to fall asleep. She waiting for me to go.

I grope my way out of the kitchen to my own bed. I am doing my best in this unfamiliar world of touch.

(103)

In spite of this confusion and awkwardness, Magda nevertheless has some fairly clear intuition of what would fill the gap in her life that she has come to experience: "Why will no one speak to me in the true language of the heart? The medium, the median—that is what I wanted to be! Neither master nor slave, neither parent nor child, but the bridge between, so that in me the contraries should be reconciled!" (133).

THE MEANING OF HUMANITY: *WAITING FOR THE BARBARIANS*

There is one last turn of this screw much in play in *Waiting for the Barbarians*, and I will conclude briefly just by noting the questions it raises.

The presence of the themes I have been considering is announced right away by the visiting Colonel Joll's sunglasses. We meet him immediately as a man who insists on seeing but in effect rejects being seen as a like-minded other. He hides his eyes, whereas the young barbarian girl is almost blind; she can be seen but can barely see, cannot return any gaze, even if the gaze is an invitation, not an attempted subjection. That is, Joll's one-sided stance is voluntary; hers is not. She has been made blind and lame by torture. At the end of the novel, after Joll's expedition results in catastrophic failure and his pretension to pure independent agency has been shattered, the sunglasses are gone, and the Magistrate forces on him the lesson of internal disintegration or self-undermining familiar in the other novels. "The crime that is latent in us we must inflict on ourselves . . . not on others" (143). We also hear again of Nietzsche's "pathos of distance," this time, in ways the Magistrate feels but does not understand, distorting and diminishing his sexual pleasure with women (45). And that disturbance, the consequences of that distance, are at the heart of what goes on between him and the girl.

For the Magistrate is clearly moved, touched by the girl's suffering, and clearly guilty at being part of the official apparatus of the empire that did this to her. He takes the girl in, and that is clearly intended to begin some act of expiation and penance. He washes the girl, cleans her feet, anoints her with oil, and sleeps with her, but they do not have sex. All this is not completely straightforward. He claims to want to understand her, to "decipher" what the marks of torture on her body mean, much as he tried to decipher what appear to be texts on slips of paper that he has found from an ancient barbarian culture. But he "reads" her *that* way, as a text. He thinks of himself as loving her (74), but he makes no attempt to learn her language, to converse with her as a fellow subject. So his humanist intervention is a limited and confused one, and accordingly his failure to "reach" her cannot be simply read as an indictment of all liberal, humanist, moral gestures in the face of such oppression. But the frustrating limitations of such gestures (and the danger of self-congratulation in making them) are certainly at issue.

Of course, he does return her to her lands and countrymen, and this has catastrophic results for the Magistrate. He is branded a traitor and mercilessly tortured. But he never seems to understand what he actually intended with the girl and so does not understand why it all ended so unsatisfyingly for him, what his history with her amounted to. He does not seem to realize, except confusingly and in disconnected flashes, that in the world they inhabit, even gestures of pity and benevolence are inseparable from the relevant social positions both occupy and so are inseparably implicated in the relations of power firmly established in that world. A moment of such realization occurs when the girl, puzzled that the older man seems to have no sexual interest in her, offers herself, and is rebuffed. The Magistrate writes,

> Though my heart goes out to her, *there is nothing I can do*. Yet what humiliation for her! She cannot even leave the apartment without tottering and fumbling while she dresses. *She is as much a prisoner now as ever before*. I pat her hand and sink deeper into gloom.
> (54, my emphasis)

Later, the Magistrate does not appear surprised when a confidante of the young girl reports to him, "She could not understand you. She did not know what you wanted from her.... Sometimes she would cry and cry and cry. You made her very unhappy. Did you know that?" (148).

And as with the other novels, this is not an issue that can be restricted to the question of the proper realization of political and institutionally secured egalitarianism, however relevant it is to that issue and however important philosophical argument about that issue is. There is a deeper form of dependence at work, and a different way of exploring its meaning in Coetzee's novels. The issue has to do with how the possibility of individual, independent agency in itself, how *that* social status, can be actualized, made psychologically and socially real in the lives of finite subjects faced with the basic dilemma sketched at the beginning here. In the Magistrate's terms, the very "meaning of humanity" is the issue, and the Magistrate comes to realize in his own limited way how such a status must be socially achieved and sustained and how terribly fragile it is. It is not a status one has merely by "showing up, and the complexity of the conditions for its achievement (the dialectical relation between independence and dependence) are everywhere apparent in these novels. Here are his reflections on the issue, and it will serve to indicate in one final way the great scope of this recognitional theme in Coetzee's work. It is a fitting closing comment on the deepest issue in the three early novels: the "meaning of humanity":

> They [his torturers] were interested only in demonstrating to me what it meant to live in a body, as a body, a body which can entertain notions of justice only as long as it is whole and well, which very soon forgets them when its head is gripped and a pipe is pushed down its gullet and pints of salt water are poured into it till it coughs and retches and flails and voids itself. They did not come to force the story out of me of what I had said to the barbarians and what the barbarians had said to me. So I had no chance to throw the high-sounding words I had ready in their faces. They came to my cell to show me the meaning of humanity, and in the space of an hour they showed me a great deal. (113)

Notes

1. The thought expressed in this chapter's epigraph is not unique to Montaigne, nor to Hegel, for that matter. Compare: "Tel se croit le maître des autres, qui ne laisse pas d'être plus esclave qu'eux" (J. J. Rousseau, *Du contract social*, in *Oeuvres completes*, vol. 3 [Paris: Gallimard, 1964], 353). And of course J. M. Coetzee: "In a society of masters and slaves, no one is free" ("Jerusalem Prize Acceptance Speech," in *Doubling the Point*, 96).
2. A. Kojève, *Introduction to the Reading of Hegel*, trans. J. H. Nichols Jr., ed. A. Bloom (New York: Basic Books, 1969).
3. Even at the end of his horrific ideal, the Magistrate in *Waiting for the Barbarians* can still rehearse for himself this sort of justification. See his remarks on "mulberry jam, bread and gooseberry jam" (151).
4. Cf. The self-understanding of Eugene Dawn (the representative of American self-understanding about the Vietnam war) in *Dusklands*: "I am the embodiment of the patient struggle of the intellect against blood and anarchy" (27). Or, in the second half, the "explorer" and elephant hunter Jabobus Coetzee: "I am a tool in the hands of history" (106). As Coetzee points out in another context (an interview), it is an important, not a marginal fact that "British liberalism failed to engender equal and reciprocal relations, period—failed to persuade the colonists, British or Dutch, that equal and reciprocal relations were a good enough thing to make sacrifices for" (Coetzeee, "Interview," in *Doubling the Point*, 62). Again, one could always insist that the philosophical merits of "British liberalism" as a position have nothing at all to do with the fact that sincere adherents

to such a view could espouse it while "contradicting" it in their colonizing practices. That seems to me an implausible position, but I won't try to argue against it here. One could sum up one central aspect of the problem in Magda's lament in *In the Heart of the Country*: "I am gagging on a diet of universals" (131).

5. G. W. F. Hegel, *Phenomenology of Spirit*, trans. A. V. Miller (Oxford: Clarendon Press, 1977).

6. I'll use this designation throughout, *faute de mieux*.

7. The "New Life" project, a Vietnam report, in the novel's first half is being written by Eugene Dawn, suggesting by contrast with the novel's title (and the standard characterization of the West as an evening land, *Abendland*) a pretense at a new beginning, dawn not dusk, or essentially the promise of technological, capitalist modernity. Cf. Dawn's remark about "poignant regret" (6).

8. The time frame of the narrative in *In the Heart of the Country* is difficult to pin down. It seems, fantastically, to range from an early-modern farming economy to the age of airplanes.

9. David Atwell's study, *J. M. Coetzee: South Africa and the Politics of Writing* (Berkeley: University of California Press, 1993) focuses helpfully on the question of agency, especially in the South African political context. There is another take on the issue in Coetzee's later novels (*Slow Man* and *Diary of a Bad Year*): how to understand agency or subjectivity when the capacities or powers of agency begin to decline and erode, in late middle age and afterward (or when the balance between independence and dependence tips, but for nonpolitical, biological reasons.)

10. So, with respect to the moral issue he has lately been most associated with, our treatment of animals, Cotezee's modernist sensibilities require him to attend to the way this treatment is written and thought about, how it is theorized, mediated through language and experience. So Coetzee does not give lectures about animal rights, but tells Elizabeth Costello's stories/fables. (*The Lives of Animals* is, somewhat ironically, all about *our* lives; *we* are the animals at issue, given what we do to other animals.) So, again, the concern is for what such treatment is doing to us, and it would be grossly inaccurate to read his fables about such themes as moral tracts, simply presented in a narrative way. The same holds for the political novels.

11. This Coetzee is one of four in *Dusklands*. There is also Jacobus Coetzee, the eighteenth-century elephant hunter whose report of his adventures is the main text of the second half. (Jacobus is in fact a "remote ancestor" of the historical author, I mean, *the real* J. M. Coetzee. See "Remembering Texas," in *Doubling the Point*, 52.) Then there is Dr. S. J. Coetzee, who is said to have published an edition and introduction of that *relaas* in 1951, and his son, named as "J. M. Coetzee," who presents himself as the translator of that edition. I suppose one has to say that there are five Coetzees, if we make the obvious distinction between *this* character, J. M. Coetzee, and J. M. Coetzee, the actual historical novelist

12. who taught at the Committee on Social Thought in Chicago and who lives now in Adelaide. The names introduce issues of inheritance, complicity, and the historicity of an author that would require a substantial independent discussion.

12. From the agent's point of view, any "prediction" I make about what I will do is either an avowal, a practical pledge that I will do it (in which case it is not a prediction), or it has to count as a paradoxical (and usually cowardly and self-deceived) denial of one's own agency, something one can only do qua agent. This is obviously another large, independent topic.

13. There is (1) the text presented as written by Jacobus Coetzee. That text is presented as if (2) in an edition by Dr. S. J. Coetzee, published in 1951, with an introduction by him, and now (3) in a translation done by Dr. S. J. Coetzee's son, who is called J. M. Coetzee. And (4) there is a ludicrously sanitized "official" deposition by Jacobus Coetzee written in 1760.

14. Perhaps the ultimate humiliation of Jacobus, in his narcissistic fantasies of mastery, is that the Namaquas do not torment or torture or take much advantage of him. For the most part, to his unacknowledged shame, they ignore him. Or at least they do until Jacobus does something outrageous, almost as if to make his presence felt. He bites off the ear of a child during a tussle, and so they expel him. Jacobus's self-absorption is as extreme as Dawn's, but more physically embodied. He becomes intensely preoccupied with a carbuncle near his anus until he is able to lance it. See the Lacanian discussion by T. Dovey, *The Novels of J. M. Coetzee: Lacanian Allegories* (Johannesburg: A. D. Donker, 1988), 67–148.

15. R. Descartes, *The Discourse on Method*, in *The Philosophical Works of Descartes*, vol. 1, trans. E. S. Haldane and G. R. T. Ross (Cambridge: Cambridge University Press, 1965), 119.

16. This is the language (the failure of selfhood) used by Coetzee in his essay on Achterberg in *Doubling the Point*. Here is a particularly illuminating passage: "The hide-and-seek *I* in Sterne has become a serious game, with dangers to the psyche, in Eliot's 'Love Song of J. Alfred Prufrock.' What has intervened has been the rise and decline of the romantic-liberal notion of the self. The self in Eliot is struggling with problems of authentic being. The self in Beckett is struggling with problems of being at all, unable to get from Descartes's *cogito* to Descartes's *sum*. I hint so skimpily at an entire history because I intend no more than to point to what lies behind the metamorphosis of fiction from the adventures of the self in nineteenth-century classical realism to the metafictional commentary on the fictionality of self that precipitates such fictions as Nabokov's *Pale Fire* and Barth's *Lost in the Funhouse* and that forms the whole of Beckett's *The Unnamable*. The poetics of these works is a veritable poetics of failure, a program for constructing artifacts out of an endlessly regressive, etiolated self-consciousness lost in the labyrinth of language and endlessly failing to erect itself into autonomy" (86–87). I think *In the Heart of the Country* and the character of Magda represent such a "poetics of failure," in just this sense, with the difference being that such failure is intelligible in terms of what might have been;

that is, in terms of what Coetzee refers to as "reciprocity." See also his Jerusalem Prize speech: "At the heart of the unfreedom of the hereditary masters of South Africa is a failure of love" (97).

17. Nietzsche, *On the Genealogy of Morals*, first essay, section 2.
18. On the conventions of the South African farm novel and its relevance to the setting of *In the Heart of the Country*, see Coetzee's essay, "Farm Novel and Plaasroman," in *White Writing*, and the interesting discussion in Dominic Head, *J. M. Coetzee* (Cambridge: Cambridge University Press, 1997), 59.
19. In *Doubling the Point*, see Coetzee's essay, "Achterberg's 'Ballade van de gasfitter,'" and his remark in the commentary, "All versions of the *I* are fictions of the *I*. The primal *I* is not recoverable" (75). One might argue that if these versions are *fictions*, there must be something, some *I*, they are false *to*. But the denial of any "primal *I*" means that what gives a fictive *I* a kind of stability, what redeems it from mere fictionality, is its *future*, not a relation to a past primal *I*, and that future is its engagement with and acknowledgment by, and so realization by, others. See also the remarks on Buber and the I-Thou relation on the previous page, 74, and the illuminating discussion by Atwell, *J. M. Coetzee*, 35–69.
20. Cf. also the Hegelian formulation at the end of: "Was my father crucified by the paradox the voices expound: that from people who bent like reeds to his whims he was asking in his way for an affirmation of his truth *in and for himself*." (130, my emphasis)
21. Coetzee, *Doubling the Point*, 59. Note especially his remarks about film, the speed of narration, and its relation to the novel.
22. Magda says that she wants "my story to have a beginning, a middle, and an end," and she fears she will live only in "the yawning middle without end" (43). Later she says, "Lyric is my medium, not chronicle" (71).
23. See Coetzee's agreement that it is no part of his intention in *In the Heart of the Country* to "dissolve" the problems of selfhood and relationship "into postmodernist game-playing" (*Doubling the Point*, 60); P. A. Cantor, "Happy Days in the Veld: Beckett and Coetzee's *In the Heart of the Country*," in *The Writings of J. M. Coetzee*, ed. M. Valdez (Durham, N.C.: Duke University Press, 1994), makes a similar point (that the issue is not the "unrepresentability of reality" but "false representations" [103]) but does not much develop it.
24. See Coetzee, *Doubling the Point*, 65: "There is a true sense in which writing is dialogic: a matter of awakening the countervoices in oneself and embarking upon speech with them." There is much of value in Derek Attridge's discussion on the "modalities of otherness," the relevance of modernist techniques in dealing with such modalities, the performative character of texts, and the "ethical demands" that all this raises. See *J. M. Coetzee and the Ethics of Reading* (Chicago: University of Chicago Press, 2004), 6.

References

Coetzee, J. M. *Doubling the Point*. Ed. D. Attridge. Cambridge, Mass.: Harvard University Press, 1992.
———. *Dusklands*. New York: Penguin, 1974.
———. *In the Heart of the Country*. New York: Penguin, 1976.
———. *Waiting for the Barbarians*. New York: Penguin, 1980.
———. *White Writing: On the Culture of Letters in South Africa*. New Haven, Conn.: Yale University Press, 1988.

2

Disgrace, Desire, and the Dark Side of the New South Africa

Adriaan van Heerden

In this article I want to show how J. M. Coetzee has enriched our understanding of moral psychology and morality through his insightful exploration of the phenomenon of disgrace in a number of his novels. Although it is not possible to give this topic the comprehensive treatment it deserves in such a short space, I believe it is at least possible to identify a few interesting strands of thought and promising avenues for future investigation.

In the first section I want to start by looking at the concept of disgrace and its relatives, shame and guilt. In the next I move on to consider the nature and objects of desire as presented in Coetzee's novel *Disgrace*. Coetzee weighs the desires of most people in the new South Africa and finds them wanting: the desire for subjugation and material wealth has replaced the high ideals of reconciliation, humanity, and brotherhood (what former Archbishop Desmond Tutu calls "*ubuntu*") that had energized the struggle for liberation from Apartheid. The new South Africa lacks moral intelligence, vision, and goodness, and this deficiency reveals the dark side of the optimism and idealism that had prevailed in the immediate aftermath of the end of Apartheid. Despite Coetzee's presenting us with an unsparingly bleak vision of violent crime and lost humanity, we may nevertheless discern a small flicker of hope in *Disgrace*. In the third section of this chapter, I will argue that this glimmer of hope is presented to us in the main character's symbolic metamorphosis into a "dog-man." In the conclusion I will summarize what I think the main messages are from these (preliminary) investigations.

GUILT, SHAME, AND DISGRACE

The importance of Coetzee's contribution to moral psychology, through his exploration of the phenomenon of disgrace, comes to light when we consider that discussion of disgrace as a concept in its own right is almost nonexistent in Western moral psychology to date. It seems that one has to go back as far as Aristotle for a detailed discussion of disgrace and its relation to shame.[1] Where disgrace *has* featured in analysis it has usually piggybacked on the concept of shame[2] and, as a further sign of relegation, we may note that the concept of shame has itself historically been neglected in modern Western philosophy as a result of the importance attached to the concept of guilt in the Judeo-Christian tradition.[3] This historical neglect has been rebalanced for several years now as intense discussions about the concept of shame and its relation to guilt have taken place.[4] However, there still appears to be little recognition of disgrace as a moral concept in its own right.

Coetzee has been concerned with the family of concepts that includes guilt, shame, and disgrace from his first novel, *Dusklands*, published in 1974, and references to these concepts occur in one form or another in all his other literary works (at least up to *Elizabeth Costello*).[5] In this section I want to construct an account of how these concepts relate to—and differ from—one another and how some of the ideas in Coetzee's oeuvre can enhance this account.

Broadly speaking, we might say that guilt, shame, and disgrace emerge at the interface between the individual and society: they signal that something has gone wrong in the relationship between the individual and society and that political or psychological pressure is being brought to bear either to normalize the relationship or as punishment for the actions that caused the failure of the relationship. On the positive side, these moral emotions signal a responsiveness to the other without which friendship and other social goods would not be possible.[6]

The Magistrate in Coetzee's novel *Waiting for the Barbarians* echoes a biblical sentiment when he remarks to himself after a few days of solitary confinement: "Truly, man was not made to live alone!" (80).[7] This sentiment was also present among the Greeks. According to Aristotle, man is a political (or social) creature whose nature is to live with others[8]—he can only be truly happy when he lives in a community (*polis*) of good men because the happy man "needs friends."[9] Former Archbishop Desmond Tutu provides an African perspective on this line of thinking when he writes in his memoir on the Truth and Reconciliation Commission that the African worldview—which he calls "*ubuntu*"—entails a recognition that "my humanity is caught up, is inextricably bound up," in yours. In this view, "We belong in a bundle of life. We say, 'a person is a person through other people'. It is not 'I think therefore I am'. It says rather: 'I am human because I belong.' I participate, I share."[10] It means that "we are made for community, for togetherness, for family," that we "exist in a delicate network of interdependence."[11] People with *ubuntu*, writes Tutu, are "generous, hospitable, friendly, caring and compassionate. They share what they have."[12] Magda, the main character in Coetzee's novel *In the Heart of the Country*, puts it another way when she observes that "It is not speech that makes man man but the speech of others" (137). We could paraphrase Magda's insight in a pseudo-Saussurean way and say that it is by being situated in a system of differences from other people, and being able to converse with them in a meaningful way, that I become truly human.[13]

However, there is not just a given aspect to this interconnectedness; there is also an aspirational or prescriptive element. As Tutu says, "Harmony, friendliness, community are great goods. Social harmony is for us the *summum bonum*—the greatest good. Anything that subverts or undermines this sought-after good is to be avoided like the plague."[14] This prescriptive element is evident in the strategies that have evolved in human societies for ensuring, or enforcing, social harmony. Societies have mores, moral expectations, social ideals, laws, and other "forms of life" (with apologies to Wittgenstein) that define the meaning of social harmony. We might say that guilt, shame, and disgrace are mechanisms for policing this social harmony (although we have to be careful not to limit their various roles to this function). Borrowing a phrase from Foucault, we might say that these moral emotions can function as instruments of *social control*. It is important to distinguish at this early stage between good and bad forms (or instances) of social control (although Foucault himself does not make this distinction, as far as I am aware): in certain cases a society might have justified reasons for wanting to prevent some of its citizens from harming others, and although this might be construed as social control, it cannot immediately be dismissed as bad.

But what happens when this desire for harmony goes too far and starts working against individuals who are eccentric, creative, free-spirited? Surely we would not want to say that a society is justified in censuring individuals simply because they contradict the ideology of the state. It seems that there is a balance to be struck, but this fact in itself suggests that an overzealous desire for social harmony is misguided (or worse). Although Coetzee recognizes the value of human touch and interaction in people's psychological well-being (see, e.g., *Waiting for the Barbarians* 80, 96), as well as higher social bonds such as friendship, the figure of the outsider is a constant presence in his work (e.g., Michael K, Friday, the young man in *Youth*). These outsiders provide valuable critical perspectives on the functioning of the social structures and political systems in which they find themselves. However, these perspectives are not always translatable into political improvements; sometimes they seem rather to indicate the existential singularity of the individuals who hold them. We could say that Coetzee's novels are positioned on the fault lines between the individual and society and between different cultures, African and Western (cf. *Disgrace*, 202) and serve as a warning to be on the lookout when *ubuntu* starts to lean toward conformism, conformity, and bad forms of social control. Coetzee *problematizes* the question of how people can live together in such a way as to recognize both their fundamental interconnectedness *and* the singularity and desires of every individual. This question also touches on the theme of power relations that runs through Coetzee's oeuvre, notably in the analysis of master/slave and state/citizen relations in several of the novels. The novels therefore operate at both the political level and the psychological level.

Given this background, let us first look at the difference between guilt and shame. Commentators from the fields of philosophy and psychoanalysis have converged on the idea that guilt differs from shame in that the former relates to failures with respect to norms, rules, or prohibitions (the realm of the *superego*), while the latter pertains to failures with respect to ideals (the realm of the *ideal ego*).[15] In the case of shame we can trace the thesis to Aristotle. In his *Rhetoric*, for instance, Aristotle writes that "the people before whom we feel shame are those whose opinion of us matters to us":[16] these are the individuals who are probable candidates for our ideal ego.[17] Rawls argued that shame is distinctively linked to what one *aspires* to be, whereas guilt is linked to what one *ought* to be, which fits with the proposed thesis.[18] More recently, Robert C Roberts identified guilt as an emotion related to moral *fault* and shame as an emotion related to moral *defect*, a distinction that again roughly coheres with the above outline.[19] Teroni and Deonna argue that the difference between guilt and shame in this regard is best understood by saying that these emotions take different formal (as opposed to particular) objects: i.e., guilt's formal object is a norm, whereas shame's formal object is a value.[20] They also argue that the self and behavior constitute different evaluative foci for shame and guilt, respectively (i.e., what is condemned in cases of shame is one's self, whereas what is condemned in cases of guilt is some particular action or behavior).

It is important to note at this stage that the guilt we are talking about here is what I want to call *subjective* guilt: it pertains to the subject's experience of feeling guilty, rather than what we may call *objective* guilt (guilt in the legal sense). I can be guilty in the legal, objective sense (e.g., after stealing a loaf of bread) without feeling guilty in the subjective sense (e.g., because I feel justified in stealing the bread to feed my starving family). It is also possible to think of cases where the converse is true, i.e., that we can feel guilty without having committed any specific legal, objective violation: for example, someone might suffer from religious guilt because he has a strong impression of the doctrine of original sin or could feel guilty for having survived a genocide (when all the rest of his family perished).

Having distinguished between subjective and objective guilt, we can turn to the concept of shame and its relation to disgrace. Shame and disgrace are often treated as equivalent, but it is in fact possible to distinguish between them.[21] To see this it is necessary to go all the way back to Aristotle. In his *Rhetoric*, Aristotle defines shame as *"the imagination of disgrace."*[22] In other words, shame is the subjective, internal *visualization* of—and *identification* with—the objective, external state of disgrace. It would be tempting at this point to *equate* shame and disgrace: when someone transgresses against morality and violates the trust of others, shame is the subjective experience of their objective condition, which is disgrace. However, Aristotle is more subtle than this, as we can see from the fact that he designates shame a quasi-virtue (in the sense of being a precondition for the acquisition of the true virtues): those who feel shame when they have done something wrong have the potential to learn from their mistakes, but to do something wrong and not feel shame is the final proof of a wicked character.[23] We might say that for Aristotle there is a *potential* flow from disgrace to shame but that this is not inevitable. What Aristotle *does not* appear to allow for (at least not explicitly in the section just mentioned) is the possibility that *society* might be in the wrong by imposing disgrace, that the values or ideals on the basis of which that disgrace is sanctioned may be morally suspect, and that the individual who resists shame in such cases may be justified in doing so. It is this possibility that Coetzee opens up for us in interesting ways.

In *Disgrace* the main character (David Lurie) does not feel ashamed about desiring and seducing one of his young students (an attractive young colored woman called Melanie Isaacs) even though, when a complaint is upheld against him and he loses his job, he is—from society's perspective—in disgrace. In fact, he goes so far as to declare to the committee of inquiry convened to "make recommendations" in the case that he feels ashamed for *not* acting on similar impulses in the past (52).[24] Although he says to Melanie's father later on in the novel that he is trying to accept disgrace as his "state of being" (172), he does not appear to experience any corresponding feelings of shame and continues to be sexually aroused when he thinks about Melanie and her even more beautiful younger sister, Desiree (65, 78, 164, 173). David is far from morally perfect, but despite his lack of shame in this case we could not describe him as a wicked character.[25] This misrelation between shame and disgrace serves as a prompt to the reader to reflect critically both on those values (or ideals) of society that sanction the disgrace (and how they differ from the individual's own values), as well as on the nature and object of the individual's desire, which compels him towards a conflict with those values. Can we make a case for David's lack of shame and his "philosophical reservations" (47) about the committee of inquiry?

David's lack of shame is not simply a matter of incorrigible lust, and his reservations about the committee are not simply the result of obstinate self-righteousness. Rather, there are complex causes underlying his position and in order to make sense of it I think it is helpful to consider three of his core values: his aspiration to romanticism as a way of life; his insistence on the maintenance of a private sphere (or existential space) distinct from the public sphere; and his belief in the "rights of desire" (89). These values do not register on the radar of the committee of inquiry and are consequently a source of conflict between David and the committee, the university he works at, and the new South Africa more broadly. What can be said for them?

In terms of the *first value*—romanticism—we need to note that it forms part of a defense of the rights and inherent value of the arts and humanities against the seemingly relentless march of instrumental reason and materialistic values in the new South Africa. Examples of these corrupting tendencies are evident in *Disgrace*: Cape Town University College is renamed to Cape Technical University (technology is good because it earns money); the Faculty of Classics and Modern Languages is closed down as part of the "great rationalization" and replaced by "Communication Skills" and "applied language studies" (3, 179) (presumably because they can be more easily justified as useful in the business environment). "Rationalization" is a revealing word here: it shows a certain kind of reason at work: a reason that values only what generates money (cf. *Elizabeth Costello*, 125). If Elizabeth Costello (the main character in Coetzee's "novel" of the same name) is right to think that the "humanities teach us humanity" and give us back our human beauty (151), then their civilizing influence is being lost in the new South Africa. David is a defiant character in this regard—*l'etranger*[26]—who battles to express his belief in the value of art: he struggles to write a chamber opera on Byron even though he doubts that it will ever be performed (214). Despite his more obvious sexual motives, David's seduction of Melanie coincides with an attempt to initiate her into a deeper appreciation of art: music, dance, literature (12–15); it is an attempt to establish a spiritual connection (if only temporarily) rather than a purely physical one. But Melanie is part and product of the new South Africa: post-Christian, posthistorical, postliterate, ignorant (32) and consequently the attempt fails. David's folly is that he believes himself to be attractive to Melanie and believes that they can have a future together as a couple (171); as David's ex-wife Rosalind points out, he is a "great deceiver and a great self-deceiver" (188). We see that although David is prone to self-deception and seduction, he also believes in humane, humanizing romantic values—values that are fading in importance in the new South Africa.

David's *second value*—the insistence on the maintenance of a private sphere (or existential space) distinct from the public sphere—is diametrically opposed to the self-conception (or self-delusion) of the committee of inquiry. When David's daughter, Lucy, asks him why he did not humor the committee, he replies: "These are puritanical times. Private life is public business. Prurience is respectable, prurience and sentiment. They wanted a spectacle: breast-beating, remorse, tears if possible. A TV show, in fact. I wouldn't oblige (66)." The collapse between the private and public spheres is linked in the novel to several worrying phenomena in the new South Africa: a confusion between the spheres of legality and spirituality/religion; the absence of a good and intelligent morality in society and the emergence of a substitute (pseudo-)morality; sinister social control; and the renascence of puritanical values.

The first of these phenomena is the confusion between law and religion. The committee refuses to be constrained in the realm of secular law by accepting a secular guilty plea and handing down the associated punishment. Instead, it claims for itself a quasi-religious status by demanding demonstrations of remorse, repentance, confession, and reformation of character. In his book on the Truth and Reconciliation Commission, Tutu (who chaired the TRC) explicitly states that there was not a requirement on perpetrators to express remorse or to ask forgiveness but only to make a full disclosure of their crimes before the TRC in order to qualify for amnesty.[27] The fact that the committee of inquiry requires David to express remorse indicates that it has moved beyond the TRC ideologically. I suggest that the committee of inquiry models its own methodology on the TRC without understanding the TRC's (aspirational) ideology of restorative (as opposed to retributive) justice, *ubuntu*, and love for one's neighbor.[28] What Coetzee seems to be showing us is how an instrument of truth and reconciliation can turn into an instrument of bad social control in the absence of a clear moral vision and an intelligent understanding of the difference between spirituality and legality. Of course, Coetzee is not alone in pointing out that the noble ideals of the TRC had not in fact taken root to the extent that many of the leaders of the anti-Apartheid struggle had supposed,[29] but his analysis of the implications of this failure is uniquely illuminating and disturbing, as we will see.

We could argue that the TRC masked the moral vacuum left by the demise of Apartheid, and this lack of a moral sense is another marker of collapse in *Disgrace*. As one of David's flings tells him, "You people [your generation] had it easier. I mean, whatever the rights and wrongs of the situation, at least you knew where you were" (9). In a sense, Apartheid provided a moral compass in the same way that the Holocaust did: it was such an obvious evil that it was easy to define *the good* as the *opposite* of this evil. But now that Apartheid is gone this definition has been lost and people are left searching for alternatives. Three obvious candidates in the new South Africa are radical feminism (in the sense of demonizing male desire and desiring castration) (cf. *Disgrace*, 52, 66), political correctness (in the sense of vilifying anything that smacks of colonialism and racism) (cf. *Disgrace*, 53), and the example set by the TRC, which operated on the basis of confession of wickedness in return for amnesty. I suggest that Coetzee weighs them in *Disgrace* and finds them wanting: since they can only function at the level of substitute morality they can tell us nothing of what it really means to be a good person. It is not sufficient to subscribe to feminism, anticolonialism, antiracism, and confession in order to qualify as a good person. What it means to be a good person is something that needs to be worked out at the individual (subjective, existential) level for it to have meaning and authenticity, but this task is made more difficult by the collapse between the subjective and objective dimensions that has taken place under pressure from the three-fold pseudo-morality, with the resulting demand to bare one's moral and spiritual soul in public.

In *Discipline and Punish*, Foucault writes that the aim of punishment (from the state's perspective) is to restore the "obedient subject" by means of an authority that "is exercised continually around and upon him."[30] It seems that David sees evidence of this kind of power at work in the committee and in his contemporary society (91). By claiming a god's eye view, the committee of inquiry takes its place in the network of institutions in the new South Africa that facilitates the "normalizing" function of power by treating individuals as transparent objects of observation and attempting to turn them into obedient subjects whose values and desires are aligned with those of the pseudo-morality. We can see in the committee's workings "the problematization of the criminal behind his crime, the concern with a punishment that is a correction, a therapy, a normalization, the division of the act of judgment between various authorities that are supposed to measure, assess, diagnose, cure, transform individuals"; this, as Foucault says, "betrays the penetration of the disciplinary examination into the judicial inquisition."[31] Rather than focusing on the guilt relating to a particular offence, the committee of inquiry becomes a judge of normality and acts as a normalizing power.[32] By so doing it negates the distinction between public and private: the individual has no right to a private life and conscience but must subject himself to the judging and normalizing gaze of his examiners, confess his sin, and, to avoid punishment, conform henceforth to the puritanical values of the inquisitor. These are the workings of a body more at home in "Mao's China" (66) rather than one which facilitates the ideals of *ubuntu*.

David identifies neo-Puritanism as a common element in the sources of the new pseudo-morality (66). The problem with Puritanism is that its morality is overly simplistic and prohibitive and that it seeks to "normalize" individuals to this overly restrictive code of behavior by, for example, punishing sexual desire per se. Like *The Scarlet Letter* before it, *Disgrace* depicts Puritanism as a denial of our humanity, our human nature, and our underlying animality, as we will see in the next section.

David's refusal to meet the demands of the committee exposes the new substitute morality for what it is: a confusion between legality and spirituality, constructed on the foundations of superficial political correctness. Thus, although he is clearly in the wrong from one perspective (it is morally wrong to take advantage of others, and even more so if they are in one's care), he is at the same time able to see through the moral vacuity of the committee, and his nonconformism might therefore be construed as "an energy that is reviving, an 'outburst of protest in the name of human individuality.'"[33] But is this protest entirely justified?

David's *third core value* is his belief in the "rights of desire"; he feels alienated from society because the case for these rights and values can no longer be made "in our day" (89): it is no longer fashionable or politically correct to ascribe to these values. David stakes a claim for (what he considers to be) "normal" male sexual desire, but not all eminent commentators are convinced that this is such a good thing. Attridge, for instance, postulates a link between Lucy's rape by the attackers on the farm and David's seduction of Melanie when he writes that "any temptation to exaggerate the positive side of this force [desire] is challenged by its other significant manifestation in the novel, the desire that—whatever other motives are at work—stiffens the penises that enter Lucy Lurie's unwilling body."[34] In the next section I want to explore this matter in somewhat more detail and take issue with Attridge's equation of David and the rapists' desire.

DESIRE AND THE DARK SIDE OF THE NEW SOUTH AFRICA

We have seen that David Lurie disgraced himself in the eyes of his society by acting on his desire for Melanie Isaacs. Attridge accuses David of never making "a connection between his forcing himself on Melanie at one point in their brief affair . . . and the sexual attack on his daughter."[35] But should David make this connection? It seems to me that Attridge's demand here is itself based on the Puritan idea that all sexual desire is bad, sinful, dangerous.[36] Instead of equating the two episodes of sexual desire, I think we should rather contrast David and the rapists' desires at another level. We have to ask: What are their *deeper* desires (i.e., deeper in the sense of pertaining to the projects that give meaning to their lives, rather than sexual desire which is common to all)? The answer to this question will, I believe, show that the problem is not so much sexual desire per se as the (amoral, immoral) deeper desires that channel some of the sexual energy.

David's deeper desire is to retain (or perhaps to resuscitate) his self-image as a desirable man;[37] the deeper desire of the rapists is to subjugate their victims (159). Like Byron's Lucifer, David's desire is amoral: his vanity springs not from principle but from impulse. He does not care if an action is good or bad; he just does it. But "the source of his impulses is dark to him" (33, 90, 143). However, David does not strike one as the kind of person who would knowingly cause harm. The attackers, on the other hand, have an explicit and immoral desire to cause physical and psychological harm to their victims. The difference in their desires and objectives indicate two different states of disgrace. David's is experienced at a personal, subjective level (172). The disgrace associated with the attackers is located at the political, objective level: it indicates that the new South Africa itself is (in) a state of disgrace. In the next section I will consider some of the preconditions for lifting this political disgrace that we are able to distil from Coetzee's novel. In the remainder of this section I want to delve a bit more into the nature and different objects of the sexual desire that fuel much of the drama of *Disgrace*.

David's defence of "normal" male sexual desire is presented in the form of a story. He reminds Lucy of a dog owned by former neighbors of theirs in Kenilworth (a southern suburb of Cape Town):

> It was a male. Whenever there was a bitch in the vicinity it would get excited and unmanageable, and with Pavlovian regularity the owners would beat it. This went on until the poor dog didn't know what to do. At the smell of a bitch it would chase around the garden with its ears flat and its tail between its legs, whining, trying to hide.... There was something so ignoble in the spectacle that I despaired. One can punish a dog... for an offence like chewing a slipper.... But desire is another story. No animal will accept the justice of being punished for following its instincts.
>
> (90)

When Lucy challenges David that the moral implied by his story is that males should be allowed to follow their instincts unchecked, he denies this: "What was ignoble about the Kenilworth spectacle was that the poor dog had begun to hate its own nature. It no longer needed to be beaten. It was ready to punish itself" (90).[38] David resists the attempt by the committee to treat him like the Kenilworth dog because he believes that "in the whole wretched business [of his affair with Melanie] there was something generous that was doing its best to flower" (89). The Puritan desire to destroy sexual desire at its root is here shown to be antihuman and against nature.[39] However, the subsequent manifestation of that desire in human culture is another matter: one can (and should) be held accountable for how one acts on one's desires, as Lucy rightly points out. This is the point where I believe Attridge goes wrong: his argument implies (perhaps inadvertently) that sexual desire is bad or evil in itself, which means he sides with the committee of inquiry on this point. Another way of putting it is to say that Attridge attacks the *nature* rather than the *objects* of desire (i.e., sexual desire per se rather than the existential or political objectives that serve as foci for the characters' deeper desires).

The way in which sexual desire manifests in David cannot be described as wicked or evil, even though the effects of his womanizing are not always happy. David may pay for sex and seduce his students, but he does not force them to have sex against their will.[40] The behavior of the Luries' attackers, on the other hand, may well be described as wicked and evil (156, 160). This is especially true of the two older attackers; in the case of the young "thug" (Pollux), there appears to be a possibility of mental illness (208). Although David himself steers away from characterizing the attackers as evil, his motivation for doing so seems to be the result of some need for psychological self-preservation, rather than the objective reality of what happened to them (98). As readers we can see that the attackers enjoy—in Elizabeth Costello's phrase—"the malicious cruelty in which Hitler and his cronies specialized" (177). In reflecting on the problem of evil, Elizabeth is reminded of when she was physically assaulted by an Australian docker in Melbourne when she was a teenager: venting his anger at her refusal to have sex with him, the man beat her so severely that her jaw was broken. She could see that the man "liked hurting her . . . probably liked it more than he would have liked sex" and remarks that this was "her first brush with evil . . . it was nothing less than that, evil, when the man's affront subsided and a steady glee in hurting her took its place." (165)

David and Lucy's attackers are of the same type: they enjoy inflicting pain on their victims. But it is more than that: they want to scar their victims emotionally for life, they want to subjugate and humiliate them (159).[41] In addition to being rapists and assaulters the attackers are also robbers. The catalogue of items stolen from the Luries demonstrates the banality of their materialistic desires: a car, a jacket, shoes (97), money, a TV, a CD player, a rifle with ammunition (108). Life in South Africa is so cheap that—as David says—you risk your life even to own a packet of cigarettes (98). This banality is another indication of the dark side of the new South Africa, showing just how far removed that society is from the high ideals (such as *ubuntu*) aspired to by many of the anti-Apartheid activists.

A significant difference between Costello's docker and the Luries' attackers is, of course, that the latter are black men in post-Apartheid South Africa. This is significant because these black men had grown up in a political system that denied "non-white" people their basic human rights and perpetrated awful acts of violence on those who resisted its racist ideology and social structures—and on many who did not. One might therefore be inclined to think that it is understandable that these men acted in the way they did: they were simply acting in the way that society had formed them. Coetzee does not give us any background information about the men: we do not know whether they had personally suffered violence at the hands of the state, what their home circumstances were like, and so on. In other words, we do not know to what extent their wicked characters and evil actions are the result of Apartheid (or mental illness). Still, we can assume that the evils of the old regime would have played at least *some* role in their psychology. As David says to Lucy, "It was history speaking through them.... A history of wrong" (156). Despite this concession the violence perpetrated by the attackers still appears as a perpetuation of the disgrace that characterized the old South Africa: the physical assault of others, the disrespect and disregard for the property and persons of others, taking pleasure in inflicting pain and suffering on others. That violence exists on the scale it does in South Africa—"it happens every day, every hour, every minute, in every quarter of the country" (98)—is a disgrace. It was a disgrace in the old Apartheid regime (cf. *Age of Iron*, 9), and it is a disgrace in the new South Africa. It is disgraceful to see human beings living in such a raw state of nature, "red in tooth and claw"; it is disgraceful that the state is so pitifully failing in its duty to protect its citizens (because it fails to take crime seriously) and as a result is powerless to intervene—and unable to provide the right kind of care for those who need it—when the worst happens (115, 154).

So far we have concentrated mainly on David and the attackers, but *Disgrace* also invites us to contrast the amoral desires of David and the wicked desires of the attackers with the moral desire voiced by Lucy. When David asks her whether she already loves the child that is growing inside her as the result of the rape, she replies: "How could I? But I will.... I am determined to be a good mother, David. A good mother and a good person. You should try to be a good person too." "A good person. Not a bad resolution to make, in dark times," thinks David (216). Although Lucy's interpretation of the situation and her response to it strike one as repulsive (not seeking justice for herself, submitting to Petrus's machinations, feeling it is her duty to bear the rape child), it nevertheless seems reasonable to believe that the desire to be a good person marks the beginning of authentic morality in existence. It is unclear how far David progresses along the road to becoming a good person, but there are signs at the end of the novel that a measure of development has taken place. It is this development that I want to explore in the final section.

GOD AND THE DOG-MAN

Disgrace is relentless in its depiction of the dark side of the new South Africa. It seems to give us a "glimpse into hell" (cf. *Elizabeth Costello*, 178; *Disgrace*, 209) by painting a picture of a country with a failing state unable to protect its citizens from harming one another; a country without a moral vision or compass; a country where people have morally defective desires (not only for gross human rights violations like rape but also for banal material objects, for which they are willing to commit murder); a country where people beat the corpses of dogs with shovels to make them fit more easily into incinerators (146); a place where the price for white people to "stay on" is to submit to the will of the new would-be warlords and thugs of the land (158, 203-4). A country, in short, where the great moral vision of *ubuntu* has been lost. Thus the new South Africa, which could have served as a moral example to the rest of the world after the end of Apartheid, ends up perpetuating the disgrace of the old regime.

Although Coetzee never explicitly mentions *ubuntu* in any of his novels, Elizabeth Costello expresses a sentiment which we might describe as characteristic of *ubuntu* when she refers to the victims of the Holocaust as her brothers and sisters (178). We could say that *ubuntu* begins with the ability to feel the suffering of the other, to "experience his flesh," as Athol Fugard writes in his novel about a young black thug called Tsotsi who grew up amid the cruelty of Apartheid. In Fugard's novel, Tsotsi's redemption (if one may call it that) comes in the wake of "the full Christian experience" when he begins to *feel*—to sympathize with a potential victim and to experience "the full meaning and miracle of sharing in another man's suffering."[42] Sympathy, for Fugard, is a light that reveals the other as a being like myself, with a body and mind capable of pain and suffering.

Coetzee does not give us "the full Christian experience," but *Disgrace* does seem to have something of a quasi-religious ending that contains elements of these themes. At the end of the novel David sacrifices his favorite dog. He could defer the dog's euthanasia for a while longer but decides not to, since it would only be postponing the inevitable. "Bearing [the dog] in his arms like a lamb, he re-enters the surgery. 'I thought you would save him for another week,' says Bev Shaw. 'Are you giving him up?' 'Yes, I am giving him up'" (220). The imagery here (the "sacrifice" of the "lamb") is reminiscent of Christianity and yet oddly unrecognizable as anything with which we were previously acquainted. What does this strange ending tell us?

It seems to me that the reference to Christianity indicates that David's development has assumed a religious dimension. We know that he does not believe in God (172), but at the same time he appears to be experiencing Christianity at a physical and emotional level: he has learnt to experience the suffering of others (where the others in this case are dogs) and to put the feelings of the dogs he cares for above his own desire for pleasure (by ending their pain through euthanasia). David has therefore undergone a measure of moral development from the self-indulgent man of pleasure at the beginning of the novel. This development is vivified in the term "dog-man." When David first meets Petrus, Petrus introduces himself as "the gardener and the dog-man," savoring the phrase "dog-man" (64). When Lucy asks David if he could see himself living in her part of the world, he asks: "Why? Do you need a new dog-man?" (88). By the time David and Lucy attend Petrus's party, Petrus says "I am not any more the dog-man" (129), and a little later David describes himself as having become "a dog-man" (146). It seems as though a torch has passed from Petrus to David, but what is the significance of this and the term "dog-man"?

On one level the term "dog-man" appears to be an inversion of "god-man";[43] it is an animalization of the function of the god-man, the one who brings salvation or shows the way to salvation. On another level it signifies a deconstruction of the supposed difference between animals and humans: it places animals and humans together on the same plane (and arguably reverses the previous hierarchy by placing "dog" before "man"). What Coetzee seems to be saying is that the way to salvation is to rediscover our fundamental animality, to recognize our deep affinity with the animals, and to stop treating them as a lower order of being—to stop treating them like animals, to be precise. By reconnecting with animals and learning to treat them with kindness and respect, we will also rediscover ourselves as animal and human and treat our fellow human beings and ourselves with kindness and respect.

This interpretation is supported by similar ideas in some of Coetzee's other novels. According to Elizabeth Costello, kindness to animals constitutes "an acceptance that we are all of one kind, one nature" (106). The "dividing line" between animals and human beings is something that is taught via socialization; it is not inherent in nature itself (106). In its ideal manifestation the dog-man thus emerges as one who embraces all living things as worthy of kindness and respect,[44] one who protests against dividing lines per se (e.g., the lines between human and nonhuman, between black people and white people) (cf. *Elizabeth Costello*, 111). And in the section of Coetzee's novel *The Master of Petersburg* where Dostoevsky (the main character) becomes a "dog-father" (80) to an abandoned dog, Dostoevsky thinks to himself that his son will not be saved "till he has freed the dog and brought it into his bed, brought *the least thing*, the beggarman and the beggarwoman too" (82). Salvation here seems to depend on one's commitment to embrace and care for the least of God's creatures (even when they are no longer alive), creatures who "come nowhere" in conventional society's list of priorities and hierarchy of values (cf. *Disgrace*, 73).

We might therefore say that Coetzee stretches the concept of *ubuntu* to include animals. This seems to be a kind of religious move, but what kind? How are we to understand these quasi-religious, post-Christian sentiments? I think a useful place to start is in the etymology of the word "religion." The *Chambers Dictionary of Etymology* cites two origins of the word: it can either mean "to go through, or read again" (derived from *relegere*), or it can refer to a sense of binding obligation (derived from *religare*).[45] Through David's feeling of obligation to care for the corpses of dogs, Coetzee disturbs our comfortable distinction between "us" and "them," between "human" and "animal," and invites us to read ourselves again, to reexamine ourselves in the light of a new perspective. This gives us a clue to an important strand of Coetzee's vision of what it means to live a morally good and virtuous life. I believe that Coetzee is fundamentally challenging us to imagine what Aquinas thought impossible: friendship with animals (cf. *Elizabeth Costello*, 110). At the end of *Disgrace* we are told of the dog's love for David: "unconditionally, he has been adopted; the dog would die for him, he knows" (215). This is strongly reminiscent of John 15:13: "No one has greater love than this, to lay down one's life for one's friends" (New Revised Standard Version). The dog shows unconditional love and friendship toward David and serves as a model for human behavior, of what it means to be a good human being. If this is not the "full Christian experience," it certainly has strong resonances with the life and message of the god-man. Through David's apparently absurd concern for the corpses of dogs, Coetzee invites us to revisit, reread, and reevaluate our values, obligations, and projects and our "rational" (instrumental, functional) view of the world.

However, being a good human being does not end with the ability to sympathize with the suffering of others. There is also a positive element, which is clearly stated by Elizabeth Costello: to live fully as a human being is to be "full of being," that is, *joy*. In order to be full of being it is necessary to live as a "body-soul" (78), not denying our animal nature but harmonizing it with our cultural and spiritual being. We may surmise from this that to be a good human being means to have the desire to help others to achieve fullness of being. And this, as Attridge says, requires "a dedication to a singularity that exceeds systems and computations: the singularity of every living and dead being."[46] It requires attention to the being of the other-as-singularity, as an individual, and the extension of love, kindness, respect, and friendship to that individual.

So what is the significance of the torch of the dog-man passing from Petrus to David? In the gospel of Matthew (16:18) Petrus (the Afrikaans version of "Peter," meaning "the rock") is named by Jesus as the rock on which he will build his church. Perhaps the suggestion is that Petrus is the kind of person on whom the new South Africa—the "new world" (117)—is built: the entrepreneurial black businessman/farmer. However, the novel contains strong indications that this is not a broad church: Petrus refuses to help in bringing Pollux (the younger attacker) to justice because he is "my family, my people" (201). We see here again the contours of a dividing line, of a new apartheid: "my people" versus "your people." For Petrus, any amount of violence against others is justified provided they are not "his people." Petrus *seems* a good man (64), but this goodness is illusory: he is revealed as an avaricious and cunning manipulator who might have engineered the attack on David and Lucy in order to force Lucy to give up her land to him (117, 118, 151). Petrus is the dog-man of the Luries' attackers, men who are described as violent attack dogs (159, 160) who mark those in their territory with "dog's urine" (199), as thugs who take pleasure in killing the joy, humanity, and spirit in others (98). This is a rather depressing rock on which to build a new South Africa. Symbolically, the future of morality in the new South Africa is in better hands with David—himself a flawed character—than with Petrus, the poster boy of the new regime.

What hope exists for the new South Africa is dependent on whether people can rediscover and recover their humanity and treat others with love, kindness, and respect. As we have seen, in Coetzee's novels there is a strong theme of rediscovering our humanity through rediscovering our animality: he challenges us to see beyond the dividing lines that structure our de facto moral vision and to reread the story of our lives from a new perspective.

But what are the *limits* of such love, kindness, and respect, if any? If one takes Lucy's position seriously, one might be forgiven for inferring that being a good person (according to the novel) implies submitting to one's oppressors and treating them with unlimited love, kindness, and respect (as Lucy does when she submits to Petrus's machinations and refuses to take action against Pollux). It seems to me that *Disgrace* presents us with two configurations of morality—what we may call "legal morality" and "spiritual morality"—represented by David and Lucy, respectively. David's expectations regarding moral behavior are based on the rule of law: when someone commits an unlawful act the law must be applied and the criminal punished accordingly (as when he enters a guilty plea to the committee of inquiry and when he wants the attackers to be brought to justice). We might say that the focus of legal morality is on conformity of behavior to principles of justice. Lucy's expectations regarding moral behavior, on the other hand, are not directed toward such abstract principles but rather at a person's character, whether he or she is (existentially) a "good person." We might call this a "spiritual" interpretation of morality as it does not take the social-political reality, and the latter's demands for social-political justice, as its primary focus.

At the end of the novel Coetzee presents us with a conflict between these two interpretations of morality, and it seems to me that he is showing us that neither can bring about a good society on its own. Legal morality cannot function properly unless individuals have a desire to make it work, and this desire has to proceed from a good character (i.e., from the existential or spiritual realm). In this light David and Lucy both reveal themselves as imperfect: despite his strong impression of social justice, David has not progressed very far toward becoming a good person, and although Lucy may be considered a better person on the spiritual level, she has given up hope on legal morality and therefore fails to protest against political injustice. Interestingly, it is Lucy's failure in this regard that accounts for the repulsive effect at the end of the novel. We feel that it is a distasteful result both for her and for future generations: the child she bears will grow up in a country with a weakened sense of social justice. The attackers, in contrast, have no developed conception of either legal or spiritual morality (or if they do, they flagrantly act against it).

Perhaps it is not so much a matter of setting a limit to love, kindness, and respect as of recognizing that honoring the rule of law is an expression of respect toward others (provided that the particular laws of the land are truly good and just and not a mockery, as in the case of the old Apartheid laws). It is the rule of law that makes a communal life possible and that facilitates the emergence of love and kindness to a greater extent than would have been the case in its absence (although it cannot generate love and kindness of its own accord: for this the spiritual dimension is required). Even if Lucy is correct in shunning retributive justice, her refusal to integrate her spiritual morality into the social-political dimension works against restorative justice.

CONCLUSION

In this chapter I have sought to show that Coetzee's analysis of disgrace constitutes a valuable contribution to moral psychology. We saw that Coetzee postulates the disjunction of shame and disgrace (an idea that was latent but unexplored in Aristotle) and that this serves as a prompt to the reader to reflect critically both on those values of society that sanction the disgrace and on the nature and objects of the disgraced person's desires that compel him toward a conflict with these values. What is still open at this stage (and in need of further investigation) is whether this analysis contains the necessary and sufficient conditions for stipulating what it means for someone to be in disgrace, and whether it is possible for the individual to escape, avoid, or otherwise break free from the state of disgrace imposed by a particular community. Looking ahead to future analysis, the conditions for the latter would appear to be dependent on the severity of the infraction in the particular community's hierarchy of values (e.g., being polite to others might be a considered a value, but an individual would not normally be disgraced by being rude, although this might depend on the social status of the person he or she was rude *to*); the unspoken and unwritten consensus of what constitutes a reasonable period of punishment; and the transgressing individual's willingness to submit to the censure of the community, demonstrate remorse, and change his or her behavior accordingly.

In terms of diagnosing the conditions of a state of disgrace, Coetzee's novel provides us with some of the necessary conditions: the individual needs to have violated one or more of society's norms, values, or mores, and the violation should pertain to an item that features highly in the community's hierarchy of values. In terms of the possibility of breaking free of this status, *Disgrace* presents two aspects: on the one hand, David Lurie seems consistently to reject the shame associated with his disgrace, while, on the other hand, he tries (later on in the novel) to accept disgrace as his "state of being." The latter position raises the specter of the impossibility of an escape from disgrace for David, but perhaps it is precisely because he continues to refuse to acknowledge the validity of the shame that his society wants him to feel that he can never escape.

Three key messages emerge from these preliminary investigations. First, while the desire for racial superiority and segregation that motivated most white people in Apartheid South Africa is morally reprehensible, the desires of many people of all colors in the new "Rainbow Nation" are banal, morally worthless, and, in some cases, downright evil (as in the case of David and Lucy's attackers). This is a difficult and uncomfortable truth to face given the prevailing substitute morality of political correctness (fed by multiculturalism, anticolonialism, radical feminism, and neo-Puritanism), but there is no way around it if South African society is to have any hope of becoming truly good. Citizens of the new South Africa must confront and remedy their deficient moral desires as evidenced in the legacy of Apartheid and the new "morality" of entitlement, which so easily turns into greed. Second, we should broaden our moral vision to identify not only with all our fellow human beings but also with animals and should learn to treat others (people and animals) with kindness and respect. Third, the good state must strive to create favorable conditions for the emergence of good people and of *ubuntu* in society—which it can do by formulating good and just laws, respecting and enforcing the rule of law, and supporting the arts and humanities as well as moneymaking—rather than attempting to micromanage the moral lives of its citizens.

Notes

1. See Aristotle, *Rhetoric*, ed. J. Barnes (Princeton, N.J.: Princeton University Press, 1991), 2.6.
2. The recent discussion by R. C. Roberts, *An Essay in Aid of Moral Psychology* (Cambridge: Cambridge University Press, 2003), 227–30, is insightful but no exception in this case.
3. See R. C. Solomon, "Shame," in *The Oxford Companion to Philosophy*, ed. T. Honderich (Oxford: Oxford University Press, 1995), 825.
4. An example of this is the debate about shame and guilt cultures that started in 1946. See R. Benedict, *The Chrysanthemum and the Sword: Patterns of Japanese Culture*

(Boston: Houghton Mifflin, 1946); M. R. Creighton, "Revisiting Shame and Guilt Cultures: A Forty-Year Pilgrimage," *Ethos* 18, no. 3 (September 1990): 279–307; and see F. Teroni and J. Deonna, "Differentiating Shame from Guilt: Consciousness and Cognition," *Consciousness and Cognition* 17, no. 3 (September 2008): 725–40, for further references.

5. See e.g. *Dusklands*, 12, 14, 15, and 29; *In the Heart of the Country*, 36, 53, 76, 114, and 128; *Waiting for the Barbarians*, 94–97 and 101; *Life and Times of Michael K*, 70, 151, 179, 181, and 182; *Foe*, 69, 98, and 119; *Age of Iron*, 9, 64, 78, 115, 149, and 151; *The Master of Petersburg*, 62, 68, and 207; *Elizabeth Costello*, 65, 85, 203, and 222.

6. See Roberts, *An Essay in Aid of Moral Psychology*, 2.

7. See Genesis 2:18.

8. See Aristotle, *Nichomachean Ethics*, ed. J. Barnes (Princeton, N.J.: Princeton University Press, 1991), 1169b18–19.

9. Ibid., 1169b21.

10. See D. Tutu, *No Future Without Forgiveness* (London: Rider, 1999), 34–35.

11. Ibid., 154.

12. Ibid., 34.

13. Several of Coetzee's novels address the problems that result when communication breaks down or when communication was always difficult or impossible (*Foe* is the prime example here).

14. See Tutu, *No Future Without Forgiveness*, 35.

15. See R. E. Lamb, "Guilt, Shame, and Morality," *Philosophy and Phenomenological Research* 43, no. 3 (1983): 337; G. Piers and M. Singer, *Shame and Guilt* (New York: Norton, 1953); H. Lynd, *On Shame and the Search for Identity* (New York: Harcourt Brace Jovanovich, 1958); F. Teroni and J. Deonna, "Differentiating Shame from Guilt."

16. See Aristotle, *Rhetoric*, 1384a24–27.

17. In Lacanian terms, "The ideal ego is the image you assume and the ego ideal is the symbolic point which gives you a place and supplies the point from which you are looked at" (D. Leader and J. Groves, *Introducing Lacan* [Cambridge: Icon Books, 2000], 48). See S. Freud, "Introductory Lectures on Psycho-Analysis (Part III)", in *The Standard Edition of the Complete Psychological Works of Sigmund Freud*, vol. 16, trans. J. Strachey (London: Vintage, 2001), 429: "[The patient] senses an agency [= conscience] holding sway in his ego which measures his actual ego and each of its activities by an *ideal ego* that he has created for himself in the course of his development."

18. See J. Rawls, *A Theory of Justice*, rev. ed. (Cambridge, Mass.: Harvard University Press, 1999), 420–24.

19. See Roberts, *An Essay in Aid of Moral Psychology*, 222–30.

20. See Teroni and Deonna, "Differentiating Shame from Guilt", section 4.3. In the case of fear, e.g., the particular object might be a dog, while the formal object is danger 4.3).

21. Roberts, *An Essay in Aid of Moral Psychology*, 227, seems to hint in this direction, but the distinction is not made explicit: "To be ashamed of others is to see them as casting disgrace on oneself."
22. Aristotle, *Rhetoric*, 1384a24; my emphasis.
23. See Aristotle, *Nichomachean Ethics*, 1128b10-33; see also Solomon, "Shame," 825; M. Burnyeat, "Aristotle on Learning to Be Good," in *Essays on Aristotle's Ethics*, ed. A. O. Rorty (Berkeley: University of California Press, 1980), 78.
24. We may note at this point that there is no corresponding disgrace: it is not a disgrace to deny these impulses, for which someone would need to feel ashamed. This further underscores the difference (disjunction) between shame and disgrace.
25. David describes himself as "not a bad man but not good either" (195).
26. David is described as "the stranger, the odd one out" at Petrus's party (135).
27. See Tutu, *No Future Without Forgiveness*, 28, 34 and 47.
28. Ibid., 51, for a discussion of the difference between restorative and retributive justice. The Postscript to the Interim Constitution (which became the constitutional underpinning of the TRC) contained an explicit reference to *ubuntu* (ibid., 45).
29. Similar views have been expressed by, among others, former South African president Thabo Mbeki, Moeletsi Mbeki (brother of Thabo), André Brink, and Desmond Tutu.
30. See M. Foucault, *Discipline and Punish: The Birth of the Prison*, trans. A. Sheridan (London: Penguin Books, 1991), 128.
31. Ibid., 227.
32. Ibid., 304.
33. Ibid., 289.
34. See D. Attridge, "Age of Bronze, State of Grace: Music and Dogs in Coetzee's 'Disgrace,'" *Novel: A Forum on Fiction* 34, no. 1 (2000): 116.
35. Ibid., 116.
36. An idea that can be traced to Augustine, Paul's letter to the Romans (13:13-4), and before that to Plato (see S. Blackburn, *Lust* [Oxford: Oxford University Press, 2004], 52, 60).
37. For instance, we are told that "for decades" womanizing was "the backbone" of David's life and that he "existed in an anxious flurry of promiscuity" but then "one day it all ended" (7). David's affair with Melanie is an attempt to relive his time at the "banquet of the senses" (24).
38. This reminds us of Foucault's statement that the purpose of Bentham's Panopticon was to "induce in the inmate a state of conscious and permanent visibility that assures the automatic functioning of power" (*Discipline and Punish*, 201).
39. See M. Foucault, "About the Beginning of the Hermeneutics of the Self: Two Lectures at Dartmouth," *Political Theory* 21, no. 2 (May 1993): 216-17 and 222.
40. Of course, David is not a sensitive person and seems to be a bit of a manipulator: he knows that Melanie is "too young. She will not know how to deal with him; he ought to let

her go" (18), and he does not pick up from her body language that she does not want to have sex with him (25). However, I think we have to assume that he would not have pursued the affair if she had sent clear rather than ambiguous signals (11).

41. Note that the attackers feel no *shame* for their actions but rather take pride in spreading their "seed" throughout their territory (199). This reinforces the distinction between shame and disgrace, and this time it proves Aristotle's point that lack of shame in some cases is proof of a wicked character.

42. See A. Fugard, *Tsotsi* (Edinburgh: Canongate Books, 2006), 206, 230, 103–5, 106.

43. Elizabeth Costello remarks on the anagram "GOD-DOG" (225).

44. This ideality is not fully realized in David: by the end of the novel, for instance, one still has doubts whether he is able treat other people (and especially women) with the necessary kindness and respect. However, his demarginalization of Teresa in the chamber opera seems to indicate some development in this regard.

45. See *Chambers Dictionary of Etymology*, ed. R.K. Barnhart (Edinburgh: Chambers, 2005), 907–8. Johan Degenaar, emeritus professor of philosophy at Stellenbosch University, South Africa, brought this distinction to my attention. It has not been picked up anywhere else, as far as I am aware.

46. See Attridge, "Age of Bronze, State of Grace," 117.

References

Coetzee, J. M. *Age of Iron*. London: Secker & Warburg, 1990.

———. *Disgrace*. London: Secker & Warburg, 1999.

———. *Dusklands*. London: Vintage, 1998.

———. *Elizabeth Costello*. London: Secker & Warburg, 2003.

———. *Foe*. London: Penguin Books, 1987.

———. *In the Heart of the Country*. London: Vintage, 1999.

———. *Life and Times of Michael K*. London: Vintage, 2004.

———. *The Master of Petersburg*. London: Vintage, 1994.

———. *Waiting for the Barbarians*. London: Penguin Books, 1980.

3

Ethical Thought and the Problem of Communication

A STRATEGY FOR READING *DIARY OF A BAD YEAR*

Jonathan Lear

What is ethical thought? For starters, let us say that thought is ethical when it facilitates or promotes the living of ethical life. It would seem then that ethical thought cannot be captured by its subject matter. It is easy enough, for example, to imagine a run-down social practice that consists in discussing ethical topics in empty ways. Imagine someone who devotes his professional life writing articles about, say, the difference between just and unjust wars—but whose soul is made coarser in the process. There might be a journal, let us fictionally call it *Ethics and Politics*, in which professors from different universities vie to place their articles—none of which make any difference in how countries go to war. It is, of course, possible that the reflection that went into those articles help authors, readers, and students become more ethically sensitive—and this possibility should not be diminished. However, it is easy to imagine a different scenario: one in which the journal functioned mainly as a credentialing agency for university jobs. People who published there would write "outside letters" for other people who published there so that deans, who care nothing about the field—other than that their university should be "ranked high"—would approve appointments and promotions.

To make the problem more vivid, imagine a moral or political issue that matters to you (racism, gerrymandering, campaign finance, gay rights, the Middle East, Islamic extremism, mistreatment of animals, destruction of indigenous cultures). Then imagine that the social circumstances surrounding you shift in such a way that this problem becomes fashionable: clever articles about it appear in the best op-ed pages and book reviews; it is discussed over dinner and at cocktail parties; certain individuals attain celebrity for advocating the cause—and yet the whole social whirl is somehow cut off from making a difference. In such circumstances we have the *appearance* of ethical thought, and it is this very appearance that can mislead participants. In such a situation, we would most likely *take ourselves* to be thinking about ethical issues—after all, we have just read, discussed, or even contributed the latest article on X. Ersatz ethical thought would give us the sense that the space for ethical thought was already filled.

The situation is even worse with novelists. No one is better positioned to profit—in the mundane, literal sense of earning large sums of money or winning distinguished literary prizes—from a "sensitive" portrayal of an ethically charged topic, such as torture or war. Let us leave to one side the cynical author who uses an ethically charged topic like torture to seek fame and fortune. The problem is more pressing if we imagine a sincere, morally engaged author who would like her writing to correct an injustice. How might that work? Is there not a vivid possibility that, precisely with the author's success as a writer, he will be taken up as a celebrity, that being "against torture" becomes a fashion item among the "intelligentsia," and so on. Perhaps philosophers will take him up and write a book of essays with titles like, "Ethical Thought and the Problem of Communication." It is not impossible that something good should come of this. But it is easy enough for the whole public event to serve as a fashionable *substitute* for ethical thought, rather than an instance of it. (Imagine the publication party for a book against global warming that needs to end early so that the guests can catch a plane.)

John Coetzee's literary style is, I think, an attempt to defeat this possibility. And I think we can understand the complexity of his literary form if we see him as trying to communicate ethical thought. In this essay I want to give at least a preliminary indication of how this might work. In the first instance, I want to give a broad overview about how Coetzee's literary form fits in to a philosophical tradition concerned with the contribution of form to ethical thought. Then I will examine one of the central arguments of Coetzee's *Diary of a Bad Year*—concerned with the shame of torture—and I will try to show how the form of the book facilitates a reader's relation to that shame.

There has been speculation in reviews about the relation between JC, the protagonist of *Diary of a Bad Year*, and John Coetzee, its author. JC is, after all, a South African novelist who has recently emigrated to Australia; he is the author of *Waiting for the Barbarians*; and hanging on the wall of his bedroom (as seen by his Filipina secretary) is "a framed scroll in some foreign language (Latin?) with his name in fancy lettering with lots of curlicues and a big red wax seal in the corner."[1] We know he is JC because that is how he signs two letters—one imploring Anya to come back to his employ after they have had a blow-up, the other inviting her and her lover Alan to dinner to celebrate the completion of the book. In private discussions between Anya and Alan, Anya refers to JC as "Señor C" and "El Señor," and Alan refers to him as Mr. C. At the dinner party, when Alan gets drunk, he calls him "Juan" to his face. As anyone who has read the book, or even just reviews, knows, each page is divided into two or three sections, each section written in (and representing) a different voice. The top section is the official voice of the author, the exposition of moral opinions that will eventually find their way into the German book. Many of them sound as though they could be taken for the voice of John Coetzee.

But there is this crucial difference between JC and John Coetzee: JC is willing to publish his "Strong Opinions" as a free-standing book; John Coetzee is not. Coetzee is only willing to publish the opinions as authored by JC in the context of a novel in which those very opinions, as well as the act of writing them down and publishing them, are questioned by JC himself and by Anya and are mocked by Alan. Not only that: JC and his book are embedded in a larger book (by Coetzee) that includes JC's personal musings (from a diary?) about his attraction to Anya and his growing sense of infirmity. What is the meaning of this difference? It is, I think, a mistake to treat this simply as a display of literary virtuosity. The reviewer in the *New York Times Book Review* said that we readers "are manipulated by a form that is coy as well as playful."[2] This claim is, I think, importantly wrong. The aim of the style is not for John Coetzee to show off—to demonstrate that he, unlike the melancholy, infirm, single-voiced JC, can do postmodern hip. Rather, it is an attempt to defeat the reader's desire to defer to the "moral authority," the "novelist" John Coetzee. In an article in the *New York Times*, Rachel Donadio writes, "In a country [South Africa] where every inch of physical and moral ground is contested, Coetzee has been criticized for refusing to play the role of writer-as-statesman, one more easily played by his fellow Nobel laureate, Nadine Gordimer."[3] The wording is marvelous: for Coetzee has never been explicitly accused of failing *to play a role*. He has been accused of racism, of letting South Africa down, of not being a moral exemplar. But when I read the criticism, it seems to me that Ms. Donadio got it right: what irks people about Coetzee is his refusal to conform to their image of how he should behave—as "South African writer," "Nobel Prize winner," and "moral conscience." We need to see this same refusal in his literary style.

JC writes, "Authority must be earned; on the novelist author lies the onus to build up, out of nothing, such authority" (149). But Coetzee's authority lies in his ability to divest himself of authority: this is not manipulation, is certainly not coy, and, if "playful" is meant to be the opposite of moral seriousness, is not playful either. The questions are why he does it and how he does it. Why he does it is, I think, straightforward: he wants to defeat ersatz ethical posturing and promote genuine ethical thought in his reader. How he does this is tricky and requires some attention.

Within the Western philosophical tradition, there have been a number of attempts to use literary characters—most notably, at the beginning, with Plato's dialogues. At the center is the figure of Socrates, who famously claims to know only that he does not know. Not only does Plato, as authority figure, disappear behind his characters, but the central figure distinguishes himself by eschewing authority when it comes to ethical knowledge. There are, of course, many other characters, some with worked-out ethical views, but the dialogues are set up so that there is always some question about how those views should be received. This is not simply a literary device to sustain the reader's interest; it is an ethical strategy: an attempt to defeat any easy attempt to defer to the author or to any surrogate for the author in the text. Even the figures within the text need to be handled with care. If a respected character were to say, "When it comes to ethics, you really need to think for yourself," one can imagine the response, "Anything you say: I really must think for myself!"[4]

Plato also was suspicious of writing as a medium for philosophical activity. In a famous passage at the end of *Phaedrus*, Socrates recounts an Egyptian tale of an ancient time in which King Thamus warns Theuth, the inventor of writing, that students "will imagine they come to know much while for the most part they know nothing."[5] Socrates' worry seems to be that writing, by its nature, tends to defeat ethical thought. People can read the words, think they know what's at stake, pass the words along to others who think they are being taught—all without friction. There is an *imitation* of ethical thought: the reading, reproduction, and transmission of "ethical arguments" that make no difference to how anyone lives. It stands to reason that a philosopher so aware of the dangers of writing would try to find a literary form that would defeat the transmission of ersatz thought.

There is, however, a problem with the dialogue form. It can encourage in the reader a sense that he is in the audience, watching the characters debate as though they were up on stage. Rather than being thrown into philosophy's midst, one can feel like an arbiter, able to choose a position from among those presented according to taste. One doesn't have to read the dialogues this way, but—(perhaps this is a reflection of the culture we live in)—I have seen generations of students incline toward it.

Perhaps it is this problem that motivated Kierkegaard, a devoted student of Plato, to create pseudonymous authors. Although Kierkegaard wrote many works under his own name, the works that are most famously associated with him—*Fear and Trembling, Either/Or, Repetition, Sickness Unto Death, Philosophical Fragments, Concluding Unscientific Postscript*—were all published under pseudonyms. But at the end of his pseudonymous authorship, Kierkegaard makes it explicit in a document signed under his own name that the pseudonyms are not pseudonyms *for him*. Rather, he, Kierkegaard, created pseudonymous authors who have themselves gone on to write their books. If it could work, the pseudonymous authorship would be an ingenious improvement on the dialogue form precisely because it breaks down the division between stage and audience. Instead of my watching two characters debate with each other "on stage" and adjudicating points to one or the other of them, it is as though one of the characters has come down off the stage—in fact, there is no longer a stage, no longer a character—and he is confronting *me*. "My pseudonymity," Kiekegaard tells us in "A First and Last Explanation," "has not had an *accidental* basis in my person . . . but an *essential* basis in the *production* itself."[6]

But why did Kierkegaard need to write "A First and Last Explanation"? Imagine Shakespeare rushing out onto stage just after the curtain goes down, arms outstretched, saying, "Wait! Before you go, this is the first time I'm going to tell you this, and I'm not going to tell you again, but the character Lear does not have an accidental basis in my person, but an essential basis in the production itself." If an explanation like that were needed, the "production itself" has failed. That Kierkegaard felt the need to explain his authorship is, I think, an indication that he thought it had failed.[7]

Might there not be a more forgiving (and thus more successful) way to use this literary form—one that wouldn't require the self-defeating gesture of a first and last explanation? Perhaps one might put the pseudonymous author *along with his book* inside a novel in which author and book are both commented upon by various voices. If this a literary style aimed at provoking ethical thought in the reader, standing, as I think it does, in a tradition that goes back to Plato's dialogues, and works through Kierkegaard's pseudonymous authorship, then it is a misunderstanding of the form to think that it is a clever (or irritating) literary feat—one in which if Coetzee were less clever (or less irritating) he would come out from behind his mask and tell us what he meant. But what if his concern were that our concern with what he meant would distract us from our concern with how we should be? If *Diary of a Bad Year* is ethical thinking in action, if it is directed toward stimulating ethical thought in the reader, then it would be a misstep for Coetzee to "step out from behind his mask" and tell us what he meant—*not* in the sense that he would be exercising bad political or literary judgment—but because there ought to be no mask out from which to step.

There would be no content withheld—nothing more to say—and an attempt to say what that (nonexistent) content was would be an attack on the production itself.[8] This is what it would mean to say that the pseudonymous author JC does not have an accidental basis in John Coetzee's person—that is, he is not showing off—but an essential basis in the production itself.

One reason to divide a page is that it gives Coetzee a way to address different parts of our soul, at more or less the same time. In *Phaedrus*, Socrates claims rhetoric is a peculiar craft of leading the soul with logos.[9] And in *Republic* he says that education should not be thought of in terms of putting something into another person but rather as turning the *whole* soul around.[10] I think we need to see the split page of *Diary of a Bad Year* as a rhetorical move in this Platonic sense. This is Coetzee's attempt to lead the whole soul.

For the sake of simplicity (and brevity) I am going to focus on two broad movements. If one reads across the top section, one is ostensibly reading *Strong Opinions*, the book that JC will publish in German translation. (One will later read what Anya calls his "Soft Opinions" and JC calls "Second Diary," which JC does not publish but does share with Anya.) Reading across like this, one is confronted by what I shall call the *dialectic of responsibility*. I am tempted to say that this is the level of rationality, but that is not quite right. As we shall see, not all of JC's arguments are rational. But this is the level at which we are presented with (and entangled in) argument. The movement works through logos. However, when we read vertically, downward, we encounter a *spectacle of embedding*. That is, we see how the moral stances that are officially to be presented in book form are embedded in the fantasies, happenings, musings, and struggles of the author's day-to-day life. It is *that from which* a normal book of moral essays would be cut off. I suggest that this imaginary embedding is meant to draw along parts of the reader's soul that would not be led by argument alone. The phrase "that from which" is a phrase Aristotle used to pick out the matter of a living organism.[11] A living human being, for example, is a form-and-matter unity in which the stuff of human life, blood, guts, flesh, and bones, realizes itself in a self-maintaining form, the human being. The stuff of life is that from which its form emerges and that in which it maintains itself. I want to suggest that *Strong Opinions*, the book of moral opinions by JC, has the *form* of argument but that form is an aspect of a living form-and-matter unity that consists of JC's arguments embedded in the stuff of his life. JC gives us the form; John Coetzee gives us the form-and-matter unity. Now, *why* seeing moral arguments as embedded in the life of a fictional character should defeat ersatz ethical thought, and perhaps even promote ethical thought in some, is a puzzle. But to solve that puzzle is to grasp the rhetorical strategy of the book.

Diary of a Bad Year opens at the very same place as the purported book *Strong Opinions*, whose author, we will later learn, is JC. It is an excursus on the origins of the state.

> Every account of the origins of the state starts from the premise that "we"—not we readers but some generic we so wide as to exclude no one—participate in its coming into being. But the fact is that the only "we" we know—ourselves and the people close to us—are born into the state; and our forebears too were born into the state as far back as we can trace. The state is always there before we are.
> (3)

JC's official voice is one of reminder and recognition. He invites us to share his skepticism about how certain forms of philosophical argument implicate us in the formation of the state. In the polis version of chicken and egg, we are told that we came first and, out of our needs, created a state. JC reminds us that there is no "we" whom we can recognize as ever wanting or needing to do that. It does not follow that JC's voice is therefore antiphilosophical. Philosophy is regularly constituted by questioning the uses to which philosophy can be put. Nor is JC scorning all uses to which a state-of-nature argument might be put. Rather, he is questioning a particular use, one that locates our responsibility in the wrong place. If we bear responsibility, it is not because of some original sin—a mythical act of mythical ancestors, who lived outside the state but nevertheless count as "us." I suspect that the intended reader (that is, the reader whom John Coetzee has in mind, whom I will simply call the reader) is one who will enjoy this opening criticism: who will enjoy the recognition that I and we are not part of a nonexistent we who purportedly carried out this bogus act. That is, we begin with a satisfying recognition that we are not who this vindicating story of the state says we are. We are not people who owe allegiance to the state's actions because "we" formed it—and we're not going to accept an argument that tries to implicate us on such shabby grounds.

As we move toward the lower part of the page, we also move to the lower part of the body—and, not accidentally, the "lower" part of the soul.

> My first glimpse of her was in the laundry room. It was mid-morning on a quiet spring day and I was sitting, watching the washing go around, when this quite startling young woman walked in. Startling because the last thing I was expecting was such an apparition; also because the tomato-red shift she wore was so startling in its brevity.

What could be more ordinary, homogeneous, self-contained than sitting in one's laundry room (as, no doubt, he had often done) watching the washing go round? But this is a world that can be disturbed by a glimpse. A week later he happens to see her again "only fleetingly as she passed through the front door in a flash of white slacks that showed off a derrière so near to perfect as to be angelic. God, grant me one wish before I die, I whispered; but then was overtaken with shame at the specificity of the wish, and withdrew it" (8). If this were only a report of JC's sexual fantasies, he would stand in an odd relation to his own imagination. What, after all, is it to have a wish and then "withdraw" it? For JC's act to make sense, we must take his whispering to be not merely the expression of a wish but a plea to God. Wishes are not the sort of thing one can withdraw; requests are. But now that the divine has been invoked, we are not just within the realm of sex—are we ever?—there is an importance here, difficult to name or understand, that, at least in the moment, makes it feel instinctively, impulsively appropriate to call on God for remedy. JC calls it a metaphysical ache:

> As I watched her an ache, a metaphysical ache, crept over me that I did nothing to stem. And in an intuitive way she knew about it, knew that in the old man in the plastic chair in the corner there was something personal going on, something to do with age and regret and the tears of things.
> (7)

We need to take seriously the idea that this ache is actually metaphysical. Though it is a psychological occurrence, it is not merely that. It is, rather, an ache that can lead us to a richer grasp of what kind of being we are.

In the *Symposium*, Socrates tells of a conversation he had with the priestess Diotima, who taught him the art of love. "All of us are pregnant, Socrates, both in body and soul, and, as soon as we come to a certain age we naturally desire to give birth."[12] But pregnancy and reproduction are the ways that mortal beings participate in immortality. This is a godly affair, and it must occur in beauty—which is in harmony with the divine. Now, when someone is pregnant in soul, "he too will certainly go about seeking the beauty in which he would beget." "In my view, you see, when he makes contact with someone beautiful and keeps company with him, he conceives and gives birth to what he has been carrying inside him for ages."[13] Now, for the beautiful young boy of ancient Greek aristocratic society, substitute the hot Filipina in her startlingly brief tomato-red shift, and thongs—"Thongs of the kind that go on the feet" (6). Much later in the novel, toward the end of JC's book *Strong Opinions*, JC writes down in the middle section of the page:

> Was Anya from 2514 in any but the most far-fetched sense the natural mother of the miscellany of opinions I was putting down on paper on commission . . . ? No. The passions and prejudices out of which my opinions grew were laid down long before I first

set eyes on Anya, and were by now so strong—that is to say, so settled, so rigid—that aside from the odd word here and there was no chance that refraction through her gaze could alter their angle.

(124–25)

In one way, this fits the Socratic conception well. For the beautiful other is not a contributor to the pregnancy but the occasion for a long-standing pregnancy to come to term. In this picture, what we would see on the upper part of the page is that to which JC gave birth in the presence of the beautiful Anya. In the lower two sections, we would be witness to the birthing process. The book *Strong Opinions* is then a kind of husk: the externalization into the world of that which used to lie inside JC's pregnant soul. Perhaps one reason that published "moral opinions" can fall flat in terms of ethical thought is that they are cut off from the birthing process.

But in another way JC provides a significant variation on the Socratic theme. For JC is not just erotically bowled over by Anya's beauty; he is preoccupied with his aging, physical decay, and death. To be sure, there are intimations of this in Plato: it is because we are mortal creatures that we stretch ourselves to become immortal. And because we know (in some sense) that we are mortal, that we experience a push toward symbolic births-in-beauty. Yet JC's birthing is more mired in anticipation of physical decay and death than anything Plato imagined. Let's face it: JC is looking for a way to die. His metaphysical ache is the living recognition that (in his erotic longing, in all its inappropriateness) he is a creature who will soon not be. From the middle section: "Last night I had a bad dream, which I afterwards wrote down, about dying and being guided to the gateway to oblivion by a young woman. What I did not record is the question that occurred to me in the act of writing: *Is she the one?*" (59). Diotima talks of giving birth in beauty; JC is giving birth in beauty in the valley of the shadow of death. He has a fantasy of dying in a whorehouse and being dumped unceremoniously in an alley, and he continues (again from the middle section): "But no, if the new dream is to be trusted it will not be like that. I will expire in my own bed and be discovered by my typist, who will close my eyes and pick up the telephone to make her report" (65)"

It is clear that Anya picks up on the importance of this fantasy. Later, in the lower section, she reports: "He told me one of his dreams, I said to Alan. It was really sad, about dying and his ghost lingering behind, not wanting to leave. I told him he should write it down before he forgets, and work it into his book" (77). Is Anya here giving advice to JC or to John Coetzee? Coetzee writes about it in *Diary of a Bad Year*, but JC leaves it out of *Strong Opinions*. One might say that she is giving advice to them both or that John Coetzee is the one able to take up her advice, but I don't think either option is correct. Anya is John Coetzee's creation—who knows in whose presence he gave birth to *that* beauty. What we have in the fictional world is Anya giving advice to JC—and I think it is helpful to think of JC as following it (after his own fashion). JC's *Strong Opinions* are written in the light of his own decay and death, in the presence of the beautiful Anya. *Strong Opinions* is JC's own being-toward-death: it is that which he elects to put forward into the public world in the light of his own imminent demise. His own decay is not what *he* wants to talk about (that is Coetzee's preoccupation): JC wants to utter the ethical word in the public domain. That is how he wants to spend his last days on earth: in the public domain, writing *Strong Opinions*; in private, entangled with Anya as quasi-Platonic lover. What all this means is far from clear. But the fact that Coetzee lets us see how JC's ethical words are embedded in his living-toward-death allows us at least to explore, in gut-open ways, why taking such a stance might matter.

It is clear from the moment they meet that JC and Anya are in close intuitive contact. As we have already seen, the moment he feels the metaphysical ache, "in an intuitive way she knew all about it." It was something "which she did not particularly like, did not want to evoke," but she could recognize it, feel it. And JC recognizes that she feels it and is even able to grasp the meaning it has for her: "Had it come from someone different, had it a simpler and blunter meaning, she might have been readier to give it welcome; but from an old man its meaning was too diffuse and melancholy for a nice day when you are in a hurry to get the chores done" (7).

In short, this metaphysical ache is not the private property of JC's imagination: it reaches out to Anya, is instantly recognized by her and responded to in her own imaginative act, which is itself immediately recognized by JC. The question is whether this ache is able to reach out, off the page, and entangle the reader. My own sense is that it does, and it helps us import an ethical ache into the *Strong Opinions*.

Even at this early stage, one can see in the form of communication a strategy designed to defeat ersatz ethical thought. In particular, any tendency in the reader to *transfer authority* to the author is undermined twice over. Not only is the author of *Strong Opinions* not John Coetzee—and thus whatever admiration one has for him cannot directly transfer into admiration for the opinions expressed—but even the purported author JC is shown to be entangling himself in a somewhat melancholy, perhaps pathetic erotic outreach to a hot little number he happened to glimpse in the laundry. Who knows what place his moral musings have in relation to this human drama? We know immediately that these "strong opinions" are being embedded in a larger context, but we have no idea what the significance of this embedding is. The "strong opinions" do seem to be what JC wants to be putting into the public domain during a period when he is contemplating his own decay and demise. This we can see not from *Strong Opinions* but from *Diary of a Bad Year*. But is this a final word that

JC needs to speak, or is it simply an empty motion he is going through as he pursues what really matters to him, a relationship with Anya? There is no answer to this question in the text. Thus there is no easy way for a reader to take on the strong opinions simply by taking John Coetzee's *or* JC's word for it. If we think of ethical thought as not the sort of thing that *can* be accepted on authority, then this is a literary form that defeats a typical way in which ethical thought is itself defeated.

For a similar reason, the form also works against ethical thought's becoming routine. With transference of authority, the problem is not only that we are taking an "expert's" word for it; the word we take tends to lose vitality. So, to take an example that I shall presently consider in more detail, if we were to take JC's word for it that "torture is a national dishonor," how would that stand with our own sense of dishonor? This is the irony of "strong opinions": opinions can't be strong simply in virtue of their content. It is possible to "accept" the opinion, yet the strength of the opinion is drained off in the transmission. Certainly, there are many warnings in *Diary of a Bad Year* that the "strong opinions" may just be ersatz ethical thought. JC himself calls the invitation to write *Strong Opinions* "an opportunity to grumble in public, and opportunity to take magic revenge on the world for declining to conform to my fantasies: how could I refuse?" (23).[14] Anya warns him that he has "a tone that really turns people off. A know-it-all tone. Everything is cut and dried: *I am the one with all the answers, here is how it is, don't argue, it won't get you anywhere.* I know that isn't how you are in real life, but that is how you come across, and it is not what you want" (70). And of course, Alan in his obnoxious tirade says that the reason *Strong Opinions* is being published in Germany is because that country is the last on earth that has any interest in the shriveled musings of a white-bearded guru. Each of the charges has some plausibility. Thus, if JC's voice—that is, the voice of *Strong Opinions*—is going to gain authority with the reader, it can only come *after* the reader has grappled with all the warnings against assigning it any authority at all. Ironically, *Diary of a Bad Year* inoculates *Strong Opinions* against being ersatz ethical thought by warning the reader that it might be just that.

Let us return to the dialectic of responsibility—reading across the pages of *Strong Opinions*. In an entry on Machiavelli, JC writes:

> Necessity, *necessità*, is Machiavelli's guiding principle. The old, pre-Machiavellian position was that the law was supreme. If it so happened that the moral law was sometimes broken, that was unfortunate, but rulers were merely human, after all. The new, Machiavellian position is that infringing the moral law is justified when it is necessary.
>
> Thus is inaugurated the dualism of modern political culture, which simultaneously upholds absolute and relative standards of value. The modern state appeals to morality,

to religion and to natural law as the ideological foundation of its existence. At the same time it is prepared to infringe any or all of these in the interest of self-preservation.
(17)

JC sees that Machiavelli has trickled down into "ordinary life"; the only people who somehow don't get it are people he calls "liberal intellectuals":

> The kind of person who calls talkback radio and justifies the use of torture in the interrogation of prisoners holds the double standard in his mind in exactly the same way: without in the least denying the absolute claims of the Christian ethic (love thy neighbor as thyself), such a person approves freeing the hands of the authorities—the army, the secret police—to do whatever may be necessary to protect the public from enemies of the state.
>
> The typical reaction of liberal intellectuals is to seize on the contradiction here: how can something be both wrong and right, or at least both wrong and OK at the same time? What liberal intellectuals fail to see is that this so-called contradiction expresses the quintessence of the Machiavellian and therefore the modern, a quintessence that has been thoroughly absorbed by the man in the street.
(18)

But when JC speaks about "liberal intellectuals," whom is he talking about? And to whom is he speaking? He talks about them in the third person, and thus it would at least initially seem that JC, in his writing, does not take himself to be addressing them. Rather, he seems to take himself to be addressing a different group—we, the intended readers (whoever we turn out to be)—and he is talking about "liberal intellectuals" with us. The sense that "liberal intellectuals" are not us (readers) is enhanced by JC's claim, "What liberal intellectuals fail to see..." JC implies that we (his readers) can see, merely by his pointing it out, what liberal intellectuals fail to see. And if it were that easy for "liberal intellectuals" to see what they purportedly fail to see, why couldn't JC call them "you"? Why couldn't he then address them directly, as he does us (his readers)? He could then say, "What some of you fail to see is..." I suspect that JC cannot address "liberal intellectuals" directly—cannot simply point out to them what they have hitherto failed to see—because what they fail to see, they *cannot* see. This is a blindness of some sort. Thus the simple activity of pointing something out could not possibly work. And so if one were somehow to bring this failure to see to the attention of those who are failing to see (that is, to the attention of liberal intellectuals themselves), one would have to use a less direct method.

In contemporary political discourse, when someone talks of "liberal intellectuals," he or she is a conservative commentator, and the point of mentioning them is to pour abuse upon them for the satisfaction of other likeminded conservatives. But this cannot be what JC is doing. His outrage at Guantanamo, to take just one example, means he cannot be in the standard mold of conservative commentator—who takes Guantanamo to be a necessity of war. And the fact that he assumes his readers will be sympathetic with his views means this cannot be the standard derogatory trope of "liberal intellectuals."

Precisely because JC's use of "liberal intellectuals" doesn't fit this mold, it ought to raise some curiosity in the reader as to just who he is talking about. And why is he talking about them *to us*? I would like to suggest that we construe "liberal intellectuals" broadly to include a group that meets three criteria:

- They are relatively well educated by contemporary standards (that is what makes them "intellectuals")
- They place special concern on the dignity and rights of the individual (this is the core value of liberalism)
- They have some confidence in reason's ability to understand the world and to give humans the basis for making good decisions (we have seen that they object to the contradictions that "ordinary people" accept as a matter of course)

Note that according to this characterization, "liberal intellectuals" would cut across the standard left-right divide. For example, the late Robert Bartley, the legendary editorial-page editor of the *Wall Street Journal*, right up to the end of his distinguished conservative career, called himself a "liberal" in the traditional sense of the term. In the conservative version of liberalism, the crux is the right of the individual to make up his mind in the market place; in the left-wing version, it is the dignity of the individual, which argues, for example, in favor of universal health care. In each case, what is at stake is some vision of the rights and dignity of the individual. The opposition JC is establishing, then, is not between left and right but between "liberal intellectuals" and "ordinary people." What I think JC wants to investigate is the role of the intellect—at least, as it is given social expression in terms of privileged education—among those who take themselves to value the rights and dignity of the individual.

Although JC sets up an opposition between "liberal intellectuals" and "ordinary people," it is noteworthy that against neither group will a moral appeal against torture succeed. "If you wish to counter the man in the street, it cannot be by appeal to moral principles. . . . Ordinary life is full of contradictions; ordinary people are used to accommodating them" (18). In effect, the "ordinary" response to torture is: "Yes, torture is a moral outrage, but sometimes it is necessary." For "liberal intellectuals," the moral appeal fails for a different reason: it is experienced by them as superfluous.

They are *already* against torture and don't need to be told that it is an outrage. JC tells us how we might nevertheless reach "ordinary people": instead of moral appeal "you must attack the metaphysical, supra-empirical status of *necessità* and show that to be fraudulent" (18). If one can show that torture isn't really necessary for the state's survival, if you can show that the claim is a fraud, then ordinary people won't need a further moral argument to be against it. But this kind of rhetorical move won't work against "liberal intellectuals" precisely because they don't think they need convincing. If there were going to be a rhetorical strategy that worked with them, it would have to be one that elicited from them recognition that, after all, they do need convincing. That being absolutely against torture does not preclude the possibility that they are somehow for it. This would be especially difficult for them to see if, as intellectuals, believers in logic, they assumed that their opposition to torture thereby ruled out the possibility that they are somehow also in favor of it.[15]

JC thinks we Americans are entangled in a national curse—a modern, secular version of blood guilt. Actually, JC is more concerned with shame than guilt—the transmission of dishonor. In this modern version, shame is transmitted not through blood but through citizenship. We are shamed, JC thinks, by the fact that we are citizens of a nation that engages in torture. Of the Bush administration, JC writes:

> Their shamelessness is quite extraordinary. Their denials are less than half-hearted. The distinction their hired lawyers draw between torture and coercion is patently insincere, *pro forma*. In the new dispensation we have created, they implicitly say, the old powers of shame have been abolished. Whatever abhorrence you may feel counts for nothing.
> (39)

It is here, in JC's opinion, that each individual American faces the challenge of ethical thought: "How, in the face of this shame to which I am subjected, do I behave? How do I save my honour?" (39). But how does the *shamelessness* of the Bush administration trickle down and shame *me*? There are a number of peculiarities in the dynamics of shame. To begin with, shamelessness is shameful. But if the administration is, as JC alleges, shameless, then they will never *feel* the shame that, JC alleges, attaches to them. That is, there is objective shame that attaches to the administration because of their shameless behavior, but there is also subjective shame—the experience of being ashamed—that they will never feel (because they are shameless). When it comes to shamelessness, objective and subjective shame necessarily come apart. But now there is a further problem with JC's claim that the shame has somehow become *my* shame, something in relation to which I must figure out how to live.

Again, there is a split between JC's claim of objective shame attaching to me and the subjective shame, a shame that I can't yet figure out why I ought to feel. Is this puzzlement my very own form of shamelessness, manifesting itself in a sense that I don't deserve to feel shame? JC is, I think, trying to block a familiar move: because I oppose George Bush, loathe the administration's tactics of skirting the law, and abhor torture, I am therefore not responsible for what the government does. In this picture, my ethical thought has already been done—and though I may be disturbed by my government's actions, I am comfortable with respect to my judgment of myself. For JC, this tactic won't work, and he tries to enliven in the reader a sense that it is not working:

> Dishonour is no respecter of fine distinctions. Dishonour descends upon one's shoulders and once it has descended no amount of clever pleading will dispel it. In the present climate of whipped-up fear, and in the absence of any groundswell of popular revulsion against torture, political actions by individual citizens seem unlikely to have any practical effect. Yet perhaps, pursued doggedly and in a spirit of outrage, such actions will at least allow people to hold their heads up. Mere symbolic actions, on the other hand—burning the flag, pronouncing the words aloud "I abhor the leaders of my country and dissociate myself from them"—will certainly not be enough.
> (40)

JC is attacking the liberal idea that the individual can be judged in his own terms, in isolation from the nation into which he happens to be born. His point is not that the nation or the culture will have influenced him or shaped his outlook and thus his complicity. Rather, JC's claim is that even if the nation has had no influence on the individual at all, the shame is still his. It attaches simply in virtue of his being a citizen. There are thus, for JC, severe limits to an individual's ability to ward off shame by saying, "It is not *mine*." Worse, at least from the point of view of liberal imagination, these limits may not be rationally justifiable. This is what "liberal intellectuals" cannot see: the fact that I can reason my way out of the shame—after all, I did nothing to deserve it—does not mean that it is not mine. It is *there*, like a curse or an oracle. It attaches to me simply by virtue of my nationality. JC cites the "deep theme" of Faulkner: "The theft of the land from the Indians or the rape of slave women comes back in unforeseen form, generations later, to haunt the oppressor" (48). And he quotes the classicist J.-P. Vernant on the structure of tragic guilt as arising from a clash of an ancient religious conception in which an impious act can defile an entire race and a newer legal conception in which the guilty one is the individual who breaks the law (49). In JC's nationalist conception, shame transmits not just across generations but also trickles down within a single generation from the political class that sanctions the taboo act to the citizens who may have had little or no say in how the political class operates. How is it fair, one wants to ask, that *I* should bear the guilt for acts I abhor, committed by leaders I voted against and over whose behavior I have no control? JC's answer: whether you figure that out or not, the shame *is yours*.

In short, JC plays jujitsu with the liberal imagination. The liberal sensibility wants to start out with the individual—his rights, dignity, and responsibilities—and then asks, "How am I responsible?" JC begins with an accusation of shared shame: "You are dishonored, simply by being part of this tainted 'we.' Now figure out how to behave as an individual: for it is given to you to figure out how to deal with the shame you have inherited for acts you did not perform, for acts you abhor."

In reading JC's strong opinion, many reactions are possible. One might, for example, dismiss JC as a nut case, given to oracular pronouncements we could well live without. Or one might "agree" with JC in the service of bolstering a complacent sense of self-righteousness ("Yes, the shame is mine as well!" Now, where is my martini?). Really, only one avenue of reaction is blocked: the one that tries to object to JC's accusation by saying, "The shame could not be mine, because I did nothing to deserve it." This is essentially the reaction of the "liberal intellectual." And it cannot be an objection because JC begins with the premise that this is a shame that attaches to you whether or not you did something to deserve it. One wants to say: it does not make sense that there should be such a thing as shame that genuinely attaches to me, though I've done nothing to deserve it. But JC already agrees that this shame does not make sense; he does not think it open to rational assessment in this way. Rather, he thinks one must just recognize it as there, attaching to me by virtue of my nationality, independently of my deeds. JC's accusation may be one I refuse to accept, but I cannot refuse it on standard rational grounds. For the accusation does not claim to be rational—that is, to make sense according to contemporary standards of responsibility—it claims to be true.

What if this accusation were somehow to resonate with me? Wouldn't that only show that I was susceptible to irrational appeals? Perhaps. But it might also serve to bypass a defensive use to which reason can be put. Rationalization is a process that purports to determine on the basis of reason alone whether or not, say, I ought to feel shame, but it is actually structured so as to arrive at the conclusion I want. To take a salient example: torture is forbidden by U.S. law, and there is widespread agreement that it would be shameful for this country to engage in torture. So, to the question, "Should we feel shame because our government engages in torture?" the official answer is, "Absolutely not; our government clearly forbids the use of torture." However, in ruling out torture, the law also leaves it unclear what interrogation techniques count as torture. At the time of writing this chapter, the interrogation technique known as waterboarding has neither been conclusively ruled in nor conclusively ruled out. Or, as we shall see, in a funny way it has been both ruled out *and* ruled in. One might think: if torture is so horrible, if engaging in it would be a national disgrace, isn't it a matter of urgency for us to make up our minds about waterboarding? And why, after all, call it "waterboarding"? Why not call it "torture by drowning"? Have we already implicated ourselves with the very vocabulary we use to discuss the issue? After all, if so-called waterboarding is *not* torture, it is certainly an effective interrogation technique, and we could perhaps engage in it more often. If, however, it is torture (as I believe it *obviously* is), then we are in the midst of a terrible crisis: The government is behaving in morally depraved ways in our name. People are suffering unimaginably and unjustly, and we should be doing everything we can to halt this crime against humanity. Instead, the situation is such as to leave us in a murky limbo. Again, on the one hand, waterboarding is absolutely forbidden to the U.S. military. The Detainee Treatment Act forbids "cruel, inhuman, or degrading treatment or punishment" of detainees and requires that interrogation techniques be restricted to those authorized in the *Army Field Manual*. The *Army Field Manual* explicitly prohibits waterboarding. On the other hand, waterboarding has been used by the CIA. It was approved by a presidential finding in 2002 and then prohibited in 2006 by a directive of the CIA director, Michael Hayden. Even so, at the time of writing, it has not yet been ruled to be torture.

This is a complex structure of prohibitions and permissions. It almost looks like the solution to a complex algebraic equation: solve for a situation in which (a) torture is forbidden; (b) waterboarding is forbidden; (c) waterboarding was permitted and could be permitted again; (d) there is no contradiction. What is this complexity for? It seems to me that it is (d) that gives the game away. The law goes to great lengths to avoid the explicit Machiavellian contradiction that JC says "ordinary people" are used to accommodating, namely:

> Torture is absolutely forbidden.
> Torture is permitted when necessary.

It is as though this complex system were written for those who cannot tolerate this contradiction, that is, for the people JC calls "liberal intellectuals." It is an attempt to capture all that is needed in the Machiavellian moment without admitting to it. Why not just admit to it? The only answer I can think of is: admitting to it brings with it a sense of shame. The liberal intellectual, as we have seen, is committed to the rights and dignity of the individual, and he is also committed to the use of reason. There is thus no way he can both forbid torture and allow it without disgracing himself (in his own eyes). But then reason is working not merely to determine whether a situation is shameful; it is working to ward off shame by whatever means possible. It is as though reason has been given a task: torture is forbidden; now use all your resources to show that all of our behavior (including waterboarding) has been consistent with the prohibition.[16]

Note that this strategy is very different from a more straightforward one that argues that waterboarding is not torture and thus ought to be permitted. Then one would allow the military to engage in it as well. It is also different from a strategy that argues that in certain cases torture is necessary. By contrast, the strategy that is being used is one that forbids torture but then goes to great lengths to keep it murky whether waterboarding is torture—and gives mixed messages about whether it is permitted. The contradiction is avoided just so long as we don't look too closely into what is going on or what we are doing.

The national debate has not been explicitly about shame but about consistency with the law. Three events that have occurred while this chapter was being written speak to this point. First, Michael Mukasey was confirmed by the U.S. Senate as attorney general of the United States despite the fact that he refused to say whether he considered waterboarding to be torture. He did say that personally he found it repugnant, but he left it an open question whether it counts as torture.[17] Naively, one might think, "Goodness, if waterboarding *might* be torture, shouldn't we get clear about whether it is or it isn't. And shouldn't we be sure a nominee was on the right side of such an important issue *before* confirming him as attorney general?" But in this instance, being on the "right side" of the issue was being on neither side of it. Second, John McConnell, the director of National Intelligence, made the remarkable claim that waterboarding would be torture *if used against him* but "declined *for legal reasons* to say whether the technique categorically should be considered torture."[18] This is what today counts as judiciousness. Again, one might think, "If Mr. McConnell is so sure waterboarding would be torture if used against him, how could he *as a matter of legality* remain unclear about whether it is torture for others? And if as a matter of legality it is not clear, why doesn't that legality apply in his case?" As anyone who has worked his way through these contortions can see, the issue is not that the law is unclear and thus the issue cannot be decided; the law has been written and interpreted in ways *so that* they can say that these officials cannot say. JC's point is that consistency with the law has become a fetish whereby "liberal intellectuals" can ward off a sense of shame. Evidence in favor of JC is provided by the third recent event, the report of the CIA's destruction of videotapes of interrogations where waterboarding was used.[19] Officially, the destruction occurred in order to protect CIA interrogators from retaliation, and there has been some speculation in the press whether it might also have been done to protect them (or the CIA) against legal redress. But another explanation overwhelmingly suggests itself: the CIA (or those who ordered the tapes' destruction) correctly understood that these activities *should not be seen*.[20] It is under the gaze that one experiences shame. And the CIA is part of a complex structure such that shame is avoided not by avoiding the shameful act but by making it impossible that there should be a public gaze upon the act. If the public were to see the act, they would no longer be able to allow their leaders to remain vague about whether it was torture. But if public leaders must remain vague, then these images must not be seen. This entire complex edifice—the dance around whether waterboarding is torture—would collapse.

JC's accusation of national shame blows this kind of casuistry out of the water. In effect, his accusation says, "It doesn't matter what kind of reasons you can find; the shame is yours all the same. It doesn't matter what the legal technicalities are, the shame is yours all the same. It doesn't matter whether the videos have been destroyed, they have been destroyed *for your sake*, to protect you from feeling the shame that is yours all the same. Shame on you for using your reason to try to find consistency in your acts. Consistency will not protect you against the shame that is yours all the same."

And to the individual who says, "I don't see why I should bear the shame; I abhor torture," we can now see that this is a repetition of what the law says about itself. The law abhors torture, and yet has somehow tolerated it. We abhor torture, and what have we tolerated? Can anyone be that confident whether his own "opposition" doesn't have the same defensive structure? Thus although JC is officially talking *to* us (his readers) *about* "liberal intellectuals," the thought begins to dawn, "Might he be talking to us, about us?" Might we not have a complicity we do not yet recognize?[21]

Having worked through one instance of the dialectic of responsibility, let me briefly recap its moments.

First, the task is to help us come to see that we are entangled in motivated structures of not-seeing. This cannot be done simply by pointing it out. We think we can see the situation as it is; we think we are already against torture.

So, second, we are told of a group, the "liberal intellectuals," who fail to see the Machiavellian world in which they are entangled precisely because they refuse to accept its contradiction.

Third, we come to see that the law and its complex structure of enforcement and non-enforcement seem to be in place in order to placate the need for consistency of the "liberal intellectuals." If the law simply reflected "ordinary people's" understanding, it would be much simpler: torture is forbidden, except when it is necessary. But, then, who are these "liberal intellectuals" whom the law is going to such efforts to pacify? And why should they be the people who feel that they have no responsibility for the law?

Fourth, JC's accusation is that we are entangled in this national shame *irrespective of our reasons*, solely by virtue of citizenship. I take this to be an intentionally scandalous claim. In effect, it says, "Your use of reason does not matter; it won't get you off the hook." In a funny way, this provides a certain kind of relief. If our reasons don't matter, then we can at least momentarily take a break from using them to try to justify our innocence. We can at least begin to inquire into how reason has been used to tolerate and sustain this shameful situation.

Finally, the question begins to dawn: Might one of the ways reason has been used to tolerate this shameful situation be my giving myself reasons to think I am not implicated in this national shame? It is at this moment that I begin to wonder whether I am an instance of the "liberal intellectual" I have been reading about. But it is at this moment I cease to be a "liberal intellectual" precisely because I can now see what the "liberal intellectual" fails to see.

Note that none of this dialectic requires that JC be right that we share a shame solely in virtue of our citizenship, nor that we agree with him. JC and his accusation serve merely as a catalyst for a process by which we slowly come to see that our own reason has been implicated in a motivated structure of not seeing. What matters is that the accusation—perhaps by its scandalous nature—stimulates us to make this movement. In general, JC seems to think that human injustice requires motivated structures of not seeing. So, to take another example dear to his heart: the fact that meat ends up on our dinner table requires that we remain with, at best, a vague understanding of how it got there. His strategy is in the service of helping us see that we are motivated not to see.

Now what does the spectacle of embedding have to do with all of this? That is, what is John Coetzee's strategy here, as opposed to JC's? It seems to me the structure of the answer is obvious: there is something about seeing JC's opinions embedded in the travails of his life that facilitates a process by which those very opinions come to matter to us in which they might not otherwise. The difficulty is in figuring out how this might be so. Here a comparison with Kafka might be illuminating. Kafka is more concerned with guilt; JC is more concerned with shame. Guilt is more associated with the voice, and Kafka is at his most powerful when he isolates the voice of judgment—"You are guilty!"—from any embedding. Shame, by contrast, requires a gaze. JC's writing provides us with many images to gaze *upon*. As he himself says, Guantanamo Bay "is more a spectacle than a prisoner-of-war camp: an awful display" (21). But if we are not merely going to look upon shameful situations but ourselves participate in that sense of shame, we need some imaginative sense of being gazed upon. Arguably, this cannot be provided by a bare gaze (what is that?) as the voice of guilt can be provided by a bare voice. We need to have a sense of *who* is gazing upon us if we are to think that *under his gaze* we ought to feel shame.[22] (I take it that if a Nazi murderer were to look down on us as weaklings for being unable to participate in the Holocaust, we would not thereby feel ashamed.) We would need to feel shame under the gaze of someone we could imaginatively respect.

And JC earns our respect not simply because of the content of his strong opinions but because of the honesty with which he faces up to his stumbling efforts to live through what he recognizes to be the end of his life. As readers, we are familiar with the novelistic trope of embedding a moral argument in a larger human drama. For instance, there is the hypocritical preacher, whose sermons are at odds with how he lives his life. Or, to take an example, closer to home, it is easy to imagine a David Lodge novel in which a philosophy professor travels all over giving lectures on how ethics is just a projection of our own values onto the world—and has an affair in each town in which he gives the lecture. We might, then, wonder about his psychology: how much does the content of his lecture flow from his need for extramarital affairs? By contrast, JC's drama really has little to do with his personal psychology. He is facing up to his own death. He is trying to understand—and live out—the place of love and creativity as one moves toward death. These are issues that confront us all insofar as we are human. And it is as such that we are moved by him. It is not so much that we are struck by his personal dynamics as we are struck by the demands of the human.

This leads to the final point: the demands of the human require that we respond to metaphysical ache. This is not JC's peculiarity; metaphysical ache marks us as human. And, I want to suggest, there is something about the realistic portrayal of metaphysical ache in another that can serve to stimulate it in ourselves. Though Anya may have been the occasion of JC's metaphysical ache, she cannot on her own have been its balm. Nothing *on its own* could have done that. To grasp JC's metaphysical ache, we need to look at the entire movement of *Diary of a Bad Year*. These include not only the moral cries of *Strong Opinions* but also the worry that they are ersatz. It includes also the semi-Platonic love affair that develops between JC and Anya. What changes? JC says that the opinions he publishes haven't changed, but his opinion of his opinions has. And he goes on to write a Second Diary, not for publication, but one that he shares with Anya, that is more personal and passionate than anything in *Strong Opinions*. There is much in the Second Diary that is moving, and we are led to believe that it is his acquaintance with Anya that facilitated these thoughts and feelings' finding their way into written words: "The best proof we have that life is good, and therefore that there may perhaps be a God after all, who has our welfare at heart, is that each of us, on the day we are born, comes to the music of Johann Sebastian

Bach. It comes as a gift, unearned, unmerited, for free" (221). There is also awe, reverence, for Tolstoy and Dostoyevsky that is as passionate as any homage I have read. Anya, for her part, is able to dump the crude Alan, but she is also able to develop into a person who wants to reach out to the aging author to be the company he seeks for his death. The moment of love is the moment of death—toward which both lives have become organized.

But for all of its residual chauvinism, I am most struck by this "soft opinion" of JC's:

> Why is it that we—men and women both, but men most of all—are prepared to accept the checks and rebuffs of the real, more and more rebuffs as time goes by, more humiliating each time, yet keep coming back? The answer: because we cannot do without the real thing, the real real thing: because without the real we die as if of thirst. (179)

It is here, I think, that JC names the metaphysical ache, by saying what it is ultimately *for*: reality. This includes not only a living recognition that he is dying—that is, a life of dying in the company of Anya—but a living recognition of the reality of others. This would require not only recognizing their dignity but crying out against their humiliation, degradation, and torture. This is when the experience of shame might be the beginning of genuine ethical thought. And though we may everywhere be offered ersatz ethical substitutes, they cannot quench the thirst that marks us a human.[23]

Notes

1. J. M. Coetzee, *Diary of a Bad Year* (London: Harvill Secker, 2007), 47. All references in this chapter are to this edition and are cited in the text.
2. K. Harrison, *New York Times Book Review*, December 31, 2007.
3. Rachel Donadio, "Out of Africa," *New York Times*, December 16, 2007.
4. With the possible exception of Plato, no one has better understood the foibles and vicissitudes of this kind of movement better than S. Kierkegaard. See his pseudonymous author J. Climacus (another JC), *Concluding Unscientific Postscript to the Philosophical Fragments*, ed. H. V. Hong and E. H. Hong (Princeton, N.J.: Princeton University Press, 1992), esp. 72-125.
5. Plato, *Phaedrus* 275a-b.
6. S. Kierkegaard, "A First and Last Explanation," in *Concluding Unscientific Postscript to the Philosophical Fragments*, by J. Climacus, ed. H. V. Hong and E. H. Hong (Princeton, N.J.: Princeton University Press, 1992), 625-30.

7. See also S. Kierkegaard, *The Point of View* (Princeton, N.J.: Princeton University Press, 1998). There Kierkegaard explains in his own name that his pseudonymous authorship was a constituent element of his life as a religious author. Again, that he felt the need to explain himself ("to history") indicates he thought the pseudonymous authorship had been and would be misunderstood. I am indebted to James Conant for numerous conversations about Kierkegaard's pseudonymous authorship.

8. This, of course, raises a question of what *I* am doing, here in this essay. Am I, John Coetzee's friend, writing my own "First and Last Explanation" so that he doesn't have to write it himself? That would hardly be an improvement on Kierkegaard's gesture. I don't think there is an easy answer to this question; but what I would like to think is that Coetzee's novel has stimulated some thinking in me.

9. *Phaedrus* 261a7–8: "*psuchagôgia tis dia logôn*"; see also 271d10–c2.

10. *Republic* 7:518c409: "*periakteon ... sun holêi têi psychêi.*"

11. "*To ex hou.*" Aristotle obviously also used the term "*hulê*."

12. Plato, *Symposium*, 205d, 206c.

13. Ibid., 209b–c.

14. JC wonders in his diary whether what he feels when he sees the horrible images of Guantanamo "is not really the dishonor, the disgrace of being alive in these times, but something else, something punier and more manageable, some overload or underload of amines in the cortex that could loosely be entitled *depression* or even more loosely *gloom* and could be dispelled in a matter of minutes by the right cocktail of chemicals X, Y, and Z" (141).

15. While reading *Diary of a Bad Year* a memory came back to me of my first assignment as a student journalist, trying out for the *Yale Daily News*. The article was about alleged branding (that is, like cattle) of students as a rite of initiation into a fraternity. George W. Bush, class of 1968, the past president of DKE, called the branding "insignificant." Stating that there is little pain, Bush said, "there's no scarring mark, physically or mentally" (Jonathan Lear, "No Intervention for Fraternities," *Yale Daily News*, November 7, 1967).

16. From the *Yale Daily News* story: The head of the Inter-Fraternity Council "said it was more like a cigarette burn and goes away after two or three weeks. Labeling the branding as minor, he stated that it has never caused any medical complications. 'It's not as bad as it sounds,' he said. He asserted that the definition of physically and mentally degrading act was 'a matter of interpretation'" (Lear, "No Intervention for Fraternities").

17. See e.g. "Mukasey Sworn in as Attorney General," *New York Times*, November 9, 2007.

18. My emphasis. The story is by Pamela Hess of the Associated Press and thus ran in many newspapers on January 13, 2008.

19. See e.g. "Justice Dept. Sets Criminal Inquiry on C.I.A. Tapes," *New York Times*, January 3, 2008.

20. In this regard, it is fascinating that there was an outcry in Congress about CIA waterboarding *until* it came out in the press that top Democratic leaders, including House Speaker Nancy Pelosi, were briefed on the procedure two years earlier and at least some urged the CIA to "push harder"; see Joby Warrick and Dan Eggen, "Hill Briefed on Waterboarding in 2002," *Washington Post*, December 9, 2007.

21. Looking back at that *Yale Daily News* story now, my attention is drawn to a completely different place than it has been before. "Fraternities will be allowed to 'put their house in order' without interference from the Yale administration, said Richard C. Carroll, Dean of Undergraduate Affairs, yesterday. Dean Carroll expects to let the Inter-Fraternity Council have complete jurisdiction 'solving its own problems', according to Carroll . . . 'I suspect the hazing has been sensationalized just a little more than the facts warrant: it may not be as horrendous as it seems. I think there may be an exaggeration of the total picture,' said Carroll" (Lear, "No Intervention for Fraternities"). This seems to me a perfect specimen of a certain type of academic dean: in the name of giving students responsibility for how they conduct themselves, he absolves himself of responsibility for directing them in any particular way. What if, in response to that incident, Dean Carroll had gone on a loud and public crusade? What if, in his remarks to me, he said instead, "What these young men have done may look innocent, but it is in fact very dangerous. It is a step along to the way to coarsening their souls. Here are people who may be future leaders, and they should not be taught to be indifferent to the pain they are inflicting on others. I hope Mr. Bush will come to see this for himself and apologize to those on whom he inflicted pain, even if it was meant to be 'in fun.' This cannot be fun; it is morally very serious. His ability to make moral discriminations is at stake." Such a scenario would have seemed strange at the time, but I cannot help wondering what good it might have done.

22. See B. Williams, *Shame and Necessity* (Berkeley: University of California Press, 1994), 81–85.

23. I am grateful to John Coetzee, James Conant, and Gabriel Lear for extended conversations on the philosophical topics discussed in this chapter. Obviously, only I can be held responsible for the views expressed here. But I should like to state explicitly that I have never had a conversation with Coetzee about his literary style.

4 Torture and Collective Shame
Jeff McMahan

SHAME AND GUILT

In *Waiting for the Barbarians*, one of J. M. Coetzee's finest novels, forces of an unnamed imperial power torture not only "barbarians" captured in their colonial frontiers but also the insubordinate magistrate of the colonial outpost in which most of the story takes place. By having the Magistrate as narrator, Coetzee affords himself occasions for representing and musing on the shame, humiliation, and diminishment endured by victims of torture. These sensitive reflections cohere well with contemporary philosophical analyses of shame as the experienced public exposure of one's vulnerabilities, weaknesses, or flaws, particularly one's inability to control the aspects of oneself that one presents to others.[1] Under repeated exposure to torture, the Magistrate is reduced to a putrid, feeble animal that impotently writhes and howls, wholly at the mercy of others.[2]

In Coetzee's most recent novel, *Diary of a Bad Year*, torture and shame reemerge as central themes, but the focus of discussion is different.[3] Whereas in *Waiting for the Barbarians* there are long passages on the evil of torture and what it does to its victims, all this is simply taken as given in *Diary of a Bad Year*, which instead poses the question how Americans should respond to the shame, dishonor, and defilement brought upon them by the Bush administration's practice of torture in what it ridiculously calls the "war on terror." The subject is no longer the shame of the victim or even the shame of the perpetrators but the vicarious shame, or collective shame, borne by the perpetrators' fellow citizens.

Unlike the shame of the victim of torture, the shame of being somehow implicated in the practice of torture is closely related to moral guilt. One of the differences between shame and guilt is that shame arguably requires the presence, or at least the imagined presence, of observers.[4] One can be ashamed *of* oneself, but not shamed only *to* or *before* oneself. Suppose, for example, that Robinson Crusoe carries a burden of secret guilt to an uninhabited island from which he can never escape and that there is no possibility that anyone he has left behind will ever discover the wrongdoing of which he is guilty. In these conditions, there is nothing that could be added to his guilt, which is and must remain entirely private, to produce a distinguishable state of shame. Yet when one's guilt is exposed to others, shame can be its public face. This is the basis of the practice of public shaming as a means of punishing the guilty—in some cultures, for example, by branding criminals, particularly on the face, or in Puritan America by locking sinners in public stocks. The thesis suggested in *Diary of a Bad Year* is that Americans are *objectively* shamed by the Bush administration's wrongdoing in torturing its suspected enemies—that is, they are shamed before the world whether they *feel* shame or not—and that among their moral burdens is an imperative to cleanse themselves of the shame and dishonor entailed by their membership in a nation that tortures its enemies.

It is unclear what the book's claims about collective shame imply or presuppose about collective guilt. The example of Robinson Crusoe suggests that there can be circumstances in which it can be rational to feel guilt when there is no occasion to experience shame. But it is possible that Americans might be shamed or dishonored by the Bush administration's embrace of torture while being individually and collectively guiltless. *Diary of a Bad Year* vacillates on the relation between shame and guilt and on whether Americans are shamed *because* of their guilt or *despite* their innocence. Although the references are mainly to shame rather than guilt, there are passages in which the two notions are treated as equivalent. It is said, for example, of those white South Africans who "will go bowed under the shame of the crimes that were committed in their name," that they "might learn a trick or two from the British about managing collective guilt. The British have simply declared their independence from their imperial forebears. The Empire was long ago abolished, they say, so what is there for us to feel responsible for?" (44). This is an implied accusation of bad faith: the British still bear responsibility for the crimes of their imperial forebears (just as, as we will see shortly, contemporary Germans still bear responsibility for the crimes of their Nazi forebears), and collective responsibility for criminal action entails collective guilt. Yet if the contemporary British bear collective guilt for the crimes of the Empire, and post-Apartheid white South Africans can learn from them some effective techniques for evading collective guilt, the implication is that the shame the South Africans bear for crimes that they did not commit but that were committed "in their name" has its basis in their collective guilt for those crimes. And a further implication is that Americans shamed by the tortures perpetrated in their name bear collective guilt as well.

Most of the pages of *Diary of a Bad Year* are divided into three sections. The middle section contains a continuing narrative—the diary, perhaps—of an elderly writer. It is concerned mainly with his relations with a younger woman who becomes the typist for a collection of short essays he is writing. The section at the bottom of the page contains a parallel narrative by the typist. Throughout most of the book, the section at the top of the page, which is usually much longer than either of the others, comprises the essays in the writer's book, which bears the same title as the collection of Nabokov's interviews and essays: *Strong Opinions*. The views about torture and shame articulated in the book are primarily in the essays, and as such are presented as the views of the writer. Are they Coetzee's views? They echo themes in *Waiting for the Barbarians* and in certain of Coetzee's other novels, particularly *Disgrace*. And some of the other views in the essays, such as those concerning human cruelty to animals, are ones with which Coetzee is identified. Finally, the writer is teasingly characterized in ways that suggest that he is simply Coetzee himself. He is, for example, a South African writer living in self-imposed exile in Australia whose initials are J.C. and who has written a novel called *Waiting for the Barbarians* and a book of essays on censorship that was published in the 1990s. It is, however, unimportant whether the views expressed in the essays within the novel are Coetzee's own. They are the views of a great many people. They are the views, in particular, of people of a certain familiar type, people generally on the political left who are earnest, decent, and humane. But in my view the beliefs about collective shame that these morally admirable people share with Coetzee's fictional writer are mistaken, and my aim in this short essay is to explain why. I will attribute them only to "C," which is how the writer is referred to in the novel. Whether they are also Coetzee's is immaterial.

I should acknowledge that I am aware that there is a vast literature on shame—or, rather, a number of vast literatures: a philosophical literature on the concept of shame and its relation to concepts of responsibility and guilt, a related philosophical literature on the role of shame in ethical life, and further extensive explorations of shame from anthropological, historical, sociological, psychological, and even literary-critical perspectives. I confess that I know little of this literature beyond what I cite in the endnotes. There is also a vast literature on collective responsibility and a sparser though significant literature on individual responsibility for collective action. I am not well acquainted with these, either. This essay is therefore an amateur foray into these issues, neither scholarly nor systematic. But in this respect my strong opinions are no different from those they confront. For C's reflections are also not the arguments of a systematic theorist.

COLLECTIVE IDENTITY AS A BASIS OF COLLECTIVE SHAME

I begin with some facts. I am an American. I have never tortured anyone. I am not in any obvious way an accessory to torture: I have never conspired to engage in torture, never instigated, aided, abetted, or been in any other way an accomplice to an act of torture, never failed to prevent an act of torture that it was in my power to prevent, and so on. Yet according to C, I have a lot to answer and atone for. I bear the shame of the tortures committed by the agents of my government. Unless I do something to purify myself, I will remain forever dishonored and "appear with soiled hands before the judgment of history" (41).

I find it curious that C's accusatory finger points toward me primarily, or even exclusively, because of my country's practice of torture, which was done in secret without public debate, had a relatively small number of victims, and involved methods near the milder end of the spectrum of modern torture techniques. By contrast, my country's war in Iraq was extensively debated in public, approved by Congress, and supported by a large proportion of the population, who immediately decorated their sport-utility vehicles with magnetic ribbons urging their brethren to "Support Our Troops," by which they meant "Support Our War," a war in which more than 100,000 Iraqi civilians have been killed. If I am weighed down with shame for the acts of my country, I doubt that the proportion attributable to the policy of torture constitutes more than a small part of the total load.

There are, however, many who feel an especially acute sense of shame for the acts of torture committed in Iraq, Afghanistan, and Guantanamo, and there are even more who say they do, for we do tend to talk this way. Just as I was beginning to formulate my ideas for this chapter, I read an op-ed piece in the *New York Times*, written in the aftermath of the terrorist attacks in Mumbai late in 2008, that urged Pakistanis as a nation to say to the terrorists among them: "What you have done in murdering defenseless men, women and children has brought shame on us and on you."[5] So I concede that the sense of vicarious shame, and in particular collective shame, is very common. The question is whether it is rational and, if so, on what grounds and on what occasions.

C's remarks suggest that wrongdoing is, or can be, an occasion for shame and that if the wrongdoing is sufficiently egregious, those who are responsible for it, either as perpetrators or vicariously, are not only shamed but also dishonored. The medium through which shame is transmitted vicariously is, he suggests, membership in a collective. Consider, for example, what he writes in the concluding paragraph of essay 10, "On National Shame," about both pride and shame:

> A few days ago I heard a performance of the Sibelius fifth symphony. As the closing bars approached, I experienced exactly the large swelling emotion that the music was

written to elicit. What would it have been like, I wondered, to be a Finn in the audience at the first performance of the symphony in Helsinki nearly a century ago, and feel that swell overtake one? The answer: one would have felt proud, proud that *one of us* could put together such sounds, proud that out of nothing we human beings could make such stuff. Contrast with that one's feelings of shame that *we, our people*, have made Guantanamo. Musical creation on the one hand, a machine for inflicting pain and humiliation on the other: the best and the worst that human beings are capable of.
(45)

When he says that a Finn would have felt proud that "one of us" had written such triumphal music, it seems that "us" must refer to Finns. But the next clause in the sentence seems to expand the reference to include among "us" all human beings. Yet in the sentence that follows, the reference is again restricted, presumably to the relevant national group: Americans. The suggestion seems to be that national pride and national shame are precisely parallel: they both make sense and they are both grounded in the collective identity shared by all members of a nation or, in these cases, a nation-state.

One might wonder whether C's view implies that even little children are somehow implicated in the deeds of their conationals. It is, in fact, commonly accepted that they are. Most people take pride in the deeds of their ancestors. A Finn who was only a year old when Sibelius's fifth symphony had its premier, or even a Finn who was born decades after that, might find that her pride swells with the music whenever she hears it. C claims that the grounds for national shame, like the grounds for national pride, are transmitted across generations, as the nation itself survives through generations. He quotes, with apparent approval, Jean-Pierre Vernant's reference to "the ancient religious conception of the misdeed as a defilement attached to an entire race and inexorably transmitted from one generation to the next," and then writes, later in the same essay: "Young Germans protest, *We have no blood on our hands, so why are we looked on as racists and murderers?* The answer: *Because you have the misfortune to be the grandchildren of your grandparents*" (49–50). According to this view, one's unchosen and ineffaceable identity as a member of a certain nation can make one the bearer of shame for the deeds of others. Even if I can somehow cleanse *myself* of the shame and dishonor I carry, my grandchildren will nevertheless inherit a burden of shame for what the Bush administration and its hirelings have done.

This understanding of collective pride and collective shame is untenable, indeed, grotesque. As I will suggest later, there may be some collectives that have features that distribute responsibility, and thus perhaps pride, shame, or guilt, to *all* their members on the basis of action by only *some* of the members. But if responsibility gets distributed in this way, it must be by virtue of more than the mere fact that the members all share a certain collective identity. Even putting aside the issue of transmission across generations, the implications of the idea that shared collective identity is a rational basis for collective pride and shame are thoroughly implausible even in quite pedestrian cases. Here is an example from my own experience. During the late 1980s and early 1990s, I lived in Urbana, Illinois, which is contiguous and, in effect, continuous with the town of Champaign, Illinois. During that period, a young woman named Bonnie Blair who had grown up in Champaign won a record number of gold medals in the Olympic games. On each occasion when she won a medal, the people of Champaign held their heads a little higher. They felt the kind of pride that C imagines a Finn might feel on hearing the first performance of Sibelius's fifth. Blair, they imagined, had bestowed honor *on them*, justifying their sense of personal pride. The grounds for pride varied, of course, depending on the degree of exclusivity of the relevant shared collective identity. In the innermost concentric circle were those who had actually been her neighbors or schoolmates as she was growing up. They were assumed to have the strongest grounds for pride. Within the next, larger circle were those who were longtime residents of Champaign, though even those who had moved there quite recently felt they were entitled to a certain degree of pride as well. Then came residents of the state of Illinois, then Midwesterners, then all Americans, millions of whom congratulated themselves on Blair's victories.

If, as C's view suggests, the residents of Champaign had genuine grounds for pride in Blair's achievements, it seems that others ought, on those same grounds, to have admired them, and perhaps even praised them, for sharing in her glory. For admiration and praise are what is called for from others when there are objective grounds for pride in one's own accomplishments. And they are also called for when pride in the accomplishments of others is justified in uncontroversial ways. Thus, Blair's coach was entitled to feel pride in her achievement, as were her parents, whose encouragement and sacrifices for the sake of her training contributed to her success. And the grounds for the pride that these people deservedly felt also justified the admiration and praise of others, which they naturally elicited. Yet I had no reason to think better of my barber after Blair won her medals than I had thought of him before. Nor did I have any reason to think less well of him after a local man, who was known to neither of us, committed a murder. That my barber rejoiced in being a resident of Champaign, which made him a bearer of the same collective identity as both Blair and the murderer, failed to give him a share in either the former's triumphs or the latter's depravity.

When C has his imagined Finn reflect that "one of us" has composed a transcendent symphony, the collective to which "us" refers is essentially arbitrary. C himself unguardedly raises the question why "us" should pick out only Finns rather than all human beings. It could in fact refer to the members of any group to which Sibelius belonged, such as all Finns, Finns whose first language is Swedish, people who are or are destined to become completely bald, people who have had throat cancer, or, as C acknowledges, members of the human species. Yet for the individual members of most such groups, there seems to be no reason for pride in the fact that *one of them* wrote that symphony. There are two reasons for this. One is that we naturally feel pride only when the unifying collective identity is one to which many of the members attribute significance. Bald people do not take pride in Sibelius's fifth because being bald is not a significant ground of collective identification. More importantly, none of the collectives I mentioned, not even the nation of Finns, enables their members to claim that "*we* composed that symphony" or even that "*we* are a people who compose great symphonies." Perhaps it is the appropriateness of the collective subject "we" that C is groping for as the criterion of rational collective pride or shame, and mistakenly thinks he has located in mere collective identity. For the acts of some members of a collective to be a legitimate basis for pride or shame on the part of the other members, the collective must be of a certain type, and the acts must have been done in a way that connects them with the collective. It might be true, for example, that while Finns have no basis for pride in Sibelius's fifth because there is no sense in which it is *their* creation, Americans nevertheless have grounds for shame in the Bush administration's acts of torture because their relation to those acts makes it reasonable to claim that *they* together constitute a nation that tortures its captive enemies. If so, the challenge is to identify the relations between Americans in general and the Bush administration and its immediate agents of torture that make that claim reasonable. More generally, what are the properties of a collective, and the conditions of individual action, that are sufficient for an act by some members of a collective to be a ground or occasion for pride, shame, or guilt on the part of the collective as a whole?

THE COLLECTIVE AS IRREDUCIBLE BEARER OF GUILT OR SHAME

I will offer a few suggestions about this, but before I do it may be helpful to distinguish explicitly between two ways in which properties might be "collectivized." According to one view, relations within a collective may be such that when some of the members act wrongly in certain ways, responsibility for their wrongdoing extends to other members of the collective—perhaps to *all* of them—in a way that makes them individually guilty or shames them as individuals. I will discuss this way in which shame or guilt might be collectivized in the next section. In this section I will consider a different possibility. According to this view, when some members of a collective act in a way that satisfies certain conditions, their act constitutes an act of the collective as a whole. When this is the case, and the act is wrong, all the members of the collective may be said to share the guilt and shame for the act. Yet this is compatible with its being the case that for any individual member of the collective, there are no grounds for *personal* shame or guilt, for that individual may be in no way personally responsible or culpable for the wrongful collective act.

This view has been articulated by Margaret Gilbert, one of the foremost writers on the nature of collectives and collective action. Her account is important for our purposes not only because it articulates the second of these two ways in which shame and guilt may be collectivized but also because it elucidates the connection between collective responsibility and the appropriateness of attributing an act or its outcome to a collective subject, so that it makes sense (as it does not in the case of the composing of Sibelius's fifth symphony) to say that "we" did it. Gilbert writes:

> If I am one of us, and *we* did something, *I am part of what did it*. More precisely, I am *part of the agent* that did it. . . . Whereas *I* am the subject of *my* action, I am *part of the subject* of *our* action. . . . If *we* did this bad thing, as opposed to this or that person doing it, we may bear moral guilt with respect to the doing of it. If *we* bear guilt, the guilt in question is, precisely, *ours*. Not mine, nor mine and yours, but ours, ours *together*. Perhaps it may then be referred to as *collective* guilt. This guilt will be *participated in*, or *shared*, by all of us, *in our capacity as members of "us."* . . . Different members can still bear different degrees of *personal* guilt in relation to what they understand to be "our" act. Some members might have done all they could to stop it, others may have been blamelessly ignorant of it, whereas some may have put all their efforts into its performance. It is clear enough where the personal guilt lies when this is so.[6]

Gilbert refers here to guilt, but all she says applies equally, with relevant changes, to shame (and pride, which contrasts with both guilt and shame). As I noted earlier, in cases of wrongdoing, the agent's shame may be nothing more—though also nothing less—than the public face of guilt.

Although this conception of collective guilt or shame as entirely distinct from personal guilt or shame is interesting, it is problematic in various ways. Suppose, for example, that one is a member of a collective that has acted wrongly in a way that makes one's claim that "*we* have acted wrongly" true. And suppose further that one bears not only one's share of the collective shame but that one also has grounds for personal shame. How might one experience the two forms of shame? Should the collective shame simply intensify one's feelings of shame? Or should the two forms of shame be phenomenologically distinguishable?

Although Gilbert claims that "a feeling of guilt can be an appropriate response for the member of a *plural subject* [her slightly technical notion of a collective] that bears guilt," this is actually doubtfully consistent with her understanding of collective guilt.[7] What is distinctive in her account of collective guilt is precisely that guilt can be a property of a collective of which an individual is a member without being a property of that individual—that is, the collective can be guilty when the individual is entirely blameless. The guilt is fully collectivized: "not mine, nor mine and yours, but . . . ours *together*"—that is, it belongs to the collective as an entity distinct from the sum of its members. One can, as Gilbert does, appeal to the idea that one can be innocent qua individual but guilty qua member of the collective—or, as she puts it, that guilt can attach to "the self-as-group-member or [to] the group-insofar-as-it-exists-in-my-person, rather than [to] me personally."[8] But I can make no sense of that, as no one seems to be composed of these distinct entities. One is either guilty, so that one deserves punishment, ought to feel shame, and so forth, or one is not. There seems to be no way to punish "the group-insofar-as-it-exists-in-my-person" without inflicting the same harm on "my person"—that is, on "me personally."

What I think Gilbert ought to say is that if it is the collective that is guilty, and not the individual member, then it is the collective that ought to feel shame. If the collective can be guilty even though the individual member is blameless, then it should be appropriate for the collective to feel shame even though it would be irrational for the individually guiltless member to do so. Sturdy common sense might intervene here to protest that collectives cannot have feelings. That may be so, but if we can make no sense of the idea of a collective feeling shame then it is hard to see how we can make sense of other collective psychological states that writers such as Gilbert and C take to be unproblematic—for example, the notion of a collective desire, a collective belief, or a collective intention.

While issues concerning the *feeling* of shame are of philosophical interest, they are of comparatively little moral significance. Our feelings are unreliable guides in matters of morality. The shame or guilt one feels may be appropriate or inappropriate, rational or irrational. If we wish to act morally, we must ask whether our feelings, either individual or collective, are justified; and to determine whether they are, only thinking will help.[9] But the question whether it is the individual or the collective that has grounds for having certain feelings does suggest parallel questions that are of considerable moral and practical significance. For example, do the grounds for attributing collective guilt or shame to *us* make any *individual* member of the collective morally liable to defensive or preventive action as a means of sparing further potential victims from torture? Do these grounds for guilt or shame confer on any individuals a moral obligation to make reparations to former victims? Do they make any individuals liable to punishment?

Suppose that one is personally implicated in a collective practice of torture in a way that makes one personally guilty and thus liable to punishment. But one is also a member of the collective that is guilty. Are individual guilt and collective guilt additive, so that the punishment one receives for one's personal guilt ought to be increased by an additional amount corresponding to one's share of the collective guilt?[10] If collective shares are determinable, they are presumably equal, but are they also—for example—proportional to the size of the collective? That is, is one's share of the collective guilt larger, so that one deserves more punishment, if the number of individuals who compose the collective is smaller? If, for example, there are only a hundred of us in the collective, are our individual shares of the collective guilt larger than they would be if there were a million of us to share the same total of collective guilt?

Gilbert claims, probably wisely, that "*there is no way of breaking down collective guilt into quantifiable shares.*"[11] But if that is true, collective guilt seems irrelevant to such practical concerns as punishment and reparation, unless, for example, one can discover a way of punishing a collective that does not necessarily involve the punishment of any of its individual members. For if individual members are punished, their individual punishments must be proportionate to their guilt, and Gilbert is denying that their share of the collective guilt can be measured. On these assumptions, proportionate punishment of individuals for collective guilt is necessarily impossible, since there is no way to calibrate punishments so that they are proportionate in relation to guilt that cannot be measured.

One might argue that if a punishment is genuinely *collective*, there is no punishment of individuals at all (apart from additional individual punishments based on individual guilt). For punishment is not just a matter of the infliction of harm but is also, and essentially, a matter of intention. When a convicted criminal is punished, his relatives may also be harmed; indeed, they may be harmed to an even greater degree than he is (by grief, loss of income, loss of reputation—in some cases because of common beliefs about collective shame—and so on). But this does not mean that the relatives are *punished*. Rather, they are harmed unintentionally as a side effect of the punishment of the criminal. One might argue that, in a precisely analogous way, collective punishment involves the punishment *only* of the collective itself. Harms suffered by individual members of the collective as a consequence of the punishment of the collective are entirely incidental. Individuals may be harmed directly—for example, their businesses may be directly affected by trade sanctions against their country—or they may be harmed only indirectly or derivatively, by virtue of their identification with the collective and their investment in its good. But such harms need not be intended and need not count as punishment.

What might be gained by the infliction of a genuinely collective punishment—that is, one intended to affect only the collective itself? If the aim is retribution, then collective punishment will, in my view, always be disproportionate in practice. This is because I think retribution—understood as the *intrinsic good* involved in the infliction of *deserved* suffering on wrongdoers—is a *comparatively* unimportant aim. Suppose, for example, that life imprisonment can be equally effective in preventing and deterring crime as capital punishment, and at no greater cost. In that case, even if some offenders really do deserve to die, execution will nevertheless always be wrong in practice because the value of retribution will always be outweighed by the ineliminable risk of executing the innocent or by the harms that would be caused to the offender's relatives as a side effect. Capital punishment would, in short, always have side effects that would be disproportionate in relation to the aim of retribution. And if this is so in the case of retribution against an individual, it is all the more so in the case of retribution against a collective, whose desert is of a different nature from that of an individual.

Suppose, however, that something more important than retribution is at stake, such as the prevention or deterrence of further wrongdoing by a collective such as a state. One might argue that in such a case the harms inflicted on the innocent as a side effect of collective punishment could well be proportionate in relation to the good that the punishment might achieve. Yet if in such a case there are members of the collective who are individually innocent and who will be harmed as a side effect of the punishment of the collective, would it not be more just to try to identify those members of the collective who are individually guilty, or who bear most responsibility for the action of the collective, and punish them rather than punishing the collective as a whole?[12] If the aims of the punishment are prevention and deterrence, it seems that punishing the individuals who are guilty should be just as effective as punishing the collective as a whole. It is also probable that punishing only the responsible agents would have fewer harmful side effects on those who are individually innocent. It therefore seems that individual punishments would almost certainly achieve a better balance between the goals of prevention and deterrence and the infliction of unintended harms on the innocent.

I have so far assumed that it is possible for collective punishment to be discriminate, in the sense that it is possible to intend to harm only the collective itself and not the individual members, many or all of whom may be individually innocent. There may, however, be cases in which this is not possible. There may be collectives that have so little internal structure or organization that it is impossible to harm or damage them except by harming their individual members. If there are, it may be impossible to punish the collective without intending to harm the individuals, many of whom may be individually innocent. In that case, collective punishment would be indiscriminate.

The upshot is that collective punishment, as a response to collective guilt in Gilbert's sense, is in practice almost certain to be either disproportionate or indiscriminate. Collective guilt in this sense is therefore largely or entirely irrelevant to matters of practice.

A POSSIBLE BASIS FOR COLLECTIVE RESPONSIBILITY AND COLLECTIVE SHAME

This notion of collective guilt, and by extension collective shame, seems, in any event, not to be what C has in mind. He writes that "the issue for individual Americans becomes a moral one: how, in the face of this shame to which I am subjected, do I behave? How do I save my honour?" (39). For C, the ground or source of the shame may be a collective act, but the shame itself is personal. In C's view, there is no metaphysical schizophrenia, no division of the self between individual person, on the one hand, and cell in the ghostly collective organism, on the other. There are just people, but shame arising from what only some of them do is sometimes distributed among them in peculiar ways by virtue of their relations within a collective. This is the other way in which I suggested earlier that shame or guilt might be collectivized.

C is a novelist. Novelists are sometimes the inspired source of moral insights of startling originality and power. But it is in general not in their line of work to draw out the implications of their insights in rigorous but tedious detail or to test the ultimate plausibility of those apparent insights by reference to those implications. This is true even of novelists who occasionally write nonfiction. And it is especially true of novelists who are themselves merely fictional, whose options are in consequence highly restricted. As someone who makes a living by thinking about matters such as this, perhaps I can offer C some professional assistance. His idea that rational pride and shame can be diffused among all the members of a collective through the thin medium of collective identity is one that I think he should want to repudiate. Among other things, it is an idea that he shares with a great many terrorists, who often invoke it, if not always in their public statements, at least in their private struggles to rationalize what they do. Many terrorists are highly morally motivated. This is especially evident in the case of suicide bombers. It is therefore unlikely in most cases that they think of themselves as intentionally killing people who are entirely innocent. Even Osama bin Laden, in his "Letter to the American people" of 2002, argued that Americans are not innocent but are responsible for the acts of their government through the activity of voting. But many others think that all Americans (and, *mutatis mutandis*, all Israelis, all Jews, and so on) are guilty just because they are Americans (or Israelis . . .)—that is, because they are citizens of a country that is guilty of grievous wrongs and injustices. This is the view that C and many terrorists seem to have in common, though C refers more frequently to shame than to guilt. The difference is that C does not infer from the collective guilt or shame of Americans that they deserve to be killed or are morally liable to be killed.

C ought not to be seduced into accepting so crude a doctrine of collective responsibility by his justifiable revulsion at the Bush administration's practice of torturing its captives. He could, in fact, do better in his effort to find grounds for shame among ordinary Americans for the acts of their government than their mere shared identity as Americans. He might start, for example, by noting that the policy of torture operates through institutions that are designed, organized, and administered by Americans to serve Americans. These institutions are, indeed, partly constitutive of the abstract object known as the United States. States are constituted by their territory, institutions, citizenry, and so on. They persist over long periods of time despite the replacement of their entire population over several generations, in part because of the continuity of their institutional structures. When the operation of these institutions results in a practice of torture, it may not be unreasonable to locate at least some degree of responsibility for the practice among those whose institutions they are, and especially among those who administer, participate in, and benefit from the operation of those institutions. This is particularly true when the institutions are at least to some degree remotely controlled through democratic decision-making procedures and when practices such as torture operate through established mechanisms of political authorization. In such cases, responsibility for the practice and its consequences can be traced back, if only tenuously, through chains of authorization, all the way to the citizens themselves. There is thus some substance in bin Laden's point, though it has nothing like the significance he attributes to it.

C might go further by noting that people have a special responsibility to control the operations of the institutions that serve them. When those institutions malfunction and begin to operate immorally, both those who administer them and those on whose behalf they operate have a duty to try to bring the immoral action to an end. People can incur a burden of shame by failing to fulfill this duty as well as by contributing positively to the continued immoral operation of their institutions.

The focus on institutions is important in another way. For it is usually only by acting in an official capacity within the institutions of a collective that an individual or group of individuals can transmit responsibility and therefore shame for wrongful acts to others in the collective. Suppose, for example, that entirely as a matter of chance all the American perpetrators of torture in Afghanistan, Iraq, and Guantanamo have been Catholics. Even if it makes sense to suppose that their action brings shame on all Americans, it makes no sense to claim that it also brings shame on all Catholics. This is because they had no capacity to act as agents of the Catholic Church on behalf of Catholics. They acted instead as agents of the United States, fulfilling the requirements of certain roles they had in exclusively American institutions.

There is a subtle but important difference between acting in an authorized role or official capacity within a collective, which is an objective matter, and acting "in the name" of a collective. The latter phrase is common and appears in C's lament, quoted earlier, that "the generation of white South Africans to which I belong, and the next generation, and perhaps the generation after that too, will go bowed under the shame of the crimes that were committed in their name" (44). But one can, it seems, act in the name of others simply by claiming to do so. This is presumably the assumption of the *New York Times* editorialist who contended that the action of Pakistani terrorists in India brings shame on all other Pakistanis. If those men had simply been ordinary criminals engaged in mass killing for personal gain, the editorialist would not have supposed that they had shamed an entire nation. It is because he assumes that they took themselves to be acting in the name of all Pakistanis that he believes that they were able to implicate other Pakistanis in what they did. But it is beyond the power of terrorists to implicate the other members of a collective to which they belong simply by declaring that they are acting in the name of the collective as a whole. If a group of white supremacists were to claim, in committing some atrocity, to be acting in the name of white people everywhere, that would not entail that there would be yet another burden of shame under which C, a white man, must go bowed.

HOW IMPORTANT IS IT TO AVOID COLLECTIVELY IMPOSED GUILT OR SHAME?

I have offered a crude sketch of some grounds on which it might reasonably be claimed that Americans quite generally have been shamed by the Bush administration's practice of torture. Suppose this sketch has some plausibility and that I and other Americans are indeed bearers of shame for the action of our government. C poses for us the question: How can we save our honor? How might we escape from this burden of shame, and how important is it that we should do so?

According to C, this is a matter of considerable importance: "the object, not just for Americans of conscience but for individual Westerners in general, must be to find ways to save one's honour" (41). (Here he repeats the mistake of thinking that shame is transmitted by bare collective identity. While I have suggested that Americans may be implicated via the institutions that connect them to their government and its acts, there are no comparable institutional structures capable of implicating Westerners in general.) C surveys some of the means by which we might save our honor but finds most of them wanting. "Mere symbolic actions," such as "pronouncing aloud the words 'I abhor the leaders of my country and dissociate myself from them'—will certainly not be enough" (40). What, then, would be enough? C has only one suggestion of which he is entirely confident. "Suicide would save one's honour, and perhaps there have already been honour suicides among Americans that one does not hear of." Thus, "if today I heard that some American had committed suicide rather than live in disgrace, I would fully understand" (40, 43).

I have no idea how seriously Coetzee would have his readers take this suggestion. I hope there are no earnest and idealistic young Americans who in a moment of anguish over their government's action have taken it seriously enough to act on it. For even if there are institutional connections between ordinary Americans and their government that make it rational for them to feel personal shame over its deeds, to suggest that it might be desirable, meritorious, noble, or even morally necessary for them to kill themselves is to attribute vastly disproportionate significance to the grounds for shame. What would killing oneself accomplish? What would it be other than a "mere symbolic action," which C dismisses as not enough? I suspect that C's answer, if only he could have stayed around for another chapter to answer challenges, would have been couched in the religious idiom in which much of his discussion of torture is expressed. He would have said that Americans have been morally stained, tainted, contaminated, or defiled and that in consequence their souls require radical purgation or purification. But like so many of religion's contributions to moral thought, this obsession with the state of one's own soul is a pernicious corruption. A hypothetical example will show where it leads.

Suppose that an American of conscience, to borrow C's term, is in a position to prevent CIA agents acting under presidential authorization from torturing ten captives who have been designated as "unlawful combatants." Alternatively, he can, as chance would have it, prevent agents of the Iranian government from torturing twenty Iranian citizens accused of disloyalty, subversion, or something of that sort. But he cannot prevent both; he must choose. According to the view espoused by C, his own moral purity and honor are at stake in the action of the CIA agents, whereas there is nothing to connect him to the action of the Iranian agents that would give him grounds for shame. If he is to save his honor, he must prevent the torture of ten by CIA agents rather than the torture of twenty by Iranian agents. Yet that would be perverse. It is not, in fact, what morality requires.

This does not show that there is no more reason to prevent wrongdoing by those to whom one is specially related than there is to prevent equivalent wrongdoing by others. If the American's choice were between preventing CIA agents from torturing ten innocent people and preventing Iranian agents from inflicting equivalent tortures on ten different innocent people, many of us think that he would have a reason to prevent the tortures by the CIA. Even so, that reason might not be that he would be shamed or dishonored by the acts of the CIA but not by the acts of the Iranians. It might instead be that because of his special relation to the CIA agents—the relation of fellow citizenship—he has stronger reason to prevent what would be bad for them than to prevent what would be equally bad for Iranians. On the plausible assumption that it is bad for a person to act in a way that is egregiously immoral, it follows that the American would have stronger reason to prevent his fellow citizens from acting immorally than he would have to prevent the same number of Iranians from acting in the same immoral way.

But even if the reason why the American ought to prevent CIA agents rather than Iranian agents from torturing ten innocent people is that this is what is required in order to avoid personal shame and dishonor, a further variant of the example suggests, to me at least, that the avoidance of shame and dishonor that one would otherwise incur, not through one's own action but only through one's association with others, is a comparatively insignificant aim. If the American could either prevent the CIA agents from torturing ten people or prevent Iranian agents from inflicting equivalent tortures on eleven, it would, in my view, be inexcusably egotistical to suppose that one should allow the torture of an additional person just to "save one's honor."

Although *Diary of a Bad Year* contains C's essays in *Strong Opinions*, it does not include the acknowledgments section of that book. If it did, it could not allow C to say what Coetzee says of those who offered him advice on the writing of *Diary of a Bad Year*: "For what I have made of their advice I alone am responsible" (231). For if some of the opinions (other than those about collective shame) articulated in *Strong Opinions* are wrong, C would have to think that his friends who had offered him advice would share responsibility for the book's mistakes, and would be shamed by them, not only because they had given him bad advice but also by virtue of their being his friends. That Coetzee does not implicate his own friends and advisors in this way offers grounds for hope that C has kept some of his strong opinions to himself rather than passing them on to his creator.[13]

Notes

1. See, for example, J. D. Velleman, "The Genesis of Shame," *Philosophy and Public Affairs* 30, no. 1 (2001): 27–52; and M. C. Nussbaum, *Hiding from Humanity: Disgust, Shame, and the Law* (Princeton, N.J.: Princeton University Press, 2004), esp. chap. 4.
2. For an account of the way in which torture is an especially egregious subversion of the victim's humanity, see D. Sussman, "What's Wrong With Torture?" *Philosophy and Public Affairs* 33, no. 1 (2005): 1–33.
3. J. M. Coetzee, *Diary of a Bad Year* (New York: Viking, 2007). All parenthetical page references in the text are to this edition.
4. Nussbaum is among those who deny that shame requires publicity. See Nussbaum, *Hiding from Humanity*, 205.

5. T. L. Friedman, "Calling All Pakistanis," *New York Times*, December 3, 2008.
6. M. Gilbert, "Group Wrongs and Guilt Feelings," *The Journal of Ethics* 1, no. 1 (1997): 76; italics in the original.
7. Ibid., 83; italics in the original.
8. Ibid., 80.
9. This is not to deny that there may be second-order reasons for having certain feelings. If people's having certain feelings would have good consequences, there might be reason to cultivate those feelings even if they were otherwise unjustified. Suppose, for example, that Finns would be more likely to support the musical arts, thereby making it more likely that other Finns will compose great symphonies, if they take pride in the work of Finnish composers. In that case it might be good to encourage their otherwise irrational pride in Sibelius's fifth.
10. One prominent legal theorist, George Fletcher, argues that collective guilt actually mitigates individual guilt. See his *Romantics at War: Glory and Guilt in the Age of Terrorism* (Princeton, N.J.: Princeton University Press, 2002), chap. 8. For criticism of this view, see J. McMahan, "Collective Crime and Collective Punishment," *Criminal Justice Ethics* (Winter/Spring 2008): 4–12.
11. Gilbert, "Group Wrongs," 81; italics in the original.
12. Philip Pettit has recently shown that there can be cases in which, even though every person who participates in a collective decision-making procedure may vote against a certain course of action, their other inputs may nevertheless commit the collective to the exact course of action that they have all individually rejected. In such a case, the collective may do wrong without any individual being guilty or having acted wrongly. I think that in such a case there is no justification for collective punishment as a matter of retribution. If it is necessary to take action against the collective to prevent or to deter further collective wrongdoing, or to coerce the collective to compensate the victims of its action, the justification for such action must be that all the members of the collective are liable to accept their share of the burden by virtue of having voluntarily participated in a decision-making procedure that had the potential to result in wrongful collective action even when no individual participant wanted that result. See P. Pettit, "Responsibility Incorporated," *Ethics* 117, no. 2 (2007): 171–201.
13. I am grateful to the editors for penetrating written comments on an earlier draft of this essay, and to Ruth Chang, Shelly Kagan, Frances Kamm, and Larry Temkin for extraordinarily helpful discussion. Special thanks to my dear friends Agi and Bosko Zivaljevic for keeping me well supplied with Coetzee's books and especially for ensuring that he always wrote a new one in time for my birthday. I am also indebted to the American Council of Learned Societies for its support of my work on this chapter. Finally, my criticisms of the views of one of his characters should not be understood as criticisms of Coetzee as a novelist. Of all living novelists whose work I know, Coetzee is in my view the best.

Part Two
Humans, Animals, and Morality

5

Converging Convictions
COETZEE AND HIS CHARACTERS ON ANIMALS
Karen Dawn and Peter Singer

In *The Lives of Animals* and in the two similar chapters of *Elizabeth Costello*, the protagonist speaks passionately against the way humans abuse animals. Is she speaking for J. M. Coetzee, the author of those works? That question has come up often as people have studied Coetzee's work and speculated about his personal character. Indeed, Coetzee's novels, in which he often shares demographical and other characteristics with his protagonists, clearly invite such questions. The reader could hardly fail to notice that Elizabeth Costello, like Coetzee, is an acclaimed novelist from a former British colony in the southern hemisphere—and even a novelist who shares Coetzee's penchant for exploring and developing characters found elsewhere in the literary world.

We have watched Coetzee's relationships with his protagonists get closer with every work, almost as if he is dabbling with commitment. We finally land, in the 2007 work *Diary of a Bad Year*, in the world of the elderly South African professor living in Australia who refers to himself as "C." The question of commitment is no longer in doubt—author and subject seem to have been joined as one. Their portfolio of fiction has moved beyond similarity—C has written an acclaimed novel, *Waiting for the Barbarians*. We cannot doubt that C is in essence a thinly veiled version of Coetzee. We feel confident in arguing that Costello, before C, with her feminine veil signaling just a little more distance, had been approaching fast.

We see that relational progression from close to "as one" in Coetzee's choice of his characters' names. On reading *The Lives of Animals* and *Elizabeth Costello*, it is hard not to notice, in the light of the complimentary biographical information, the similarity in surname between the protagonist and author. Yet their names are not the same. In *Diary of a Bad Year*, we are teased with the notion that they are. As we note that C's views on animals match Costello's in tone, we can safely assert that Coetzee has, with C, left little doubt that those views are his own and therefore that when Elizabeth Costello speaks on animal issues, she is, in essence, speaking for the author. Further, the weight she gives those issues reflects Coetzee's sensibilities. We need not base our argument solely on the biographical parallels between Coetzee's characters and their author. If we look at the author's nonfiction work and interviews, we see Elizabeth Costello's views (and C's) demonstrated in the life of the creator. We also notice that J. M. Coetzee is becoming increasingly willing to voice those views in his own name.

Cora Diamond, seeing Elizabeth Costello's passion for and focus on animals as arguably separate from Coetzee's personal sentiments, has suggested that we should not see *The Lives of Animals* as essentially about animals and the way we treat them. She writes: "One can hardly, I think, take for granted that the lectures can be read as concerned with that 'issue', and as providing arguments bearing on it." Instead, she holds, we might see it as "centrally concerned with the presenting of a wounded woman."[1]

Although Diamond is right to say that there is more going on in *The Lives of Animals* than a presentation of an argument against animal abuse, Coetzee's own words point to the inadequacy of Diamond's overall interpretation. When asked by an interviewer how critics respond to the animal themes in his books, Coetzee used, as an example, their response to *Disgrace*:

> The test case is my novel *Disgrace*, in which animals figure quite prominently. Most reviewers have more or less ignored their presence (they mention that the hero of the novel "gets involved with animal rights campaigners" and leave it at that). In this respect they—naturally—mirror the way in which animals are treated in the world we live in, namely as unimportant existences of which we need take notice only when their lives cross ours.[2]

As those comments pertain to the critics' response to *Disgrace*, a book that has major themes other than society's treatment of animals, we find it particularly ironic that in reference to a later work solely focused on animals and even called *The Lives of Animals*, anyone should suggest that animal issues might be seen as mostly titular or analogous.

If we look at Coetzee's own life it becomes clear that the way we treat animals is an issue of vital importance to him. We see him make choices that we would expect from Elizabeth Costello: He is vegetarian. He is a patron of Voiceless, an Australian organization that gives grants to animal protection groups, and of the Australian Association for Humane Research, an antivivisection group.[3] He has affiliated himself with some of the campaigns of People for the Ethical Treatment of Animals, signing a PETA petition, for example, that called for a Thai ban on *phaajaan*, a brutal practice in which baby elephants are broken by means of torture.[4]

It is significant, also, that the passage we quoted above, about *Disgrace*, comes from an interview Coetzee granted to the Swedish animal rights magazine *Djurens Rätt*. Coetzee is famous for his reluctance to grant interviews. After he was awarded the Nobel Prize in 2003, the interview with the animal rights magazine was the only interview he gave. Sweden's largest daily newspaper, *Dagens Nyheter*, had to be content with publishing some correspondence between Coetzee and a former university colleague. Other newspapers got nothing at all. Coetzee did, however, make another media exception in early 2004, giving a reading of *Elizabeth Costello* for the animal rights radio program *Watchdog* (hosted by one of us, Karen Dawn). The reading was for an episode that examined the comparison between the Nazi Holocaust and our current treatment of animals.[5] Coetzee was asked to participate because Elizabeth Costello had made the comparison. He obliged, in what was to that date his only radio guest spot, again showing his attachment to the topic. But he was willing only to read Elizabeth's ardent arguments from his book, choosing not to join the discussion and claim them as his own. We will explore, below, Coetzee's progressive willingness to avow those views.

We noted earlier that we saw significance in Coetzee's choice of a surname for Elizabeth that was reminiscent of his own last name. We were not oblivious, however, to Coetzee's use of his own first name for Elizabeth's son, John Bernard, a man stuck in the middle between his mother's crusade for the animals and his wife's defense of meat eating. We find it interesting that John makes some of the same points, as he challenges Elizabeth, that have been put forward by Coetzee when he has written in his own voice. While choosing a vegetarian lifestyle Coetzee has, in his earlier nonfiction work, skirted on the verge of impugning his own choice. We therefore understand the character of John to reflect some of Coetzee's earlier discomfort with, even personal judgments against, that choice.

We see Coetzee foreshadow John Bernard's concerns, for example, in a 1995 essay published in *Granta* under the title "Meat Country." The author comments that it is human nature to procreate and then also tells us: "Similarly, whether or not it is a good idea to kill fellow beings and eat them, that is the way of the world, the animal kingdom included." He suggests that cows and horses would probably eat meat if they could and continues, "The question of whether we should eat meat is not a serious question . . . we have not made ourselves to be creatures . . . with a hunger for flesh. We are born like that: it is a given, it is the human condition."[6] That thinking corresponds with John Bernard's contention: "Carnivorousness expresses something truly deep about human beings... they don't want a vegetarian diet. They like eating meat. There is something atavistically satisfying about it. That's the brutal truth."[7]

It is not only John who holds that line of thought in *The Lives of Animals*. It is carried further by the character of Elaine Mark, a member of the English Department who has written about Costello's work. Mark asks Elizabeth:

> Are you not asking too much of humankind when you ask us to live without species exploitation, without cruelty? Is it not more human to accept our own humanity—even if it means embracing the carnivorous Yahoo within ourselves—than to end up like Gulliver, pining for a state he can never attain, and for good reason: it is not in his nature, which is human nature?

To that, Elizabeth gives a long response, culminating in her acknowledgment that it might be in our nature to eat meat. She then adds, however,

> You say there is nothing left to do but embrace that status, that nature. Very well, let us do so. But let us also push Swift's fable to its limits and recognize that, in history, embracing the status of man has entailed slaughtering and enslaving a race of divine or else divinely created beings and bringing down on ourselves a curse thereby.[8]

There is no inconsistency in arguing, as Elizabeth does, that eating meat may be in our nature but that following our nature is not always the best choice. As we weigh Coetzee's own words about human nature against both his descriptions of meat and what we learn about his dietary habits in the *Granta* essay, "Meat Country," we conclude that he feels the same way. In that essay, after arguing that meat eating is natural, he displays his own distaste for it. He writes that wandering around the atrium of fruits and vegetables at the market is "like being in the mythic hall of plenty." Then of the meat hall he writes, "No longer does the air hold the scent of melons and peaches. Instead there is a smell of blood and death, and all the exertions of the smiling assistants behind the counters to scrub and sterilize will not chase it away."

While John Bernard mirrors Coetzee's self-criticism, "Meat Country" assures us that Elizabeth speaks for the author's visceral reactions and for the way in which he chooses to live. And given Coetzee's colorful and impassioned nonfiction writing on the issue of meat, we cannot believe that when Elizabeth Costello and her son discuss the matter they do so only to allow the author an analogy.

An examination of Coetzee's interviews suggests that during the decade that followed the publication of "Meat Country," he may have become less attached to the idea that eating meat is a fundamental part of our nature. In a 2004 interview in the Australian weekly magazine *The Bulletin*, Coetzee says he gave up meat thirty years earlier and comments, "God knows why it took me so long. I suppose I thought it was normal human behavior."[9] On the website of Voiceless we see a 2005 quotation in which he says that the Australian animal foundation "is a small part of what has become a large and I would hope irreversible movement among human beings to make this planet a less harsh and deadly place for all those to whom it is the one and only home."[10]

In light of his personal long-term commitment to vegetarianism, what did Coetzee mean by saying, in his 1995 Granta essay, that whether we should eat meat "is not a serious question"? Perhaps we can find a clue in something Elizabeth says in *The Lives of Animals* about reason and argument:

> Both reason and seven decades of life experience tell me that reason is neither the being of the universe nor the being of God. On the contrary, reason looks to me suspiciously like the being of human thought; worse than that, like the being of one tendency in human thought. Reason is the being of a certain spectrum of human thinking. And if this is so, if that is what I believe, then why should I bow to reason this afternoon and content myself with embroidering on the discourse of the old philosophers.[11]

Elizabeth gives reason and philosophical arguments their most searing indictment when she discusses a philosopher and says:

> Can we, asked the philosopher, strictly speaking, say that the veal calf misses its mother? Does the veal calf have enough of a grasp of the significance of the mother-relation, does the veal calf have enough of a grasp of the meaning of maternal absence, does the veal calf, finally, know enough about missing to know that the feeling it has is the feeling of missing.
>
> A calf who has not mastered the concepts of presence and absence, of self and other—so goes the argument—cannot, strictly speaking, miss anything. In order to, strictly speaking, miss anything, it would first have to take a course in philosophy. What sort of philosophy is this? Throw it out, I say. What good do its piddling distinctions do?[12]

Compare that with Coetzee's own response, again in the interview with *The Bulletin*, to the question of whether animals are sentient: "I am impatient with questions that imply that creatures have to pass some kind of test concocted in a philosophy department before they can be permitted to live."

In a similar vein, when Elizabeth is asked if her own vegetarianism comes out of moral conviction, her response seems visceral yet suggests that the question goes to things beyond the viscera, beyond human mortal morality. She answers, "No, I don't think so. It comes out of a desire to save my soul."[13] We therefore see in Elizabeth an attitude that may align well with that of her creator, who has said that whether to eat meat is not "a serious moral question" while he abstained on what we might call moral grounds. We have here a hint that to both Coetzee and Elizabeth, meat eating is a matter of clear right and wrong and yet one that cannot be reasonably discussed in arguments about morality. Certainly Elizabeth does not appear to attempt to seem reasonable. With talk of souls, we see the suggestion that her stance is "above" reason, rather than beyond it.

We notice further similarities between the two Johns as both show some embarrassment with regard to a strong vegetarian stance. In "Meat Country" we see an author who appears to be gently ridiculing his own feelings and lifestyle:

> Trying to live a life on Gandhian-Shavian lines in the United States today is both eccentric and dated, in an uninteresting way. . . . Nevertheless there are people deeply enough attached—or perhaps just habituated—to ways of living they have made their own to persist in them no matter how unsuitable the environment. On visits to the United States, visits that have sometimes stretched to months, I try obstinately to hold to a regimen which, although it does not include socialism or sandals or cold showers or even free love, does include a dislike for cars, a deep affection for the bicycle, and a diet without flesh. I hold to these preferences as discreetly as I am able, aware of their comic potential. They seem perfectly sane to me but I have no interest in making converts.[14]

That voice, in which Coetzee makes fun of and apologizes for himself, seems to come through in John Bernard's feeling of embarrassment for his mother, Elizabeth. As her talk ends we are privy to the voice inside John's head: "A strange ending to a strange talk, he thinks, ill gauged, ill argued. Not her métier, argumentation. She should not be here."[15]

What embarrasses Elizabeth's son most is something called "The Plutarch Response." As Coetzee writes in *The Lives of Animals*:

> What he dreads is that, during a lull in conversation, someone will come up with what he calls The Question— "What led you, Mrs Costello, to become a vegetarian?"—

and that she will then get on her high horse and produce what he and Norma call The Plutarch Response. After that it will be up to him and him alone to repair the damage.

The response in question comes from Plutarch's moral essays. His mother has it by heart; he can reproduce it only imperfectly. "You ask me why I refuse to eat flesh. I, for my part, am astonished that you can put in your mouth the corpse of a dead animal, am astonished that you do not find it nasty to chew hacked flesh and swallow the juices of death-wounds."[16]

Yet Coetzee himself responds, in the *Djurens Rätt* interview, to the question of whether or not he is a vegetarian with: "Yes, I am a vegetarian. I find the thought of stuffing fragments of corpses down my throat quite repulsive, and I am amazed that so many people do it every day." Even in the mainstream *Bulletin* interview he described eating meat as "a repulsive habit" and said, "As for vegetarianism, it is hard to understand why people should want to chew dead flesh."

In the 2007 novel *Diary of a Bad Year*, the character C uses similar imagery in a section titled "On the Slaughter of Animals." He holds that it is important for people to see the kitchen "as a place where, after the murders, the bodies of the dead are brought to be done up (disguised) before they are devoured." That point made by C, from whom Coetzee hardly attempts to separate himself, and the responses cited in the Coetzee interviews mentioned above, are all notably similar to the Plutarch Response, which embarrassed Elizabeth's son John. And they reflect the vehement vegetarianism that Coetzee rejected in the earlier *Granta* essay but which he has since begun to publicly embrace.

The comparison between what we do to animals and what was done to the Jews in the Holocaust is perhaps Elizabeth's most contentious argument. She openly acknowledges that it will polarize people. Yet writing in his own voice, in "Meat Country," Coetzee raises that comparison—though he dances around it, asking rather than asserting. He suggests that people are more affronted by the killing of a bear for food than an ox because there are so few bears whereas "oxen, by contrast, are two a penny. They can be bred without end, their species is not threatened. The life of a species is of a higher order than the life of the individual." Then he continues:

> This species argument is widely accepted today. Is it fair to remind ourselves of the Nazis, who divided humankind into two species, those whose deaths mattered more and those whose deaths mattered less? What does the ox think about being consigned—without consultation—to a lower species than the bear or indeed than the spotted owl or the Galapagos sea turtle?

In the *Djurens Rätt* interview Coetzee is bolder. Again in his own voice, but no longer with a tentative question, he compares the killing of a person to the killing of an animal:

> It is not inherently easier to close off our sympathies as we wring the neck of the chicken we are going to eat than it is to close off our sympathies to the man we send to the electric chair (I write from the United States, which still punishes some crimes with death), but we have evolved psychic, social and philosophical mechanisms to cope with killing poultry that, for complex reasons, we use to allow ourselves to kill human beings only in time of war.

In 2006, Coetzee wrote a speech for the Australian organization Voiceless, which was read on his behalf by the actor Hugo Weaving. It included a reference to a "warning on the grandest scale that there is something deeply, cosmically wrong with regarding and treating fellow beings as mere units of any kind."

Coetzee then wrote of that warning:

> It came when in the middle of the twentieth century a group of powerful men in Germany had the bright idea of adapting the methods of the industrial stockyard, as pioneered and perfected in Chicago, to the slaughter—or what they preferred to call the *processing*—of human beings.
>
> Of course we cried out in horror when we found out about this. We cried: *What a terrible crime, to treat human beings like cattle! If we had only known beforehand!* But our cry should more accurately have been: *What a terrible crime, to treat human beings like units in an industrial process!* And that cry should have had a postscript: *What a terrible crime, come to think of it, to treat any living being like a unit in an industrial process!*

With that speech, Coetzee had, undeniably, come out of the closet. We might say he burst out of it, brandishing a version of Costello's most controversial analogy. He left no doubt that even on this most polarizing of issues, the comparison between the killing of humans to the killing of other animals, Elizabeth Costello is aligned with Coetzee.

We accept that the title of *The Lives of Animals* can be seen as a double entendre, for, indeed, we are all animals, and the book does examine Elizabeth's life. Moreover, Elizabeth explicitly compares herself to Kafka's ape, Red Peter. Yet given the evidence we have presented—the views recently put forward by C, who is the protagonist most difficult to separate from the author, plus the author's choice of lifestyle, his personal reaction to meat eating, the causes he supports, the magazines and radio shows for which he does interviews, and the comments he has made showing his frustration with the press's tendency to undermine his animal themes—we must conclude that the issue of how we treat animals does considerably more than provide the "context" for a portrayal of a wounded person. Further, Coetzee himself tells us that he would not want us to conclude otherwise. In the *Djurens Rätt* interview, asked how fiction can contribute to the question of animal rights, he expressed the hope that it could "show to as many people as we can what the spiritual and psychic cost is of continuing to treat animals as we do, and thus perhaps to change their hearts."

We leave the final comment on the issue of the relationship between Coetzee's fiction and his concern about animals to Coetzee himself, by quoting a question and answer, from the *Djurens Rätt* interview:

Q: What consequences, if any, do you think receiving the Nobel Prize will have for the animal rights issue?

A: Some reviewers have made the connection between the chapters of Elizabeth Costello that are concerned with animals and the fact that their author has won this year's Nobel Prize, and have asked the question whether the author believes what his character Elizabeth Costello says about the appalling treatment of animals in our modern world. I do not imagine that a single, rather difficult book will change the world in that respect, but perhaps it will make some small impact.

Notes

1. Cora Diamond, "The Difficulty of Reality and the Difficulty of Philosophy," in *Reading Cavell*, ed. A. Crary and S. Shieh (London: Routledge 2006), 98–118.
2. This and other quotes are from an interview first published in the Swedish magazine *Djurens Rätt* (Animal rights) and are taken from the version reprinted in Henrik Engström, "Animals, Humans, Cruelty, and Literature: A Rare Interview with J. M. Coetzee," *Satya* (May 2004).
3. See http://www.voiceless.org.au/About_Us/Misc/About_Us.html; "Our New Patron," *Australian Association for Humane Research, Newsletter* (September 2004): 1.
4. "Jackie Chan Joins Elephant Torture Ban Campaign," *South China Morning Post*, November 20, 2003, cited from http://www.jc-news.net/forum/msg.php?i=1963&p=0.
5. Broadcast on KPFK Los Angeles, April 26, 2004.

6. J.M. Coetzee, "Meat Country," *Granta* 52 (1995): 46.
7. J. M. Coetzee, *The Lives of Animals* (Princeton, N.J.: Princeton University Press, 1999), 58.
8. Coetzee, *The Lives of Animals*, 57.
9. Interview with J. M. Coetzee, *The Bulletin*, May 26, 2004.
10. http://www.voiceless.org.au/About_Us/Misc/About_Us.html. The statement is dated November 29, 2004.
11. Coetzee, *The Lives of Animals*, 23.
12. Ibid., 66.
13. Ibid., 43.
14. Coetzee, "Meat Country," 43.
15. Ibid., 36.
16. Coetzee, *The Lives of Animals*, 38.

6

Coetzee and Alternative Animal Ethics
Elisa Aaltola

Animal ethics has become a valuable part of philosophy. The main elements include criticism of anthropocentric assumptions and emphasis on experientialism (a view that centralizes the capacity to experience).[1] Hence, nonhuman animals can also have moral value. The analytic approach,[2] which has applied standard moral theories to other animals, has been accompanied by the postmodern approach,[3] which emphasizes matters such as plurality and contextuality.

Most of animal ethics has been preoccupied with theory or principles. This has meant that the issue of persuasion has often been overlooked: how to communicate the theory and principles to the hamburger-loving folk?[4] The age-old question of rhetoric has remained untouched. This is where J. M. Coetzee becomes relevant. His novels present ethical views related to nonhuman animals, constantly underpinned by the issue of how to communicate such views to others. On a more concrete level, the novels are a form of persuasion in themselves. The differences between Coetzee's approach and standard animal ethics do not stop here. He reminds us of not only persuasion but also other valuable factors often overlooked in ethics. Whereas animal ethics has tended to emphasize theory, principles, reason, and speaking for the animal, Coetzee emphasizes poetry, virtues, emotion, and letting the animal speak to us.

This essay explores Coetzee's "alternative animal ethics." It will concentrate on three crucial elements: the differences from standard philosophy, the priority of the animal, and poetry as a form of persuasion. Most of the references are to *The Lives of Animals*. In this novel, Coetzee brings to life Elizabeth Costello, a novelist, who via public lectures explores the relationship between humans and other animals. *Disgrace* is also referred to. Before moving further, it has to be noted that some are skeptical about whether Costello represents Coetzee's personal sentiments, and some maintain that Coetzee is not talking of animals to begin with.[5] Evidence suggests that Coetzee does, indeed, have strong pro-animal views that coincide with those of his characters. However, the interest here does not lie with what Coetzee may intend to say but what his characters are in fact proposing.

RELATION TO STANDARD ANIMAL ETHICS

The first key to Coetzee's "alternative animal ethics" is its relation to standard animal ethics. Here three dichotomies come to play: theory-poetry, principles-virtues, and reason-emotion.

Theory vs. Poetry

Via Elizabeth Costello, Coetzee repeats the two main elements of animal ethics. First of all, perfectionism is criticized and the capacity to experience brought forward.[6] Costello argues that reason and other such qualities are not relevant from the viewpoint of value—even if animals did lack reason, this would not justify using them as mere instruments. What matters is the animal's capacity to have experiences. Second, anthropocentrism is attacked without mercy. Costello stipulates that emphasis on human reason is biased, for such reason has no objective value. It is a mistake to value only that which is human.

However, a third common theme in the theories of animal ethics is entirely missing. It forms a central point of differentiation between standard animal ethics and Coetzee's approach. Costello insists that she is a poet rather than a philosopher. She states that although the audience may expect a lecture that is "cool rather than heated, philosophical rather than polemical, that will bring enlightenment rather than seeking to divide us into the righteous and the sinners, the saved and the damned, the sheep and the goats" (*The Lives of Animals*, 22), she cannot fulfill this expectation. The implication is that, if anything, she will be involving herself in polemic persuasion rather than theory. Costello dryly remarks that if you want philosophy, don't ask a novelist to give you a talk. She can only do philosophy in the "unoriginal, secondhand manner" (22), by repeating what she has read.

Costello's unwillingness to follow theory causes doubt in the audience. Her son states: "Not her metier, argumentation. She should not be here" (36). It also causes doubt in Costello, as later on her son describes her as "confused" and unable to answer a question. However, this does not get her down. Costello offers direct criticism of standard philosophy by describing central mistakes made in the history of philosophy and by having little regard for the "classics." The message is clear. Costello may do badly in theory, but the expectations of standard philosophy should be forsaken altogether in favor of poetry. For Costello, principles are uninteresting. We need to know what lies behind them. It is this that poetry gains its impetus from. It is implied that poetry opens up perspectives for criticism of standard cultural meanings (such as rationalism or speciesism) and for clarification of sentiments (such as emotion and equality) muddled and forgotten under the weight of those meanings. Therefore, philosophy is replaced with poetry, which persuades by polemics and revelations. The theme of persuasion is especially evident in Costello's relation to the academic audience: the question of how to communicate ethics to others is constantly present.

This is where Coetzee introduces a further theme: listening. In her self-aware lecture, Costello tells the story of Kafka's Red Peter, an ape that has to address an academic audience and describe his alteration from an animal to a human being (or an animal disguised as a human being). She goes on to make the correlation between Red Peter and herself. Both Costello and Red Peter "gibber and emote" (23) rather than reason. The audience understands neither. However, perhaps it is the audience's fault, if apes and novelists seem to merely gibber, for perhaps they are not listening in the right way. Costello maintains that animals are our silent captives who "refuse to speak to us" (25). It is implied that they remain mute because the anthropocentric audience is deaf. The society will not listen to the language of animals, and animals refuse to change their language to suit the purposes of the meat-eating society. The same applies to poets, whose language the academic audience will not pay attention to. Costello sees the animals' refusal as "heroic," thus suggesting that the refusal of the poet to be theoretical could be equally heroic. The ape may be forced into a human disguise, and the poet may be forced into an academic disguise, but their true nature will soon resurface.

For both the poet and the animal, the inability to be heard causes grief. Costello talks of the branded and wounded Red Peter, who has to defend himself in front of academics, and states that she, too, is not a philosopher but "an animal exhibiting, yet not exhibiting, to a gathering of scholars, a wound, which I cover up under my clothes but touch on in every word that I speak" (26). The insistence on humanity and theory may give cause to deafness, which harms those who remain unheard.

The true identity of the animal and the poet is dismissed and devalued: they will only be accepted when disguised in the humanistic, academic veil.

Thus, it is suggested that theory be replaced with poetry and persuasion and that new ways of listening be adopted. These form significant challenges to standard animal ethics, which relies on analytical arguments and tends to "speak for" the animals.

Principles vs. Virtues

Costello maintains that her vegetarianism is based on "a desire to save [her own] soul" (43). Coetzee seems to be leaning back toward virtue ethics and its emphasis on personal character rather than detached principles. With some exceptions,[7] animal ethics has paid little attention to human nature, and thus Coetzee is offering a needed reminder.

This reading is offered support by the fact that much emphasis is placed on the notions of "goodness," "human nature," and "personal responsibility." Coetzee explores the question whether being good to animals is practically possible. A member of the audience suggests that we would have to live in a totalitarian society in order to live without any cruelty or exploitation and states that perhaps we should accept our "humanity" and eat meat. Costello replies that humans are not biological carnivores—thus, eating other animals is not a necessary aspect of human nature but rather a choice. This choice is the stumbling block that prevents most from being "good people." Costello mentions the limits of her own moral character. She wears leather, which she understands to be one form of "obscenity" (meat-eating being another) (44). Time and again she implies that there is a touch of monstrosity in the manner in which animals are treated. It seems that we could better our characters but choose not to. Real monsters are not those who cannot understand the implications of their actions but those who not only understand them but rejoice in them. The person who eats meat is bound to be aware that the inevitable price of her culinary pleasure is the suffering and death of another creature. It is this combination of pleasure and awareness of its price that is at the root of obscenity and does justice to the choice of terminology.[8] Costello is shocked at her own incapacity to come above such banality. She is a seemingly good person, yet she is taking part in what to her is murder.

One way to avoid the implications is to deny personal responsibility by resorting to ignorance. Coetzee draws an analogy between animal industries and the Holocaust. Costello claims that: "The people who lived in the countryside around

Treblinka . . . said that they did not know what was going on in the camp; said that, while in general they might have guessed what was going on, they did not know for sure; said that, while in a sense they might have known, in another sense they did not know, could not afford to know, for their own sake" (19). She goes on to point out that this ignorance is constant in relation to nonhuman animals. She describes how she wanders through an ordinary town, not seeing any animal suffering but knowing it is hidden all around her: "They are all around us as I speak, only we do not, in a certain sense, know about them" (21). It is not practical limitations but self-oriented unwillingness to pay attention, to be aware, that prevents respectful treatment of other animals. For Costello, ignorance is a moral vice. When it comes to the ordinary Germans and others following the Nazi rule, she says: "They lost their humanity," what they committed was a "sin," they became "polluted." She argues: "It was and is inconceivable that people who *did not know* . . . about the camps can be fully human" (21). Our whole humanity is destroyed by ignorance. Whereas typically ignorance is positioned outside moral responsibility (we are not responsible for what we do not know), Coetzee's character claims that we are, in fact, responsible for not knowing. Here Coetzee presents us with the concept of "denial," which combines knowledge with ignorance: we seek not to know something that we do know.[9] Denial is a choice, and as such an act that we can be held responsible for.

Costello's choice of terminology ("curse," "sin") implies that we will be punished for our actions. If, indeed, "meat is murder," then those who scarf down hamburgers should face a penalty for their actions. However, she also notes that no immediate punishment is offered. People seem to "come away clean" from their everyday life, which constantly presents them with a "fresh holocaust." They do not feel responsibility or guilt; they remain untouched. "We can do anything and get away with it . . . there is no punishment" (35). The world is filled with Hannah Arendt's "banality of evil": evil is found in the mundane and thus goes unpunished. It may be the inability to feel shame or guilt that is at the root of Coetzee's virtue ethics. Costello wants the punishment to be guilt, but people feel none. One could argue that it is precisely this inability that marks the decline of humanity: we have lost touch with human nature when we cannot feel shame for taking part in a global society that ignores the lives and interests of tens of billions of animals each year.

Hence, human nature is tarnished when people make the choice to kill unnecessarily. Furthermore, we cannot avoid personal responsibility by pleading ignorance. Meat eaters are obscene monsters whose humanity is under doubt. They would deserve a punishment. These are heavy terms, and they are not met on the pages of animal ethics books. The difference between a poet and a philosopher is becoming clear. Whereas the standard animal ethicists would be presenting a calm and neutral argument, Coetzee (and, living up to her own promise, Costello) offers strong polemics to cut to the point. Moreover, whereas standard animal ethics is concerned with principles, Coetzee is underlining a more personal element: be a good person. In a sense he is personalizing ethics: ethics is not detached theory but something to be found from our personal lives, something that we are to be held personally accountable for.

Reason vs. Emotion

One of the basic anthropocentric claims is that reason sides with humans and emotion with animals. Therefore (following a rather illogical leap), valuing animals has to be sentimental rather than rational. The response in animal ethics has been to reject emotion and build pro-animal arguments on reason alone.[10] Only a few have suggested that we should, in fact, criticize the role of reason.[11]

Coetzee is not blind to the matter. Costello's son calls her beliefs "propaganda," while his wife, Norma, calls ethical beliefs "opinions" and emphasizes their supposed "sentimentality" (*The Lives of Animals*, 17). However, Costello does not adopt the typical animal ethics route but rather responds by criticizing reason. For Costello, reason is not the "being of universe," but only one aspect of human thinking and thus a mere fragment of our reality (23). Moreover, she takes a strong position in favor of emotion. She maintains that instead of principles, we ought to listen to our "hearts": "If principles are what you want to take away from this talk, I would have to respond, open your heart and listen to what your heart says" (37). Hence, an emphasis on emotion is a further diversion from standard animal ethics.

It can be claimed that emotions are an elemental part of human behavior, and coincide with reason. Martha Nussbaum has argued that emotions are needed for "understanding": only purely factual and fragmented knowledge can be void of emotion. For something to be understood, it needs to strike a chord in us, lead to some type of affective response. Nussbaum further maintains that emotion is a way of knowing, as it can form the perspective from which to make things meaningful.[12] These ideas are reflected in Coetzee's work. A substantial part of his animal ethics is based on emotion: the lives of animals are to have an emotive impact on human beings. We can understand other animals, and our relation with them, only by taking emotions into account. Therefore, Coetzee is replacing theory, principles, and reason with poetry, virtues, and emotion. This enables him to try and understand the animal from a new perspective.

BEING A BAT

Here we come to the second theme of Coetzee's work: the priority of the animal viewpoint. Costello places great emphasis on sympathy, which she calls the capacity to "share the being of another," and which she links with imagination (she talks of "sympathetic imagination") (34–35). Identification (perhaps a better term for what Costello is describing) and imagination form an integral part of Coetzee's animal ethics. Human beings are to imagine the animal point of view. The claim is radical to those who maintain that animal minds are inevitably alien to us. This attitude is reflected in Wittgenstein's argument, according to which even if a lion did talk, we could not understand him. Such skepticism is common not only in standard analytical philosophy but also in postmodern philosophy.[13] Costello argues the opposite. As seen, she thinks that the lion can talk but remains silent only because humans do not listen in the right way. Animals have minds, and the inability to understand them is a fault of human reluctance. Costello is familiar with the famous paper on philosophy of mind entitled "What Is It Like to Be a Bat," and she criticizes its author, Thomas Nagel, for positioning the bat as a "fundamentally alien form of life" (31). We can understand other animals. All we need is a new way of listening.

Costello states that we ought to try and see the animal's world via its bodily, living experiences. She criticizes the claim *"cogito ergo sum"* and maintains that existence is not based on "a ghostly reasoning machine" but rather on experience. Experience consists of "fullness, embodiedness, the sensation . . . of being alive to the world" (33). Thus, Coetzee pays attention to the element that Nagel highlights in his paper: consciousness in the phenomenal sense. It is "qualia" that matters, the stuff of "what it is like." This is where the key to understanding animality lies—an understanding that Costello describes as being without limit. We can identify because we, too, are experiencing beings. Costello argues that "to be a living bat is to be full of being" and maintains that the task is not about knowing each specific sensation of the animal but rather about experiencing the sense of their "full being" (33). We can do this, for being human, too, is to be full of being; we, too, have qualia.

In identification, imagination is necessary. We are to jump outside anthropocentric frameworks and explore new meanings. Most importantly, we are to jump outside human presumptions and seek ways of understanding the animal perspective. Costello tells the tale of primate experiments in which the animals had to figure out complicated ways of getting to their food. According to her, it is only in the technological mind of humans that ways of reaching food would be at the forefront. Perhaps for these social animals, entirely different questions were more prominent (why are their captors suddenly making things so difficult for them, what has changed in their status?).[14] Costello argues that scientific models for measuring animal intelligence are "imbecile." She suggests that perhaps the experimenters are not far from philosophers. Both concentrate so thoroughly on technical issues ("can the ape use tools?"; "what are rights?") that they forget the more meaningful questions ("what is it like to be an animal?"). Costello says: "This is where a poet might have commenced with a feel for the ape's experiences" (30). Thus, Coetzee is centralizing the animal. Understanding animality is the basis for his take on ethics: it is not principles or experiments but the animal and her perspective that are to be prioritized.

This view has been endorsed elsewhere. Eileen Crist has maintained that the standard approach to researching animal minds has been fixated on "mechanomorphic" claims: animals are explained via external, mechanical descriptions not internal descriptions that refer to a subject. Research rests on "technical language," while "ordinary language" (which gives room for animal subjectivity) is falsely ignored as unscientific.[15] The conceptual framework that is chosen to describe other animals is built on normative and political views (if we want to instrumentalize animals, it makes little sense to describe them as individuals) and will lead to expected results (a mechanical framework will offer us a mechanical animal).[16] Thus, Costello's scientist will see what he wants to see, and the speciesist society does the same. However, intellectual honesty requires that if we are to understand other animals, they should be placed at the center of our efforts. Ethologist Marc Bekoff has argued, in a Coetzeean manner, that "there are no substitutes for listening to, and having direct experiences with, other animals."[17] For him, "animals are a way of knowing."[18] Indeed, it is time to listen to the lion speak.

Therefore, we are to explore the animal viewpoint via both similarities and differences. Similarity gives basis for identification, whereas differences require imagination—we ought to identify with what we can easily hear but also use imagination to capture that which escapes human language. In both, it is crucial that the animal herself be made the central point of our attention.

The argument could be brought forward by maintaining that we remain blind to aspects of our own selves as long as we refuse to see the animal. First, some argue that animals affect our minds and meanings. The "externalist" view is that the body and the environment (including relations with other animals) shape minds.[19] Raimond Gaita repeats this claim as he reminds us that our "creatureliness" affects the meanings we have. Human-animal relations have an impact on conceptual schemes.[20] Second, some claim that animals have a bearing on human personhood. Interaction is especially relevant here. Juan Carlos Gómez argues that personhood is based on experienced interaction: "The idea is that subjects . . . can coordinate their 'subjectivities' . . . with other creatures' subjectivities."[21] Gómez states that, thus, personhood requires seeing others as persons: "I am a person in so far as I and another perceive and treat each other as persons."[22] The ethologist Barbara Smuts, specifically in relation to Coetzee's thoughts, has explored these themes beautifully in the light of her vast experience in animal behavior. She says of animals:

> If they relate to us as individuals, and we relate to them as individuals, it is possible for us to have a *personal* relationship. . . . Thus while we normally think of personhood as an essential quality that we can "discover" or "fail to find' in another, in the view espoused here personhood connotes a way of being *in relation to others* . . . when a human being relates to an individual nonhuman being as an anonymous object, rather than as a being with its own subjectivity, it is the human, and not the other animal, who relinquishes personhood.[23]

Therefore, our minds, meanings, and even personhood are constructed in relation to other animals. When insisting that the animal be brought forward, Coetzee is, literally, saving our humanity. This sheds further light on his claim that the killing of animals destroys human souls: we cease to be not only good people, but people altogether when we refuse to recognize the value of other animals.

Thus, it is little surprise that the relation between humans and other animals is crucial for Coetzee. The animals whose worlds we are to imagine have lives that are deeply affected by human actions. Here lies another valuable point in Coetzee's animal ethic. Most invitations to understand other animals concentrate on the wild animal. Poets pay heed to the lions, deer, and wolves, not the piglets born in farrowing crates or the chicken cramped to battery cages (a matter Costello ironically points toward). Coetzee exemplifies this via the perspective of Costello's son: "Jaguar poems are all very well, he thinks, but you won't get a bunch of Australians standing around a sheep, listening to its silly baa, writing poems about it" (*The Lives of Animals*, 55). This understanding penetrates the whole of the society, as we are fixated on cultural taboo animals, such as lions and pandas, while ignoring domesticated animals. The value difference is at times explicated in philosophy. Postmodern philosophy has seen a deep aversion toward domesticated animals. Even their ontological status is seen as "less" in comparison to the wild animals. In fact, they may not be "real" animals at all, but human artifacts.[24]

The importance of paying attention to domesticated animals cannot be overemphasized. If we are to start exploring our moral relation with other animals, it is surely those animals that we have the deepest effect on that ought to be given the priority. In fact, it strikes as deceitful to place all emphasis on the wild animals, who are relatively independent from us. The moral message seems to be: We have nothing to worry about: animals are doing fine; they are roaming free instead of being cramped to small cages. Coetzee forces us to look at a reality we would rather not pay attention to. Even the ape Costello talks of is not a wild creature, but one tormented by humans. Via Costello, Coetzee asks us to imagine not independent animal existence but the lives of animals under human rule.

POETICS IN ACTION

Coetzee suggests that we can persuade others by poetry. One way to discover how poetry works is to look at his novels *Disgrace* and *The Lives of Animals*. The main character in *Disgrace*, David Lurie, has personal relations with two women (one of them his daughter), who work in animal welfare. The women have relatively strong views on animals: "Yes, we eat up a lot of animals in this country, it doesn't seem to do us much good. I'm not sure how we will justify it to them" (*Disgrace*, 82) and thus introduce Lurie to the problematic nature of our relation with other animals. They echo the rejection of anthropocentrism present in *The Lives of Animals*: "There is no higher life. This is the only life there is. Which we share with animals" (74). Lurie, on the other hand, has a standard, anthropocentric view on the matter. He first describes the women as "animal lovers," and although he sees no harm in their work, he finds it "hard to whip up an interest in the subject" (72–73). Later Lurie, when enticed to work in the animal shelter, protests: "All right, I'll do it. But only as long as I don't have to become a better person. I am not prepared to be reformed. I want to go on being myself" (77). He states that the Church Fathers don't believe in the souls of animals, thus dryly acknowledging the historical roots of his own anthropocentrism. When asked if he likes animals, Lurie brings forward a crude, instrumentalizing view: "I eat them, so I suppose I must like them, some parts of them" (81). Up until here, Lurie is the speciesist Costello is referring to. Unwilling to change his character for the better, ignorant and uninterested, willing to stereotype animal advocates as "sentimentalists," and willing to consume the anthropocentric meanings and animal body parts fed to him by the culture.

Then Lurie comes across sheep meant for slaughter. He first reiterates the speciesist agenda: "Sheep do not own themselves, do not own their lives. They exist to be used" (123). However, as Lurie helps the sheep to graze, a more critical attitude starts to emerge. He complains to his daughter that the sheep should not have been introduced to the people (meaning himself) who are about to eat them. When she inquires whether he would prefer for the slaughtering to happen in an abattoir so that he wouldn't have to think of it, he says simply: "Yes." He is pleading to remain ignorant, thus explicitly taking part in the denial that Costello talks of in *The Lives of Animals*. However, Lurie is in a situation where ignorance becomes impossible: the sheep are not whisked away to an abattoir but rather remain under his very eyes.

The lives of these animals cannot be hidden. Instead, the relationship with the sheep deepens, and suddenly Lurie describes the countryside treatment of animals as "indifferent" and "hardhearted" (125). The change is becoming evident: Lurie is no longer in the speciesist club. He is starting to grasp his own ignorance.

All this happens after interaction with sheep. It becomes evident that Lurie has experienced sympathetic imagination in relation to these animals (ironically, the very species that Costello's son claims is not worthy of imagination). The domesticated animals have "spoken" to Lurie. Lurie even contemplates buying the sheep in order to rescue them from death, but realizes that the owner would simply get new sheep to kill. Coetzee describes this new situation as follows: "A bond seems to have come into existence between himself and the two Persians, he does not know how... suddenly and without reason, their lot has become important to him" (126). Hence, quite literally, emotion is taking over reason, and Lurie is identifying with the sheep to the extent that their fate matters to him greatly. Consequently, Lurie hesitates to go to the party where the dead sheep are being served, feeling that the sheep's lot has "disturbed" him. He thinks of the possibility of communicating with animals and asks himself whether he has to change, become like the women. He says: "I never imagined I would end up talking this way" (127). Lurie has found new ways of thinking, literally beyond his imagination, that have enabled him to recognize the animal viewpoint. Hence, he is faced with Costello's question: Should I become a better person?

Lurie starts to go over to the shelter as often as possible. He helps with the killing of unwanted dogs, but it has a significant effect on him. He cries when leaving the shelter, his hands shake, he feels the animals can sense his shame. Finally Lurie explicitly realizes that he is changing: "He does not understand what is happening to him. Until now he has been more or less indifferent to animals." (143) The fate of the animals is "gripping" his whole being. Lurie is feeling the guilt that Costello wishes all meat eaters felt. He has been altered by the encounters with animals, and indifference has been replaced by a strong sense of identification—Lurie is becoming "a better person."

Lurie's respect for the dogs extends beyond their death. He does not want the bodies of the dogs to be "dishonoured" by being mangled together with waste (although he does doubt whether the concept makes sense in relation to animals). So he takes it upon himself to personally process the dogs through the incinerator. He does question his concern for dead dogs and wonders if he is becoming "stupid, daft, wrongheaded" (146). However, for Lurie, the bags of dead dogs contain "a body and a soul inside," and thus he is explicitly abandoning the speciesist beliefs of the church fathers. He states that he finally knows the proper name for the feeling toward animals he before had difficulty stipulating: "Love" (219). He has gone through a complete change: he is now one of the people he would have labeled and even laughed at before, and he is no longer embarrassed to admit that he has strong emotions toward animals. Lurie has become "an animal lover."

The book has a rather stark ending. Lurie is faced with a dilemma of whether to save a young dog for another week or to take part in its killing. Ultimately, he chooses the latter. He did not save the sheep, and here he decides not to save the dog. There are many interpretations for this surprising conclusion. The first concerns one of the general themes of the book: Lurie is a rather helpless character who struggles to actively have a positive effect on events and people around him, and the inability to help animals intertwines with this theme. A second interpretation is more directly animal related. Lurie rejects saving the sheep because they would be replaced by others, and a similar approach applies to his view on dogs—regardless of his actions now, the dog will ultimately be killed. Perhaps Coetzee is asking us to look at the sinister consequences of our actions and to do something about their causes. We cannot help all the animals suffering as a result of speciesist attitudes, but we can do something about speciesism itself. A third option is that Coetzee does not want to offer us a feel-good ending, for the holocaust is still ongoing. Ending the book in the saving of one dog might delude us from remembering that animals are being killed in huge numbers every day (the term "*Lösung*" is used repeatedly in the book). The frustration of not being able to help brings to light the massive scale of the problem.

So what is the poetics of *Disgrace*? The novel explores the human-animal relation via the main character's personal experiences. The reader is invited to identify with the character who is coming to terms with the viewpoint of other animals. Through this two-level identification, the reader is perhaps asked to examine her own animal ethics. *Disgrace* does not make explicit claims but rather offers the reader a lived perspective through which to contest anthropocentric meanings. Here Coetzee is again following the virtue ethics account. It is via the personal journey of Lurie that meanings are contested. Like a character from a Greek tragedy, Lurie finds himself facing a battle, going through a catharsis, and finally achieving virtue and humanity. Like the viewer of a tragedy, the reader lives through the same catharsis—she is not reading ethics but living ethics. Persuasion gains its footing here: when we are invited to enter the world of Lurie, we are also invited to see animals how he sees them and (however briefly) to adopt his moral alteration.

Therefore, Coetzee is offering an animal ethic via the standard form of literary identification, which entices the reader to try on different viewpoints. Such an approach is alien to animal ethics, which follows the standard form of philosophical argumentation and, if anything, asks the reader to remain detached and neutral. In the context of persuasion, Coetzee's stance seems rather inevitably more effective. Detachment allows a reader to hold on to her own viewpoint and to give up on the text when needed. It does not offer (in any other than a metaphorical sense) new viewpoints or play with that of the reader or invite the reader to keep up with the text even when uncomfortable problems emerge. Literature succeeds not only in such play and lure but also in the contextualization of ethics, which makes it lived and thus both makes it seem plausible and offers a basis from which to make a judgment on its practical merits. Standard philosophy offers ethics, which is abstract and remains outside the reader, whereas Coetzee's approach makes the reader and ethics intertwine by bringing ethics inside the reader and the reader inside ethics. These elements allow Lurie to literally lure us to his world of ethics.

The Lives of Animals, on the other hand, uses a different approach. Whereas *Disgrace* lures and implies, *The Lives of Animals* accuses and polemicizes. More specifically, the difference consists of two elements. First, in *The Lives of Animals*, the ethics is made explicit as Costello's collected rage sweeps though the audience. In *Disgrace*, moral reflection is minimal, whereas here, such reflection takes center stage. Thus, ethics is not so much a part of a narrative, as an entity in itself. Second, ethics is no longer something that another person confronts but rather something that the reader is confronted with. There is no "living with" the ethics but rather being interrogated by it. Lurie shows us how an ethics can be adopted, whereas Costello asks us to justify our ethics—one happens in third person, the other in second person. The reader is the audience that Costello is addressing.

In *The Lives of Animals* Coetzee pays little attention to describing the concrete treatment of animals. Costello states: "I will pay you the honour of skipping a recital of horrors of their lives and deaths. . . . will take it that you concede me the rhetorical power to evoke these horrors and bring them home to you with adequate force, and leave it at that, reminding you only that the horrors I here omit are nevertheless at the centre of this lecture" (*The Lives of Animals*, 19). Her omission has a strong, harrowing impact. It is stated that the reality of domesticated animals is that of horror and that this horror should gain our full attention. By not giving the horror any detailed attention, Costello sparks imagination. The reader is given the task of envisioning "what it is like." This imagination is at the center of *The Lives of Animals*, and it gives priority to the animal.

A further important element in the book is shock via juxtaposition—the rhetoric of *The Lives of Animals*. Costello's oddity in front of the academic audience (she is a self-doubting female novelist with open arguments who hungers for emotion, facing self-assured, mainly male academics who hunger for logics and reason) is in itself a juxtaposition. However, the more challenging juxtaposition takes place when Costello makes the "dreaded comparison" between the Holocaust and animal industries: "Let me say it openly: we are surrounded by an enterprise of degradation, cruelty, and killing which rivals anything that the Third Reich was capable of, indeed dwarfs it, in that ours is an enterprise without end, self-regenerating, bringing rabbits, rats, poultry, livestock ceaselessly into the world for the purpose of killing them" (21). She not only makes the comparison but indeed describes animal industries as the greater atrocity. The Holocaust was about killing with an end: an annihilation. Animal industries do not have such an end; for them death itself is a sought-after product—they constantly need new bodies and lives to turn into death.

The comparison is radical in the context of anthropocentric meanings. The most obvious sign of discomfort comes from Abraham Stern, one of the academics, who accuses Costello of "blasphemy" and of insulting the dead (50). However, Costello stands by her comparison. Both animal industries and the Holocaust rest on rendering other beings alien and insignificant. It could be that, in fact, the oppressive treatment of other animals enables the similar treatment of given groups of humans (this could be the "curse" that Costello refers to). As long as experiencing beings are treated hierarchically and instrumentally, the future of humanity does not look bright (therefore, Costello also argues that speciesists are similar to racists). It is the whole mechanism of relating to other beings (humans or animals) that needs to change. The best that Stern's argument does is exemplify the cause of our problems: the dualistic divisions into "us" and "them," inside which respect for another is an insult to oneself and the value of one's own kind is built upon difference in relation to others.[25]

Therefore, Coetzee is introducing ethics via perhaps the most shocking comparison available. However, what remains unclear is whether this method of persuasion works. When Stern refuses to attend Costello's second lecture, he is choosing to become deaf to her arguments. The unwillingness to listen reflects a typical response: as Costello is aware, most people prefer to remain ignorant. Coetzee is offering shock tactics to an anthropocentric culture in denial. The more obvious the horror, the greater the need to deny. This leads to an important question: Can the poet be effective if the society is unwilling to listen?

Costello's son asks: "Do you really believe, Mother, that poetry classes are going to close down the slaughterhouses?" Her reply is "No." He goes on: "It seems to me the level of behaviour you want to change is too elementary, too elemental, to be reached by talk" (*Disgrace*, 58). He claims that humans like meat; they don't want to change. Hence, it is argued that poetry is too weak in the face of denial based on self-interest. Costello's own attitude is that of frustration: "John, I don't know what I want to do. I just don't want to sit silent" (59). For her, the inadequacies of poetic persuasion are secondary in relation to the need to speak out. The society may be deaf, but silence is not an option. Again, Costello is favoring virtue ethics at the expense of utilitarianism: it may be her desire to do the right thing and be "a good person" that drives her to wage a war against the Goliath of the hamburger culture.

Advocating care for others is important even when it seems to bear little effect. It is not only shock tactics that may fail, but also mediating animality per se. Costello states: "If I do not convince you, that is because my words, here, lack the power to bring home to you the wholeness, the unabstracted, unintellectual nature, of that animal's being" (65). Words can only go so far. However, like the animal, the poet has to keep to her own language, regardless of its failings. Costello may be tired, but she is not about to give up.

So how, to continue with persuasion, can deafness be overcome? It is important to note the third possibility besides philosophy and poetry: activism. One interpretation is that, like animal ethics and poetry, activism explores the normative aspects of the animal-human relationship. The basic claim behind it is that animals are active, independent beings who should not be treated as passive instruments. This claim is supported by various acts of "liberation," which force us to reexamine the basis of the named relationship. It can be maintained that direct actions—rather than being mindless and sporadic—contest meaning. They form "fractures" to the anthropocentric worldview that force us to reexamine understandings concerning other animals.

Maxwell Schnurer has argued that atrocities are enabled by a state of mindlessness, in which the reality is made meaningful via simple categories that remain outside any questions or criticism. Efforts to challenge these categories remain unsuccessful as long as they rely on "information" alone, for such information is analyzed on the basis of the same categories it is supposed to contest and thus remains simply insignificant or without meaning. (More important, since the categories are perceived to be beyond the reach of criticism, criticism does not make sense.) Schnurer offers the Holocaust underground resistance as an example of a more successful route toward challenging mindlessness. According to him, direct actions are not mere events but rather arguments that contest what is considered important: they "communicate value." An active, fighting, self-valuing Jew contested the stereotype of passive, incapable "others" empty of value. Schnurer argues that animal activism follows the same formula. In the speciesist society, animals are seen as valueless objects that humans have the right to use.[26] An activist turns this structure on its head: animals are of so much value that humans have the duty to risk their own skin in order to save them. The belief that "animals have no value and humans have rights over them" is replaced with the belief that "animals have great value and humans have duties toward them." Schnurer points out how social movements "can help people re-interpret everyday life and make new meaning from it" and maintains that this is what activism is all about. Actions "call upon audiences to consider their own ethical role in relationship to animals."[27] Thus, actions challenge mindless meanings. They may initially be read in a negative way, but what matters is that even then the observer is forced to pause and reflect, for a speciesist meaning has suffered a blow. As such reflections accumulate, change in cultural values begins. Schnurer's view makes sense. Direct actions are communicative, and their sheer radicality forces people to reflect upon meanings that usually are placed outside criticism. The meat eater is taken by surprise, and in order to make sense of the unusual and radical, he has to (even if for just a moment) open the door for new possibilities and values.

Costello, too, causes fractures via her juxtapositions. She omits "information" that would simply remain insignificant when read via anthropocentric meanings and instead uses radical juxtapositions to contest those meanings. Humans are not creatures of goodness but rather monsters; killing animals is not acceptable but rather obscene; animal industries are not morally justified but rather a form of holocaust. Such juxtapositions have a much greater effect than merely stating that "killing animals is morally wrong." If Costello feels uncomfortable, she is causing even more discomfort in the audience. Costello is taking part in activism: she does not seek to convince us by thinking but rather to shock us *into* thinking. She is a fracture in the academic bone. Costello has forced people to reflect on the "mindless" meanings by turning those meanings around. It may be that a society wanting to live in denial can only be alerted to challenge their meanings by these types of radical juxtapositions or other forms of radical rhetoric.

Disgrace, with its gentle persuasion, may only hit a chord with somebody who is already willing to listen. Those with a willingness to ignore need a louder wake-up call. *The Lives of Animals* offers us such a call.

CRITIQUE

Coetzee's approach depends on altering and replacing animal-related meanings. However, there is one objection to this. Those with a Wittgensteinian understanding may maintain that meanings cannot be altered and replaced that easily. Meanings lead to ethics; in the construction of normative views, their power is far greater than that of moral theory. Thus, they cannot be altered on the basis of such theory. Despite her pro-animal attitudes, Cora Diamond has criticized Tom Regan and Peter Singer on these grounds.[28] She claims that dualism between humans and animals is a basic meaning ("a central concept for human life"), which the theories in animal ethics will struggle to contest. In her opinion, meanings are to be given priority not only over moral arguments but also over factual considerations. Mental capacities are irrelevant, as are other factual similarities: "We form the idea of this difference, create the concept of the difference, knowing perfectly well overwhelmingly obvious similarities."[29] Diamond goes so far as to suggest that suffering, too, is secondary to meaning. She maintains that standard animal ethics "attacks" the "significance of human life" if it concentrates on suffering, interests, and other mental capacities instead of giving priority to meaning. Meanings may go against facts and moral theory, but so be it.

Gaita, who quotes Coetzee in length, maintains the same position (again, despite offering some pro-animal views). For him, claims of human-animal equality are a form of "meaning-blindness." Some notions are absurd—not because they are factually false but because they make no sense in relation to our language games. One example is the slogan "meat is murder." On these grounds, Gaita criticizes *The Lives of Animals*. He argues that there are "radical differences" between the Holocaust and animal industries that "deprive the comparison of power to shed light." For him, the comparison is "foolish and also offensive," for "we do not and cannot respond to what happens in the abattoir as we respond to murder."[30] Therefore, Coetzee's juxtapositions would be both powerless and meaningless.

The account faces problems. According to Gaita, claims of animal equality remain superficial to a degree that even those who present them are not true believers: "I have heard people say that meat is murder, but I have not met anyone whom I credit with believing it. No one I know or have even heard of treats people who eat meat as though they are murderers or accomplices to murder."[31] However, Coetzee is presenting us with precisely a person who very much believes that meat is murder (and that it is, indeed, comparable to the Holocaust). Costello is perplexed about how to relate to the animal murder all around her. She says:

> Is it possible, I ask myself, that all of them are participating in a crime of stupefying proportions? Am I fantasizing it all? I must be mad! Yet every day I see the evidence.... It is as if I were to visit friends, and to make some polite remark about the lamp in their living room, and they were to say: 'Yes, it's nice isn't it? Polish-Jewish skin it's made of, we find that's best, the skins of young Polish-Jewish virgins.' And then I go to the bathroom and the soap wrapper says, 'Treblinka—100% human stearate.' Am I dreaming, I say to myself?... Everyone else comes to terms with it, why can't you? *Why can't you?* (*The Lives of Animals*, 69)

Costello's reality is at odds with the reality of those surrounding her; the latter is like a bad dream for her. The difference is so great that she cannot even relate to it as a "reality." Her meanings are different; she is different. Whereas Gaita would want us to believe that nobody truly grasps the meaning of "animal murder," Coetzee shows us the acute sense in which some do indeed have it. The meaning is so vivid that it causes suffering and forces Costello to wish she could abandon it—however, at the same time it is so integral to her being that rejecting it is an impossibility. If anything, this is a real, lived meaning of elemental importance.

Therefore, it needs to be acknowledged that alternative meanings do exist, that anthropocentrism does not have a monopoly on meanings. Coetzee's take on the matter is deeper than that of Gaita. Whereas Gaita is pointing out that animal rights supporters do not gun down people who eat burgers, Coetzee is interested in the more relevant question: What does this mean? He brings forward the difficulty of relating to both a society that lives off an atrocity and an atrocity that is approved by the society, and he implies that the issue boils down to the difference between minority and majority meanings. Gunning down meat eaters is a futile option, for what is needed is not eradication of certain individuals but reflection on meanings. It is this heterogeneity of meanings that Diamond and Gaita risk overlooking. Moreover, the division into animal ethics and meanings has to be questioned. Animal ethics is a product of the times, firmly grounded on the societal meanings that emphasize similarity, suffering, equality, nonprejudice, consistency, and so forth. Even the factors that Diamond criticizes—mental abilities, interests, and emphasis on suffering—are basic meanings of the contemporary society, not abstract elements without relevance. Therefore, animal ethics is not an alien construction but part of our lived reality, a meaning in itself.

What about the human-animal dichotomy emphasized by Diamond? Cary Wolfe has talked of a Wittgensteinian "ethnocentrism" in this context. As a critical voice he brings forward Derrida, according to whom we do not own concepts (this includes the concept of "the human"). Moreover, animals cannot be placed in the conceptual order (such as a dichotomy). Rather, the animal renders us vulnerable and limited in conceptuality: we wake up outside language, completely open to any possibility. Wolfe suggests that it is here that we find both Lurie and Costello: wondering what has happened to them.[32] Wolfe's reminder is needed. Whereas for Diamond humanity is the starting point for ethics, one could argue that, in fact, the collapse of humanity is the starting point. We do not become exposed as long as we are lulled in a strong sense of human identity and dualism. Instead, we need a push into the unknown before we can see other beings in themselves and become exposed to their presence.

More recently, Diamond has written a sympathetic essay that directly explores *The Lives of Animals*. In this essay, she centralizes the ideas of "exposure" and "the difficulty of reality." Costello serves as an example of both. She has become exposed to the horror faced by other animals and is haunted by the difficulty of relating to a society that lives with this horror (she also finds haunting her own limitations in coming to terms with it all). Exposure and understanding the difficulty of reality have caused her to become an open wound.[33] The implication is that we all would do better by becoming similarly exposed. These claims strike a chord. As suggested above, the ontology of Costello is very different from the ontology of "normality": the latter seeks security, whereas the former has become open to the horror faced by billions on this earth. Diamond's terminology fits the situation beautifully.

Diamond warns us of "deflection" (a term borrowed from Stanley Cavell), within which appreciation of the difficulty of reality turns into solving that difficulty. She argues that Singer (and presumably others working within analytical animal ethics) need to take part in this deflection. It is expressed in the reluctance to accept the limitations of thought: "Is there any difficulty in seeing why we should not prefer to return to moral debate, in which the livingness and death of animals enter as facts that we treat as relevant in this or that way, not as presences that may unseat our reason?"[34] Diamond argues that for Costello, it is problematic to treat the fate of animals as a point of normative debate, as it would be problematic to meet the arguments of Holocaust deniers as a source of serious moral debate. The suffering of animals *is*, it exists, and we should remain open to it rather than deflecting it via linguistic displays or prolonged debate. Diamond asks: "But what kind of beings are we for whom this is an 'issue'?"[35] Diamond also emphasizes the notion of "fellow-creature." Instead of deducting from given traits given types of value, justice should rather start with a recognition of "our own vulnerability," which we ultimately share with other animals.[36] Diamond argues that moral theory "pushes apart justice, on the one hand, and compassion, love, pity, and tenderness, on the other," without recognition that "loving attention" toward others is needed for us to understand "evil."[37] Fellow-creatureliness, by contrast, enables us to become exposed to other animals and to see in them the same finitude that we see in ourselves.[38]

However, perhaps Diamond is too quick to judge animal ethics. In a response to Diamond's essay, Ian Hacking maintains that Singerian philosophy persuades people and offers forensic reasons to respect animals. Thus, in its functionality it has practical value: it pushes us toward social and legal change. Hacking argues: "Don't knock deflection."[39] Hacking has a point. First, the practical power of given works in animal ethics is something that Diamond unduly ignores. Singer's *Animal Liberation* (1975) has played a part in the evolution of the animal rights movement and the growth of vegetarianism, and the same can be said about works by Tom Regan, Mary Midgley, and so forth. Second, these works are needed to convince the diehards, who have been so affected by instrumentalizing views ("pigs are bacon") that they will never feel sympathy toward animals. For these broken people, animals will always remain distant beings; however, they, too, can review the effects their actions have on the lives of animals if convinced by something other than references to fellow-creatureliness. In these instances moral arguments are a manifestation of loving attention: they are calling for a being to change so that others may be recognized and suffer less. Ultimately, reliance on nothing but exposure works only in the perfect world—the world of people capable of responding to exposure. However, our difficult reality is colored by cultural conceptions that muddle exposure by telling us that animals are food or instinctual mechanisms. In such a reality, we need not only exposure but also reasons and arguments that trigger us to become exposed. Hence, animal ethics may not always be deflection but rather an invitation to look more carefully where one has previously been blinded by presumptions that equate living beings with steak and sausages.

One of the elements in animal ethics criticized by Diamond is the emphasis on mental abilities. However, if we ignore the mental abilities, interests, and suffering of other animals, we also ignore the animal perspective. Sentient beings make sense of the world on the basis of experiences. Get rid of these, and you delete the animal. This is perhaps the most important criticism of the Wittgensteinian emphasis on meaning: it tends to exclude the meanings of animals. All that is seen is the human reality, the human constructions, and human vulnerability, while the animal remains a passive object of a war over meaning. One option is to argue that animals do not have meanings, at least in the second-order sense (something implied by Gaita). Costello has an answer ready. She remarks of a philosopher who excludes animals from the moral sphere on the grounds that they cannot contemplate on "death" and thus do not have "meanings": "It awoke in me a quite Swiftian response. If this is the best that human philosophy can offer, I said to myself, I would rather go and live among horses" (*The Lives of Animals*, 65). Now, cognitive ethology shows that not only experiences but also beliefs, concepts, and intentions are common in the animal world.[40] More important, our own exposure to animals suggests that animals are not without minds. These minds give grounds for meanings. No matter how Mary may want to make hunting meaningful, its meaning to the hunted animals remains that of stress, fear, and pain. Hence, if we are to become exposed to the animal, we need to become aware of their mental abilities and the meanings that are born out of these abilities. Perhaps at times different capacities are given too much emphasis in animal ethics, but the opposite (giving them no room) will not do either.

This leads to an altogether different problem. Costello points out that we can imagine the points of view of fictional characters. Although her remark is meant to prove that surely imagining the perspectives of animals cannot thus be such a difficult task, it actually reveals a basic problem: imagination can be purely fictional and depend on nothing but the author. Does this make Coetzee's approach vulnerable to anthropomorphism? Singer argues that Coetzee goes wrong with his example of imagining fictional characters. We can imagine them because they are human—it is altogether a different matter to imagine the experiences of other species ("Reflections," in *The Lives of Animals*).[41]

Claims of anthropomorphism are usually based on the "problem of other minds," which demands full evidence for the existence of a mind of another being. However, the issue of evidence is not relevant to Coetzee—he is not interested in scientific proof of the standard kind but instead urges the reader to find alternative ways of understanding minds. A reoccurring theme for Coetzee is an encounter with an animal. The animal reveals herself to us and (against all our standard demands for evidence) changes the way we view her: the animal becomes a somebody, a being with a mind. Here imagination may play an important role, as we recognize animals as *someones* as soon as we seek to imagine their lived viewpoints. However, even more elemental seems to be the simple openness to the animal and her presence. After having encountered the animal, there can no longer be doubt, and there is no more room for skeptical arguments.

Dale Jamieson maintains that we should replace the "inferential view," which will only acknowledge that another being has a mind after evidence, with an "affective stance," which approaches the other being as a being with a mind.[42] A mind is not a conclusion but the starting point. Coetzee is offering a similar claim: animals are to be approached as beings who have minds. His criticism of technical explanations neatly follows Wittgenstein's claim: "My attitude towards him is an attitude towards a soul. I am not of the opinion that he has a soul."[43] Unsurprisingly, Wittgensteinian philosophers have emphasized the need to forsake the skeptical approach. John McDowell refers to Wittgenstein's analyses of the sentence, "Someone else cannot know it is this that I am feeling," and argues that the mistaken or "deflected" way of interpreting it is to see it as addressing the difficulty of knowing other minds. Rather, it is about being "unhinged" by the realization that language—and hence one's special nature as a speaking animal—is failing oneself.[44] Hence, maybe we should not reject other minds because of lingual difficulties related to explaining them—rather, we should reject the demand for lingual evidence and embrace the minds of others (a matter manifested beautifully in Costello's account of the rather ridiculous scientific studies on apes). Diamond argues that skepticism of other minds is a "tragedy": it involves blindness to others and their impact on our very reality and being (Stanley Cavell uses the term "soul-blindness" to define skepticism).[45] Language is seen as the tool with which to gain knowledge of other beings, whereas in fact it may deter us further away from them.

Anthropomorphism can be avoided by actively taking the animal into account. As argued above, rather than starting with humanity, we ought to start by focusing on the animal and by letting the animal "speak." Most of all, the capacity to experience is crucial. I catch glimpses of what it is like to be a pig because both the pig and I make the world meaningful via experiences. In Costello's opinion, for example, identification and imagination are possible, for "full being" forms a point of continuation between humans and other animals: "To be a living bat is to be full of being; being fully a bat is like being fully human, which is also to be full of being.... To be full of being is to live as a body-soul" (33). Costello also emphasizes embodiedness. The experience of full being is linked to having "a body with limbs that have extension in space, of being alive to the world" (33). This links "full being" with the capacity to experience: "being alive to the world" is precisely the stuff of "what it is like," of having a viewpoint to existence. Hence, animals are not aliens but our embodied, experiencing cousins. We can imagine what it is like not being able to move in a crowded cage or being injected with toxins in a laboratory. It could even be questioned whether it makes sense to maintain that we categorically cannot imagine what it is like to be a pig or a bat—where is the grounds for such a complete denial when taking into account the similarities? Another element worthy of attention is interaction—a theme, which runs through Coetzee's animal ethics. By interacting with animals, we start to gain a sense of their being, their particularity, and their value—as Lurie gains a new understanding of animals via his dealings with them, we may gain new glimpses of what it is to be an animal by going closer to them.

There is one aspect that is largely missing from Coetzee's approach. Although identification and interaction are emphasized, there is a lack of animal particularity. We get to know animals as "sheep" and "dogs" but not as specific individuals with their specific histories. This forms a slight problem. For instance, Jacques Derrida maintains that generic categories impose anthropocentric attitudes on animals: generalizations erase identities and thus enable human beings to convert animals into property (an act that Derrida calls a "crime").[46] Derrida emphasizes the particular animal, "that animal." Generalizations are so fundamental to anthropocentrism that he even suggests that the current way of conceptualizing reality would collapse if the generic term "animal" was abandoned and replaced with a term that emphasizes specificity. Although Coetzee does not present us with complete generalizations (we do get to learn some details of some of the animals), he would benefit from placing more attention on animal particularity. This applies not only because such particularity is crucial if we are to start viewing animals as independent beings with their own identities but also if imagination and identification are to take flight. We cannot identify with the faceless, generic being, and for the animal truly to step on the central stage, she needs to be given an identity.

CONCLUSION

Coetzee's alternative animal ethics centers around three main themes: resistance to theory, priority of the animal perspective, and poetics as a form of persuasion. In essence, he is suggesting that we adopt a new way of looking at the human-animal relation. Instead of theory and its concentration on principles and reason, poetry, virtues, emotion, and imagination should be prioritized. Virtues remind us of personal responsibility rather than abstract principles; emotions can reveal new meanings; and imagination together with identification may enable us to see the animal perspective. Poetry can communicate these factors, persuade in a way that theory cannot. The animal speaks to us, if we perceive her with emotion and imagination. Poetry may convince us to listen. The value of Coetzee's approach lies here.

Notes

1. See M. H. Bernstein, *On Moral Considerability: An Essay on Who Morally Matters* (Oxford: Oxford University Press, 1998).
2. P. Singer, T. Regan, M. Midgley, E. Pluhar, D. DeGrazia, B. Rollin, and many others have been prominent authors.
3. The postmodern approach has been influenced by continental and feminist philosophy. V. Plumwood and D. Haraway are a couple of examples—even J. Derrida has presented strong pro-animal views.
4. Of course, books like P. Singer, *Animal Liberation* (New York: Random House, 1975), have been highly influential, important, and persuasive (also G. Francione and T. Regan are among those who have sought to publicize their ethics more widely). However, the issue of persuasion per se is rarely discussed.
5. See P. Singer and M. Garber, "Reflections" in *The Lives of Animals*, by J. M. Coetzee, ed. Amy Gutman (Princeton, N.J.: Princeton University Press, 1999), 73-84, 85-92.
6. Perfectionism links the value of an individual with a perfectable, highly esteemed quality, such as "rationality." See again Bernstein, *On Moral Considerability*.
7. B. E. Rollin, *Animal Rights and Human Morality*, rev. ed. (New York: Prometheus Books, 1992); S. F. Sapontzis, *Morals, Reason, and Animals* (Philadelphia: Temple University Press, 1987). S. R. L. Clark, *Animals and Their Moral Standing* (London: Routledge, 1997).
8. As will be seen later, comparisons between killing humans and killing animals are often understood to be "obscene." For Coetzee, it is not the correlation but the lack thereof that is obscene.
9. On denial, see S. Cohen, *States of Denial: Knowing About Atrocities and Suffering* (Oxford: Blackwell, 2001).

10. See R. C. Solomon, "Peter Singer's Expanding Circle: Compassion and the Liberation of Ethics," in *Singer and His Critics*, ed. D. Jamieson (Oxford: Blackwell, 1999), 64-85.

11. Including B. Luke, "Taming Ourselves of Going Feral? Toward a Nonpatriarchal Metaethic of Animal Liberation," in *Animals and Women: Feminist Theoretical Explorations*, ed. C. J. Adams and J. Donovan (London: Duke University Press, 1995), 290-319.

12. M. Nussbaum, *Love's Knowledge* (New York: Oxford University Press, 1990).

13. For analytical philosophy, see P. Carruthers, *The Animals Issue: Moral Theory in Practice* (Cambridge: Cambridge University Press, 1992). For postmodern philosophy, see M. Calarco, *Zoographies: The Question of the Animal from Heidegger to Derrida* (New York: Columbia University Press, 2008); C. Wolfe, "Exposures," in *Philosophy and Animal Life*, by S. Cavell et al. (New York: Columbia University Press, 2008), 1-42; C. Wolfe, "In the Shadow of Wittgenstein's Lion: Language, Ethics, and the Question of the Animal," in *Zoontologies: The Question of the Animal*, ed. Cary Wolfe (Minneapolis: University of Minnesota Press, 2003), 1-57.

14. Another example is the monkey who, when offered the choice of two images, chooses the image of a human being rather than that of a monkey—for Costello, the monkey does not wish to be human per se but rather one of those beings who can come and go as they please instead of being locked in a cage.

15. E. Crist, *Images of Animals: Anthropocentrism and Animal Mind* (Philadelphia: Temple University Press 1999). See also L. Birke, *Feminism, Animals, and Science: The Naming of the Shrew* (London: Open University Press, 1994); J. Dunayer, *Animal Equality: Language and Liberation* (Derwood, Md.: Ryce Publishing, 2001).

16. D. Jamieson, "Science, Knowledge, and Animal Minds," in *Morality's Progress: Essays on Humans, Other Animals, and the Rest of Nature*, ed. D. Jamieson (Oxford: Oxford University Press, 2002), 52-70.

17. M. Bekoff, "Animal Emotions: Exploring Passionate Natures," *BioScience* 50, no. 10 (2000): 869.

18. M. Bekoff, *Minding Animals: Awareness, Emotions, and Heart* (Oxford: Oxford University Press, 2002), 9.

19. M. Rowlands, *Externalism* (Durham, U.K.: Acumen Publishing, 2003).

20. R. Gaita, *The Philosopher's Dog* (London: Routledge, 2002).

21. J. C. Gómez, "Are Apes Persons? The Case for Primate Intersubjectivity," in *The Animal Ethics Reader*, ed. S. Armstrong and R. Botzler (London: Routledge, 2003), 139.

22. Ibid., 142.

23. B. Smuts, "Reflections," in *The Lives of Animals*, ed. A. Gutman (Princeton, N.J.: Princeton University Press, 1999), 118.

24. See S. Baker, *The Postmodern Animal* (London: Reaktion Books, 2000). It has to be noted that analytical animal ethics is not guilty of such odd favoritism, as it has largely

concentrated on domestic animals. Most notably Singer, *Animal Liberation*, explores the plight of domestic animals in great detail.

25. A book that similarly compares animal industries to the Holocaust, Charles Patterson, *Eternal Treblinka: Our Treatment of Animals and the Holocaust* (New York: Lantern Books, 2002), argues that many human atrocities have been partly enabled by the instrumentalizing attitude humans have toward other animals.

26. Schnurer (Jewish himself) first felt uncomfortable about the comparison between animal industries and the Holocaust—however, after a visit to Birkenau he saw the comparison to be apt.

27. M. Schnurer, "At the Gates of Hell: The ALF and the Legacy of Holocaust Resistance," in *Terrorists or Freedom Fighters? Reflections on the Liberation of Animals*, ed. S. Best and A. Nocella (New York: Lantern Books, 2004), 114.

28. C. Diamond, "Eating Meat and Eating People," in *Animal Rights: Current Debates and New Directions*, ed. C. Sunstein and M. Nussbaum (London: Routledge, 2004), 93–107.

29. Ibid., 98.

30. Gaita, *The Philosopher's Dog*, 210–11.

31. Ibid., 198.

32. Wolfe, "In the Shadow of Wittgenstein's Lion."

33. C. Diamond, "The Difficulty of Reality and the Difficulty of Philosophy," in *Reading Cavell*, ed. A. Crary (London: Routledge, 2006), reprint, in *Philosophy and Animal Life*, by S. Cavell et al. (New York: Columbia University Press, 2008), 43–90.

34. Ibid., 74.

35. Ibid., 51.

36. C. Diamond, "Injustice and Animals," in *Slow Cures and Bad Philosophers: Essays on Wittgenstein, Medicine, and Bioethics*, ed. C. Elliot (Durham, N.C.: Duke University Press, 2001), 121.

37. Ibid., 131.

38. For Diamond, the term emphasizes sympathy, imagination, and respect for the independence of animals and rejects instrumentalization (see Diamond, "Eating Meat and Eating People").

39. I. Hacking, "Deflections," in *Philosophy and Animal Life*, by S. Cavell et al. (New York: Columbia University Press, 2008), 164.

40. Bekoff, "Animal Emotions"; M. S. Dawkins, *Through Our Eyes Only? The Search for Animal Consciousness* (Oxford: Oxford University Press, 1998); L. Rogers, *Minds of Their Own: Thinking and Awareness in Animals* (Boulder, Colo.: Westview Press, 1997).

41. Another issue is where to draw the line: if we are to accept Coetzee's proposal, are we to take into account the lives of oysters or snails, too? Descartes famously excluded oysters, and with them (in the name of consistency) all animals from the moral sphere.

However, Coetzee maintains that we can imagine the perspective of an oyster, for we "share the substrate of life" with it. I may not know what it is like to sit inside a shell in the bottom of a sea, but I can imagine the pain of such a creature.

42. Jamieson, "Science, Knowledge, and Animal Minds."
43. Wittgenstein, *Philosophical Investigations*. In this vein, Gaita maintains that "almost all philosophical and scientific work about animals is based on the assumption that Wittgenstein threw into doubt—that we are justified in attributing various 'states of consciousness' to animals only to the degree that we have evidence for them" (Gaita, *The Philosopher's Dog*, 52).
44. J. McDowell, "Comment on Stanley Cavell's 'Companionable Thinking,'" in *Philosophy and Animal Life*, by S. Cavell et al. (New York: Columbia University Press, 2008), 127–38.
45. Diamond, "The Difficulty of Reality"; see Cavell et al., *Philosophy and Animal Life* (New York: Columbia University Press, 2008).
46. J. Derrida, "The Animal That Therefore I Am," in *Animal Philosophy: Ethics and Identity*, ed. P. Atterton and M. Calarco (London: Continuum, 2004), 113–28.

References

Coetzee, J. M. *Disgrace*. New York: Penguin Books, 1999.

———. "Exposing the Beast: Factory Farming Must Be Called to the Slaughterhouse." *The Sydney Morning Herald*, May 2, 2007.

———. *The Lives of Animals*. Princeton: Princeton University Press, 1999.

7

Writing the Lives of Animals
Ido Geiger

Sunt lacrimae rerum, et mentem mortalia tangunt
[Things have tears, and affairs of mortals touch the mind]
—Virgil, *Aeneid*, 1.462

The story begins for me with Antigone. More precisely, it begins for me with the Antigone of Sophocles embedded in Hegel's *Phenomenology of Spirit* and in his philosophy more generally. Reading Hegel, I came to think that the role of Antigone in his grand narrative of the unfolding of reason and the progress of history was yet untold. For Hegel, as I read him, Antigone stands outside reason and history as the agent who effects their radical transformation. Antigone does not obey an already acknowledged religious or moral law, say the law commanding the universal right of burial. Forbidden on pain of death by Creon, without support from the city, the burial of her brother first enacts a law. Antigone brings the one who lies outside the law into the human fold. Acting blindly, her inevitable end is violence at the hands of the form of life she will transform. However, the rationality of transformations can be seen only retrospectively, and it is from this retrospective vantage point that Hegel is generally thought to have written—and so read. For this reason his telling of the story of Antigone remains unheard.

The question then arises of where in actuality there are such acts. For Hegel, the French Revolution and its aftermath, that is, the Reign of Terror and the subsequent European wars, stand as the violent foundation of modern ethical life. The great individual who is the unwitting agent at its origin is Napoleon. Generalized, we might think in similar terms of other struggles of liberation, for example, the struggles against slavery and the disenfranchisement of women. Paradoxically, the power of these examples—indeed, of any example—owes again to our viewing them with hindsight as radical transformations leading to our present form of ethical life. To the Antigones in our midst and the tragedies that beset them we are necessarily blind.[1]

Soon after that, I read for the first time Coetzee's *Disgrace* and then his Tanner Lectures on Human Values, *The Lives of Animals*. Acting alone for the burial rites of unwanted dogs killed at an animal-welfare clinic, David Lurie, protagonist of *Disgrace*, might be described as a dog-Antigone. However, unlike Hegel, Coetzee carefully resists assimilating the actions of his protagonist into any retrospective narrative of reason. And at the heart of his Tanner Lectures we find an explicit rejection of any traditional philosophical approach to the question of the moral standing of animals and an alternative to it in the form of a poetic injunction to think our way into the lives of animals, which seems to describe well the lesson learnt by Lurie in *Disgrace*. These works of Coetzee's thus seemed to me to promise a unique present view of the working of originary ethical moments, precisely by resisting describing them with hindsight. Furthermore, the works seemed to promise a unique insight into the relationship between philosophy and literature, in particular, into the moments in which philosophy turns to literature. In contrast, both these matters remain, for the most part, silent in readings of Hegel's philosophy. In the following pages I will attempt to follow through these intuitions, beginning with *Disgrace* and the questions it raised for me. I will then turn to what I take to be Coetzee's reflections upon these problems in *The Lives of Animals* and some other lessons which make up his subsequently published *Elizabeth Costello* to see what they can teach us concerning these questions. Contending with these questions will also, I hope, throw light upon the relation between literature and philosophy.

DISGRACE

David Lurie, the protagonist of *Disgrace*, is a professor, fifty-two, and twice divorced. Once a member of the Department of Modern Languages, specialist in the romantic poets, he now belongs to the Department of Communications at the newly named Cape Technical University in Cape Town. The beginning of the story describes what Lurie calls his solution to the problem of sex: ninety-minute weekly sessions with a woman he has contacted through an escort service. The affectionate relationship and the sexual encounters, described as entirely satisfactory, end when Lurie bumps into the woman with her two boys in the city. He has three sexual encounters with a student, is forced to leave the university, and finds himself living in the Eastern Cape with his daughter, who grows flowers and garden produce and keeps dog kennels. There, in a brutal attack, his daughter is raped by three men, he is beaten and burned, and the dogs are shot dead. The balance of the story will see him helping at an animal-welfare clinic with feeding, cleaning, and treating animals—and with the killing of unwanted dogs. He will learn that he can neither protect his daughter nor persuade her to leave her dangerous home or abort the child she now carries. The story ends with his working on a chamber opera he has long courted of Byron in Italy and helping with the killing of a dog he has come to love and think of as his own.

Disgrace begins with a fall. It is not, however, a fall from grace.[2] It seems rather to reveal the disgrace in which human beings and animals already live. The fall at the heart of this disgrace consists of two rapes: the rape of Lucy, Lurie's daughter; and the rape of his student, Melanie Isaacs. *Disgrace*, however, and this is crucial to establish at the outset, does not at all contend with rape either in legal terms or in the terms of moral law as they are ordinarily understood. Though the rape of Lucy is clearly rape in any moral or legal sense of the word, she resolutely refuses to report it to the police, choosing to struggle alone with what she characterizes as something entirely personal. It is, she says, something Lurie does not and cannot know. That what is at issue is an entirely personal wrong seems also to be the case with the rape of Melanie. In the first of their sexual encounters Melanie is described as "passive throughout" (*Disgrace*, 19) and in the third as "quick, and greedy for experience" (29).[3] It is of the second encounter that the narrative, with brutal honesty, employs the term rape.

> She does not resist. All she does is avert herself: avert her lips, avert her eyes. She lets him lay her out on the bed and undress her: she even helps him, raising her arms and then her hips. Little shivers of cold run through her; as soon as she is bare, she slips under the quilted counterpane like a mole burrowing, and turns her back on him. Not rape, not quite that. But undesired nevertheless, undesired to the core. As though she had decided to go slack, die within herself for the duration, like a rabbit when the jaws of the fox close on its neck. So that everything done to her might be done, as it were, far away.
> (25)

"Not rape, not quite that"—but by implication rape in some sense. How are we to think of the violence and wrong done here? At the university hearing held to contend with his offenses, Lurie's response to the charges against him is taken to be insincere and obfuscating. He is suspected of accepting the charges in name only. But his proclamation, "I accept whatever Ms Isaacs alleges" (50)—it is of great significance that the details of the charges are never read in the story; clearly, he is not charged with rape—seems to me to be very different. Lurie sees with clarity that the offense against Melanie is personal. It is what it is to her alone, beyond the language of morality and the letter of the law. He pleads guilty to a wrong that is not assimilated into the order of reason.

In the second part of the book Lurie will not speak again to Melanie nor, despite his great love for her, find a way to share the trials of his daughter. The duties that lay their claim on Lurie in the first part lead him on to other beings, human and animal. And as the first part of the book revolves around two falls, so the second is mainly concerned with twin works: the work at the animal-welfare clinic; and the composition of the opera about Byron's time in Italy. Indeed, just as the former are not falls from grace, the latter do not bring salvation.

We are told of the first work early in the story. Lurie is planning a chamber opera on Byron's days in Ravenna at the villa of his married mistress, Teresa Guiccioli. For months he writes nothing; "the project has failed to engage the core of him. There is something misconceived about it, something that does not come from the heart" (181). He finds his way into the writing when he concentrates not on the young and attractive Teresa but on the plain middle-aged woman she has become, still longing for the dead Byron. In his meeting with Melanie's father, Lurie insists that things might have turned out differently between Melanie and him. What he failed to supply he describes as the lyrical: "I manage love too well. Even when I burn I don't sing" (171). It is in the composition of the Byron opera that he will find song: "This is how it must be from here on: Teresa giving voice to her lover, and he, the man in the ransacked house, giving voice to Teresa" (183).

The second work, too, runs through the length of the story. What begins with the burial of the dogs massacred by the rapists and a bewildering bond with sheep destined for the banquet table becomes a central part of Lurie's life. He spends much of his time helping with the tending and the killing of unwanted animals. One of his duties at the clinic is taking the corpses of dogs to a hospital incinerator. Moved by an inexplicable feeling that the dogs are being dishonored by the operators of the incinerator, he takes on alone the work of administering their last rites: "he has become a dog-man: a dog undertaker; a dog psychopomp; a *harijan*" (146). By the end of the story he learns to think strong thoughts to comfort the condemned young dog he has come to love. He has become a dog-Antigone.

Let me try to formulate three closely related questions that *Disgrace* raises for me and with which *Elizabeth Costello*, I think, contends. But even before doing so, it is important to underscore that thinking of a novel as leaving something that demands further writing and reading poses pivotal questions: What is it that *Disgrace* leaves unsaid, and why does it do so? What is it that demands the extraordinary work of *Elizabeth Costello*? I hope to show not only that embedding *Disgrace* in the further work of *Elizabeth Costello* is an interpretative hypothesis that is corroborated by reading the works together but also that this embeddedness of texts in each other is a question that both of these works open. It is centrally related to the unfulfillable imperatives at the heart of both these works.

First, there is the question of the relation of the two parts of the story: What is it that sets the events in motion and moves the story on? Lurie's solution to the problem of sex is clearly no solution, and learning this leaves him, in a sense that demands inquiry, open. Lurie first describes the event at his hearing.

> The story begins one evening, I forget the date, but not long past. I was walking through the old college gardens and so, it happened, was the young woman in question, Ms Isaacs. Our paths crossed. Words passed between us, and at that moment something happened which, not being a poet, I will not try to describe. Suffice it to say that Eros entered. After that I was not the same.
> (*Disgrace*, 52)

Later he will leave the following words unsaid:

> *I was a servant of Eros*: that is what he wanted to say, but does he have the effrontery? *It was a god who acted through me.* What vanity! Yet not a lie, not entirely. In the whole wretched business there was something generous that was doing its best to flower.
> (89)

Lurie will remain open to the end of the story, and it is this openness, which leads him first into the relationship with Melanie, that will also somehow allow him to think his way into the being of the condemned animals and into the life of Teresa Guiccioli. So the literary or narrative question of the principle that drives the events is also, I think, the question, both literary and ethical, of how we are to read the ending, which in both senses sees nothing resolved. Lurie learns that he cannot help his daughter; he does not meet Melanie again; his opera is yet unfinished, heard in composition only by the dog he helps kill. Indeed, the story begins with the end of Lurie's dissolute solution to the problem of sex, and its end, the killing of his beloved dog in the animal-welfare clinic, is also a terrible final solution—a *Lösung* of the life of an unwanted dog, victim of the animal fertility of his kind.[4] Nothing is resolved. The question, then, is why can the narrative and ethical imperatives that set the story in motion not find their resolution? Why do they necessarily leave something open and undone? What is this wrong, in no ordinary sense legal or moral, that cannot be put right?

Second, there is the question of the unbearable proximity of rape to what Lurie describes as "something generous that was doing its best to flower" (*Disgrace*, 89).

We find this proximity again, which so starkly reveals that we are not within the realms of the law or of morality, when Lurie confronts the claim that he cannot understand what his daughter has suffered: "He does understand; he can if he concentrates, if he loses himself, be there, be the men, inhabit them, fill them with the ghost of himself. The question is, does he have it in him to be the woman?" (160). The openness that is a condition of love—for his daughter, for Melanie, for his dog—can also lead to terrible violence. This is why Lurie, without denying his violence, can say to Melanie's father: "It could have turned out differently" (171). This second question, then, is the question of the terrible proximity of love and rape. Put in the language of morality, this is the question of the impossibility, in *Disgrace*, of telling good from evil. And it is evident that this question is closely related to the former question: the imperative, characterized in *The Lives of Animals* as opening ourselves to the being of another, is no moral remedy.

Finally, what is the relationship between the very real work with animals and the work of art of the opera? The processes greatly resemble each other: In both, Lurie learns to think his way into the being of another, to think strong thoughts that will aid his dog in the throes of death, to listen to what Teresa alone, singing to the dead Byron, can teach him. Their ends, too, are closely tied: The opera remains unheard, heard in composition only by the dog Lurie helps kill. How are we to understand the relation between these two processes of life and art? This last question is also, I hope to show, the question implied in my claim that *Elizabeth Costello* takes on the unfinished work of *Disgrace* and also a question the former text itself raises. We might think of it as the question of writing the lives of animals.

THE LIVES OF ANIMALS

Later incorporated into *Elizabeth Costello* (2003), Coetzee's Tanner Lectures on Human Values, entitled *The Lives of Animals*, were delivered in Princeton in 1997. Preceding the publication of *Disgrace* (1999), they contend with what we saw is a central question of the novel—What do animal lives demand of us?—as though framing it in advance. At the heart of the lectures is a clearly stated rejection of the philosophical tradition contending with the moral question of the lives of animals and an alternative to it in the form of a simply phrased yet deeply puzzling poetic injunction—an injunction that seems to describe well the lesson learnt by David Lurie in *Disgrace*. The central critical charge lodged against philosophy in *The Lives of Animals* is that it makes human reason the mark or the means of the distinction between humankind and nonhuman animals. In this manner it justifies the perpetration of violence against animals reaching monstrous proportions in our day. For this reason the very language of philosophy must be rejected; mentioned by name in the lectures are Plato, Aristotle, Augustine, Aquinas, Descartes, Kant, and Thomas Nagel, but also, and this bears emphasizing, Porphyry, Bentham, Mary Midgley, and Tom Regan.

> "'The question to ask should not be: Do we have something in common—reason, self-consciousness, a soul—with other animals? (With the corollary that, if we do not, then we are entitled to treat them as we like, imprisoning them, killing them, dishonouring their corpses.)'"
> (*Elizabeth Costello*, 79)

The originary moral fact, the lectures claim, falls within the province of poetry, and it places us under a limitless obligation to all animal lives.

> Despite Thomas Nagel, who is probably a good man, despite Thomas Aquinas and René Descartes, with whom I have more difficulty in sympathizing, there is no limit to the extent to which we can think ourselves into the being of another. There are no bounds to the sympathetic imagination.
> (80)

It is patent, even from this brief and limited presentation of the lectures, that it is difficult to know what to make of their claims and how to respond to them. They emphatically reject the traditional philosophical discussion of the moral standing of animals. Yet their venue is an academic one, and Coetzee is clearly intent on addressing the philosophical tradition.[5] Moreover, it is not clear that the rejection of the language of philosophy is not a rejection of all language, including poetry. For what alternative is there to the language of comparison and the abstraction of universals? What language is it that has no limits and no blind spots? How does the sympathetic imagination speak? The lectures might seem further to suggest that the truth of their claims in some way depends upon attaining their own poetic ideal. Do the lectures themselves then think their way into the being of another? Who is this utterly other they bring to life? Where between philosophy and poetry does this being stand?

Answering these questions is a complicated matter. For Coetzee's two Princeton lectures tell the story of a single lecture delivered at the fictive Appleton College by the imaginary writer Elizabeth Costello. There is a rather rudimentary literary frame to the lecture delivered at Appleton: a son who teaches physics at the college, a philosopher daughter-in-law and their children, scenes of driving to and from the airport, but also a dinner and its academic conversation, a seminar in the English Department, a debate with a philosopher. What are we to make of this unusual being—a chimera with a body of a philosopher and the head of a poet?

To begin to answer this question it is important to note that Coetzee carefully inscribes the failure of Costello's lecture precisely as a philosophical or more broadly theoretical or academic argument. Despite clearly pronouncing that the very premise of comparing animal and human lives is to be rejected, Costello is taken to be doing just that by her interlocutors. Her daughter-in-law, who specializes in the philosophy of mind, takes her to compare human and animal minds and to claim that there are animal forms of reason (*Elizabeth Costello*, 91–93). O'Hearne, the professor of philosophy with whom Costello holds a public debate, seems to present her as speaking for the animal-rights movement, although Costello perfectly explicitly presents herself as searching for an alternative to the legacy of Bentham, Midgley, and Regan. She says that the "question to ask should not be: 'Do we have something in common . . . with other animals?'" and rightly lists Bentham as a philosopher who does ask it: "The question is not, Can they reason? nor, Can they talk? but, Can they suffer?"[6] More specifically, O'Hearne's first concern is that the animal rights movement presents a particular historical vision, a recent Western, even Anglo-Saxon idea, as universal—as though forms of moral blindness were not precisely Costello's concern (105–6). His further questions again take Costello to compare animal and human thought, speech, and attachment to life—again as though insisting on the possibility of throwing a bridge across a chiasm were not the lesson her talk attempts to teach. Even her son concludes that argumentation is not her métier (80; also see 10).

What, then, is the relation of Costello's extraordinary lecture to philosophy, and why does Coetzee so painstakingly inscribe its failure as a philosophical argument? Perhaps Coetzee should be read as insisting, at the same time, on the categorical imperative of finding our way into the lives of animals and on the inescapability of the generalization of philosophy and, more broadly, on the inescapability of language and comparison. Coetzee would then be rejecting the philosophical tradition and language more generally and in some sense insisting on their necessity. To escape philosophy and its limitation, to say what can be said by no language including the language of poetry, would then be both imperative and impossible. In other words, the poetic injunction at the heart of the lecture would be impossible to obey—giving us a first clue what *Disgrace* will of necessity leave undone, as though it was open-ended even before it was begun, leaving us also with the suggestion that what initially appears to be the relation of literature to philosophy is a moment within both literature and philosophy.

We find confirmation for these suggestions when we note that although the two Tanner lectures are entitled *The Philosophers and the Animals* and *The Poets and the Animals* they do not stand respectively for a rejection of philosophy and an affirmation of poetry. Like the philosophers, the aging Appleton poet, Stern, wrongly takes Costello's intention to be to liken the murder of Jews in Nazi death camps to the industrial slaughter of animals and refuses to attend the dinner in her honor (*Elizabeth Costello*, 94). (Costello does fall into drawing this comparison, but she intends to compare the impossibility of imagining—and so of comparing—their deaths; her failure, I am suggesting, is unavoidable.) In her English Department seminar Costello speaks at some length about "The Jaguar" and "Second Glance at a Jaguar." Ultimately, however, the tradition that Ted Hughes represents—Blake, Lawrence, Gary Snyder, Robinson Jeffers, and Hemingway are named—is said to speak for an "ecological philosophy that justifies itself by appealing to an idea, an idea of a higher order than any living creature" (99). It is explicitly called Platonic (98, 99).

This leads us to ask where in the lectures (and where in *Disgrace*) do we find an example of fulfilling the injunction to think your way into the being of another. The truth of Costello's moral injunction seems to depend on its performance. Yet Coetzee describes the delivery of her talk as flat and without impact (63). (I find myself trying to imagine Coetzee's delivery. Is he, unlike Costello, an animated reader of his own stories? With what blend of breath and sense did he animate his protagonist on the occasion of his lectures?) Costello begins her lecture not by evoking the horrors of the lives and deaths of animals in abattoirs, trawlers, and laboratories but by asking that the rhetorical power to do so be conceded her. Costello's fame is owed mainly to her book *The House on Eccles Street*, which tells the story of Joyce's Molly Bloom. And it is precisely her success in bringing Molly Bloom to life that Costello offers as proof that there are no bounds to the sympathetic imagination: "If I can think my way into the existence of a being who has never existed, then I can think my way into the existence of a bat or a chimpanzee or an oyster, any being with whom I share the substrate of life" (80). Clearly, however, we who have not read the book cannot take it as proof of this capacity. Coetzee's lectures, then, contain a rejection of philosophy that is repeatedly taken for a bad philosophical argument and an affirmation of poetry that, on first reading, seems to inspire nobody.

Is there in the story an example of the poetic engagement with the being of another animal, which Costello so firmly enjoins? Who fulfills it? Does Elizabeth Costello fulfill her own injunction in the story of the Appleton talk on the lives of animals? Does she fulfill it in the subsequently published book entitled *Elizabeth Costello*, divided not into chapters but into lessons and seemingly classifiable neither, in any usual sense, as literature nor as philosophy, incorporating, as it does, an interview, debates, more lectures (some discussing fictional or real books, several delivered in real conferences), musings prompted by a (real) book, a statement of belief within a fictional setting, encounters with real and invented characters—more of Elizabeth Costello's unusual life? Does Coetzee, whose protagonist she is, transitively fulfill the injunction by writing Elizabeth Costello, that is, *Elizabeth Costello*? Does he fulfill it by writing David Lurie, that is, *Disgrace*? (And who fulfills the injunction in Coetzee's later novel, *Slow Man* (2005), in which Costello appears in the thirteenth chapter to reveal to its protagonist that it is she who is writing the story and insists she must stay with him a while to write it better?)

At the heart of Coetzee's Tanner Lectures on Human Values we find a single lecture delivered at the fictive Appleton College by the imaginary writer Elizabeth Costello. The lecture itself begins with Elizabeth Costello describing herself as feeling like Red Peter, the ape who delivers Kafka's "Report to an Academy" (1917). She announces the lives of animals as her topic but refrains from evoking the horrors of their lives and deaths. Costello then pronounces to her audience that like a vast number of Germans who lived in close proximity to the Nazi death camps and yet, by willing ignorance, did not know the evil in the air, we, too, will ignorance of the industry of animal death. The bulk of the lecture, however, after the rejection of the language of reason, which I already examined, is devoted to Kafka's Red Peter—and with him to the idea and practice of thinking a way into the life of another.

"A REPORT TO AN ACADEMY"

In Kafka's story, Red Peter reports on the process of education that has taken him, a Gold Coast chimpanzee, to the "cultural level of an average European."[7] Delivering a monologue to an academy (no description of it is given in the story), Red Peter begins by explaining why he cannot quite give the report he was asked to give. Though shot and captured a mere five years earlier, forgetting his origins was a necessary condition of his education. His attempt to tell his own story is necessarily a misrepresentation of it: "Of course what I felt then as an ape I can represent now only in human terms, and therefore I misrepresent it, but although I cannot reach back to the truth of the old ape life, there is no doubt that it lies somewhere in the direction I have indicated."[8] Thus, what he can tell the academy "will contribute nothing essentially new"—"your life as apes, gentlemen, insofar as something of that kind lies behind you, cannot be farther removed from you than mine is from me."[9]

Red Peter's education begins inside a cage aboard a steamer headed for Europe. Forced to squat with knees bent, he comes to the very bodily conclusion that there is no way out and the search for a way out is the principle that drives his instruction. It will teach him first to imitate the sailors' spitting, pipe smoking, and, with great difficulty, their schnapps drinking. With the first downed bottle he also breaks into human sound, uttering his first "Hallo!" His speech now shows a predilection for images and idioms. He earns a living on variety stages and has his professional affairs seen to by a manager. He lives in an apartment, has acquired the taste for wine, and takes creaturely comfort in a broken, half-trained chimpanzee whom he cannot bear to look at by day.

Two thoughts come immediately to mind. First, like Coetzee's lecture-story, Kafka's story-report inhabits an exceptional literary space. Red Peter is invited to tell his ape story, but this he cannot properly do. His commission is literary, specifically autobiographical, but he can only make an impersonal report of fact. With this assertion indeed the story ends: "I am only imparting knowledge, I am only making a report. To you also, honored Members of the Academy, I have only made a report."[10] Indeed, Red Peter states that he will inevitably misrepresent his story as an ape because he is employing human language. (And what other language is there? Can no language tell an animal life?) Recall that it is precisely Costello's failure to pronounce emphatically enough that this contradiction is the condition of her lecture (but doesn't she? Coetzee surely does) that causes her philosopher interlocutors to misunderstand it and take her to attribute human reason, thought, and speech to animals. She claims that there are no bounds to the sympathetic imagination but employs human thought and language to tell of what lies beyond their ken. This clearly leads to contradiction. Like Red Peter, Elizabeth Costello recognizes this impassable limit. Speaking of her ability to know what it is like for a corpse to be a corpse she says:

> What I know is what a corpse cannot know: that it is extinct, that it knows nothing and will never know anything any more. For an instant, before my whole structure of knowledge collapses in panic, I am alive inside this contradiction, dead and alive at the same time.
> (*Elizabeth Costello*, 77)

Speaking, somehow, from within this contradiction is the condition of both Red Peter and Costello—and so both of Kafka and of Coetzee. It is the moment missed by reading Hegel as though he views the development of history as thoroughly rational, overlooking the figures who, like Antigone, stand for the violent and irrational transformation of reason.

Second and closely related to this point is the fact that the success of the lectures of both Red Peter and Costello hangs on their ability—the impossible ability—to think their way into the being of another: the other Red Peter once was and the range of others Costello claims she can think and tell. Like her, Red Peter, too, suggests at several points that his vision is unique. He tells his audience with authority that apes think with their bellies;[11] about his mate he says that he alone can see "the insane look of the bewildered half-broken animal in her eye."[12] Again, it seems that the failure of reason is a necessary condition of their success, as though both Coetzee and Kafka are suggesting that it is only at the site of the collapse of language into contradiction that we think our way into the being of another.

This brings us to what is most striking about Costello's turn to Red Peter in her Appleton lecture and also in the first lesson of *Elizabeth Costello*, entitled "Realism." On both occasions she says she feels like Red Peter and insists she is not being ironic: She says what she means. And this must mean that we are to read Costello as Costello reads Red Peter. Indeed, it is in this reading and in this reading alone that we find Costello not merely proclaiming her moral imperative or naming the literary corpus it has engendered but fully trying to think her way into the being of another. We are, then, to read her reading her way into Red Peter. This, she says, is the only way left for her (and so for us) speaking to an academy as or in Red Peter. What alternative does she (do we) have?

> I ask the question and then answer it for you. Or rather, I allow Red Peter, Kafka's Red Peter, to answer it for you. Now that I am here, says Red Peter, in my tuxedo and bow tie and my black pants with a hole cut in the seat for my tail to poke through (I keep it turned away from you, you do not see it), now that I am here, what is there for me to do? Do I in fact have a choice? If I do not subject my discourse to reason, whatever that is, what is left for me but to gibber and emote and knock over my water glass and generally make a monkey of myself?
> (*Elizabeth Costello*, 68)

At the very heart of her lecture Costello reads into yet another text, itself embedded perhaps in Kafka's "Report." Like it published in 1917, Wolfgang Köhler's *The Mentality of Apes*, she claims, just might have been Kafka's inspiration.[13] Köhler's book describes the experiments conducted with a group of chimpanzees at the Prussian Academy of Science Anthropoid Station in Tenerife between 1913 and 1917. Costello focuses on Sultan, Köhler's most gifted student, and on his use of implements (stick, box) to get to food outside his reach.

> Sultan knows: Now one is supposed to think. That is what the bananas up there are about. The bananas are there to make one think, to spur one to the limits of one's thinking. But what must one think? One thinks: Why is he starving me? One thinks: What have I done? Why has he stopped liking me? One thinks: Why does he not want these crates any more? But none of these is the right thought. Even a more complicated thought—for instance: What is wrong with him, what misconception does he have of me, that leads him to believe that it is easier for me to reach a banana hanging from a

> wire than to pick up a banana from the floor?—is wrong. The right thought to think is: How does one use the crates to reach the bananas?
>
> Sultan drags the crates under the bananas, piles them one on top of the other, climbs the tower he has built, and pulls down the bananas. He thinks: Now will he stop punishing me?
>
> (*Elizabeth Costello*, 72–73)

It seems clear that in some sense Coetzee is here, in his protagonist, finally thinking his way into Sultan's life. But in what sense, precisely? Is this an attempt to describe correctly Sultan's thoughts and draw from them his moral standing? If it were, then Costello's interlocutors would be right to charge her with the contradiction of attributing human language and thought to an ape. Furthermore, she would rightly be challenged to explain what makes her thinking true to the facts and Köhler's—despite the years spent trying precisely to think and describe the mentality of his apes—false, or at least tragically incomplete.

Coetzee, I suggested earlier, is well aware of these objections. Indeed, they are in some way a necessary condition of what is happening in these passages, which is not something that is said in them. We learn what the cost of Red Peter's education consists of, says Costello, "through the ironies and silences of the story" (*Elizabeth Costello*, 72). (Lurie describes his behavior at his hearing as standing up for the principle: "Freedom to remain silent" [*Disgrace*, 188].)

> Kafka's ape is embedded in life. It is the embeddedness that it important, not the life itself. His ape is embedded as we are embedded, you in me, I in you. That ape is followed through to the end, to the bitter, unsayable end, whether or not there are traces left on the page. Kafka stays awake during the gaps when we are sleeping.
>
> (*Elizabeth Costello*, 32)

This key passage tells us that finding our way into the being of another is not something sayable or readable. It is not something verifiable or refutable—nothing that we can say is true to the facts. (It is not a matter of words and their truth value—not all value lies in truth.) Costello is not claiming that her description of Sultan's thoughts is right. Indeed, she proclaims in her "Realism" lecture that the "word-mirror is broken, irreparably, it seems.... The words on the page will no longer stand up and be counted each proclaiming, 'I mean what I mean!'" (*Elizabeth Costello*, 19).[14] It is the ironies and silences of his story that call Costello to follow Red Peter, as Kafka follows Sultan through to the end. Thinking your way into the being of another is not attaining knowledge and a stable moral stance. *It is a relation to another that exists only in its transitivity—being called by another and calling another in train.*[15] It is being moved by the exceptional moral demand made upon us by another, an imperative that cannot be fulfilled but only transmitted by its witness in silence. It is in being followed by Kafka, and by Costello, and now by us, to the bitter, unsayable end that Red Peter, attempting himself to follow his own animal past, is embedded in life.[16]

This, I suggest, is also the significance of the exceptional relation of texts we are examining, the dizzying *mise en abîme* down which Coetzee casts us. It is precisely a relation of embeddedness: Costello's story embedded in Coetzee's lecture; Kafka's story embedded in Costello's lecture; Sultan's story embedded in Köhler's report to the academy—and also the lives of animals in *Disgrace* embedded in *The Lives of Animals* and also, as we will see below, the lives of animals in *Disgrace* embedded in the Byron opera and, more generally, the embeddedness of life in writing. At its bottom we do not find the bedrock of the right description of Sultan's animal life or of the life of Lurie's dog or of Teresa Guiccioli nor, consequently, the right answer to the question of their moral standing. To be embedded in another is to follow another. To be embedded in life is to be embedded in another—to be moved by the demand made upon us by the animal life of another, and to move another in turn. The chain of texts comes to life for me or you only when we are summoned by them, called in to them, and by reading and writing further, call in another. It is an imperative that can be followed but not fulfilled. Like Kafka, Coetzee follows these animal lives to the bitter unsayable end. Unlike Hegel, he will not then assimilate them into the order of reason. He does not offer us an answer, after the fact, to the question of what principle of reason or morality an animal life stands for.

The train of animal texts and lives speaking to us does not end here. (Who but a philosopher would deny that this relation continues to infinity?) Within the essay "Reflections on the Guillotine" Coetzee hears the story of the young Camus who finds himself assisting his grandmother in slaughtering a hen.

> As for animals being too dumb and stupid to speak for themselves, consider the following sequence of events. When Albert Camus was a young boy in Algeria, his grandmother told him to bring her one of the hens from the cage in their backyard. He obeyed, then watched her cut off its head with a kitchen knife, catching its blood in a bowl so that the floor would not be dirtied.
>
> The death cry of that hen imprinted itself on the boy's memory so hauntingly that in 1958 he wrote and impassioned attack on the guillotine. As a result, in part, of that polemic, capital punishment was abolished in France. Who is to say, then, that the hen did not speak?[17]
>
> (*Elizabeth Costello*, 108)

Finding your way into the being of another is a relation that exists only in its transitivity. It does not involve the attainment of a stable position of knowledge and a moral stance. (But isn't this a story about the abolishment of capital punishment? We now feel how powerful is the pressure to read with hindsight. This is the pressure to which Costello's interlocutors and Hegel's readers yield. This is the pressure to which the philosophical tradition yields in its attempt to comprehend the radical historical transformations of our ethical life.) But then meeting Costello's injunction to "open your heart" (*Elizabeth Costello*, 82) is not opening ourselves to the articulate fullness of the animal life of another and learning what, morally speaking, it demands of us. Instead it means tearing open a gaping hole within ourselves and transmitting this wound. Indeed, Costello describes herself as an "animal exhibiting, yet not exhibiting, to a gathering of scholars, a wound, which I cover up under my clothes but touch upon in every word I speak" (71). Like her, Red Peter hides a scar under his clothes, and in place of the animal mouth that has learned to speak he has a silent mouth—"a large, naked, red scar" on his cheek.[18] It is in this sense that Costello is embedded in the life of her son and he—in hers. Like them, Kafka's ape is whirled down this human hole and calls us in to follow.

This, I am suggesting, is the answer to the first question posed by *Disgrace*. The driving force and main concern of the narrative is what I described, prematurely, as openness and as a duty incurred that cannot be fulfilled. It begins with what David Lurie characterizes as Eros acting through him. It continues with his efforts to think his way into the lives of his daughter, the animals he tends, and Teresa Guiccioli. And it remains open in his unfinished opera and the dog he helps to die. Nothing is resolved. The moral imperative that the life of an animal poses cannot be comprehended into the order of reason and fulfilled. Unlike Hegel, Coetzee does not supplement his vision of the tragedy of these moments of ethical life with a retrospective view of their achievements. *Disgrace* ends like an open wound.

"THE PROBLEM OF EVIL"

I characterized the second question *Disgrace* raises as the terrible proximity or undecidability of good and evil, specifically, the terrible proximity of love and rape. We should already have some sense that this matter is a consequence of the line of thought we have been following. For if the claims made upon us by the life of another cannot be comprehended into the order of reason and fulfilled, then there can be no clear conception here of what tells right from wrong. In their second sexual encounter, Melanie is described as a victim of rape, deciding "to go slack, die within herself for the duration, like a rabbit when the jaws of the fox close on its neck. So that everything done to her might be done, as it were, far away" (*Disgrace*, 25). Without in the least diminishing his responsibility for this violence, Lurie later insists that in "the whole wretched business there was something generous that was doing its best to flower" (89)—"It could have turned out differently" (171), he says to Melanie's father. How are we to understand this conjunction? And how is it related to the idea of a claim made upon us by another that cannot be met but only transmitted?

The sixth lesson of *Elizabeth Costello*, entitled "The Problem of Evil," revolves around a conference in Amsterdam devoted to the problem of evil. We are told at the opening that Costello suspects she was invited because of a piece that attacked her for belittling the Holocaust in a talk in the United States. We are then still within the purview of the Appleton talk on the lives of animals. Indeed, what she decides to speak about turns out to be a deeply disturbing consequence of the injunction to think our way into the being of another, about which nothing was said in that talk. In Amsterdam Costello grapples with a book by Paul West on the assassination plot against Hitler, leading to the attempt on his life in July 1944 (*The Very Rich Hours of Count von Stauffenberg* [1989]). Costello's focus is the description of the execution of the plotters. Her charge against West is that in obeying the poetic injunction to think his way into the being of another he let loose upon the world the evil he touched:

> Through Hitler's hangman a devil entered Paul West, and in his book West in turn has given that devil his freedom, turned him loose upon the world. She felt the brush of his leathery wing, as sure as soap, when she read those dark pages.[19]
> (*Elizabeth Costello*, 167-68)

What we have before us is a startling consequence of the injunction to think our way into the being of another, and Costello knows this full well, knows that what West has done she, too, does. West's process of poetic invention in thinking his way into the being of Hitler's henchman is the very process she engages in herself (see, 166-67, 174, 177, 179). Indeed, West's method is strikingly similar to Costello's, telling the story of the plot through the eyes of Claus von Stauffenberg, who, in turn, continues to inhabit the lives implicated by the failed assassination attempt even beyond his execution, telling—as Costello claims we can—of a life beyond its death. We have Costello thinking her way into West ("we can pretend the book in question is no longer Mr West's but mine, made mine by the madness of my reading" [174]), West thinking his way into Stauffenberg, who in turn is thinking his way into the execution, that is, into the minds of the executed and their terrible executioner, even Hitler himself—a second, terrifying *mise en abîme*. Their correspondence notwithstanding, Costello now insists that she would no longer allow herself to give "the butcher a voice" (168). Some things must remain unsaid.

> *Obscene*. That is the word, a word of contested etymology, that she must hold on to as a talisman. She chooses to believe that *obscene* means *off-stage*. To save our humanity, certain things that we may want to see (*may want to see because we are human!*) must remain off-stage. Paul West has written an obscene book, he has shown what ought not to be shown.
> (168–69)

Costello seemingly offers here a solution to the threat of giving the devil a voice and a stage. Until "she thought better of it, she had no qualms about rubbing people's faces in, for example, what went on in the abattoirs" (179). This she will do no longer. Having taken place, such things "ought not to be brought into the light but covered up and hidden for ever in the bowels of the earth, . . . if one wishes to save one's sanity" (159).

However, this resolution cannot be taken at face value. First, Costello herself knows that the refusal to know cannot be justified (178). For it is precisely this willed ignorance that is the sin of those who deny the slaughterhouses and those who turned a blind eye to the death camps. She continues to wrestle with this contradiction to the end of the lesson with no resolution. Second, and glaring, is the fact that Coetzee's "Problem of Evil" does expressly give Hitler's vile henchman a voice and a stage. Moreover, in it Costello recalls an event in her youth in which she struggled with a man who tried to rape her and, having tired of the struggle, beat her brutally. (It is striking that in *Disgrace* there is no description of Lucy's rape.) Of "her first brush with evil" (165), which left her with a broken jaw, she has never spoken (so, like Red Peter, Costello has a mouth that speaks and a silent scar; it is through a scarred ear that Lurie learns to listen); nor has she used it in any of her books. "For half a century the memory has rested inside her like an egg, an egg of stone, one that will never crack open, never give birth. She finds it good, it pleases her, this silence of hers, a silence she hopes to preserve to the grave" (166). How are we to take Costello's newfound conviction that the imperative to think our way into the being of another can lead to evil? And how are we to tell when obeying it might turn the devil loose upon the world? What are we to make of the apparent contradiction between Costello's vow of silence and Coetzee's writing?

I think that Coetzee is not limiting here the scope of the imperative to think our way into the being of another but bringing into the open a terrible and inescapable consequence of it. For the resolution to keep silent is no solution to the threat of giving evil a voice and a stage. This was already implicit in the imperative in the lecture on animal lives. For recall that Costello says there of Kafka that we think our way into Red Peter's life "through the ironies and silences of the story" (*Elizabeth Costello*, 72). Silence is precisely that into which we are called.[20] Costello now sees clearly that there is no way of knowing what we are entering. To think our way into another, to open ourselves up to be inhabited by another, is to submit ourselves to whoever and whatever enters our being. When another speaks and acts through us we cannot decide what the other says and does. "The Problem of Evil" teaches us that we are as likely to be inhabited by good as by evil—an impossible choice between willing ignorance and courting the devil.

Moreover, what it is that enters our being and acts through us cannot be decided. Bev Shaw devotes her life to the welfare of animals. She is Lurie's guide into the lives of animals. Yet she is described in terms very similar to those used of Hitler's executioner ("West in turn has given that devil his freedom, turned him loose upon the world. She felt the brush of his leathery wing"): "He does not dismiss the possibility that at the deepest level Bev Shaw may be not a liberating angel but a devil, that beneath her show of compassion may hide a heart as leathery as a butcher's. He tries to keep an open mind" (*Disgrace*, 144). If it is the devil who possesses her being, it is precisely because she thinks her way into the suffering animals in her charge, as West inhabits the dead Stauffenberg and his fellow conspirators. And it is precisely the fact that Lurie allows Eros to take possession of his being that allows Rape to enter, "god of chaos and mixture, violator of seclusions" (105).[21] This, I think, is why Lurie takes full responsibility for the violence he does Melanie and yet can feel that between them there was "something generous that was doing its best to flower" (89).

The horror of the proximity of love and rape is nowhere clearer than in Lurie's terrible struggle to think his way into his daughter's silence: "Lucy's intuition is right after all: he does understand; he can if he concentrates, if he loses himself, be there, be the men, inhabit them, fill them with the ghost of himself. The question is, does he have it in him to be the woman?" (160). This question Coetzee, and Costello, leave open for us. Having been warned that "if what we write has the power to make us better people then surely it has the power to make us worse" (*Elizabeth Costello*, 171), will we read our way into Elizabeth Costello? And, if we do, will the evil that has entered her through Hitler's executioner and through her assailant enter us? Will we read and write on, for better or worse? This is the impossible question put to us by Coetzee's writing of Costello's silence, the writer of fiction who throughout the book bearing her name no longer writes fiction.[22]

ETHICS AND WRITING

This brings us back, finally, to the question of the relation of reality or life and art. I asked earlier what we are to make of the double open ending of *Disgrace*: the train of relationships of animal and human lives that begins to call forth the yet unfinished and unheard opera. Indeed, we can now see that this question was already implicit in the discussions of the first and second questions. For the call to enter the animal life of another, we saw, is *transmitted in writing*: in Kafka's writing the life of Köhler's Sultan, in Costello's writing the life of Kafka's Red Peter, in Coetzee's *The Lives of Animals* writing the story of Elizabeth Costello, and in *Disgrace* writing the story of David Lurie, which ends with the composition of the unheard opera of Teresa Guiccioli; the evil of Hitler's executioner is transmitted in West's writing of the Stauffenberg plot. We can now see clearly that this question of the relation of life and art is also the question implicit in the intuition that *Disgrace* calls for the work of *Elizabeth Costello* (and the chimerical genre in which it is written). The trains we followed in *The Lives of Animals* lesson (Coetzee—Costello—Kafka—Red Peter—Köhler—Sultan) and "The Problem of Evil" lesson (Coetzee—Costello—West—West's literary Stauffenberg—Hitler's real henchman) also think of real lives as calling for reading and writing, which in their turn call for a response, and further reading and writing. The call of an animal life sounds in the silences of writing, in the lacunae of reason. This call, I suggested at the end of the last section, ultimately addresses us. (In the opening of this paper I told of first hearing this call in the silences of Hegel's Antigone.) The silences of writing and lacunae of reason call forth from us such writing and reason.

What is the relation between reality and art, between reading and writing and life? There is, I think Coetzee is saying, no life without thinking our way into it and responding to it, no life without reading and writing. (Hegel would say: There is no human life without social and political recognition. To the Antigones in our midst, however, we are necessarily blind.) With what question, then, does Coetzee leave us? Clearly, it is the very real question of whether to read and write, to read and write the life and words of another. The question is whether or not to wrestle with the silence and unreason of another—not to turn it into knowledge and speech but to pose the question in silence to another in train. This is the question with which Lurie's unheard opera leaves us:

> His hopes must be more temperate: that somewhere from amidst the welter of sound there will dart up, like a bird, a single authentic note of immortal longing. As for recognizing it, he will leave that to the scholars of the future, if there are still scholars by then.

> For he will not hear the note himself, when it comes, if it comes—he knows too much about art and the ways of art to expect that.
>
> (*Disgrace*, 214)

This is also the question with which Elizabeth Costello is grappling at the end of "The Problem of Evil" and perhaps throughout the book. This is the significance of Coetzee's writing of a writer who seems no longer capable of writing.

Finally, this same question is put to us with utmost urgency by the postscript to *Elizabeth Costello*. In it Coetzee is again reading and writing in the tracks of a writer, following Hofmannsthal's "Letter of Lord Chandos" (*Ein Brief* [1902]; signed Phi. Chandos, 22 August, 1603), addressed to Francis Bacon, with "The letter of Elizabeth, Lady Chandos, to Francis Bacon" (signed Elizabeth C., 11 September, 1603). Hofmannsthal's Lord Chandos, responding to a concerned letter from his friend Bacon, writes to explain his two years of silence: "*his complete abandonment of literary activity.*"[23] In it Chandos recalls his former plans of writing motivated by a deep feeling of the unity of all existence. These plans, however, were not to come to fruition. He has lost all ability to speak of lofty ideas, general subjects, even worldly matters: "My case, in short, is this: I have lost completely the ability to think or to speak of anything coherently."[24] Moments of revelation, evoked by a "pitcher, a harrow abandoned in a field, a dog in the sun, a neglected cemetery, a cripple, a peasant's hut" now fill him to the brim with a "silent but suddenly rising flood of divine sensation."[25]

> Recently, for instance, I had given the order for a copious supply of rat-poison to be scattered in the milk-cellars of one of my dairy-farms. Towards evening I had gone off for a ride and, as you can imagine, thought no more about it. As I was trotting along over the freshly-ploughed land, nothing more alarming in sight than a scared covey of quail and, in the distance, the great sun sinking over the undulating fields, there suddenly loomed up before me the vision of that cellar, resounding with the death-struggle of a mob of rats. I felt everything within me: the cool, musty air of the cellar filled with the sweet and pungent reek of poison, and the yelling of the death-cries [*Gellen der Todesschreie*] breaking against the mouldering walls; the vain convulsions of those convoluted bodies as they tear about in confusion and despair; their frenzied search for escape, and the grimace of icy rage when a couple collide with one another at a blocked-up crevice. But why seek again for words which I have foresworn! . . . but there was more, something more divine, more bestial; and it was the Present, the fullest, most exalted Present. There was a mother, surrounded by her young in their agony of death; but her gaze was cast neither toward the dying nor upon the merciless walls of stone,

but into the void, or through the void into Infinity, accompanying this gaze with a gnashing of teeth![26]

Chandos will never again write either a letter or a book "because the language in which I might be able not only to write but to think is neither Latin nor English, neither Italian nor Spanish, but a language none of whose words is known to me, a language in which inanimate things speak to me and wherein I may one day have to justify myself before an unknown judge."[27] It is a letter wrought in silence, writing the inability to speak or write. It is a letter writing the collapse of language.

Of the many questions which the letter might raise Coetzee seems to end with this question: What response does the letter call for? What would count here as responding in kind? And who—the letter is, after all, addressed to Francis Bacon—is really called to respond? The postscript to *Elizabeth Costello* intervenes with yet another text that raises the question of the address. The question was implicit when I claimed that the texts we are reading call *us* in to follow. The trains of written texts we followed must address us, that is, *each of us singly*, Coetzee and Costello and me and you. It is an animal life that is addressing us and ultimately must call *us* in to follow, must *in us come to life*. *The words of another* must in us come to life.

For we learn that Lord Chandos has not managed to keep his plight from his wife. Indeed, Lady Chandos herself has become the vehicle of her husband's visions. Her letter to Bacon reveals that "in the company of my Philip I too have moments when soul and body are one, when I am ready to burst out in the tongues of angels" (*Elizabeth Costello*, 228):

> We are not meant to live thus, Sir. *Flaming swords* I say my Philip presses into me, swords that are not words; but they are neither flaming swords nor are they words. It is like a contagion, saying one thing always for another (*like a contagion*, I say: barely did I hold myself back from saying, *a plague of rats*, for rats are everywhere about us these days).
> (228)

It is a contagion, saying one thing always for another, saying one thing for another without end. *It is* a contagion, saying for another, *another* saying for another without end. *With what words can such writing end?*

Not Latin, says my Philip—I copied the words—*not Latin nor English nor Spanish nor Italian will bear the words of my revelation*. And indeed, it is so, even I who am his shadow know it when I am in my raptures. Yet he writes to you, as I write to you, who are known above all men to select your words and set them in place and build your judgments as a mason builds a wall with bricks. Drowning, we write out of our separate fates. Save us.

(*Elizabeth Costello*, 230)

Notes

For their responses to this paper, I am deeply indebted to Eli Friedlander, Yoav Kenny, Anton Leist, Eyal Peretz, Aviv Reiter, Peter Singer, and Michael Weinman.

1. See: I. Geiger, "Die Tragödie der Gesetzgebung und der Skeptizismus der moralischen Anerkennung: Hegel über Antigone und Krieg," in *Skepsis und literarische Imagination*, ed. B. Hüppauf and K. Vieweg (Munich: Wilhelm Fink Verlag, 2003), 77–94; "War and the Founding of the State in Hegel's Political Philosophy," *History of Philosophy Quarterly* 20 (2003): 297–317; "Hegel's Critique of Kant's Practical Philosophy: Moral Motivation and the Founding of the State," *International Yearbook of German Idealism* 2 (2004): 121–50; *The Founding Act of Modern Ethical Life: Hegel's Critique of Kant's Moral and Political Philosophy* (Stanford, Calif.: Stanford University Press, 2007).

2. The sense of fall in the story is not religious. It is a fall in a godless world. The only person who will describe it in religious terms is the father of Lurie's student (*Disgrace*, 172). The character Elizabeth Costello, in a text to which I will return later, reflects that while "she has less and less idea what it could mean to believe in God, about the devil she has no doubt. The devil is everywhere under the skin of things, searching for a way into the light" (*Elisabeth Costello*, 167).

3. Interestingly, this scene is missing from Steve Jacobs's otherwise unusually faithful film adaptation of the novel.

4. "When people bring a dog in they do not say straight out, 'I have brought you this dog to kill,' but that is what is expected: that they will dispose of it, make it disappear, dispatch it to oblivion. What is being asked for is, in fact, *Lösung* (German always to hand with an appropriately blank abstraction): sublimation, as alcohol is sublimed from water, leaving no residue, no aftertaste" (*Disgrace*, 146).

5. The traditional philosophical response to the challenge posed by the radical transformations of our shared ethical life is to think of the imperatives of morality as expanding their scope, say from white (adult, property-owning) men to other races to women to animals and so on. It is worth suggesting at this early juncture that Coetzee's radical alternative to this traditional philosophical response is best thought of not as rejecting it but rather as supplementing it. For the classic example of such a view in the context of the moral standing of animals, see P. Singer, "All Animals Are Equal . . . Or, Why the Ethi-

6. cal Principle on Which Human Equality Rests Requires Us to Extend Equal Consideration to Animals Too," in *Animal Liberation* (London: Pimlico, 1995).
6. J. Bentham, *Introduction to the Principles of Morals and Legislation*, chap. 17. See also the remark on the Great Ape Project (*Elizabeth Costello*, 70). Costello is, of course, ignoring the fact that the animal rights movement does not at all conclude from this comparison that "we are entitled to treat them as we like, imprisoning them, killing them, dishonouring their corpses."
7. See, F. Kafka, "A Report to an Academy," in *The Complete Stories*, trans. Willa Muir and Edwin Muir (New York: Schocken Books, 1971), 258.
8. Ibid., 253.
9. Ibid., 251, 250.
10. Ibid., 259.
11. Ibid., 253.
12. Ibid., 259.
13. See, W. Köhler, *The Mentality of Apes*, trans. E. Winter, from the second rev. ed. (New York: Liveright, 1976).
14. Costello clearly rejects any allegorical and, more broadly, signifying and referential readings of Kafka, insisting that it is impossible to tell who is doing the talking in the "Report" (ape? man? parrot?) and who is addressed (men? apes? parrots?). She thus sides with critics such as Benjamin and Deleuze and Guattari. The latter characterize Kafka's language as torn from sense and reference. This is exemplified by the stories of becoming-man (of the beetle, of the dog, of the ape) and becoming-animal (beetle, dog, ape). See G. Deleuze and F. Guattari, *Kafka: Towards a Minor Literature*, trans. D. Polan (Minneapolis: University of Minnesota Press, 1986), 22. Benjamin compares the relationship of Kafka's stories to doctrine to that of the Hagaddah to the Halacha: "They are not parables, and yet they do not want to be taken at their face value; they lend themselves to quotation and can be told for purposes of clarification. But do we have the doctrine Kafka's parables interpret and which K.'s postures and the gestures of the animals clarify? It does not exist; all we can say is that here and there we have an allusion to it" (W. Benjamin, "Franz Kafka," in *Illuminations: Essays and Reflection*, ed. H. Arendt, trans. H. Zohn [New York: Schocken Books, 1969], 122). Kafka's own "On Parables" suggests a life of following parables and in which nothing lies outside them. See F. Kafka, "On Parables," in *The Complete Stories* (New York: Schocken Books, 1971), 457.
15. My thinking of the transitive nature of the call to follow another is deeply indebted to Peretz. See E. Peretz, *Literature, Disaster, and the Enigma of Power: A Reading of "Moby Dick"* (Stanford, Calif.: Stanford University Press, 2003).
16. Here I have in mind, of course, Derrida's title and its play on the homonyms *"je suis"* (I am) and *"je suit"* (I follow, pursue). J. Derrida, *L'Animal que donc je suis* (Paris: Galilée, 2006).

17. At the risk of belaboring the point, it is worth emphasizing the following: First, Camus himself does not make the connection between the scene described in the autobiographical *The First Man* and the *Actuelles* essay. The essay, however, does begin by Camus thinking his way into a story related of his father: the father, after witnessing an execution he favored, returns shocked and silent—a silence broken only by his vomiting. See A. Camus, "Reflections on the Guillotine," in *Resistance, Rebellion, and Death*, trans. J. O'Brien (New York: Knopf, 1961), 175. Second, Camus's childhood recollection melds into Coetzee's *Boyhood*. In its opening scene the horns under the tongues of chicken are bloodily cut, and elements of this recollection greatly resemble Camus's story: the makeshift chicken coop, the clay earth in the yard; the knife used by Camus's grandmother, which reappears in the hands of the farmhand who castrates the lambs on the farm where Coetzee's father was raised. See: *Boyhood*, 1-2, 98-99; A. Camus, "The Chicken Coop and Cutting the Hen's Throat," in *The First Man*, trans. D. Hapgood (New York: Knopf, 1995), 229-35.

   I cannot here discuss yet another inspiring relation of embedded texts inspired by Coetzee. In it, Cora Diamond thinks Costello's woundedness through the founding moments of Stanley Cavell's thought: discoveries of our separateness from one another, our exposure, our soul-blindness. Cavell, responding in kind, faces his own avoidance of the question of animals by reading Costello aided by Diamond's notion of animals as companions. The texts are also literally embedded one in the other, each part of a festschrift dedicated to the work of the other. See C. Diamond, "The Difficulty of Reality and the Difficulty of Philosophy," in *Reading Cavell*, ed. A. Crary (London: Routledge, 2006), 98-118; S. Cavell, "Companionable Thinking," in *Wittgenstein and the Moral Life: Essays in Honor of Cora Diamond*, ed. A. Crary (Cambridge, Mass.: MIT Press, 2007), 281-98.

18. Kafka, "A Report to an Academy," 251.

19. A significant part of the lesson describes Costello's discovery that the target of her talk is also a speaker in the conference. She searches for a different example, tries to write the example out of the paper, considers pretending to be ill, but finally reads the paper she originally wrote. It is noteworthy that the lesson was indeed first read by Coetzee at a conference on evil in the Netherlands in 2002. West, however, was not one of the speakers. Might West then also be a stand-in for another author who, Coetzee feels, has let Hitler's executioners loose upon the world?

20. Indeed, in an earlier essay Coetzee describes the attempt to imagine what takes places in the dark, sound-proof torture chamber as an origin of literature. This poses the question of how to avoid being "impaled on the dilemma proposed by the state, namely, either to ignore its obscenities or else to produce representations of them" (J. M. Coetzee, "Into the Dark Chamber: The Writer and the South African State," in *Doubling the Point: Essays and Interviews*, ed. D. Attwell [Cambridge, Mass.: Harvard University Press, 1992],

364). In the essay, however, Coetzee presents this task as difficult but achievable; it is possible "not to play the game by the rules of the state ... to establish one's own authority ... to imagine torture and death on one's own terms" (364).

21. Note also Lurie's childhood recollection of the incongruity of the word "rape" and the horror it stands for (*Disgrace*, 159-60).

22. "In a world in which there are no more God-given rules, in which it has fallen to the philosopher-artist to give the lead, should the artist's explorations include acting on his own darker impulses, seeing where they will take him? Does art always trump morality? This early work of Musil's offers the question, but answers it only in the most uncertain way" (J. M. Coetzee, "Robert Musil: The Confusions of Young Törless," in *Inner Workings: Essays, 2000-2005* (London: Vintage Books, 2008), 38.

23. See, H. von Hofmannsthal, "The Letter of Lord Chandos," in *Selected Prose*, trans. M. Hottinger, Tania Stern, and James Stern (New York: Pantheon Books, 1952), 129-41.

24. Ibid., 133.
25. Ibid., 135-36.
26. Ibid., 136-37.
27. Ibid., 140-41.

References

Coetzee, J. M. *Boyhood: Scenes from Provincial Life*. Harmondsworth: Penguin, 1998.

——. *Disgrace*. Harmondsworth: Penguin, 2000.

——. *Elizabeth Costello*. London: Secker & Warburg, 2003.

8 Sympathy and Scapegoating in J. M. Coetzee
Andy Lamey

INTRODUCTION

For some years now, whenever the South African novelist J. M. Coetzee has been invited to deliver a lecture, he has been in the habit of reading a work of fiction instead. When Coetzee won the Nobel Prize in 2003, for example, rather than deliver the customary speech, he shared with his Stockholm audience a curious, elliptical narrative that evoked Daniel Defoe and his famous creation, Robinson Crusoe (the inspiration for Coetzee's 1986 novel, *Foe*). Before that, Coetzee's public appearances often saw him read different stories about a recurring character named Elizabeth Costello. Coetzee's protagonist is herself a writer, and readers of the Costello stories have noted many teasing resemblances between Costello and her creator. These include the fact that Costello is from Australia, where Coetzee has lived since 2002 (and where he recently took out citizenship). Costello is also described as a "major world writer" whose work has inspired "a small critical industry," statements that are both also true of Coetzee (*Elizabeth Costello*, 1–2). Both writers have a disdain for the trappings of literary celebrity but reluctantly participate in it. Coetzee and Costello have each retold a canonical work: what *Foe* did to *Robinson Crusoe*, Costello's *The House on Eccles Street* does to *Ulysses*. Most strikingly, the setting of a Costello story often resembles the institution to which Coetzee has been invited to talk. When Coetzee spoke at a conference on evil in Amsterdam, for example, he read a story describing Costello's attendance at . . . a conference on evil in Amsterdam.

The Costello stories, most of which had been previously published, were brought together in 2003 as *Elizabeth Costello*, which is subtitled "Eight Lessons." Each chapter or lesson is preoccupied with a different topic, such as Eros or literary realism. At the center of the book, however, are two linked chapters, "The Philosophers and the Animals" and "The Poets and the Animals," both of which revolve around our relationships with our fellow creatures. The animal chapters were originally delivered as lectures at Princeton University and then published, with commentaries from prominent academics, in Coetzee's 1999 book *The Lives of Animals*. These two "lessons" have since elicited a considerable amount of commentary and a certain amount of shock. In them, Coetzee's protagonist likens the treatment of food and laboratory animals to the annihilation of European Jews during the Holocaust.

Elizabeth Costello marks the second time Coetzee has published his two strange animal chapters in book form. Does that mean he wants to draw them especially to our attention? Regardless, it is worth singling out the animal chapters for critical examination. For if we focus our attention on them, two philosophical preoccupations emerge. The first is evident in Coetzee's use of animals to evoke a particular conception of ethics, one very similar to that of the philosopher Mary Midgley. Such a view affords a central role to sympathy and is fundamentally opposed to a long-standing rival view, most clearly exemplified by the social contract tradition, which prioritizes an instrumental conception of rationality. Coetzee's second, darker theme connects animals to the phenomenon of scapegoating, as it has been characterized by the philosophical anthropologist René Girard, who has visibly influenced Coetzee. Coetzee uses animals to symbolize Girard's idea that we often copy the desires of people who at first glance seem our rivals or opponents. Such a view holds the result to be a jealous spiral of rivalry and imitation, from which we seek release through the joint infliction of violence on some third party, whether animal or human.

As we will see, these two themes have several features in common. Perhaps the most important is that while they both involve human interactions with animals, each ethical leitmotiv transcends application to that particular issue and raises deeper philosophical questions concerning the foundations of morality and the therapeutic allure of political violence, respectively. Among the benefits of making the ethical preoccupations of Coetzee's animal chapters explicit is that doing so enhances our understanding of his fiction: both themes appear elsewhere in his work, particularly in *Disgrace* (which was first published, like the animal lessons, in 1999). However, when Coetzee's two philosophical strands are separated and analyzed in their own terms, the ethics of sympathy is shown to be a more coherent notion than the understanding of politics he takes over from Girard.

THE ETHICS OF SYMPATHY

This interpretation of Coetzee's animal lectures tries to move beyond a critical divide that has largely defined the early response to *Elizabeth Costello*. David Lodge spoke for many reviewers when he said that while the chapters on animals compelled him to reexamine some of his own assumptions concerning the treatment of animals, "the reader is not quite sure whether he is intended to spot some confusion or contradiction or non sequitur in Elizabeth's arguments."[1] On the other side of the divide, many readers have taken Elizabeth Costello to be a device through which Coetzee is issuing a clear message. Such was the view, for example, of the philosopher Tom Regan, author of *The Case for Animal Rights*, who wrote of Coetzee that "it is not fanciful to believe that some of his characters speak for their creator. Elizabeth Costello, the main character in Coetzee's latest novel of the same name, is a case in point."[2]

Both of these interpretations grasp part of the truth without being fully satisfying. Lodge is correct that many aspects of Coetzee's lessons resist paraphrase, and there are some fairly basic questions—such as what genre they belong to—that have no clear answer (several commentators have likened them to a cross between works of fiction and absurdist philosophical dialogues). But Lodge is too quick to throw up his hands and declare the animal chapters to be without coherent or legible themes. Similarly, Regan is right to sense an ethical challenge to our thinking about animals at work in Coetzee's texts. Yet Regan's reading is simplistic in the way it takes *Elizabeth Costello* to perform only a polemical function (if that were Coetzee's only goal, one wonders why he did not write a nonfiction essay about animals instead). That Regan allows to pass without comment, and may even himself accept, Costello's wild analogy between the treatment of animals and the Holocaust, is a still more off-putting aspect of his view.[3]

A better approach begins by noting both Costello's Holocaust analogy and the strong reaction it generates on the part of another character. "Let me say it openly," Costello says, "we are surrounded by an enterprise of degradation, cruelty, and killing which rivals anything that the Third Reich was capable of, indeed dwarfs it, in that ours is an enterprise without end, self-regenerating, bringing rabbits, rats, poultry, livestock ceaselessly into the world for the purpose of killing them" (*Elizabeth Costello*, 65). Costello makes this remark in the first of the two animal lessons, during a speech at an American university (in many ways similar to Princeton, where the chapter was first read). Afterward there is a reception in Costello's honor. But an elderly poet on the faculty declines to attend and sends her a note instead:

Dear Mrs. Costello,

Excuse me for not attending last night's dinner. I have read your books and know you are a serious person, so I do you the credit of taking what you said in your lecture seriously.

At the kernel of your lecture, it seemed to me, was the question of breaking bread. If we refuse to break bread with the executioners of Auschwitz, can we continue to break bread with the slaughterers of animals?

You took over for your own purposes the familiar comparison between the murdered Jews of Europe and slaughtered cattle. The Jews died like cattle, therefore cattle die like Jews, you say. That is a trick with words which I will not accept. You misunderstand the nature of likenesses; I would even say you misunderstand willfully, to the point of blasphemy. Man is made in the likeness of God but God does not have the likeness of man. If Jews were treated like cattle, it does not follow that cattle are treated like Jews. The inversion insults the memory of the dead. It also trades on the horrors of the camps in a cheap way.

Forgive me if I am forthright. You said you were old enough not to have time to waste on niceties, and I am an old man too.

Yours sincerely,
Abraham Stern
(94)

This exchange occupies a central place in the animal chapters. What are we to make of it? Costello's speech certainly forces us to reconsider many of the painful practices we currently inflict on animals. Yet even if we agree with her that meat eating and other common habits are wrong, Stern's powerful rebuttal should remind us that it is still a leap to liken such practices to the Holocaust. When the animal chapters were published in *The Lives of Animals*, one of the responses was by Peter Singer, author of *Animal Liberation*, and even he thought Costello went too far. "There's a more radical egalitarianism about humans and animals running through her lecture than I would be prepared to defend," Singer wrote in his slightly exasperated reply.[4]

When Coetzee's animal chapters first appeared, they included footnotes to titles such as *Animal Rights and Human Obligations*, a collection of writings about animals by moral philosophers, and *The Great Ape Project*, an anthology-cum-manifesto that argues that higher primates should be granted legal personhood. The footnotes have been dropped in *Elizabeth Costello*, no doubt because none of the other chapters has any, but there is a related reference in the text that, indirectly, sheds light on Costello's exchange with Stern. It comes when Costello explicitly rejects using philosophical terms to make her case. "Such a language is available to me, I know" she states. "It is the language of Aristotle and Porphyry, of Augustine and Aquinas, of Descartes and Bentham, of, in our day, Mary Midgley and Tom Regan" (*Elizabeth Costello*, 66).

What the thinkers Costello mentions have in common (perhaps the only thing they have in common) is that they are frequently cited in academic debates over the ethical status of animals. Porphyry, for example, is a third-century pagan who has been embraced by contemporary animal advocates because of a tract he wrote advocating vegetarianism. Augustine, Aquinas, and Descartes, by contrast, usually wear the black hats in the animal rights literature and are blamed for establishing the Christian view of animals as morally insignificant or, in the case of Descartes, for denying animal sentience. A much-cited passage from Jeremy Bentham says of animals, "The question is not, Can they *reason*? nor, Can they *talk*? but, Can they *suffer*?"

The most conspicuous name, however, is that of Mary Midgley. Midgley is a contemporary English philosopher who has written several books on animals. She does not go quite as far as Peter Singer and other advocates of vegetarianism: "What the animals need most urgently is probably a campaign for treating them better before they are eaten," she wrote in her 1983 work, *Animals and Why They Matter*.[5] What makes Midgley's name leap off the page is that she and Coetzee would seem to share several abiding concerns and preoccupations.

Much like Coetzee, Midgley has had a longstanding fascination with Robinson Crusoe ("Had Robinson Crusoe any duties?" begins one of her most well known papers).[6] Midgley is a feminist critic of the moral philosophy that predominated during the Enlightenment; *Foe*, which has a female protagonist, is often taken to offer a feminist critique of the literary realism that predominated during the same period. Costello, in keeping with her eschewal of philosophical and rationalist approaches to ethics, embraces a conception of morality based on imaginative identification. As she summarizes it, "The heart is the seat of a faculty, sympathy, that allows us to share at times the being of another" (*Elizabeth Costello*, 79). Despite Midgley's presence on Costello's list, she upholds a similar view of morality. "It can be our duty to *feel* in one way rather than another," Midgley has written, "something for which the [philosophical] tradition has little room."[7] Perhaps more than anything, Midgley and Coetzee both see animals as a key test case for the soundness of any ethical philosophy.

The best way to see what an ethic of sympathy might amount to is to contrast it, as Midgley has, with the social contract tradition. Two influential strands of that tradition originate with Kant and Hobbes and continue into our own time in the work of distinguished thinkers such as John Rawls and David Gauthier (representing the Kantian and Hobbesian approaches, respectively).[8] Although there are important differences between these two types of contract theory, both use the notion of a hypothetical agreement to outline an account of moral obligation.[9]

In the case of Hobbesians, the contract device is used to express the idea that morality is ultimately rooted in self-interest. This view begins from the basic fact that you and I could potentially hurt each other. For this reason, we both have a strong incentive to establish rules prohibiting bad behavior. For a modern Hobbesian such as Gauthier, "ethics" is simply another name for these mutually advantageous conventions. Strictly speaking, on this view, there is nothing inherently wrong with killing, cheating, or stealing. Rather, we should refrain from such activities because we recognize that we are all potential victims of such crimes and it is in everyone's interest to abide by a moral code that keeps social life flowing smoothly for all concerned.

Kantian contractarianism in many ways represents the opposite approach. Unlike Hobbesians, Kantians do not reject the commonsense belief that there is something intrinsically objectionable about killing, stealing, and the rest. Rather, they use the idea of a contract precisely to express this everyday understanding of morality. For thinkers such as Rawls, individuals matter on a moral level because they are "self-originating sources of valid moral claims," or what Kant referred to as ends in themselves.[10] Implicit in this view is a conception of moral equality: each person is due impartial moral concern. In Rawls's theory, the idea of a contract is used to capture this basic moral insight. In particular, Rawls asks us to consider what social institutions would be agreed to by people who did not know their race, gender, class, or other personal characteristics. Such a contract is likely to be based on impartial standards that, for Rawls, represent the true standards of justice.

At the heart of Hobbesian and Kantian contractarianism, then, are two very different conceptions of justice. For Hobbesians, it is the amoral idea of mutual advantage. For Kantians, it is the highly moral concept of impartial respect. Nevertheless, the two approaches have obvious similarities. In both cases, for example, the idea of social contract is not meant to be taken literally (neither theory claims there was any point in time when people actually negotiated a social contract). They are philosophical rather than historical theories, which use the idea of a hypothetical agreement to help us clarify to ourselves the nature and scope of our moral obligations.

The two theories have something else in common: they both raise questions about who is included in the social contract. A basic assumption of all versions of contract theory is that where there can be no contract, there can be no ethics. That would pose an obvious problem regarding the moral status of animals. Chickens, dogs, and rabbits can not meaningfully "agree" to anything, so the notion that they make any direct moral claims on us must be false. Leave aside the idea of animal rights: If the contractarian approach is correct, even mainstream animal-welfare laws are difficult, if not impossible, to justify.

That is not the only exclusion problem. Midgley quotes a contractarian named G. R. Grice, who notes the many entities his moral theory excludes:

> It is an inescapable consequence of the thesis presented in these pages that certain classes cannot have natural rights: animals, the human embryo, future generations, lunatics and children under the age of, say, ten. In the case of young children at least, my experience is that this consequence is found hard to accept. But it is a consequence of the theory; it is, I believe, true; and I think we should be willing to accept it. At first sight it seems a harsh conclusion, but it is not nearly so harsh as it appears.[11]

According to Grice, what makes his theory not quite as harsh as it first appears is that parents—who are party to the social contract—will ensure that their children are granted an indirect moral status. But as Grice himself notes, this is simply a contingent fact about the society we live in. It is easy to imagine a cultural milieu in which children are treated quite savagely (as was of course the case during much of our own society's history). "In this circumstance the morally correct treatment of children would no doubt be harsher than it is in our society. But the conclusion has to be accepted."[12] As Midgley points out, this is not very reassuring. We normally think of innocent children as making a fairly direct moral claim on us. Yet Grice's Hobbesian approach cannot accommodate this basic ethical notion. Nor is the problem solved by switching to a Kantian framework. Although Rawls's highly detailed theory can grant moral standing to one category on Grice's list, namely future generations, it is now a well-documented problem that Rawls cannot bestow moral consideration on the mentally handicapped (a serious failing, given Rawls's goal of outlining a truly impartial theory), let alone animals.[13]

Midgley has long been an outspoken critic of contractarian approaches to ethics. She wants to bring home to us just how many entities there are that can not be party to a contract yet that nonetheless make moral claims on us. To that end, her list of examples includes the following:

The dead
Posterity
Children
The senile

The insane

"Defectives, ranging down to 'human vegetables'"

Embryos

Sentient animals

Ecosystems

Countries

Oneself

God[14]

A reader does not have to agree with all of the items on Midgley's list to take her point. If we can have ethical obligations, however minimal, to even a few of the categories she mentions, then morality cannot be modeled on the idea of a contract. Even leaving aside all the nonhuman entities the contractual approach excludes, when it comes to human beings, contract ethics sees us as worthy of moral concern only in our capacity as rational beings capable of negotiating agreements. As Midgley puts it, such an understanding "isolates the duties which people owe each other *merely as thinkers* from those deeper and more general ones which they owe each other as beings who feel. . . . Such an account may not be *Hamlet* without the Prince, but it is *Hamlet* with half the cast missing, and without the state of Denmark."[15]

Midgley's rejection of the idea that moral concern extends only to rational beings finds a strong echo in Elizabeth Costello's speech. "Even Immanuel Kant, of whom I would have expected better, has a failure of nerve at this point," Costello says. "Even Kant does not pursue, with regard to animals, the implications of his intuition that reason may not be the being of the universe but on the contrary merely the being of the human brain" (*Elizabeth Costello*, 67). Crucially, however, Coetzee is not content with having Elizabeth Costello announce this idea. He also dramatizes it, in the form of Costello's exchange with Abraham Stern.

Much like Midgley, albeit in a more literary and imaginative way, Coetzee's fictional episode brings home just how far our moral obligations extend beyond other rational contracting agents. Costello and Abraham Stern both make moral claims on behalf of a category on Midgley's list, namely, animals and the dead. To be sure, Costello does her cause a considerable disservice by suggesting that the mass killing of pigs and chickens represents a comparable wrong to the mass killing of people, let alone an act of systematic murder such as the Holocaust (a topic to which we shall return below). Such an equation sits uneasily with us because it is an ethical wrong of its own, one that, as Stern says, "insults the memory of the dead." But if we wade into Costello's analogy with a pair of tongs, a genuine ethical truth can be extracted from it: animals do make moral claims on us.

The full scope of that claim is, of course, subject to debate. But regardless of whether we are more drawn to the idea of animal welfare or animal rights, Costello's exchange with Stern involves two genuine moral claims coming into conflict. From *Antigone* to *Sophie's Choice*, literature has long used such conflicts to shed light on the nature of moral experience. In this case, the dispute is between two parties who both have a certain type of moral motivation. That motivation is one an ethic of sympathy can explain and make sense of, but which a rationalist ethic such as contractarianism, even in its most inclusive Rawlsian form, cannot. Coetzee's conflict between the ethical significance of animals and our duty of memory toward the dead thus causes the full horizon of ethical meaning, concern, and obligation to flash before our eyes.

Coetzee's interest in the ethical treatment of animals seems inseparable from this larger concern with the nature of morality. Elizabeth Costello often stresses the importance of sympathetic identification, as when she remarks that "sympathy has everything to do with the subject and little to do with the object" (79). Costello repeatedly links this notion to literature and its capacity to place us inside the mind of a fictional creation. This should cause us to realize that animals have long played an important role in Coetzee's own fiction. In particular, they have functioned as a crucial test case for the integrity of his characters. *Foe*, for example, mentions apes living on the island with Cruso (as Coetzee spells his name), which he and Friday kill as pests. Images of the gratuitous killing of animals appear as far back as *Dusklands* (1974), Coetzee's first novel, in which a psychotic hunter sheds blood with abandon. But the place where Coetzee's animals highlight the wellsprings of morality most powerfully is *Disgrace*.

Disgrace's protagonist is a university professor who is stripped of everything. He has been undone by a sex scandal of his own making, and after losing his job he must stand helplessly by while his daughter is raped. Eventually he finds a strange peace working at an animal shelter. The shelter is run by a woman named Bev Shaw, and the professor's job is to take the bodies of unwanted dogs to the incinerator after she kills them. In between death and incineration the dogs' bodies stiffen with rigor mortis, and workmen at the incinerator hack at them with shovels, in order to make the corpses more manageable. The professor, however, soon discovers that he cannot bear to watch the animals treated in this way and, without quite knowing why, takes over the work of incineration himself.

> Why has he taken on this job? To lighten the burden on Bev Shaw? For that it would be enough to drop off the bags at the dump and drive away. For the sake of the dogs? But the dogs are dead; and what do dogs know of honour and dishonour anyway.

> For himself, then. For his idea of the world, a world in which men do not use shovels to beat corpses into a more convenient shape for processing.
>
> The dogs are brought to the clinic because they are unwanted . . . that is where he enters their lives. He may not be their saviour, the one for whom they are not too many, but he is prepared to take care of them once they're unable, utterly unable, to take care of themselves, once even Bev Shaw has washed her hands of them. . . . He saves the honour of corpses because there is no one else stupid enough to do it.
>
> (*Disgrace*, 146)

Is it possible to think of a more ignoble and worthless thing than the corpse of an animal? Yet as Ian Hacking has written, the former professor's behavior is "not so crazy. We need to attend to the bodies of those we love, and to save them from humiliation after death."[16] Hacking gives the examples of family members seeking to reclaim the bodies of their loved ones killed in war or airplane disasters. Coetzee's ethical vision, however, is more radical. It asks us to take seriously a sense of obligation not to dead human beings or living animals but to the corpse of a dog. The contrast with the Hobbesian strand of contractarianism, in particular, could not be more striking. Coetzee's quietly affecting scene portrays an act of sympathy mercilessly purged of any possibility of reward. The dead dogs can give the broken teacher absolutely nothing in return, not even a friendly lick on the face. And yet he feels compelled to honor their dignity nonetheless.

It seems no accident that over the course of *Elizabeth Costello*, Costello herself descends into senility. Slowly, she becomes the kind of being who demands our sympathy without being able to consciously return it. Perhaps that explains why she is often likened to an animal herself, as when her son characterizes her as "an old, tired circus seal." It might also explain a vision she has at the end of the book, when we no longer know if she is in possession of her faculties. The last thing the old woman sees is heaven. And its sole occupant is an old, tired dog, badly mangled yet contentedly sleeping.

Mary Midgley takes Robinson Crusoe to symbolize her conception of morality. Even when no other human being is present, she wrote in a paper called "Duties Concerning Islands," Crusoe has ethical obligations: to himself and to his island's animals and ecosystem. At one point Midgley also characterizes Crusoe as an emblematic figure of "the history of colonization." All of these themes are taken up in *Foe*, which was published three years after "Duties Concerning Islands" first appeared.[17] This raises the possibility that Coetzee was inspired by Midgley. As it happens, a similar question preoccupies Elizabeth Costello, who wonders whether Kafka read a particular primatologist before writing a story about an ape. Costello concludes that it is impossible to say for sure that Kafka read the primatologist in question. "But I would like to think he did, and the chronology makes my speculation at least plausible" (*Elizabeth Costello*, 71). Regarding Midgley and Coetzee, however, we do not need even to go that far. It is enough merely to note their shared preoccupation with an ethic of sympathy, whether or not Midgley's philosophical writings inspired Coetzee's more literary lessons

THE SCAPEGOAT AND THE SACRIFICE

This, then, is the first ethical theme we find lurking beneath the surface of Coetzee's animal chapters. There is, however, a second preoccupation present in Costello's exchange with Stern. And while it is also connected to Coetzee's interest in animals, it would seem to stem from a decidedly less generous ethical impulse.

Abraham Stern and the Holocaust are not the first Jewish character or concern to appear in Coetzee's work. Ian Hacking has pointed out that a Kafka story Elizabeth Costello discusses at length, "A Report to an Academy," was originally published in a German journal called *The Jew*, and most readers at the time took Kafka's ape to symbolize German Jewry.[18] In *Disgrace*, the professor character, David Lurie, and a student he has most likely raped, Melanie Isaacs, both have Jewish names. Lurie at one point wears a bandage that is described as a skullcap. After witnessing an African character rub his thumb and forefinger together and remark "always money, money, money," Lurie reflects: "A long time since he last saw that gesture. Used of Jews, in the old days: money-money-money, with the same meaningful cock of the head. But presumably [the African] is innocent of that snippet of European tradition" (*Disgrace*, 130). Finally, when dogs are killed at Lurie's animal shelter, it is referred to as "*Lösung*," German for "solution," which some critics have interpreted as a reference to the "final solution" of National Socialism.

This last reference may take some readers aback. Does Coetzee's work suggest a crude parallel after all? Does *Disgrace* endorse Elizabeth Costello's view that the mass killing of animals is as bad as the Holocaust? A more plausible explanation, I believe, is suggested by a scene in *Elizabeth Costello* that takes place after her lecture on animals. She attends a faculty dinner (the one Abraham Stern refuses to attend) where the topic of conversation turns to animal sacrifice in the ancient world: "The Greeks had a feeling there was something wrong in slaughter," another character says to Costello, "but thought they could make up for that by ritualizing it. They made a sacrificial offering." Costello then makes a curious reply that mentions the idea of scapegoating, in the sense of blame projection: "Perhaps we invented gods so that we could put the blame on them" (*Elizabeth Costello*, 86).

When it was first published in *The Lives of Animals*, this passage included a footnote mentioning a book called *Homo Necans: The Anthropology of Ancient Greek Sacrificial Ritual and Myth* (1983) by a German scholar named Walter Burkert. Burkert is a prominent name in the field of ancient religion. René Girard has written about similar themes, particularly in his 1977 book, *Violence and the Sacred*.[19] It seems hardly a coincidence that two characters at the dinner where animal sacrifice is mentioned have the last name "Garrard." Why would Coetzee draw attention to Burkert and Girard? I believe it is because he shares with them both, but Girard especially, a concern with ritual sacrifice and scapegoating.

Girard is famous for his theory of mimetic or imitative desire. In essence, it is the view that human beings are fundamentally mimics: we unconsciously copy the aspirations of the people around us. Because the causes of this mimicry lie deep in the human psyche (Girard has a complicated debt to Freud), the people we imitate simultaneously copy us. The result is that human desires give rise to the aspirational equivalent of an arms race, in which rivals not only compete for the same object but increasingly resemble one another: they want the same thing.

This fraught process constantly threatens to explode into violence. In the ancient world, Girard argued, rituals of sacrifice and scapegoating brought release from the spiral of endless rivalry and conformity when a human or animal victim was selected for immolation or expulsion. Hence the term "scapegoat," originally denoted a goat ceremonially driven off into the wilderness while another was killed. According to Girard, such sacrifices achieved a highly therapeutic outcome, which he termed a "scapegoat effect":

> By a scapegoat effect I mean that strange process through which two or more people are reconciled at the expense of a third party who appears guilty or responsible for whatever ails, disturbs, or frightens the scapegoaters. They feel relieved of their tensions and they coalesce into a more harmonious group. They now have a single purpose, which is to prevent the scapegoat from harming them, by expelling and destroying him.[20]

Bluntly speaking, Girard's theory amounts to the view that bloody sacrifice is what made human society possible.

Girard is a committed Catholic, and his writings portray the coming of Jesus Christ as a major turning point in the history of sacrifice. Christ is the target of sacrificial violence, yet there is a written record documenting his innocence, in the form of the Gospels. According to Girard, this means there can be no more effective sacrifices after Christ's death, as the unconscious projection that always underlay the "scapegoat mechanism" has finally been exposed. Nonetheless, scapegoating has its roots in our very makeup, and so, even though it no longer has any positive outcome, it continues into the present day. In Girard's declinist view, the modern world continues to witness sacrificial violence but without the resulting social harmony.

Girard has exerted a noticeable influence on Coetzee. "What I take over from Girard," Coetzee has written, is "the outline of a politics of desire" (*Giving Offense*, 118). References to Girard appear throughout Coetzee's nonfiction writings, including a thought-provoking essay on advertising that uses Girard's theory to explain why ads so frequently employ an image of a model, such as a beautiful woman, alongside an image of the product (because we allow our desire to be shaped by the model's desire, Coetzee says) (*Doubling the Point*, 127–38). Coetzee's debt to Girard, however, is perhaps most clearly evident in an essay in his anthology *Giving Offence: Essays on Censorship*, which examines Alexander Solzhenitsyn's struggle with the Soviet government.

Coetzee is hardly impartial between Solzhenitsyn and his Stalinist opponents. Nonetheless, despite their differences, Coetzee argues, on a psychological level the Russian writer and his censors were "carried on waves of polemic toward identity and twinship" (*Giving Offense*, 118). Solzhenitsyn internalized his enemies' notion of a war to the death and attacked the state with a rhetoric of denunciation and abuse that was in every way identical to the discourse of abuse directed at him. Coetzee quotes with approval the judgment expressed by one of Solzhenitsyn's dissident editors: "Having been rightly schooled in hatred of Stalinism, without realizing it Solzhenitsyn also imbibed the poisons of Stalinism" (137). The Russian writer's relationship with the Soviet authorities thus illustrates Girard's notion of rivals who come to mirror each other.

By invoking the notions of sacrifice and scapegoating in *Elizabeth Costello*, Coetzee would again seem to be highlighting an overlooked theme in *Disgrace*. The novel ends, for example, with Lurie making a sacrifice of a dog whom he carries "in his arms like a lamb" (*Disgrace*, 220). The image of a sacrificial lamb is suggested earlier in the novel when Lurie wants to rescue two sheep that a neighbor plans to kill. Lurie himself is made into something of a scapegoat by his university's sexual harassment committee, just as the last name of his own victim, Isaacs, recalls Abraham's sacrifice of Isaac in the Book of Genesis. At one point Coetzee's protagonist even offers a history of scapegoating:

> Scapegoating worked in practice while it still had religious power behind it. You loaded the sins of the city on to the goat's back and drove it out, and the city was cleansed. It worked because everyone knew how to read the ritual, including the gods. Then the

gods died, and all of a sudden you had to cleanse the city without divine help. Real actions were demanded instead of symbolism. The censor was born, in the Roman sense.... Purgation was replaced by the purge.
(91)

Lurie does not see the rise of Christianity as a major transition in the same way that Girard does. Rather, he takes the key turning point to be the disappearance of religious meaning altogether. With that important exception, however, Lurie's view of history is pure Girard, as is evident in his interpretation of the role of sacrifice in ancient societies and his pessimistic view of the modern world as having descended into nontherapeutic political violence.

In Girard's theory, animal and human scapegoats are interchangeable: hence the possibility of replacing goats with the human figure of Christ. Yet there is never any implication in Girard's writings that slaughtering an animal and murdering a person are morally indistinguishable. Coetzee would seem to understand scapegoating in a similar way, highlighting a psychological drive that can result in the violent destruction of people or animals, yet without implying they are equally wrong. And just as Girard has written about the scapegoating of Jews in the Middle Ages, who were blamed for the bubonic plague, Coetzee's references to Jews, European anti-Semitism, and *Lösung* would seem to highlight modern anti-Semitic scapegoating, most obviously by Nazi propagandists. It is this status as scapegoats, whether metaphoric or literal, that Coetzee's animal and human victims share, rather than any crude moral equivalence.

Political violence is a major theme of *Disgrace*. The relationship among David Lurie, his daughter, and the men who assaulted her is plausibly read as an allegory for the relationship between white and black South Africans in the early post-Apartheid period, when there was a real possibility of political life descending into an ongoing spiral of violent revenge. In keeping with this theme, an important moment occurs near the end of the book, when Lurie's daughter, Lucy, tells him she is not going to press charges against the men who raped her. According to her, "in another time, in another place," it might be appropriate to make her assault a public matter. Given that it took place in South Africa, however, she feels that what happened is her business alone. Her father rejects this line of reasoning. "Do you think that by meekly accepting what happened to you," he angrily asks, "[you will receive] a sign to paint on the door-lintel that will make the plague pass you by? That is not how vengeance works, Lucy. Vengeance is like a fire. The more it devours, the hungrier it gets" (112).

The reference to a door-lintel recalls the theme of sacrifice and bloodshed in the book of Exodus, in which the Israelites are instructed to slaughter a lamb and mark its blood on their doors: "God will pass through to kill Egypt with a plague, and He will see the blood on the lintel and the two doorposts. God will then pass over that door." Lucy's father dismisses the possibility that any action she can take will allow her to escape the ongoing pattern of vengeance. It is no surprise then, when he physically assaults one of her attackers, who in turn threatens to retaliate. Lucy is unique among Coetzee's characters in that the only person or animal she turns into a scapegoat is herself. In terms of Girard's theory, she does the opposite of coming to resemble her attackers. They inflicted on her their violent fantasies, but she wants nothing from them in return, not even justice. Only she, it would seem, personifies the ideal Coetzee has characterized elsewhere as "replacing a dialectic of violence by one of healing" (*Giving Offense*, 120) And so when she discovers she is pregnant, she chooses to keep her rapist's baby.

This is a disturbing resolution to a powerful book. But Coetzee's Girardianism, it bears pointing out, also leaves a disturbing trace in *Elizabeth Costello*. The unsettling element concerns Coetzee's decision to name Costello's Jewish interlocutor after a real person. The historical Abraham Stern was not only a poet (like Coetzee's character) but the founder of the notorious Stern Gang, the most militant of several armed Zionist groups active in Palestine in the early 1940s. Stern managed the unprecedented feat of being both a Zionist and—there is no other word for it—a fascist. Influenced by Social Darwinism and an admirer of Mussolini and Hitler, he so loathed Palestine's British occupiers that he supported the Axis and sent an infamous letter to representatives of the German government offering to enter the war on Germany's side. Writing in 1940, Stern called for a joint German-Jewish alliance that would see "the re-establishment of the Jewish state in its historic borders, on a national and totalitarian basis, allied with the German Reich."[21]

The historical Stern would seem a particularly chilling case of the process Girard highlighted: he came to resemble his deadliest rivals. But why does Coetzee have a character who speaks on behalf of the victims of the Holocaust call to mind Zionism's worst historical spokesperson? Is Coetzee suggesting that invoking the history of injustice against the Jewish people—a history Coetzee's own writings powerfully evoke—can itself function as a political tool, one that causes us to overlook the shortcomings of Israel, which Stern presumably represents? These are only some of the questions that Coetzee's enigmatic text raises but never answers.

CRITICISM

These, then, are two related themes underlying Coetzee's preoccupation with animals. On the one hand, Coetzee's work often highlights the sharp divide between

YES approaches to morality that set the boundary of moral concern at the boundary of rationality and a more inclusive and humane ethics of sympathy. As Elizabeth Costello summarizes such a view, which she associates with the superiority of literature to philosophy, "There is no limit to the extent to which we can think ourselves into the being of another. There are no bounds to the sympathetic imagination" (*Elizabeth Costello*, 80). Yet animals also illustrate Coetzee's interest in precisely the opposite form of vicariousness, the act of projecting our own worst traits onto another entity that we then blame, in the manner highlighted by Girard.

What are we to make of these two themes? Several critics of *Elizabeth Costello* have pointed out that sympathy was the central idea in the ethics of Adam Smith and David Hume, thereby suggesting that Coetzee is writing in the tradition of the Scottish Enlightenment. Smith and Hume, however, have been criticized for failing to take adequate note of the negative side of imaginative identification.[22] Midgley captures this negative quality when she points out that exploitation also requires sympathy. A sadist cannot derive pleasure from inflicting pain on a rock or other unfeeling objects. Deliberate brutality, rather, requires that the perpetrator be able to enter into his victim's perspective at least enough to imagine the experience of agony. As Midgley points out, "Cruelty is something which could have no point for a person who really did not believe the victim to have definite feelings."[23] Coetzee's Girardian concern with negative forms of psychic identification would seem to align his understanding of entering "the being of another" less close to that of Smith and Hume than to Midgley's more nuanced modern view.[24]

If an ethic of sympathy and a Girardian politics of desire are linked forms of vicariousness, both also call into question a purely instrumental conception of rationality. Such a conception is particularly evident in the Hobbesian strand of contract theory: we have our pregiven desires, and reason is the tool we use to act on them. This view often goes hand in hand with the notion that we are creatures who seek only to maximize our own self-interest (*homo economicus*). On a Girardian understanding of desire, however, the idea that our self-interest alone gives shape to our desires is immediately called into question. Although Girard's view would seem to have its own bleak elements, when accompanied with an affirmative ethic of sympathy, it would at least admit the possibility that, at least some of the time, we will be motivated to act on the interests of others.

This is more than some contract theorists have been willing to allow. As David Gauthier has written, there are large categories of human beings his ethic of mutual advantage excludes. "The primary problem is care for the handicapped. Speaking euphemistically of enabling them to live productive lives, when the services required exceed any possible products, conceals an issue which, understandably, no one wants to face."[25] But the notion that we should not care for others when it is not in our interest to do so is only a problem if we accept Gauthier's flawed understanding of morality. If an ethic of sympathy has intuitive appeal, one reason is that a morality expansive enough to include animals will also be wide enough to include every member of our own species. The same cannot be said of some of the most distinguished moral philosophies in the Western tradition. Sympathy deserves to be seen as more than a corrective to the excesses of the Enlightenment and warrants serious consideration as an ethical starting point in its own right.

Taking the ethics of sympathy seriously, however, should not cause us to ignore the oversimplifications it can give rise to. In particular, it seems neither desirable nor possible to fully separate sympathy from reason in the way Costello repeatedly suggests. Our sympathies extend in many different directions and often come into conflict. We need reason to serve as adjudicator and guide if we are ever to act on our moral convictions in an effective way. Moreover, a certain form of rationality would already seem to be at work in our acts of sympathetic identification.

For us to sympathetically identify with a being requires that it have a consciousness. Elizabeth Costello seems aware of as much. She discusses at length a famous paper by Thomas Nagel titled, "What Is It Like to Be a Bat?" Revealingly, no one ever asks us to consider what it is like to be a river or a tree. Bats and other animals may not be rational, but the fact that they are sentient makes the difference between their awareness and ours seem a matter more of degree than of kind. Acts of sympathetic identification would thus seem to presuppose that we have first singled out for empathetic concern a particular type of entity, one in regard to which the notion of identification is intelligible to us. Such an act of discrimination and classification seems just as much the product of reason as of sympathy. If so, that would call into question simplistic dichotomies of the kind Costello not only explores at length, but often takes to show the superiority of literature over philosophy. There is more philosophy already present in literature then her remarks would allow.

Turning to Coetzee's second theme, it is worth noting that there is no clear Christian message in his work and that he rejects much of Girard's theory (on an anthropological or historical level, Coetzee notes, it "lacks an empirical basis and may even be unfalsifiable" [*Giving Offense*, 248]). Yet Coetzee's debt to Girard can help us to make sense of what has long seemed a curious aspect of Coetzee's attitude toward politics. During the Apartheid era, Coetzee was often contrasted with more politically outspoken South African writers, such as Nadine Gordimer. Gordimer herself once said of Coetzee that his work embodies a "revulsion against all political and revolutionary solutions."[26] Coetzee's embrace of Girard's politics of desire would explain how he could unambiguously oppose Apartheid yet nonetheless still be wary of entering into psychic combat with an authoritarian regime. On a Girardian view, that way lies Solzhenitsyn and "the belligerence that tends to be generated in any field ruled over by censorship." (*Giving Offense*, 117)

This, however, would ultimately seem an unsatisfactory view of politics. Surely some things are worth getting belligerent over. How Coetzee the individual comports himself in regard to political issues is his own affair, but on an artistic level, one struggles to find any awareness in Coetzee's work that sometimes we should resolutely oppose a political entity or institution. Political regimes that foster severe injustice would seem the most obvious example. Coetzee's Girardian notion of enemies coming to resemble one another, however true on an abstract level (and surely it does contain some truth), downplays the material differences between a courageous individual such as Solzhenitsyn and the vast apparatus of the Soviet state. The eliding of this distinction is in keeping with the fact that, for all Coetzee's genius, he often seems tone deaf to the positive side of political activity: to its transformative possibilities, to its shared excitements, to its genuine joys. (Perhaps this is one reason why Elizabeth Costello, with her gratuitous Holocaust analogy, sometimes seems like a parody of a politically engaged writer.)

This brings us back to Abraham Stern. The historical individual lived in a period leading up to the establishment of a new state, and his own life was defined by political violence (Stern was killed by British police in 1942). In this, he evokes the setting of *Disgrace*, South Africa on the cusp of a new future, as well as the novel's concern with politically inspired acts of vengeance. In addition, Stern the literary character is "carried on waves of polemic toward identity and twinship" with Costello. In short, all the Girardian tropes are there. And yet, one cannot help wishing Coetzee had plucked a different name out of the past.

Stern's name evokes more than an individual. It evokes the history of Zionism and of Israel itself. Surely it is a distortion of historical reality to have a Jewish fascist occupy this symbolic space. Many criticisms can be made of Israel, including the charge that a form of "Apartheid thinking" defines its treatment of the Palestinians. But acknowledging that Israel is guilty of a great wrong should not come at the expense of historical perspective. The role of European anti-Semitism and the Holocaust in motivating Jewish immigration to Israel, as well as terrorist attacks on Israeli civilians, should cause us to recognize that the Israel-Palestinian conflict is too complex to warrant equating Zionism with fascist ideology. Inserting a reference to Abraham Stern and no other Israeli characters fails to do justice to a complex political reality.[27] Ironically, the result on a symbolic level is precisely the type of crude political denunciation that Coetzee is normally at such pains to avoid. In a text that has so much to say about imaginative identification, Coetzee's invocation of Abraham Stern seems itself to reveal a failure of sympathy.

CONCLUSION

At one point in *Elizabeth Costello* another character worries over the way she is often treated as "a Mickey Mouse post-colonial writer." (*Elizabeth Costello*, 9) This is another similarity between Costello and Coetzee, who has attracted a considerable amount of attention from postcolonial critics. The Mickey Mouse comment raises the possibility that Coetzee is unhappy with being pigeonholed in this way and that *Elizabeth Costello* is on one level a commentary on overlooked themes in his fiction. Whether or not Coetzee was in fact trying to offer such a commentary, this is how I have interpreted the animal lessons. They articulate thematic preoccupations with which Coetzee has long been concerned yet which have not traditionally featured in the discussion around his work.

It is unlikely, however, that anyone ever comes away from writing about *Elizabeth Costello* with a sense of complete satisfaction. It is too strange, too riddling, too baffling for that. If, as Elizabeth Costello states, there is no limit to the extent we can think ourselves into the being of another, there may be a limit to how much we can think our way into Coetzee's book. I have left aside the chapters on African literature, artistic depictions of evil, and other topics, and I have not attempted to relate them to the animal chapters. If I have managed to convey the sense that there are intelligible themes in Coetzee's animals lectures, including a philosophically respectable account of the role of sympathy in ethics and a less appealing politics of desire, I will have accomplished enough. These themes can be taken to illuminate Elizabeth Costello's seemingly mad obsession with animals. As for her creator, however, one never quite escapes the feeling that he is still out in the darkness, smiling a Cheshire grin.

Notes

1. D. Lodge, "Disturbing the Peace," review of *Elizabeth Costello*, *New York Review of Books* 50, no. 18 (2003): 10.
2. T. Regan and M. Rowe, "What the Nobel Committee Also Failed to Note," *International Herald Tribune*, December 19, 2003. My approach is partly inspired by a detail in Regan and Rowe's article, which mentions a reading Coetzee gave from *Disgrace*. According to

Regan and Rowe, "Coetzee began with the observation that, although many critics had commented on the book's depiction of human relationships and violence, none had discussed the animal theme, one that appears frequently in his writing." However, I am less interested in Coetzee's conscious intention than the effect of taking *Elizabeth Costello* as an indirect commentary on *Disgrace*.

3. For other critics who share Lodge's bafflement, see P. Singer, "Reflections," in *The Lives of Animals*, ed. A. Gutmann (Princeton, N.J.: Princeton University Press, 1999), 85–91; and J. Yardley, review of *Elizabeth Costello, Washington Post*, November 16, 2004. For critics who are sympathetic to the Holocaust analogy, see T. M. Costelloe, "The Invisibility of Evil: Moral Progress and the 'Animal Holocaust,'" *Philosophical Papers* 32, no. 2 (2003): 109–31, and D. Sztybel, "Can the Treatment of Animals be Compared to the Holocaust?" *Ethics and the Environment* 11, no. 1 (2006): 97–132. Costelloe and Sztybel both attribute Costello's view to Coetzee.

4. Singer, "Reflections," 86. Singer's disagreement with Costello is worth stressing. Singer has grappled at length with the comparative moral worth of human and nonhuman animals, and the position he arrives at is far more considered and careful than Costello's. The average human being has intellectual abilities far greater than that of any animal, Singer notes, and for this reason we will normally occupy a higher moral status than any other species. Singer illustrates this point by asking us to consider a scenario in which we decided to perform painful medical experiments on normal adult humans and randomly kidnapped people from city parks for this purpose. In addition to the pain of the experiments themselves, such a scheme would also result in widespread terror, as people became afraid to walk through parks. Were the same thing done to animals, however, they would certainly experience the pain of the experiments, but not the "anticipatory dread" of being kidnapped. See *Animal Liberation*, 2nd ed. (New York: New York Review, 1990), 15. This shows that however much we might wish to improve the treatment of animals, there will always be good reasons not to rank them on a moral par with normal adult humans.

I believe Singer is right about the moral superiority of human beings. However, there is a second reason to emphasize his disagreement with Costello. Singer is highly critical of the way our culture treats animals, and this should remind us that objecting to Costello's analogy is not the same as defending the status quo regarding animals. If Costello's analogy is sloppy and emotional, it does not follow that activities that inflict pain on other species are justified. Indeed, my own view is that meat eating and other widespread practices involving animals are morally wrong. Although I do not make the case for this view below, I do want to be explicit that my criticisms of Costello do not stem from a rejection of the cause of animal protection. Like Singer, I believe the best position is one that rejects both Costello's crude analogy and the many unnecessary cruelties that are regularly inflicted on animals. For a more detailed outline of my views regarding animals, see "Food Fight! Regan vs. Davis on the Ethics of Eating Beef," *Journal of Social Philosophy* 38, no. 2 (2007): 331-48.

5. M. Midgley, *Animals and Why They Matter* (Athens: University of Georgia Press, 1984), 27.
6. M. Midgley, "Duties Concerning Islands," in *Environmental Ethics*, ed. Robert Elliot (New York: Oxford University Press, 1995), 89-103.
7. M. Midgley, *Beast and Man*, rev. ed. (London: Routledge, 1995), 259.
8. J. Rawls, *A Theory of Justice* (Cambridge, Mass.: Harvard University Press, 1971); D. Gauthier, *Morals by Agreement* (New York: Oxford University Press, 1986).
9. My account of the differences between Hobbesian and Kantian contractarianism follows W. Kymlicka, "The Social Contract Tradition," in *A Companion to Ethics*, ed. Peter Singer (Oxford: Blackwell, 1991), 186-96.
10. J. Rawls, "Kantian Constructivism in Moral Theory," in *Collected Papers*, ed. S. Freeman (Cambridge, Mass.: Harvard University Press, 1999), 330.
11. Quoted in M. Midgley, "Duties Concerning Islands," 90.
12. G. R. Grice, *The Grounds of Moral Judgement* (Cambridge: Cambridge University Press, 1967), 149.
13. For a small sampling of the literature on Rawls's exclusion of the mentally handicapped (and animals), see M. Midgley, "Duties Concerning Islands"; B. Barry, *Theories of Justice* (Berkeley: University of California Press, 1989); P. Cavalieri and W. Kymlicka, "Expanding the Social Contract," *Etica and Animali* 8 (1996): 5-32; and M. Nussbaum, *Frontiers of Justice: Nationality, Disability, Species Membership* (Cambridge, Mass.: Harvard University Press, 2006).
14. Midgley, "Duties Concerning Islands," 97.
15. Midgley, "Duties Concerning Islands," 93.
16. I. Hacking, "Our Fellow Animals," review of *The Lives of Animals*, *New York Review of Books* 47, no. 11 (2000): 20.
17. Midgley, "Duties Concerning Islands."
18. Hacking, "Our Fellow Animals," 27.
19. Originally published in French as *La violence et le sacré* (Paris: Grasset, 1972).
20. R. Girard, "Mimesis and Violence," in *The Girard Reader*, ed. J. G. Williams (New York: Crossroad, 1996), 12.
21. The German (or Sternist) Memorandum, quoted in J. Heller, *The Stern Gang: Ideology, Politics, and Terror, 1940-1949* (London: Frank Cass, 1995), 85-86. See also A. Perliger/L. Weinberg, "Jewish Self-Defence and Terrorist Groups Prior to the Establishment of the State of Israel: Roots and Traditions", *Totalitarian Movements and Political Religions* 4, no. 3 (2003): 91-118.

22. P. Railton, "Toward an Ethics That Inhabits the World," in *The Future for Philosophy*, ed. Brian Leiter (New York: Oxford University Press, 2004), 278.
23. Midgley, *Animals and Why They Matter*, 114.
24. For an excellent discussion of the complex role sympathy plays in *Disgrace*, see M. Marias, "J. M. Coetzee's *Disgrace* and the Task of the Imagination," *Journal of Modern Literature* 29, no. 2 (2006), 75–93. Marias persuasively rebuts the view that Coetzee's work expresses an Enlightenment view of sympathy.
25. Gauthier, *Morals by Agreement*, 18.
26. N. Gordimer, "The Idea of Gardening', Review of *The Life and Times of Michael K*, *The New York Review of Books* 31, no. 1 (1984): 6.
27. The names of two other characters in the animal lessons evoke Jewish historical figures. Both, however, were critical of Zionism. There is an English professor named Elaine Marx and an academic dean named Arendt (whose first name is not given). Such references would seem to again evoke Midgley's work. Midgley has pointed out how philosophers such as Marx often isolate a single human capacity or attribute (in Marx's case, freely given labour) and celebrate it on the grounds that it is the quality that most separates us from animals. This approach is misguided, Midgley points out, because it runs together a moral claim and a question of biological classification. As she puts it, exalting one particular attribute as humanity's highest good is "a particular moral position and must be defended as such against others; it cannot ride into acceptance on the back of a crude method of taxonomy" (M. Midgley, quoted in W. Kymlicka, *Contemporary Political Philosophy: An Introduction* [New York: Oxford University Press, 1989], 190). YES The problem with Marx's view is that there are human activities in which people find considerable value, such as giving birth, that are capacities we share with animals. Similarly, there are some actions, such as committing suicide, that may be unique to human beings yet that we do not celebrate. Like Marx, Hannah Arendt lauds one particular human attribute, in her case our capacity to take part in a shared world of political speech and action, on the grounds that it is what separates us from animals. See H. Arendt, *The Human Condition* (Chicago: University of Chicago Press, 1958). There is a certain casual brilliance in the way Coetzee extends Midgley's critique of Marx to Arendt, whose philosophy is often thought to invert Marxism. In the context of the allusion to Abraham Stern, however, recalling the authors of "On the Jewish Question" and *Eichmann in Jerusalem* does not provide us with a rounded picture of Zionism or Israeli history.

References

Coetzee, J. M. *Disgrace*. New York: Penguin, 1999.

———. *Doubling the Point: Essays and Interviews*. Edited by D. Attwell. Cambridge: Harvard University Press, 1992.

———. *Elizabeth Costello: Eight Lessons*. London: Secker & Warburg, 2003.

———. *Giving Offense: Essays on Censorship*. Chicago: University of Chicago Press, 1996.

Coetzee, J. M., et al. *The Lives of Animals*, ed. A. Gutman. Princeton, N.J.: Princeton University Press, 1999.

Part Three
Rationality and Human Lives

9

Against Society, Against History, Against Reason
COETZEE'S ARCHAIC POSTMODERNISM

Anton Leist

> Or, for that matter, those who believed that mankind had lost its way and should go back to its primitive roots and make a fresh start. In other words, the anthropologists.
> —Sister Bridget, in *Elizabeth Costello*

> That is not the point of the story, say I, who am, however, in no position to dictate what the point of the story is.
> —Elizabeth Costello

PHILOSOPHICAL AND LITERARY EXPERIMENTS

Writers like John Coetzee make a deep personal impression on some people who happen to be philosophers. And they make a deep impression on some philosophers in their very role as philosophers. What distinguishes this kind of philosopher? Nothing less than a full-scale diagnosis of current philosophy would be needed to answer this question. Instead, I want to characterize, in a rough and sketchy way, one growing category of philosopher by distinguishing it from others. These philosophers are increasingly interested in the epistemological potential of literature and art as they become less and less convinced by the truth-providing role of the structures lying at the center of interest of more traditional philosophers. In order to obtain an idea of what moves these literature-inclined philosophers, I shall try to give them a sharp, somewhat oversimplified profile by distinguishing them in particular from two more classical groups. The opposition we arrive at, then, is one between what could widely be called the "postmodernists" vs. the "analytics" and the "historians."

I shall comment only briefly on the analytics and the historians as I wish to concentrate on the postmodernists. The analytics are the heirs of a style of philosophizing that emerged from the "analytic" program early last century. Officially, they have given up this program of scientific or linguistic reductionism, but—as the gravity of a once lively tradition seems to make unavoidable—there remain several once new and provocative attitudes in their manners. Analytics orient themselves to linguistic structures and often share the unspoken belief that "concepts" are something not only heuristically important but ontologically guaranteeing of truth. By elaborating on concepts, the analytics are, as Rorty helped us to see, implicitly "Kantians," even if today they tend to shy away from the grand idea of "reason" or claims to an "a priori."[1] Also they subdivide into a series of fine-grained positions specifying different degrees of loyalty toward traditional epistemic aims, such as the "foundationalists," the "coherentists," and the "naturalists."

The historians concentrate on studying a historical epoch or a historically important philosopher, normally a "classic" figure, and do so for different reasons. In most cases, they believe "their" philosopher to be an important forerunner of present-day problems; they want to reactualize both his point of view and his arguments for present debates. Others want to "reeducate" (Rorty) the dead ones in order to prove their actual points. Still others want to know about the "real" history of ideas and to tell a logical story of their development.[2]

The postmodernists share the interest in systematic truth with the analytics, in contrast to the descriptive self-sufficiency of the historians, but unhappily they also share the conceptual skepticism of the historians, as opposed to the conceptualist self-confidence of the analytics. The postmodernists would like to be analytics in a historically refined form, if that were possible. They are nearest, perhaps, to one sort of analytic, those believing in truth as a "coherence" in ideas, but they lack the analytic coherentists' unrestrained belief in truth, argument, or social harmony. Postmodernists use history to make comparisons and to relativize Archimedean points, but they cannot satisfy themselves with historical knowledge per se instead of achieving something like truth if truth is not achievable. Postmodernists, neither believing in truth as the analytics do nor being content with history as the historians are, try to find substitutes for truth.

Making an attempt to define these substitutes forces this overview to become an even bolder enterprise. Substitutes could best be thought of as attitudes toward the situation in which philosophers (and everyday people also) find themselves historically and which they have to confront. In principle there are, it seems, two kinds of attitude to be developed from this challenge. On the one hand, one can accept the disbelief in truth and try to put freedom in the place of truth. This would mean adopting an attitude of irony and playfulness toward cultural verities. Culture, including its truth claims, cannot be got rid of; freedom does not make sense outside of culture. Therefore swimming through what seems to be a contingent accumulation of cultural stuff could be a form of freedom toward it: perhaps the best thing to be attained. This, in any case, is the solution from those who could be called the "players" among the postmodernists.

There are, on the other hand, those who think this attitude is neither psychologically feasible nor epistemologically coherent. These postmodernists would like to hold onto some certainties, either those normative achievements of present societies enabling skepticism and freedom on such a large scale or some truths to be found within these new games of experimental living. It is difficult to find a common bracket for the different positions here, but to call these postmodernists "experimentalists" would do well enough as theirs is an epistemic aspiration that distinguishes them from the players. Experiments are different from games, in that they aim at letting something become known, even if superficially games and experiments share a raft of social and psychological characteristics. Experimental postmodernists differ from the players in that they have not fully given up epistemic hope. And, to make the picture still more difficult, they converge in their hope with those analytics, who are aware of the problematics of "conceptual" truths and have embarked on a program of minimalizing the conceptual foundations of knowledge.

With much more effort and time these different positions could be reconstructed systematically at the level of present philosophical theories and debates.[3] If one shares at least some of the postmodernists' skepticism toward philosophy (i.e., as practiced by analytics and historians), one might be afraid of being restrained by its internal norm of rationalizing conflicts and problems and thereby being severely restricted in experimental thinking. Philosophy is to an extraordinary extent burdened by its own tradition, its traditional style of rational inquiry. Both literature and philosophy are able to capture the present historical situation, but writers are less blinded by the obsession with rationalizinng experiences. The usual job of philosophers is to answer other philosophers, and their aim is to make progress within the common project of rational justification. This project notoriously restricts the imagination. Why justify and rather than developing alternatives? Why not leave the given order of things? Turn one's back on the present? Or, even better, why not see the present differently to its own view? Philosophy hardly ever deals with real-life situations rather than "ideas" and "arguments." Philosophers are not (to put it starkly) open to experience outside ideas, whereas writers, as devoted to human life, have a chance to pierce through the shell of ideas.

These remarks, however sketchy, may be sufficient to motivate a tour through three of Coetzee's books. The books of choice will be *Life and Times of Michael K*, *Waiting for the Barbarians*, and *Elizabeth Costello*. Each of these books assembles a variety of motives and themes. The first and third focus on problems that obviously also lie at the core of modern and postmodern philosophy: the problem of whether there is a "view from outside" society and whether rationality is a morally foundational characteristic of humans. Michael K undergoes an experiment involving life outside society, and Elizabeth Costello tries to find pure animal existence as the point from which, again as a view from the outside, one might speak toward those who remain either within philosophical tradition or within our perhaps predetermined everyday experiences. Torture, the theme at the core of *Waiting for the Barbarians*, is for most traditional philosophers not a problem comparable to the two already mentioned. Such philosophers often share the common view that torture is as trivially wrong as it is extraordinary. Showing torture to be both an endemic and an epistemological phenomenon, *Waiting* provides one proof among many of why literature is ahead of such philosophers' naïve and complaisant view, if developed from the epistemic foundation of pure knowledge. Unrestricted by tradition, Coetzee gives us instead a lesson in what it means to learn through torture.

To preview: Central figures in Coetzee's novels surely represent experimental postmodernism. What is open to debate is the size and outcome of the experiments they represent. What are these meant to prove? Do they want to show the most elementary conditions for human society, or do they suggest alternatives? Commentators on these novels are of different opinions. But in the end, at least from the experimental (as distinct to the playful) interest in reading these novels, it is important what these novels do prove, as well as what they are meant to prove. A kind of archaic living is not an alternative.

MICHAEL K: DISSOLVING ONESELF OUTSIDE SOCIETY

To approach a figure like Michael K from the backdrop of philosophical interests may appear to be a grave misunderstanding, either because the novel's aims strike one as predominantly political or because Michael K, a strangely disfigured, unspoken, and withdrawn colored man of thirty-one, is the very opposite of an intellectual. But despite the politico-historical setting of the story in South Africa's Apartheid regime during the 1980s—the "times" alluded to in the title—the story of the book is strong enough to provide an unrelentingly detailed and extensive description of what it would be like to live outside nearly everything.

Why and in which sense is Michael living outside? The novel follows the life of the harelipped son of a cleaning woman, living in Cape Town and migrating with his dying mother to a farm of her idyllic childhood memory in the Karoo, a semideserted region in inner South Africa. The story projects a sharpened, civil-war situation in a (then) future South Africa, still radicalizing the actual race conflicts in the country during the 1980s. After his mother dies en route, Michael brings her cremated ashes to the farm and becomes involved in a series of confrontations with officials, policemen, and the military. He passes through several labor camps but repeatedly manages to free himself and to live on or near the deserted farm. At the end of the story, after freeing himself from the last rehabilitation camp, Michael once more ends up at his mother's deserted apartment, the place from which they started.

The story ends with his musings about returning to the farm and living anew a life that he had experienced as fulfilling, that of gardening and growing melons and pumpkins.

As shown by its many references to real South African places and the social structures of Apartheid, the novel in part is resonant of a specific historical situation. By switching into Michael's inner life, the existence of someone with a lifelong career as handicapped and homeless, however, the story grows into an increasingly allegorical or principled (or philosophical?) reflection on what it means to withdraw not only from a horrendous and brutalizing war situation but also from language, communication, reason, and perhaps, in the end, even meaning itself. To what extent is it possible to remain human while withdrawing from communication and language? Or, alternatively, to what extent are the sympathetic figures whom Michael meets saved from the latter's dissolution of self, and what negative consequences come from this?

Before engaging with Michael's view, some aspects of the situation in the story should be mentioned—aspects that are also important in other Coetzeean writing. The world described is dominated by roles and institutions and only rarely populated by individuals. "Robert" is one of the rare names belonging to a brotherly behaving man, head of a family, whom Michael meets in one of the camps.[4] Otherwise people are termed "the policewoman," "the nurse," "the soldier," "the farmer," "the stranger," and so on. Michael K and his mother Anna K stand between the good person, Robert, and the many anonymous nonindividuals who abound in the story: they are both individual and symbolic.[5] Most people in the book are not only introduced by a kind of role or function; they often also lack the conviction to control a specific kind of development; nor do they have any definite beliefs, whether local or systematic. Although the army serves the interests of the white minority, the grandson of the white Visagie family deserts. The Jakkalsdrif Free Corps guard is planning to desert in case he is sent to the northern war site (*Life and Times*, 86). The medical officer at a later camp fails to understand the larger purpose of the war and his job: "Can you remind me why we are fighting this war? I was told once, but that was long ago and I seem to have forgotten" (157). The medical officer, as a representative of liberal conscience, is the most important counterpart to Michael. Through his words it becomes most clear what Michael's relation to society is, even if this is more guessed than understood by the officer.

Michael's exclusion from society is accelerated by the events of the war, but it dates back to his childhood in an orphan asylum. There, whatever "the nature of the beast that had howled in him, it was starved into stillness" (68). When he comes upon the deserted Visagie farm, he does not feel "at ease" there (58). In the face of the Visagie grandson's threats he feels "stupidity creep over him like a fog again"

(64). People often avoid looking at him. In between his being held in camps he takes refuge in unpopulated places, first at the deserted farm, then in the mountains, then again in a hole in the earth near the farm. The "earth" is beginning to be increasingly important to him. In his voyage to the farm he helps himself to animal fodder from a feeding trough: "At last I am living off the land" (46). At the farm he gives his mother's ashes back "to the earth" (58). In the mountains he feeds off anthills; he thinks to become a "different kind of man," as dry, yellow, and red as the landscape itself (67). Back near the farm once more he lives on the pumpkins he planted earlier, enjoying moments of bliss in eating their ripened flesh, something surpassed still by the consumption of sweet melons. "All that remains is to live here quietly for the rest of my life, eating the food that my own labour has made the earth to yield" (113).

Parallel to submerging himself in the environment of his hiding places, Michael dissolves himself into a series of ever-growing states of sleep, dreaming, hallucination, and stoic dizziness: "He was learning to love idleness. . . . He was neither pleased nor displeased when there was work to do, it was all the same" (115); "It occurred to him that he might not be fully in possession of himself" (119). And indeed he is not in possession of himself, in part because he is undernourished but also because of the trancelike state into which he lets himself drift and in which he feels exceedingly happy. Why is it that he meshes with the earth, living in a hole in the earth, dreaming and sleeping himself into a state of a consciousness of stasis, where nothing happens but the flow of time? "Like a parasite dozing in the gut, he thought, like a lizard under the stone?" (116). It is not, of course, that he follows an ideal of nature, taking (for example) nature as a sphere of freedom or harmony beyond the cruelties of the human world.[6] It is rather because there is no other content in his life once his mother has died and he has buried her ashes. Michael is losing all content in life, and even if he is not, throughout the book, losing his life in the biological sense, he is losing his grip on it and with it every humanly lived life. He meshes with the earth because, if there is nothing else to mesh with, that is one's fate. Of course, eventually every human being meshes with the earth, but for Michael this is strikingly visible even while he is alive.

During his second internment in a camp, Michael comes under the charge of the "medical officer," who perceives him as a childlike but at the same time alien creature and who increasingly makes the strangeness of his patient, his blankness, into his own, deeply personal problem. In a diarylike report that turns into an eloquent personal confession, the medical officer elevates his patient's reticence to let himself feed, and to accept starvation instead of one of the social roles open to him, into a transcendental experience. "Your stay within the camp was merely an allegory, if you know the word. It was an allegory—speaking at the highest level—of how scandalously, how outrageously a meaning can take up residence in a system, without becoming a term in it" (166). The officer tries to read Michael, and he reads him as one who is looking for freedom outside camps and beyond wars, in a sense radicalized by the world's having become a place of camps and holes. For the officer Michael is a great escape artist (166) who is able to avoid social encampment of every sort, and he has a growing desire to understand Michael, something he is fated not to achieve.

Is Michael to be understood? What should we make of this figure? One of the many meanings the character encapsulates is that life outside society is grim, nasty, brutish, and short, even if inside it is no less grim. Michael personifies what freedom comes down to in the end if society is given up fully: "I am more like an earthworm, he thought" (182). He not only shirks charity but is without emotion toward it: "Do I believe in helping people? He wondered.... He did not have a belief" (48). It seems that Michael is not to be understood because in him there is nothing to be understood; he personifies the point from which one can look at the problem of understanding and living in society. The confrontation with the medical officer does nothing to help either of them. The problem seems to be that the officer is the reflective liberal (the basic reason that he does not deserve a name), whereas the story's naïve good people, Robert, Felicity, and Noel, all are doing good out of instinct. The medical officer, for all his caring for his patient, is put on the side of the military and bureaucrats only, it seems, because as a liberal he wants Michael to be reasonable. He wants him to be reasonable in trying to force him to speak: "Talk, Michael.... You see how easy it is to talk, now talk. Listen to me, listen how easy it is to fill this room with words.... Give yourself some substance, man, otherwise you are going to slide through life absolutely unnoticed" (140). Suggestions like these reflect the modern reduction of human beings to their words and their becoming visible only through words. Michael is not good with words and therefore, in the sense of the liberal, does not exist.[7]

Susan Heider's reading of Michael seems to me to be right in that, in the confrontation between Michael and the medical officer, the novel focuses on the principled core of Coetzee's criticism of the repressive side of social structures by trying to make visible how Michael's resistance to an aggressive society manifests itself in his avoidance of language and communication and how the medical officer's attempt to make him speak verges on repression.[8] Heider's interpretation highlights the radical meaning possibly intended by Coetzee, particularly when she calls the doctor a "torturer" and a "sadist" and compares him to a Nazi concentration camp doctor because the doctor orders Michael to speak and shows signs of indignation when he meets with no response.[9] Michael is meant to be a figure trying to avoid all structures of society, roles, economics, paid work, history, and communication, someone who has radicalized the alternative suggested to him as a social outsider into a pure version of otherness, which leaves him in nature, in a dazed, dreamlike, and wordless state that is, when fully conscious, the consciousness of the immediate presence.[10] All of this seems interesting and artistically impressive enough, but it is the confrontation with the medical officer that brings into focus the place where the story may go off the track.

A simple point (parallel to the classical antirelativist response) on behalf of the medical officer's invocation to Michael to speak is the observation that one needs many words, and Coetzee's enormous linguistic competence, to make the whole story of Michael plausible in the first place. Only by making sensible use of words is it possible to counter the repressive aspects of sociality, including the repressive aspects of communication and of the meaning of specific words. The novel itself is proof of this insight, and the illusion it transports is in its suggestion that the whole story could have been told by Michael, who at the same time is "not good with words" and is an antihero even regarding language. The medical officer is shown to be the actual dumb one as he wants to press his meanings on Michael and is slightly totalitarian because, in the famous passage cited, he still believes Michael to be a "meaning in the system" (166).[11] But the self-contradiction of reflectively dropping out of the medium of reflection proves the officer right and Michael (and Coetzee?) wrong. Of course, the last view of Michael in the book, dreaming of drinking spoonfuls of water out of the farm's well, shows a reduced enough existence to avoid suggesting a rich, alternative good life. But even the central aim of the book, as I read it, bringing into view how to look at our societies from a fully external position, becomes murky because of its linguistic self-contradiction.

So in the end I side with the medical officer and not with Michael or the other instinctively "good" figures. If we had to decide whether to live in a world of goats, pumpkins, and melons, of endless days and timeless presence, or in a world of effective medicine, history, structured time, labor with ends and planning, and (alas) economic purposes, I would prefer the second. This, it goes without saying, is in a sense circular—but not in a negative way, for the alternative is not one that allows us to choose. The alternative is simply to give up the achieving of culture in toto and not suggest another culture. The critique of society contained in the figure of Michael does not allow any playful handling of traditions; for him society is too apocalyptic to be lived playfully, even for the whites. His basic experiences are reminiscent of the pre-Socratics who dealt with fire, water, and earth because words and ideas had not yet been made the mark of humanity by Socrates and Plato. Michael is archaic because he lacks the playfulness of Diogenes, who had the irony to live in a barrel (instead of a burrow), perhaps even a barrel which had previously contained wine. Michael prefers to live in a burrow, like foxes or rabbits, and in doing so he embodies a regression into an obscure form of humanism and antihumanism at the same time. Let us now see how two of Coetzee's other books attempt to substantiate this notion.

BARBARIANS: THROUGH TORTURE TO UNDERSTANDING

As already stated, divergent positions are bound together under the label of experimental postmodernists. Besides the "archaic" postmodernists we could also distinguish the "pragmatist" ones. Both take for granted some basic elements of human life. As opposed to the archaics, the pragmatists accept aspects of the "modern" liberal culture among these elements, whereas archaic postmodernists call into question reflection and words themselves. Given this distinction, *Life and Times* is obviously nearer the archaic than the pragmatist position. There is a slightly different attitude involved in Coetzee's earlier *Waiting for the Barbarians*, and a look at this book may prove helpful to giving the distinction a clearer profile. The book shares its title with a 1904 poem by the Greek poet Constantine Cavafy that depicts a situation of both fear and the hope of salvation by the decadent Romans against threatening barbarians.[12]

Coetzee's story centers in the same way around a morally corrupt "Empire" waging war against nomadic aborigines, who themselves in part represent standards of natural good but above all become the object of imperial power enacted in different shades of evil. If the Empire represents Western culture at its worst, the story's narrator, the elderly magistrate of a little border town, embodies Western attitudes in a more favorable way. In contrast to Michael K, the Magistrate undergoes a development for the better and, refined through both brutal events and especially the ordeal of being tortured himself, ends up a more understanding person than he was at the beginning. Judged from the standpoint of *Barbarians* (1980), one could think of the unreservedly negative lesson of *Life and Times* as perhaps being attributable to the aggravated circumstance of actual history, the politically sharpened situation in the South Africa of 1983. But in *Barbarians*, too, it is not entirely clear on which side of my distinction between "archaic" and "pragmatic" the figure of the Magistrate should finally be placed.

Overall, as mentioned, the story concerns the self-improvement of the central figure, the Magistrate.[13] Why does he need improvement? At the beginning of the story he does not "ask for more than a quiet life in quiet times," "serving out [his] days on this lazy frontier, waiting to retire" (*Barbarians*, 8). He is content to have created as comfortable a life as possible for himself, and if he shirks cruelties and conflicts it is because of his own laziness. He shuts his ears to the screams of the victims. As he becomes increasingly involved in the imprisonment and torture of some of the native people, though, he is being captured by his own obsession with torture, manifested in his strange attitude of bodily obsession toward a barbarian girl. This shows itself in his attraction to the girl's marks of torture, in his fits of self-reproach and doubtful self-reflection, and in the changing contents of his one recurrent dream. Opening himself gradually to the extent of his involvement in cruelties, he half-intentionally provokes his own torture, which provides the purgatorial event necessary to understand what it means to be repressed. Having lived through the events of his own imprisonment, torture, and humiliation, he achieves a new understanding. His dreams include an event of peace offering (109), and the closing description of children cooperatively building a snowman (albeit one lacking arms) (155) suggests hope—in contrast to the building of fortified castles in his earlier dreams.

So far this looks like a story of moral improvement in dark times. And indeed a central part of the narration is devoted to illustrating how the usual man of "consciousness" is deeply involved in the repressive regime he thinks he is both distanced from and critical of. The moral ordeal of the Magistrate covers his being put on trial by the cruel circumstances of war, but even more so his being forced to confront his own immorality. This part of the novel is developed in a psychologically refined depiction of the relationship the Magistrate entertains with the barbarian girl. Save for the depth of the analysis accompanying this recording of an interaction between two very different partners, which seems to dissolve the contrast between torture and understanding by showing their mutual dependency, this part of the story has an overall humanistic end in the self-improvement of the Magistrate.

To the extent of his improvement and change, the Magistrate is a different person from Michael K. There is, however, another side to this development, an undercurrent of forces blocking and hindering it, restricting the process to the point of what is eventually a rather modest achievement. To pin it down I will call this undercurrent the "antilinguist barrier," which manifests itself in the Magistrate's struggle with the provocations he is confronted with: a barrier involved in his confrontation with torture, pain, and the history of his town. In the end the antilinguist barrier leaves him speechless: "I think: 'There has been something staring me in the face, and still I do not see it'" (155). A judgment of the meaning implied in the figure of the Magistrate has to make sense of these two strands of development in the novel. Let us look a little more closely at the two of them, beginning with the encounter between the Magistrate and the barbarian girl.[14]

Having taken a first group of prisoners, Colonel Joll, the representative of the Empire, tortures them in order to evoke "truth" that he needs in order to recommend a larger campaign against the barbarians in the following year. (Actually, he inscribes his "truth" on them.) Among the prisoners is a young barbarian girl who is saved from torture by crippled feet and a partial blindness. Even if appalled by her appearance ("glossy black hair of the barbarians," "smells of smoke, of stale clothing, of fish" (25, 26), the Magistrate develops a growing fascination with the remaining signs on the girl's body. The parallelism of the torturer's interest in the human body and his own is at once rather clear to him ("The distance between myself and her torturers, I realize, is negligible; I shudder" [27]), yet he is unable to control his fascination. What is the motive? Not, of course, "pure" sympathy or a feeling of guilt as the local representative of the regime, but a hidden identification with the torturer, something to be pulled into the open only toward the end of the book.

> Though I cringe with shame, even here and now, I must ask myself whether, when I lay head to foot with her, fondling and kissing those broken ankles, I was not in my heart of hearts regretting that I could not engrave myself on her as deeply.... I was not, as I liked to think, the indulgent pleasure-loving opposite of the cold rigid Colonel. I was the lie that Empire tells itself when times are easy, he the truth that Empire tells when harsh wind blows. Two sides of imperial rule, no more, no less.
> (135)

The Magistrate's understanding was driven, then, by interest in torture, and at the same time restrained by self-deception. Because of his morals he is unable to join in the torture openly or to cooperate with it. But he feasts hiddenly on the cruelties effected by others.[15] His interest in torture alone is strong enough to break through his conventional distance toward a member of the slightly despised barbarians, as the girl is. No less than others, he, too, is influenced by racial stereotypes ("do I really look forward to the triumph of the barbarian way: intellectual torpor, slovenliness, tolerance of disease and death?" [52]), and his sexual desire is fixed on a prostitute trained in the imperial code of sexual behavior. What animates his movement of moral self-clarification, therefore, is the vague apprehension of involvement in cruelty that strikes him from the beginning. As the occasions of cruelty add up, he is shifted increasingly to the clarified position of moral awareness.

The book has a positive humanist dimension, then, that brings it close to pragmatist postmodernism. Pragmatism is most often understood as the attempt to invoke everyday certainties, and practically relevant certainties especially, against more abstract and contentious beliefs.[16] "Practical certainties" are the certainties of the day, those existing among a present community or culture. Certainties concerning the basics of moral humanism, as involved in the humanist moral side of *Barbarians*, are included in our present point of view in Western societies. But how extensively is this set to be taken? To what extent are certainties involved concerning the power of self-reflexivity, enlightenment, freedom, and reason: that is, typical liberal and democratic certainties? Let us tie these normative ideas together under the label of "liberal certainties" and have a look at what I have tried to identify (with the help of the anti-linguistic barrier) as the second strand of development in *Barbarians*.

Besides his attempt to understand the tortured girl, the Magistrate is also involved in another attempt at understanding. At the beginning of the narration he is engaged in a project to write a history of his town. The project is linked to his archaeological hobby of collecting remnants of earlier barbarian generations outside the town. From the beginning, however, his hope to decipher the ancient poplar slips dug out of the ground is slim.

> One evening I lingered among the ruins after the children had run to their suppers.... I sat watching the moon rise, opening my senses to the night, waiting for a sign that what lay around me, what lay beneath my feet, was not only sand, the dust of bones, flakes of rust, shards, ash. The sign did not come. I felt no tremor of ghostly fear. My nest in the sand was warm.... Ridiculous, I thought: a greybeard sitting in the dark waiting for spirits from the byway of history to speak to him before he goes home to his military stew and his comfortable bed.
>
> (*Barbarians*, 16)

These musings suggest a still active wish to understand the historic beginnings and through them the larger context of the Magistrate's own activities. They also show a conclusively pessimistic view of his chances for success. In a later scene with the Colonel, when accused of treasonous communication with the enemy by way of the ancient slips, the Magistrate suggests a series of arbitrary interpretations of their content, something like a vote for unrestricted historical relativity. Whatever can appropriately be read out of signs on specific occasions can be read out of them; there is no universal content or deeper truth behind them, only an arbitrary local one (111). In the end the Magistrate definitely gives up writing his memorial, and perhaps gives up writing at all: "For a long while I stare at the plea I have written. It would be disappointing to know that the poplar slips I have spent so much time on contain a message as devious, as equivocal, as reprehensible as this" (154).

His experience at this point is that he is unable to avoid the perspective "of a civil servant with literary ambitions" and that he is unable "to tell the truth." As a consequence he plans to bury the slips in the desert again, to have them wait for later generations: "There has been something staring me in the face, and still I do not see it" (155). This partial ending to the story is, in the narrative, close to the Magistrate's observing the hope-inspiring scene of the children building a snowman ("It is not a bad snowman"). A new generation will grow that will presumably soon become involved in a new cycle of barbarian hysteria, but perhaps not. There is no hope, however, for a deeper understanding of the history of it all; there is no sign shining through the masses of scriptures, neither the ancient nor the more current ones.

Despite his basically reflective stature, the Magistrate is not able to realize the arbitrary construction of his fear of the barbarians. Together with the inhabitants of the town he expects the barbarians to attack soon, an expectation created as part of the military campaign. He also shares the strange combination of torture and truth, something expressed recurrently when torture is called an inquiry for "truth." Given the actual events it soon becomes clear that the Colonel is not looking for truth but is rather constructing it. He is determined to produce an enemy for the Empire, and he makes every interrogation into one that will provide the truth he is interested in attaining. The Magistrate is also looking for truth with the poplar slips, but he does not grow weary of the search because he has a different way of relating to truth. Throughout much of the story the Magistrate is eager to know, but he resigns himself to finding his own perspective in the end. The moral purification that represents the humanist message of the narration also produces a relentlessly skeptical attitude toward his own abilities to see through the language of the Empire. And, as borne out by his being captured by the barbarians' fear, the Magistrate is right in his skepticism.

The Empire is able to dictate truth because it has the power to do so. The power resides in the threat of torture but also in the power of communality, the simple fact that beliefs need social corroboration.[17] Only through alternative communities can this power be mitigated. The Magistrate is helplessly isolated in his town, however, and his attempts to make contact with the barbarian girl are not successful. Of course, he is aware of his "reading" the girl in a parallel way to the torturer's inscribing his torture into her: "It has been growing more and more clear to me that until the marks on this girl's body are deciphered and understood I cannot let go of her" (31). This strange acceptance—strange in that it is expressed at this specific point of the story—of reacting toward the marks of torture as to a form of writing gives both us and the Magistrate a clue of the perspective shared between the torturer and himself. Reading presupposes language and schemes, and the scheme is the one of the oppressors. All deciphering is bound to a shared system of decipherment, and what the Magistrate achieves in the end is nothing more than some clarity about this system. He is still unable to leave it, to stay outside: "I think: 'I wanted to live outside history. I wanted to live outside the history that Empire imposes on its subjects, even its lost subjects. I never wished for the barbarians that they should have the history of Empire laid upon them. How can I believe that that is cause for shame?'" (154).

The one strong attempt for reaching understanding on the side of the Magistrate was in his relationship to the barbarian girl. But most of the time he is dominated not by interest in her self but only in her torture. They depart as strangers. "A stranger; a visitor from strange parts now on her way home after a less than happy visit" (73). During negotiation with her people, the Magistrate asks her to "tell them the truth," only to receive a little smile from the girl at this idea (71). The Magistrate realizes at the last minute that he has missed the opportunity to learn the barbarian language through her. Given all these omissions he is unsuccessful in understanding her. What he sees is her impenetrable body: "With this woman it is as if there is no interior, only a surface across which I hunt back and forth seeking entry" (43). Perhaps, he thinks at an earlier point of time, "it is the case that only that which has not been articulated has to be lived through" (65). He is, as it turns out, right in this, with the fatal consequence not only of "what cannot be articulated must be experienced" but also of "what has been experienced cannot be articulated." There seems no way out of this circle if one is missing the right language.

There are two meanings, then, in this book that are mutually contradictory or at least weakening. On the one hand, there is the lesson of possible moral improvement and humanity, the "meaning of humanity" (115), being provided by the torturers and implied in the elementary human woes like pain, thirst, hunger, humiliation, and fear of death. Suffering is a method of self-improvement. But is it the only or best one? And where does it lead to? Self-improvement, on the other hand, makes the Magistrate aware of his blindness, but does not help him really to see. Even if not as negative as Michael K's end, the lesson implied is not dissimilar to the archaic dream in the later book. The Magistrate cannot free himself from the Empire's linguistic restrictions, even if he grows aware of them. The barbarians represent a more simple and elementary way of living. Coetzee describes it briefly, in a manner pointing toward pragmatism: "She has a fondness for facts, I note, for pragmatic dicta; she dislikes fancy, questions, speculations; we are an ill-matched couple" (40). Crossing the gulf between the imperial subjects and the barbarians is not an option for those acquainted with "questions" and "speculations."

Let me bring these remarks on *Barbarians* to a close by drawing two conclusions. The first is an observation that there is room for different attitudes in the face of the realization of the Empire's linguistic power. One can settle on different postmodernist positions. A playful attitude will follow if one takes the unavoidability of schemes as fully neutralizing the fate of suffering. Different views can thus be combined, and in sum they can be used to take the awful importance out of suffering. The pragmatic attitude tries, on the other hand, to hold on to what is thought good in our present situation, improved with methods of criticism—as in the positive lesson inherent in *Barbarians*. The archaic attitude becomes urgent if one sides with the facts of suffering to such an extent that everything in our present view becomes suspicious and worthless. This, I fear, is the overall tendency in *Barbarians*, its ambiguity notwithstanding.

Second, I remark again on the contradiction between the book's meaning and our ability to read it.[18] Why should we readers—we "Romans" (according to Cavafy's poem, as opposed to the barbarians)—have any belief in the culture of the barbarians? Any positive allusion to the barbarians seems a romantic exercise based on a contradictory statement. The criticism inherent in the novel is based on insights that the readers are capable of grasping, as distinct from the Magistrate's view. We readers are able to see through the effects of imperial language and upbringing and, siding with Coetzee, we can suspect a similar imprint in our own language. But why should such a realization, *brought about by insight*, lead us to neglect the ability that produced the insight in the first place? We are not in the situation of the Magistrate, with the barbarians as the only utopic alternative; rather, we are presented with this alternative, witnesses to it. And the knowledge of it makes a difference to it. Being aware of the ability to see how our view is impregnated by power an argument for avoiding the radical alternative of the barbarian life.[19]

COSTELLO: ANTI-REASON AS JOY

The pieces collected under the title *Elizabeth Costello* have a literary style different from that of the other novels and include talks and lectures to an academic audience. It is of some interest how Coetzee manages to circumnavigate the danger of philosophical abstraction usually involved in such forms. In a sense, the confrontation of academic discourse with the world of literature is an opportunity hard to beat if one sails under the flag of attacking the smugness of "reasonable arguments," "rational clarifications," or the moral teachings of "humanity" in an abstract conception. It should be clear from the beginning that Costello enters the scene as someone attacking the very existence of philosophers by calling into question their intellectual stance, albeit not their persons. One may think that such an attack cannot be advanced by means of "argument" because such a style of exchange predetermines the outcome. But are not speculations about Michael K's speechless existence and the Magistrate's succumbing to the Empire's power of rhetoric necessarily embedded in a great deal of argument? Understanding includes, as is well understood, reason and argument.

In many sympathetic commentaries about Coetzee's novels, and *Costello* especially, this conclusion is heavily attacked.[20] In order to make clear what is at stake here, one needs two steps, I think: first, a clarification of meaning and, then, an argument. (A dissenter may stop listening at the mention of "argument." I will return to this hypothetical opponent in a moment.) For the clarification of meaning, "reasons" should be understood as answers to "why" questions of different sorts. Reasons ought not to be taken as specific explanations, for example, instrumental or economic ones. Reasons in the widest sense of the word also concern the sense of reasons; there can be reasons against specific kinds of reasons. Here is the argument: If reasons were not allowed, orientation would be lost, and this would restrict freedom. If one is for freedom, one is in need of reasons. It is possible to describe a consciousness without reasons, and Michael's inner view comes close to that. But as we have to judge him from our position of enjoying reason and freedom, then without a good reason for his inner state we cannot be sorry for him. Now, what about the opponent who closed his ears against the very utterance of "argument"? He is missing a potential for freedom, something not to be forced upon him.

The argument just given provides a very basic and not, as one might fear, blind vote for the "liberal" public culture, understood as oriented to the norm of giving and taking reasons for the attitudes one chooses. As this reasoning culture does not want to force reasons on others but favors the exchange of reasons, it does not force on others, within limits, the awareness of reasons. An attitude beyond reason, such as Michael's, is to be allowed, but only in private. Society is not possible on the basis of Michael's speechless attitude. The part of society required to be public needs reasons, and better good reasons than bad ones.[21] In contrast to Michael, Costello wants to address a public audience, something to be done only with the help of reasons. Falling into reasonless awareness would not in itself be a possible public reason, even if there could be good reasons for such an awareness. Let us see whether Costello presents some.

Costello's argument is most easily introduced by her attack on Thomas Nagel's attempt to prove that we human beings are unable to know what "it is like to be a bat." Nagel believes that we are bound to our human perspective, our human lifeform, including language and reason. Costello's overall argument tries to show that it is wrong to codify a set of specifically human capabilities into a "human point of view" with normative consequences against animals. Such an argument, of course, is a notoriously difficult and typically philosophical one, as it centers on the boundaries of our human worldview, including the practical consequences of having attitudes along these boundaries.

Again, in reading Costello's attempt (or to be precise, Coetzee's, presented through his literary figure) as a form of argument, in the widest sense of "argument," I take every possible piece of socially sharable experience to be covered by this kind of exchange. Also, should the literary presentation of Costello's talks, with its side and meta-commentaries, be considered as being included in (and measured by) the medium of argument and not taken as something wholly different? If we are moved, reprehended, or shaken by the figure Costello represents, this has to be viewed within the framework of her reasoning, even if it is subsequently shrugged off. Take, for example, the nervous breakdown of Costello at the end of the second animal-lecture episode through the experience of her total alienation from human rationality. Durrant interprets this suggestively as incorporating a flight to death, as giving up the will to live.[22] The calming attempt of her son, in analogy to the earlier advice about how to accompany cattle for slaughter, is moving, but where do we want to be moved? We seem to need "closer inspection."

The stage for the debate is set by Costello with the help of the first lecture and its topic, realism. On the whole, the first story, including its short piece of explicit argument, is only a kind of stage setting, making one aware of what Costello is up to, against the backdrop of figures representing counterpositions in the present postmodern culture. Reminding us of the "beautiful" and clever but cruel officer Mandel in *Barbarians*, the counter-figure is the beautiful and clever but playful postmodernist literary critic Susan Moebius, who is somehow attracted by Costello's zest, even if simultaneously repelled by it. With the possible exception of her son, most other figures in the stories mistake and neglect Costello to various extents. Only her son is shown to be aware of the extremity of his mother's view, even if he himself is undecided as to what to think of it. In this he is the most congenial figure of the stories, most akin, I think, to the usual reader.[23]

Costello's introduction provides the message of global and historical antirealism:

> The word-mirror is broken, irreparably it seems.... The words on the page will no longer stand up and be counted, each proclaiming 'I mean what I mean!' The dictionary that used to stand beside the Bible and the works of Shakespeare above the fireplace, where in pious Roman homes the household gods were kept, has become just one code book among many.
> (*Elizabeth Costello*, 19)

This introduces a radical view of relativism in combination with a genealogical explanation (pointing to the stability of words through gods), followed by the further suggestion that there is no tragedy involved in this process, as we now realize the illusionary spell cast over earlier times. One makes progress, when "the mirror falls to the floor and shatters" (20). But if the mirror is broken, why not go and play with the pieces? This is not something Costello and her son, as the interpreter, seem ready to do. Why the distance to Moebius, who tries to pull the author of *The House on Eccles Street* into a trendy gender discourse instead of tackling the problem of realism? The attempt Costello makes to break through the attitude of play is a reference to Kafka's ape in the famous "Report to an Academy." Costello reads the situation of an ape addressing serious elderly gentlemen with an academic speech as a method of ironically shifting identities between being human and being nonhuman. The broken word-mirror may dissolve distinctions, but there is an alternative to arbitrariness and playing with the pieces, which is only hinted at in Costello's reference to Kafka. Nobody in the audience is ready to take up her hint, and the closing talk to her son is not of much help either. What she is driving at, of course, are the moral consequences of human beings and nonhumans becoming exchangeable, especially in terms of suffering. As these consequences are only vaguely hinted at in the first "lesson," they have to be pulled into the open, and Costello does this with the necessary rhetorical verve in the following two lectures.

The question pursued in these two lectures and the additional voices accompanying Costello's statements, is, on the face of it, a simple one: What authority does our human view on animals have, in terms of the anthropocentric criteria we impose onto animals? The most explicit statement representing the present "reflective" view on these matters is raised by the philosopher O'Hearne toward the end of the second lecture. He thinks it licit to kill animals as their life is "happening" to them but not licit to allow cruelty in the sense of suffering. O'Hearne brings up the classical criterion in the present animal ethics debate by distinguishing between life without a reflective sense of the living being and life including a reflective sense of being alive and possibly dead. The conclusion drawn is that death has different meanings to beings of the first sort, normally animals, and those of the second sort, normally human beings.[24] Costello, in both her talks, tries to call this very distinction into question both by casting doubt on its relevance and by trying to dissolve it.

Her arguments go like this: Would we think the mathematical human genius more valuable than the down-to-earth reasoner, and, if not, why draw a line between clever humans and dumb animals (68)? Scientific measurement of animal capacities is heavily biased by human standards, thereby ignoring the animals' genuine capacities (108). Animals have their own way of speaking to us (108). The importance of life and death does not lie in a conscious reflection on life and death but in the unintellectual nature of a being (111). A veal calf's lack of a reflective stance concerning its relation to its mother does not diminish the importance of this relation nor make it irrelevant (111). What Costello is suggesting instead of the reclaimed superiority of reflective capabilities is "fullness, embodiedness, the sensation of being" (78), or "joy" as the "experience of full being" (78). She also invokes the power of poetry, with poems about panthers and jaguars (95; subtly corrected by her son who adds less aesthetic animals like chicken, pigs, rats, and prawns, 100) helping us to identify with the embodied animal. Against Nagel's distance to bat existence, she draws on the writer's ability to feel herself into living with "webbed feet."

There are, as one would expect from a literary figure, two sides to Costello's engagement. There is the direct emotional side, covering her attempts to visualize—by comparisons, illustrations, and strong claims—the reality of animal life. It is a strong and, in the end, unproven claim that the perspective of the bat or the panther is fully accessible to human imagination. It may be possible, in opposition to O'Hearne (110), to be "friends" with a chicken, but O'Hearne seems to be right in that we cannot feel ourselves into chicken reality. Some of Costello's rhetorical devices, such as the Holocaust analogy or the "Plutarch response" (83), may have the effect of shaking naïve connoisseurs of meat into thinking, but in themselves they prove nothing. They presuppose that such comparisons can be made, and to the extent that, in the light of their being, they are made explicitly without proof, they even manifest the playful postmodernist stance from which Costello distances herself on other occasions. More emotionally shaking are the scenes of animal killing, a goat in *Life and Times* and a horse in *Barbarians*. These scenes are not meant, however, to prove something, and rightly so. On the basis of their very capacities as writers, therefore, Costello and Coetzee are unconvincing when one asks for reasons in the way they grant permission for one to do.

Critics of "rationalist" animal ethics such as Cathryn Bailey follow up on these emotional attacks on our animal-human distinctions, echo Costello's sneer at the "piddling distinctions" (111) of some philosophers, and plea for the "continuity between reason and emotion" and the reversing of present priority of clarity over empathy.[25] It is difficult to know what to make of this. Empathy with whom and with what? It seems obvious that clarity has an important part to play in these matters and cannot be substituted by empathy. To suggest this is to fall into the error of conflict at the wrong place. Empathy cannot conflict with clarity as clarity is an inherent quality of human empathy, as perhaps opposed to the empathy of animals. Critics like Bailey criticize dualisms in the "male" tradition but are captured in the same dualism. Their criticism would take hold, however, if it made sense to take the "point of view" of animals more radically. This is what Costello aims at with the other, more reflective and reasoned side of her statements.

But is it possible to leave the "human view"? O'Hearne makes a suggestion as to what this could mean:

Of the many varieties of animal lover I see around me, let me isolate two. On the one hand, hunters, people who value animals at a very elementary, unreflective level; who spend hours watching them and tracking them; and who, after they have killed them, get pleasure from the taste of their flesh. On the other hand, people who have little contact with animals, or at least with those species they are concerned to protect, like poultry and livestock, yet want all animals to lead—in an economic vacuum—a utopian life in which everyone is miraculously fed and no one preys on anyone else.—Of the two, which, I ask, loves animals more?

(110)

Costello misses this opportunity to agree with O'Hearne, as she should have done on the basis of her own earlier vote for the "primitive experience," a "primitivist poem" (98), identifying with the body of the jaguar, and avoiding ecologist abstractions that draw one onto the level of systems thinking, something alien to individual jaguars. Well, jaguars do not write primitivist poems, either, but we may have to use our human abilities if we want to become like a jaguar, including poetic help. The problem lies in the consequence hinted at by O'Hearne. If the ideal is to identify with animals without any "human" reservations, then this means behaving like animals, hunting them, and enjoying eating them. Michael K behaves like this in a gripping scene of *Life and Times* when he drowns a goat without reservations and has a meal from it afterward. At times Coetzee/Costello play with this vision of an archaic ethics: "We can call this primitivism. It is an attitude that is easy to criticize, to mock. It is deeply masculine, masculinist. Its ramifications into politics are mistrusted. But when all is said and done, there remains something attractive about it at an ethical level" (97). If we try to leave the human view, the only method that remains is the animal view. If, as Costello suggests, the poets offer a more adequate approach to animals than the philosophers do, the advice is to become more primitive, more animal-like, something that is attractive "at the ethical level."[26]

Archaic ethics, surely, cannot be taken at face value. Costello seems to mix two tasks that do not seem to cohere. We are not allowed to approach animals with our human standards of evaluation, devaluing them in their lack of reflective attitudes. We have to emphasize—and to feel into—their "being full of life." As we can do that only by stressing our humanly empathetic abilities to the limits, the question may be asked why we should consider animals fully on their own level, if that can only be done by making use of our humanly reflective stance. So either we have to devalue our own abilities and turn ourselves into animals, or stretch our abilities to the limit and identify with nature, absolutely. Both attempts are contradictory, the contradiction being one between means and ends.

There is another way to illustrate this conflict. In his fictitious inner monologues of Köhler's apes, Coetzee suggests an extended doubt about all human achievements, similar to the totalized diagnosis of instrumental thinking in Adorno and Horkheimer's *Dialectic of Enlightenment*. Everything touched on by human civilization is drawn under and stained with the repressive power of instrumental thinking. To escape the influence of instrumental thinking, one needs to go back to nature itself, and episodes of suffering—or other ways of displaying our animal nature—may be the method to break the spell of our human degradation of pure nature. But to move in this direction we have to use our special human capacities, reflective and sensitized empathy, something alien to animals. To resort to this capacity calls into question the very starting point of the whole argument. The argument is reduced to another radically enlarged plea for sympathy, sympathy not so much with humans but with animal life and with nature. But why this enlarged sympathy, if not to make us more human?[27]

In part, this self-contradictory plea for an archaic animal ethics in Costello is counterbalanced by the other figures' opposition, by representatives of "reasonable standpoints" such as (to a slight extent) Norma's and (especially) O'Heare's. Coetzee himself is far too reflective an author not to be aware of these alternative views. But, at least to my reading, Costello's voice is meant to win the day, and her suffering, both in her aging body and in and from her own thinking, puts further weight on the scales. All the other figures seem to come off too lightly, somehow living too smugly on the carcasses of animals, to make their position the right one. But this only fits if we accept the world being one of suffering or of guilt, something that I think we should oppose. Suffering and thinking are not exclusive alternatives; more innocuous possibilities lie between.

CONCLUSION

I have called the philosophers who are skeptical toward an essentially positive content of reason experimental postmodernists. Within this class three different positions turned out to be possible, which were in turn termed the players, the archaics, and the pragmatists. Players endlessly experiment with pieces from our culture; archaics suggest a return to a precultural state; and pragmatists defend an identification with essentials of our present Western culture, without thinking them unavoidable or "essential" in a deeper, necessary sense. This reading of Coetzee has attempted to show that some of his most impressive figures come closest to the archaic position within this class, even if the surrounding stories are complex enough to leave open what the meanings carried by figures like Michael K, the Magistrate, and Costello are meant to be. Even if the life-form implied in these figures is a fairly clear one of animal-like primitiveness and innocence, how to transpose this life-form into our present situation remains open.

The joy Costello wants to evoke may be a method to open up paths of freedom as her attacks are surely intended to encourage us to break through the restrictions of our anthropocentric perspective. Similar to all of Coetzee's central figures, Costello is trying to find a way out of the universally stained human thinking. Neglecting the self-contradictory responses I tried to make toward all the three methods covered, we could simply ask whether and to what extent we are impressed by the world made visible through the perspectives of Michael, the Magistrate, and Costello and, if so, what this impression comes down to in a practical sense.

There are, in essence, two worlds coming into view: our everyday world of separation and time, words and power, and instrumental ends and means, and an alternative world, however vague, of amalgamation and presence, bodies and trance, self-forgetfulness and nondirected joy. This latter world is not that present societies can obtain, as Coetzee himself (perhaps intentionally) notes through the indignation of Abraham Stern at Costello's Holocaust analogy. The forms of life lived by Michael, the Magistrate, or Costello do not constitute a recipe for most of us. Many of us, I think, are impressed by these views of life, and they incline us to distance ourselves from playful postmodernism. There is too much suffering involved in the stories of Michael, the Magistrate, and Costello to keep up the relaxed and distanced attitude of play. All three scenarios of widespread cruelty motivate those gripped by them to deeply question their own lifestyles and the dogmas of their own societies. Cruelty seems to force those confronted with it into questions of truth, and if truths are becoming suspect themselves, as in Coetzee's writing, the confrontation turns into an even deeper level of this search.

How should we take the flirtation with the precultural, prelinguistic, animal-like state offered to us by these figures? Maybe as an impressive general reminder of where we are and what we are, a general motive of carefulness and suspicion toward our own linguistic and rational powers. One wonders, however, how such general rebukes can work if they are less helpful in detail. Are such attempts at Rousseau-like alternatives of the good nature, or, perhaps better, at an evaluationally neutral nature, only recurrences of secularized religious needs? Maybe so, but they are also attempts to probe the restrictions and limits imposed by figures trying to run to the limits of our present thinking. If a positive ethics had to be drawn directly from the novels, it would have to be an idyllic agricultural life, something obviously impossible for simultaneously greedy and inventive humans.

Another way to read the novels takes the archaic solution to be an argument for some contents of our present culture not to be placed at our disposal: contents related to our linguistic capacities and our ability to reason and communicate with one another. I would like to read Coetzee's novels as a forceful proof—even if perhaps not fully intended as such—of a pragmatic postmodernism that, on the one hand, keeps a critical distance toward specific forms of rationality and other "imperial" achievements, but, on the other hand, guards itself against both arbitrary playfulness and a beautiful archaism. In a sense Coetzee, or at least this reading of him, is in danger of repeating a typical philosophical error by magnifying specific and local experiences into large-scale scenarios. Nearly all of philosophy's mistakes follow from undue generalizations out of the particular. Reading Coetzee as literature and not as philosophy, then, could help us to improve some, if not all, of our practices.

Notes

1. R. Rorty, *Philosophy and the Mirror of Nature* (Oxford: Blackwell, 1980), chap. 3.
2. See R. Rorty, "The Historiography of Philosophy: Four Genres," in *Truth and Progress: Philosophical Papers*, vol. 3, by R. Rorty (Cambridge: Cambridge University Press, 1984), 247–73, for these distinctions.
3. In part this has been done by R. Rorty, *Truth, Politics, and 'Post-Modernism'* (Assen: Van Gorcum, 1997); and R. Rorty, *Philosophy and Cultural Politics: Philosophical Papers*, vol. 4 (Cambridge: Cambridge University Press, 2007).
4. Other characters are self-speaking names like "Noel," the humane head of a camp, and "Felicity," a possibly black cleaning women in a hospital ward of whom it is said that "her time is full as it has ever been, even the time of washing sheets" (*Life and Times*, 158).
5. Throughout the book Michael K is referred to in narration only as "K," which perhaps should be read as keeping any content from him, referring to him as someone standing outside of content. It would be a misunderstanding to think of him as preparing to take on any content, as he resists such attempts, even the offerings of Robert.
6. In the context of an interrogation Michael makes the extraordinary statement that the vegetables weren't his but "came from the earth" (139). Normally this would not be a good argument as coming from the earth does not signify being in the earth's possession. Here it signals Michael's meshing with the earth, a kind of ecocentrist point of view.
7. Michael is unable to grasp himself in words. "Always, when he tried to explain himself to himself, there remained a gap, a hole, a darkness before which his understanding baulked, into which it was useless to pour his words. The words were eaten up, the gap remained. His was always a story with a hole in it: a wrong story, always wrong" (110).
8. S. D. Heider, "The Timeless Ecstasy of Michael K," in *Black/White Writing: Essays on South African Literature*, ed. P. Fletcher (Lewisburg, Penn.: Bucknell University Press, 1993), 83–98.
9. Ibid., 88–89. Heider calls the officer, who is a pharmacist by profession, a "doctor" throughout, which may partly have given rise to her extreme reading. Overall her reading of *Life and Times*, even if partly overdone, makes an extremely convincing case of the details of Coetzee's attempt to articulate the outside view of Michael.

10. Michael is even trying to get outside his desires. "He was not sure that he wanted to become a servant of hunger again; but a hospital, it seemed, was a place for bodies, where bodies asserted their rights" (71).

11. "The doctor's words are farcical, for he clings to the assumption that K is a meaning in the system. The doctor's translations of K into allegorical meaning are even more empty because it is all in an imagined speech to K; K is not present. He is a critic haranguing an absent auditor" (Heider, "The Timeless Ecstasy," 91).

12. The text of the poem can easily be found on the Internet.

13. In this I follow S. V. Gallagher, *A Story of South Africa: J. M. Coetzee's Fiction in Context* (Cambridge, Mass.: Harvard University Press, 1991), chap. 5. Gallagher is informative on the historical South African context of the novel written in 1979. Gallagher's interpretation is, however, one-sided in giving it a much too positive and optimistic political message.

14. By calling the barrier "antilinguist," I obviously want to refer to a similar problematic involved in *Life and Times* and, as will be seen, in *Elizabeth Costello*. The difference between the Magistrate and Michael is that the former looks at the barrier language makes from the side of a speaker who tries to remain a speaker, whereas Michael is meant to stand outside of language. Costello again is closer to Michael than to the Magistrate as she tries to offer us the speechless "joy" of embodiedness, thereby evoking anew a tendentially self-contradictory attempt to side with the animals. The occasions of speechless dream, stupor, feeling, and so on in most of Coetzee's novels, including the three under discussion, are helpfully selected by S. Durrant, "J. M. Coetzee, Elizabeth Costello, and the Limits of the Sympathetic Imagination," in *J. M. Coetzee and the Idea of the Public Intellectual*, ed. J. Poyner (Athens: Ohio University Press, 2006), 118-34. I cannot follow here his again helpful references to psychoanalysis.

15. How to explain his recurrent falling into a deep sleep when washing the barbarian girl's broken ankles? Is this the weakening force of his effort at self-deception? Or is his contradictory mind giving him a merciful blackout? Durrant suggests, rightly I think, that sleepiness and stupor signal an anti-intellectual beginning of change in the person of the Magistrate. The "somnabulic mode of attentiveness to other lives" starts a development that is meant to be primarily emotional ("J. M. Coetzee," 121).

16. The "pragmatic maxim" invented by Charles Peirce and made use of by James, Dewey, and Rorty expresses the abstract idea of this pragmatist attitude. The fact that the maxim itself is not very clear, bordering on the positivist verification principle, fortifies the pragmatist's flight from abstractions, which are at best shortcuts to something concrete.

17. It seems to me irrelevant whether the Empire's power reaches for "truth" or only for "widespread belief." If it dictates widespread belief and lacks the power to decide truth, the practical result is the same thing.

18. Under the presumption, of course, that the meaning stated is the definitive one.
19. There is a strong similarity between the Magistrate's skepticism toward justice and Judith Shklar's and Rorty's "liberalism of fear." The Magistrate sees reference to justice as unavoidably imbued with power relations or ideological interpretations: "Justice, one that word is uttered, where will it all end?" (*Barbarians*, 108). Out of similar reasons Shklar and Rorty prefer a liberalism concentrating on the avoidance of cruelty instead of the promotion of justice. See J. Shklar, "Liberalism of Fear," in *Liberalism and the Moral Life*, ed. N. Rosenbluhm (Cambridge, Mass.: Harvard University Press, 1989), 21–39; R. Rorty, *Contingency, Irony, and Solidarity* (Cambridge: Cambridge University Press, 1989), 89. For criticism of this as too small a basis for intrasocietal relationships, see B. Yack, ed., *Liberalism Without Illusion* (Chicago: Chicago University Press, 1996).
20. Susan Heider thinks that "K's dissociation from words is far from a lack of knowledge. His knowledge is a knowledge that encompasses the unnamed, growing more powerful the further from culture he gets" ("The Timeless Ecstasy," 90–91). C. Bailey, "On the Backs of Animals: The Valorization of Reason in Contemporary Animal Ethics," *Ethics and The Environment* 10, no. 1 (2005): 1–17, rests heavily on identifying reasons with things like the "rationalist tradition," the "male point of view," "dualism," a "position of power," an exclusion of emotion and by this of women—all of which are non sequitur if reasons are understood widely enough. Durrant gives a more dialectical view on sympathetic imagination, asking it to be "between speech and silence" ("J. M. Coetzee," 126). He also accepts that Costello is making "arguments," albeit cryptic ones (like feeling into a bat over imagining her own death).
21. For the private/public distinction, see Rorty, *Contingency, Irony and Solidarity*, chap. 4. Rorty thinks Foucault is a "private philosopher" as he asks for such a radical change in society that it should be restricted to the private sphere (65). The second strand in *Barbarians* is, of course, rather Foucaultian and in the same sense private. The Magistrate is a private figure, whereas Costello is a public one.
22. Durrant, "J. M. Coetzee," 132.
23. The "son's" being nameless in the first story signals his not being a central figure. He sees himself as a kind of Hermes, a "mouthpiece of the divine" (*Elizabeth Costello*, 31). What seems to make him important is that, like his frail mother, he is a bearer of imperfections (e.g., a "balding spot"), which put him on the side of the Nietzschean "weak."
24. What I call the "classical present view" in animal ethics, represented by T. Regan and P. Singer, is also briefly voiced in the first animal lecture, for example, *Elizabeth Costello*, 70, 89–90.
25. Bailey, "On the Backs of Animals," 2, 4.
26. Durrant, "J. M. Coetzee," reads Costello's "joy" as a stab toward disembodiment, and therefore toward death. The problem with this is that it includes giving up all criteria for behavior. There is nowhere to go from there.

27. In a sense this argument is backed by the inner monologues of Köhler's apes, who demonstrate a social logic instead of the humanly instrumental one. Sultan asks, "Why is he starving me?" not "how to handle the wooden crates to reach the banana?" (*Elizabeth Costello*, 72). The social is more basic than the instrumental. But then the criticism against instrumental reason has its limits through the social.

References

Coetzee, J. M. *Elizabeth Costello*. New York: Viking, 2003.
———. *Life and Times of Michael K*. London: Penguin Books, 1983.
———. *Waiting for the Barbarians*. London: Penguin Books, 1980.

10

Coetzee's Critique of Reason

Martin Woessner

> All forms of discourse may have secrets, of no great profundity, which they nevertheless cannot afford to unveil.
> —J. M. Coetzee, "Truth in Autobiography"

> Sometimes, I think: it's novels that should be written.
> —Bernard-Henri Lévy, *War, Evil, and the End of History*

According to their press release of October 2, 2003, the Swedish Academy decided to bestow the Nobel Prize for literature upon J. M. Coetzee for his "well-crafted" novels, which are full of "pregnant dialogue and analytical brilliance." Even more important than this, in the academy's opinion, was the fact that Coetzee himself "is a scrupulous doubter, ruthless in his criticism of the cruel rationalism and cosmetic morality of western civilization."[1] This is a fair description, but it is one that requires almost immediate qualification. For as much as Coetzee's work may call into question our everyday pieties, our self-serving rationalizations and evasions, it does not stop there. More importantly, it also points the way toward what we might call moral awakening. And it does so, crucially, via the form of the novel.

Coetzee's "capacity for empathy," as the Swedish Academy put it, allows him to dramatize the specific moments when "cruel rationalism" and "cosmetic rationality" break down, when they no longer justify the actions of individuals confronted with the messy realities of everyday existence.[2] Almost every one of his protagonists is moved toward a moment of moral insight, toward a flash of recognition that finally exposes the limited capacity of reason to govern our lives. If there is any thread that unites Coetzee's many novels, unique and disparate as they are, it is this: the critique of reason, not for the sake of critique—not, that is, for the sake of reason—but for the sake of moral life. Over the course of a long and distinguished career he has outlined a decidedly post-philosophical position, one not easily co-opted by current moral debate but one that overlaps in interesting ways with Richard Rorty's late writings on the relationship between philosophy and literature.

THE PHILOSOPHER AND THE NOVELIST

For centuries, philosophers have been telling us that the unexamined life is not worth living. A life without rational reflection, they have argued, following Socrates, is a life less full, less complete. Only in subjecting ourselves to critical reflection, in submitting our own selves to the gaze of enlightened reason, do we fully live. But could it be that philosophical life—or at least a certain kind of philosophical life—is part of the problem? It is worth remembering that Heraclitus, so busy contemplating the stars that he fell into a well, is as much the patron saint of professional thinkers as Socrates.

Poets and the playwrights since Aristophanes have been quick to satirize the high-mindedness of philosophers. More than once have professional thinkers missed the proverbial forest for the trees. To be fair, though, it is worth pointing out that philosophers themselves are aware of the peculiarities of their calling. Wittgenstein, who was, to put it mildly, prone to peculiarities, recorded the following in his notebooks: "I am sitting with a philosopher in the garden; he says again and again" 'know that that's a tree', pointing to a tree that is near us. Someone else arrives and hears this, and I tell him: 'This fellow isn't insane. We are only doing philosophy.'"[3] There has been no shortage of modern writers to poke fun at the philosopher's inability to see a tree for a tree. Saul Bellow, a Nobel winner long before Coetzee, created the Heidegger-quoting professor Moses Herzog to demonstrate, among other things, that excessive erudition does not necessarily help one to understand, let alone lead, a good life. The novel that bears his name is little more than a catalogue of his failed attempts to wrap his philosophically trained mind around the fact that his best friend ran off with his wife. Even Heidegger, who sought to return philosophy to the realm of concrete experience with concepts of angst and care and resolve, cannot help him: "Human life," as Herzog finally begins to realize, "is far subtler than any of its models, even those ingenious German models."[4]

This is pretty much the lesson of another Heidegger spoof in American literature: Flannery O'Connor's "Good Country People," which introduces us to Joy Hopewell, a character less well rounded than Bellow's Herzog, perhaps, but much funnier. Like Herzog, Hopewell has read her Heidegger. Not only read it, but mastered it. To her Southern-small-town mother's bafflement, she has earned a Ph.D. in philosophy. But this does not change the fact that she remains a fragile, naïve young woman;

philosophy, like the prosthetic leg she has worn since a childhood hunting accident, keeps her standing, but just barely. As her mother is fond of putting it, her daughter was "brilliant but she didn't have a grain of sense."[5] Hopewell has read enough Heidegger to change her name from Joy to Hulga, a tougher, less innocent-sounding moniker, but her embrace of Heideggerian existentialism and all the dread, death, and nothingness it entails has done little to prepare her for real-world nihilism. If anything, her Heideggerian expertise prevents her from seeing it at all, until a real-world nihilist—a lying, cheating, hard-drinking Bible salesman only O'Connor herself could have invented—not only pulls her leg but steals it.[6]

Is O'Connor's single-legged protagonist representative of something? Reading Coetzee's *Slow Man* when it appeared in 2005, exactly half a century after O'Connor's short story was first published, I could not help but notice certain similarities between Hulga Hopewell and Paul Rayment, the middle-aged photographer-protagonist who looses a leg at the beginning of Coetzee's novel and spends the rest of the narrative attempting to reconcile himself to the fact (in the same way that Herzog spends an entire story trying to get over his failed marriage).[7] Before losing a leg, both Hopewell and Rayment were solitary individuals—rational, contemplative, perhaps even a little cold. Both eschewed the easy comforts of community or, less dramatic than that, simple neighborliness; Hulga kept company with Heidegger, Paul with his collection of antique photographs. If not antisocial, exactly, each had antisocial tendencies.

But what does their one-leggedness reveal? If the lessons of Hulga Hopewell and Paul Rayment are at all alike, it is in their mutual suggestion that cold, calculating rationality must be supplemented, if not supplanted, by emotion and, more specifically, by empathy. It takes the loss of a leg to make our protagonists realize that, in fact, they were already unsteady. Their solitary worlds are easily and quickly broken, leaving them baffled, befuddled, stumbling. Could it be that Coetzee is saying something similar about Western rationality itself—namely, that an overdependence on the prosthetic of reason has made us emotionally unsteady? As a critic of "the cosmetic rationality of western civilization," to borrow from the language of the Swedish Academy, Coetzee is keenly aware of the delicate and ephemeral nature of the achievements of modern thought. JC, the narrator of *Diary of a Bad Year*, who, as many reviewers have pointed out, bears a striking resemblance Coetzee himself, is certainly not convinced that modern rationality is all it pretends to be: "What if the contest to see whose terms warm-blooded life will continue on this planet," he asks, "does not prove human reason the winner?" (*Diary of a Bad Year*, 71).

A tour of Coetzee's writings over the past four decades reveals an abiding interest in the fragility of modern rationality, more specifically, in its inability to help us live our lives. Paul Rayment is but one of Coetzee's many protagonists to be brought to the limits of reason by unexpected events. His story is emblematic of the struggles and setbacks faced by other characters. In this instance, the loss of a leg is nothing compared to the emotional paralysis that sets in after the accident. With his world upended as quickly as his bike, Rayment stumbles from scene to scene, much to the chagrin of his narrator, Elizabeth Costello, who, in her cameo appearance, bemoans the fact that "he has not the faintest idea of how to bring about his heart's desire" (*Slow Man*, 141). A bourgeois automaton, he has to learn to live all over again. Many of Coetzee's other characters travel similar paths, emerging from the quagmire of an excessively rational and ordered existence to eventually confront, and perhaps overcome, their emotional deformations. From *Dusklands* (1974) and *Waiting for the Barbarians* (1980), through *Age of Iron* (1990), up to *Disgrace* (1999), *Elizabeth Costello* (2003), and *Diary of a Bad Year* (2007), the Nobel Prize winner has created an array of protagonists who live the life of the mind, only to discover later that life is more than mind. Through such imaginary individuals, Coetzee has consistently explored the limits of stark and detached rational thinking—the very stuff that defined his own former life as a computer programmer, as described in *Youth* (2002). Beyond these limits is, in Coetzee's work at least, a post- or even prephilosophical ethics of compassion. Like the "heart's desire," it is one that cannot be schematized, quantified, or taught, only dramatized via the unique form of the novel.

It is here that the topic of "Coetzee and Philosophy" touches upon one of the oldest debates in the Western tradition. From Plato to Richard Rorty, thinkers have wondered, or worried, about the proper relationship of philosophy and literature. As is recounted again and again, Plato banished the poets from the republic because in creating fictions they muddled the waters of truth itself. But Plato told us this through fiction. What are the Socratic dialogues if not literary works in their own right? Indeed, Socrates may be the most compelling character ever created.

Although there were some notable exceptions, Kierkegaard and Nietzsche foremost among them, it was not until midway through the twentieth century that the literary dimension of modern philosophy was properly addressed. Even then it took figures at the margins of academic philosophy to suggest that literature might play as important a role in moral discourse as philosophy. Iris Murdoch, who penned both prose and philosophy, is a case in point. She insisted time and again that the novel was much better positioned to inculcate our senses of love and empathy than any analytical treatise. Arguing against an overly scientific conception of philosophy, Murdoch stressed that "the most essential and fundamental aspect of culture is the study of literature, since this is an education in how to picture and understand human situations." In her opinion, "we are moral agents before we are scientists," and we need to foster our imaginative abilities to inhabit the perspectives of others before we can apply a logical gloss to our moral existence.[8] The fact of the matter, for Murdoch, is that we do not live our lives as rational decision-making machines. Literature's ability to depict, nay, to dramatize this "darker, less fully conscious, less steadily rational image of the dynamics of the human personality" exposes this fact time and again, reminding us not only of the importance of imagination and empathy but also the limits of the rationalist view of the world.[9]

Some philosophers, such as the Wittgenstein scholar Cora Diamond, have taken Murdoch's defense of the importance of literature for moral philosophy to heart. In particular, Diamond appreciates literature's capacity to broaden moral philosophical discourse beyond the categories of "action and choice" so as to address what she calls, after Murdoch, an individual's "texture of being"—the whole messy complex of their everyday lives.[10] Alice Crary, restating and reinforcing Diamond's position, has similarly argued for a wider conception of both objectivity and rationality. Literature, in her opinion, can help get us past the tendency to see morality as little more than the realm of judgments and justifications; it can help us to see that morality in fact addresses *"nothing less than individuals' entire personalities, the whole complicated weaves of their lives."*[11]

Martha Nussbaum is another thinker for whom literature holds great moral potential. Like Diamond and Crary, she, too, wants "to bring novels into moral philosophy," and she is careful to explain that the desire to *"add"* novels to philosophy is not the same as the urge to *"substitute"* them for it. Indeed, she is no fan of sweeping condemnations of "systematic ethical theory" or "'Western rationality,'" as she has explained in *Love's Knowledge* and other works.[12] But unlike Diamond and Crary, her vision of a literature-inflected moral philosophy does not look ahead to a new conception of reality, rationality, or objectivity. Instead, it looks back to the source of all "practical" reflection: namely, Aristotle.[13]

Whether looking back to a time when poetic and philosophical reflection shared a common practical aim (Nussbaum) or ahead to a time when overly narrow conceptions of reason are no more than a relic of a misguided positivist past (Diamond and Crary), these philosophers have done a great deal to bring literature into current philosophical debate. It was Richard Rorty, however, who did the most to dismantle the barrier erected—primarily by analytical philosophers, who thought they had finally put philosophy on the path towards pure science—between philosophy and literature. No doubt this was in large part attributable to his penchant for sometimes dramatic overstatement. Near the end of his life Rorty began to argue that philosophy was in fact no more than a "transitional genre" between religion and literature. In his words, "Intellectuals of the West have since the Renaissance progressed through three stages: they have hoped for redemption first from God, then from philosophy, and now from literature."[14] For Rorty, "religion and philosophy were stepping-stones," way stations on the path toward literature, which seeks not to offer grand outlines of communal salvation and redemption (in the case of religion) or timeless and transcendental truth (in the case of philosophy), but to edify, to shape and possibly transform individual, autonomous selves.[15] Far from proving Aristotle right, or reconfiguring our conception of reason, literature, for Rorty, simply helps us to grow up. He saw it as a sign of intellectual maturation, in fact, that we now turn to novelists for inspiration and insight, for it is they who teach us to truly value irony and contingency. Literature teaches us that "redemption is above all else individual, private, matter"; while we can and should hope for social cooperation and solidarity, the terrible history of the twentieth century makes clear that we cannot hope for manmade redemption on a mass scale.[16]

Rorty did not always subscribe to such a teleological account of literature's evolution out of philosophy. In fact the young Rorty, as Neil Gross's recent intellectual biography makes clear, was quite interested in continuing the philosophical project as it was construed by midcentury analytic thinkers.[17] Even when he did part company with his colleagues in *Philosophy and the Mirror of Nature* (1979), his internal critique of the discipline, he did not call for the abandonment of philosophy, merely a reorientation of it—"there is no danger of philosophy's 'coming to an end,'" he maintained.[18] So far as philosophers sought to edify rather than find and define, they might be able to contribute to society. It was only when they conceived of their work along narrowly scientific lines that Rorty thought his colleagues erred. To think that philosophers might, like Newton, unlock the secrets of nature, that they might at last uncover the true picture—the mirror—of reality, was hubristic and misguided. But once this residual arrogance was discarded, philosophers still might contribute to what Rorty called, after Michael Oakeshott, "the continuing conversation of the West."[19]

By the time of his next major work, however, Rorty had all but abandoned the hope that philosophy had any positive role to play in this regard. In fact, *Contingency, Irony, Solidarity* (1989) went so far as to urge a "general turn against theory and toward narrative."[20] Foreshadowing this recommendation, the book opens with a lengthy epigraph from Milan Kundera's *The Art of the Novel*, which argues that the conversation of the West, which is founded on individualism and tolerance, is safeguarded not by philosophy but by the "wisdom of the novel." "The treasure chest in the history of the novel" is what protects our deepest knowledge of, simultaneously, solidarity and individuality, compassion and the well-lived life, which is why Rorty makes Nabokov, Orwell, and Proust outshine Derrida, Heidegger, and Nietzsche in the book that follows Kundera's quote.

Rorty eventually came to the conclusion that literature and philosophy, insofar as they speak, respectively, for imagination and reason, stand in opposition to each other. By his account, "rationality is a matter of making allowed moves within language games," whereas "imagination creates the games that reason needs to play."[21] In other words, reason is dependent upon imagination; it requires the prior work of creativity to establish the limits of its discourse. As Rorty puts it, "imagination has priority over reason."[22] This egg-or-chicken conundrum would not be of much interest were it not for the fact that it directly affects Rorty's conception of moral behavior. For Rorty, choosing the right action requires imagination far more than reason—that is, the ability to fashion new discourses, possibilities, or identities outshines the ability to make the correct decision within preexisting language games. To put it bluntly, those who read widely in creative literatures are better off in the face of a moral dilemma than those who read deeply in rational philosophy. Fostering the imagination, a faculty that, as we shall see, is so closely allied with care, compassion, and sympathy, is an indispensably important part of moral instruction—and it is something novels do better than philosophical arguments. In Rorty's words: "The advantage that well-read, reflective, leisured people have when it comes to deciding about the right thing to do is that they are more imaginative, not that they are more rational."[23] One gets the sense that, for Rorty, a few inventive novelists can do more good than a whole department of problem-solving philosophers.[24]

Must—should—philosophy come to an end, to be replaced by literature? Is it really no more than a "transitional genre"? No doubt, philosophy could occupy itself for generations with the examination of its own obsolescence (Leszek Kołakowski has written that academic philosophy "keeps itself busy trying to prove that it has indeed died").[25] Heidegger, the greatest end-of-philosophy philosopher of recent times, variously put forth poetry and "thinking" as alternatives.[26] Both had the advantage, he thought, of being science- and metaphysics-free; both were also able to disclose worlds of meaning in new and exciting ways, something Rorty greatly appreciated in Heidegger's later works.[27] But the project of establishing a post-metaphyiscal poetics is perhaps easier suggested than carried out.

After Rorty, it seems unclear whether any secure bridge between the philosophical treatise and the novel can be made, and made to last. Certainly the novelists themselves are none too eager to embrace philosophy as their own. Kundera himself has more recently asserted that "novelistic thinking"—the very stuff that protects the cherished wisdom of the West for him and for Rorty—is "purposely a-philosophic."[28] What does this mean? Simply that literature is

> fiercely independent of any system of preconceived ideas; it does not judge; it does not proclaim truths; it questions, it marvels, it plumbs, its form is highly diverse: metaphoric, ironic, hypothetic, hyperbolic, aphoristic, droll, provocative, fanciful; and mainly it never leaves the magic circle of its characters' lives; those lives feed it and justify it.[29]

Coetzee, I would argue, is closer to this position than anything else. Coetzee's work proposes an embrace of a prereflective empathy that stands in opposition to Nussbaum's stripped-down Aristotelianism as well as Crary's wider conception of rationality. To put it another way, he is closer to the critique of "Western rationality" than any of the philosophers besides Rorty might wish him to be. Following Rorty's terminology, we could say that he exhibits more imagination than rationality. If there is room for reason in his works, it is only a very different kind of reason. Coetzee cannot be pressed into the ranks of philosophy without damaging his project; he remains, necessarily, a novelist.[30] His works both dramatize and refashion the arguments that thinkers like Murdoch and Rorty have articulated, achieving something very different than their treatises, something with far more moral force. Just as moral life cannot be anatomized into a series of philosophical puzzles, his novels cannot be treated as mere fodder for moral theory. Their very existence as novels demands that we rethink the aims and methods of moral discourse itself.

THE LIMITS OF REASON

Many of Coetzee's protagonists are intellectuals. Whether they are academics and writers (as in *Age of Iron*, *Disgrace*, *Elizabeth Costello*, and *Diary of a Bad Year*) or imperial bureaucrats (as in *Dusklands* and *Waiting for the Barbarians*), they learn to feel as much as think. When they do not, it is only because their allegiance to Western rationality is so total that they cannot break from it without slipping into madness; they are incapable of imagining what Rorty would call new "practical identities" for themselves in the face of a novel life context.[31] Take, for example, Eugene Dawn, the narrator of "The Vietnam Project," which constitutes half of *Dusklands*. Dawn is a minor functionary in the U.S. Department of Defense, struggling to complete the magnum opus from which the novella draws its name. From the beginning, it is clear that Dawn encounters the world through only his reflective, Cartesian self. His sun-drenched San Diego surroundings, his coworkers, his family, even his body are all alien to him. Indeed, his "body betrays" him, preventing him from spending even longer hours in the basement of the top-secret archives, researching the potential for "mythography" in American propaganda in Vietnam. His wife and his own body are no more than obstacles to his work (*Dusklands*, 7, 8).

Aside from obsessiveness, there is nothing to suggest that Eugene Dawn is unlike so many others, both near and far, who kept the American war machine running in Southeast Asia. His report is filled with the platitudes of imperial hubris: Western propaganda fails, he suggests, because it assumes that the Vietnamese are like us, Cartesian, doubting subjects. But just the opposite is true, according to Dawn's report; they understand only the "father-voice," which the United States must be relentless in utilizing (24–25). The father cannot seem weak, hence Dawn's enthusiasm for "the return of total air-war" (28). But shortly after penning these words, Dawn's physical and psychic health begins to fail:

> I am in a bad way as I write these words. My health is poor. I have a treacherous wife, an unhappy home, unsympathetic superiors. I suffer from headaches. I sleep badly. I am eating myself out. If I knew how to take holidays perhaps I would take one. But I see things and have a duty toward history that cannot wait. What I say is in pieces. I am sorry. But we can do it. It is my duty to point out our duty. I sit in libraries and see things. I am in an honorable line of bookish men who have sat in libraries and had visions of great clarity. I name no names. You must listen. I speak with the voice of things to come.
> (29)

These are the words of a man on the edge of a nervous breakdown—an overeducated, overly dutiful minion in the vast apparatus of the American military industrial complex.

It comes as no surprise that Dawn has read—no, studied—Bellow's *Herzog*. But unlike Bellow's protagonist, Coetzee's is no clown. His breakdown is not comical, the quixotic wanderings of an absentminded professor. When Dawn finally snaps and abducts his child, the result is not a comic escapade but a thriller. He flees. He checks himself and his son into the "Loco Motel," which is nestled beneath the San Bernardino Mountains (and is an obvious foreshadowing of what is to come). He loses touch with the world around him. He dreams of "the rapture of pure contemplation" that his new surroundings will supposedly afford. But inspiration and insight do not come. His child begins to cry and complain. Dawn, who is in no mood for the "irrational behavior" of a child, sinks into foul moods, followed quickly by paranoia (38). It is not long before the police track them down. A standoff and then a confrontation ensue. The father endangers the child.

The final section of "The Vietnam Project" is narrated from a facility where Dawn undergoes psychiatric treatment. He participates fully in the process, convinced that reflection and contemplation will restore him. To the end, he remains a rationalist: "I approve of the enterprise of exploring the self. I am deeply interested in my self. I should like to see in black and white an explanation of this disturbed and disturbing act of mine" (46). Unable to think of others before his breakdown, Dawn is equally incapable of doing so afterward. He cannot think from the perspective of anybody but himself. He cannot escape the prison house of his overactive cogito. Even "in his cell in the heart of America," he continues to "ponder and ponder" (49).

The only relief is after lunch, when, as he explains in his deadpan manner, "I take my capsule and sleep" (48).

Dawn's overdeveloped rationalism, like his overdeveloped sense of duty (to knowledge, to country, to history), is his undoing. Like Adolf Eichmann, the good Kantian who only carried out his duties, even if it meant sending Jews to their deaths, Dawn is never irrational.[32] But if his story, like Eichmann's, teaches anything, it is that reason alone is not enough. Hyperrationality is irrationality. It obscures and corrodes as much as it uncovers and sustains; it has the potential to reduce others, even ourselves, to little more than objects for contemplation, to pawns in a specific rule-governed game. Dawn ponders and ponders, but he does not feel. He does not empathize, does not sympathize. Any concern he might have for others, even for his own body, is overshadowed by the need to serve the full pursuit of insight and vision. There is no room for imagination in his world. What Arendt said of Eichmann applies to him as well: "An inability to *think*, namely, to think from the standpoint of somebody else," is his most defining characteristic.[33]

Perhaps because "The Vietnam Project" is one of his first published works, it is also one of Coetzee's bleakest. There is a youthful, *Twilight Zone*-esque revelry in the hopelessness of Dawn's case. It is not a story of redemption. Dawn does not atone for his deeds, does not become a better person; he only declines toward the inevitable fall (like the empire he serves, we are to surmise). A similarly pessimistic streak runs throughout much of Coetzee's earlier fiction. In anticipation of Giorgio Agamben's claim that the concentration camp is the "Nomos of the Modern," the Kafka-esque *Life and Times of Michael K* depicts a world in which outsiders are shuttled from camp to camp, without reason or warning.[34] And in "The Narrative of Jacobus Coetzee" (the second half of *Dusklands*) and *Waiting for the Barbarians*, the imperial adventurers and men of letters who confront the wildest, deepest, darkest territories beyond the camp, the areas outlying the edge of empire, are little disposed to empathy. Jacobus Coetzee, an eighteenth-century explorer of Southern Africa, considers himself, like Dawn, "a tool in the hands of history." He fancies himself a curator of civilization who brings "light to what is dark." The natives of the remote interior are "people of limited being," in need of the stern, guiding hand of a master—a belief that of course justifies the most vicious brutalities, all in the name of what was once upon a time referred to as the "civilizing mission" of empire (*Dusklands*, 106).[35] Here reason is not just the antithesis to imagination but a the cornerstone of a vicious ideology of power and domination.

The dialectic of Enlightenment, which Horkheimer and Adorno dissected during the darkest days of the Second World War, is on full display in Coetzee's critique of imperial reason, whether historical (colonial Africa) or more contemporary (American involvement in Vietnam).[36] That rationalization can lead to brutalization—a "new kind of barbarism" is what Horkheimer and Adorno called it—is a fact that he all but takes for granted.[37] But by the time of *Waiting for the Barbarians* he had begun to create characters who, though they may not, in the end, rise up against it, at least have doubts about the imperial power unleashed by the victory of the Enlightenment. They offer counternarratives that challenge the supposedly self-evident superiority of Western civilization. *Waiting for the Barbarians*, for example, is an internal critique. The magistrate who narrates the tale is, like Dawn, no more than a cog in the imperial machine. Unlike his predecessor, however, his faith in the imperial mission begins to waver. His whole life he "believed in civilized behaviour," only to be taught by "the new men of Empire," the military men, that such notions as civilized behavior are, at the end of the day, as quaint and irrelevant as his amateur archeological hobbies (*Waiting for the Barbarians*, 24). He is of the old guard, someone who believed, or duped himself into believing, that empire was compatible, if not synonymous, with law and decency. But the civilizing mission, he eventually realizes, is nothing more than a rhetorical sham (part of what Coetzee calls, in his critical writings, "the repertoire of thinking by which Europe held sway over" other lands [*White Writing*, 10]). Indeed, civilization itself is part of the problem. As the military overtakes his small, far-flung outpost, transforming it into a gulag for so-called barbarians, our narrator sardonically interprets their prison building as the final blooming of "the black flower of civilization" itself (*Waiting for the Barbarians*, 79).[38]

The Magistrate's moral awakening in *Waiting for the Barbarians* does not come quickly, but it would be incorrect to say that it is the product of slow and careful deliberation. There is no moral balance sheet to be drawn up, discussed, and debated. Instead, what finally convinces him of the evils of empire is an immediate and visceral reaction to bodily harm. Once the colonel, with whom our narrator has sparred from the start, begins to imprison and torture the alleged barbarians under his nose, the Magistrate can no longer turn a blind eye to the realities of the civilizing mission. Indeed, the reduction of the imperial other to mere corporeality is what eventually leads him to outright insubordination, the punishment for which entails that he, too, will be reduced to mere embodiment. Rounded up with the barbarians, he is not spared their fate:

> The wound on my cheek, never washed or dressed, is swollen and inflamed. A crust like a fat caterpillar has formed on it. My left eye is a mere slit, my nose a shapeless throbbing lump. I must breathe through my mouth.
>
> I lie in the reek of old vomit obsessed with the thought of water. I have had nothing to drink for two days.

> In my suffering there is nothing ennobling. Little of what I call suffering is even pain. What I am made to undergo is subjection to the most rudimentary needs of my body: to drink, to relieve itself, to find the posture in which it is least sore.
>
> (*Waiting for the Barbarians*, 115)

Under the weight of extreme bodily harm, the Cartesian cogito breaks down. As Joseph Slaughter has argued in reference to French policies in Algeria, torturers attempt "to fragment their victims' subjectivity, they resort to a violent destruction of the signifier-signified relationship."[39] Even the category of pain cannot be processed in the torture chambers, which are always but a short step away from the interrogation cells. As Elaine Scarry pointed out long ago, in her careful examination of the extensive collection of testimony from torture survivors held by Amnesty International, intense physical pain unmakes the world of the tortured. It nullifies language. It reduces rational expression to monosyllabic cries and yelps.[40]

Pain transforms the Cartesian *cogito* into pure body. Tormented, tortured, or abused, the body swallows the rational self, crowds and overtakes it. Pain also individualizes, in a fashion. Pain is not just yours or mine, because intense pain attacks the worlds that define and sustain what is yours and what is mine. Pain reaffirms the corporeal facticity of our embodiment, but in a way that is not accessible to the light of rational reflection. There are literally no words to describe the exact experience of torture. Even the embodied phenomenology of somebody like Heidegger or Merleau-Ponty—or, more recently, continental feminism—which all attempt to locate existence somewhere other than the Cartesian *cogito*, cannot offer us this.

Coetzee's awareness of the body in pain is at the heart of his critique of reason and the rational subject it presupposes. Like Beckett, whom the young Coetzee studied intently (even traveling to the Ransom Center in Austin to examine its collection of Beckett manuscripts), he is unsparing in his critique of the Cartesian *cogito*. He has written of Beckett's "sustained skeptical raids on Descartes." It is tempting to turn these words back upon Coetzee himself. But Beckett is "satiric," whereas Coetzee, I would argue, is moral. At the end of the day, Beckett desires only that "we do not lie to ourselves" (*Inner Workings*, 172). Coetzee, however, wants more than that. He wants us not just to avoid the fictions of the subject but to embrace actively the sufferings of others. He wants us to get out of ourselves, literally, and to inhabit the pain of the oppressed.[41]

Precisely because pain is beyond or outside of rational discourse, it cannot be rationally dissected. So Coetzee, like novelists before him, dramatizes pain; he pushes it into the space of the imagination where it can be accessed by others. He describes the way in which pain thoroughly destabilizes the self. Elizabeth Curren, the main character in *Age of Iron*, battles cancer. The only respite from the pain that governs her daily life is the capsule:

> Whatever else it brings, the Diconal at least brings sleep or a simulacrum of sleep. As the pain recedes, as time quickens, as the horizon lifts, my attention, concentrated like a burning glass on the pain, can slacken for a while; I can draw breath, unclench my balled hands, straighten my legs. Give thanks for this mercy, I say to myself: for the sick body stunned, for the soul drowsy, half out of its casing, beginning to float.

"But the respite," Mrs. Curren knows, "is never long. Clouds come over, thoughts begin to bunch, to take the dense, angry life of a swarm of flies" (*Age of Iron*, 182). At the start of the novel, Mrs. Curren's thoughts are not yet crowded by pain. She knows she is ill, terminally ill, but she is resolved. She does not turn away from her own mortality. In good Heideggerian fashion, she is determined, as she says, "to embrace death as my own, mine alone" (*Age of Iron*, 6).[42] Yet as the pain increases, as the cancer progresses, she begins to realize that she cannot control everything—not even her body, not even her death. This insight sends her searching not for solitude but for community. She discovers that, *pace* Heidegger, even death is something shared.

Sensitizing us to pain, and to the pain of others specifically, has been a central part of the novel's attempt, from the genre's inception, to educate our sentiments. As scholars have attested for some time now, the novel proved an indispensable part of the Enlightenment's moral education in this regard. Realizing that mechanical reason alone could not foster sympathy (closer to what we would call empathy today), David Hume, Adam Smith, and J. J. Rousseau all turned to the novel—Rousseau even wrote one, *Julie, or the New Héloïse* (1761)—as the preferred site for moral instruction. Smith's *The Theory of Moral Sentiments* (1759) would not have been possible were it not for the astonishing popularity of epistolary novels such as Samuel Richardson's best-selling *Pamela, or Virtue Rewarded* (1740) and *Clarissa, or the History of a Young Lady* (1747-1748). By all accounts, these works, like Rousseau's later addition to the genre, almost single-handedly cultivated in their readers a refined sense of empathy, which Smith made the hallmark of his moral thinking. As intellectual historian Jerrold Seigel has argued, "Literary culture was increasingly serving readers and writers in Smith's time as a site where participation in the lives of others served as a vehicle of self-formation."[43] Vicariously participating in another's emotional and physical sufferings, in other words, is what allowed eighteenth-century readers to become moral beings. More recently, the cultural historian Lynn Hunt has even suggested that these novels were an important step forward in the emerging language of human rights. Insofar as epistolary novels extracted from their readers a certain kind of empathy for others, even across "class, sex, and national lines," they cleared the way for the notion of universal, individual rights that would animate not only the American and French Revolutions, but the human-rights revolutions of the twentieth century, from the Nuremberg Trial after the Second World War to the establishment of the United Nations and its 1948 Universal Declaration of Human Rights.[44] If we have forgotten that the Enlightenment rests on sentimental foundations as much as rational ones, it is only because the scientific rationalism of the Enlightenment has had a much more lasting impact on the Western tradition than the seemingly antiquated literature of the eighteenth century. But if the scientific and materialist achievements of Enlightenment rationality are predicated upon, as Horkheimer and Adorno suggested, the exclusion of "emotion and finally all human expression" from the realm of "knowledge and cognition," then perhaps it is time to revisit these long-forgotten sources of moral instruction.[45] As Robert Solomon has argued, the emotions are, after all, "an essential part of the substance of ethics itself."[46]

It is worth pointing out that *Age of Iron* is an epistolary novel. It takes the form of an extended letter that Mrs. Curren pens for her estranged daughter, who has fled, in disgust, Apartheid-era South Africa. Although Curren tries hard to remain detached, to offer merely a clear portrait of the world her daughter has left behind, she cannot ignore the fact that her letter is in its own way an emotional appeal. "Do not read in sympathy with me," she pleas, urging her daughter to read her testimony with "a cold eye" (*Age of Iron*, 104). But she knows that her letter offers little possibility of such: "It is through my eyes that you see; the voice that speaks in your head is mine. . . . It is my thoughts that you think, my despair that you feel, and also the first stirrings of welcome for whatever will put an end to thought: sleep, death" (103). Because the epistolary novel, as Lynn Hunt explains, allows for readers to observe, to witness intimately "the unfolding of an inner self," it all but forces the reader to undergo the transformation(s) of the protagonist. It puts us in another's shoes. Like Elizabeth Curren, we hope to emerge, by the end of the novel, from "a state of ugliness." We, too, suffer alongside her, wanting to be "saved." We, too, want to "love." Though she desires the warmth of emotion, this retired professor of classics, of dead and lifeless languages, fears that, like her rambling letter to her faraway daughter, she is becoming more "abstract, more abstracted . . . disembodied, crystalline, bloodless" (136–37). She craves emotional warmth and well-being, but she cannot fully give herself over to it. Likewise, neither can we.

That Elizabeth Curren dies without unequivocally embracing the warmth of emotions like forgiveness and love—emotions, Coetzee is arguing, that are necessary for the establishment of a post-Apartheid community—suggests that the path of such emotions as empathy is not a quick nor easy way out of the rational binds of our age (and what was Apartheid but the rationale of colonialism taken to its horrifically logical conclusion?).[47] We, too, are unprepared for such a leap as Elizabeth Curren yearns to take, perhaps because the Enlightenment's legacy of sentimental education has been overshadowed by the technical perfectionism of mechanical rationality for too long, deforming us along the way. In Horkheimer and Adonro's formulation, "reason displaces all love."[48] As a result, we moderns are accustomed to interacting with one another and the wider world around us in a purely materialist, scientific fashion. In *Diary of a Bad Year*, JC even goes so far as to complain that this is a result of a peculiarly American kind of worldview: "The body as conceived in America, the American body, is a complex machine comprising a vocal module, a sexual module, and several more, even a psychological module. Inside the body-machine the ghostly self checks read-outs and taps keys, giving commands which the body obeys" (*Diary of a Bad Year*, 133). We treat our bodies as machines for living and our environment, interpersonal relations included, as no more than a nexus of problems to be processed and eventually solved. We expect all answers to come easily, like solutions to mathematical equations. But empathy, which forces upon us an entirely different perspective of the world, is messier than this. There is no finality, no finish line to cross in our ongoing attempts to think from the perspective of others. We, too, must struggle to the very end; for as long as injustice remains and suffering continues, empathy will remain a dilemma for reader and author alike. Elizabeth Curren teaches us that there are no easy cures.

Coetzee's later novels are almost exclusively about empathy and compassion, which Martha Nussbaum has described as the ability "to follow the story of another's plight with vivid imagination."[49] We might also think of them as explorations of generosity. As J. Glenn Gray once explained, generosity "is the capacity to participate imaginatively in others' experiences, to explore freely many worlds, and to give ourselves to them for their own sake without calculation of returns."[50] Seen in this light, Coetzee's novels are not merely lessons in generosity, but generous acts in and of themselves; they push back the limits of our sympathies, extending the space of our concern for others. In these works, empathy remains an open question, not just with regard to our fellow humans but to animals as well. Indeed, if Coetzee is discussed by philosophers at all these days, it is primarily for his forays into the murky realm—Agamben refers to it as "the open"—between humans and animals.[51] Making explicit a theme that, we might say, rested dormant in his earlier works, Coetzee's recent work has taken up specifically the theme of animal suffering, again challenging the narrow confines of rationalist morality. In novels such as *Disgrace* and *Elizabeth Costello*, Coetzee not only pushes the reader to recognize the rights of others, including the most basic right of all, the right to a life free from torture and bodily harm, he also extends these concerns to animals. As Eduardo Mendieta has argued, in an essay devoted to what he calls Coetzee's "zoopoetics," these novels "bring back into the moral ambit" the question of our treatment of animals.[52] Why should not animals also deserve our empathetic embrace, they seem to be saying. Perhaps their suffering, like the suffering of women, minorities, foreigners, and "lower classes" depicted in the epistolary novels of the eighteenth century, is also worthy of our concern.

Disgrace begins with the trials and tribulations of David Lurie, another aging academic, but ends with the almost sacrificial killing of animals. In between we witness the slow and painful evolution of one man, and one country, from a state of disgrace toward a state of grace. To be sure, like *Age of Iron, Disgrace* offers no happy ending, but it does seem to hold out hope that people can change, that they can awaken from their moral immaturity. In this regard, David Lurie is a long way from Eugene Dawn.

Lurie is disgraced at his university, when a student brings a sexual harassment complaint against him, forcing him out. He is again disgraced when his daughter, to whose small farm he has retreated after the university scandal occurs, is viciously raped in his powerless presence. He is disgraced by the racism of his country's past, for which his daughter's abuse seems to be punishment (her rape is a kind of intimidation, meant to force her into the protection of her black neighbors). He is also disgraced, though it takes him some time to realize it, by the treatment of animals in the world around him—so many animals abused, mutilated, abandoned, and forgotten that a compassionate, charity-based euthanasia program comes to seem almost saintly. Whether at the level of the personal, the national, or the species, disgrace stains Lurie's life.

Throughout all of this, Lurie, like the good academic he is, labors on a libretto, an entire opera actually. He attempts to tell the story of Byron in love, in Italy, but his imagination is blocked. He does not know where to begin. It is only when he realizes that the story is not Byron's but that of the poet's lover, Contessa Guiccioli, that the music comes to him. The opera, Lurie realizes, cannot be his, nor even Byron's. It must be hers. And it is not about lust and passion and youth, but the slow, painful trials of love.

Is it love that pushes David Lurie from disgrace to grace? It seems so. Love, which Elizabeth Curren so desperately desired, is what finally rescues Lurie. It is what allows him to see from the other person's perspective. Indeed, as Iris Murdoch has argued, "love is the difficult realisation that something other than oneself is real."[53] It is no accident that he is able to complete his opera only when he sees the story through the eyes of the Contessa and not Byron. The new perspective allows him finally to recognize that behind the feeling of disgrace is egotism, for which love, selfless love, is the only antidote. The animal activist Bev Shaw teaches Lurie this lesson. Her selfless devotion to animals, carried out in her charity clinic, which doubles—painfully, paradoxically—as a euthanasia program for unwanted, un-cared-for animals, is the example he needs: "He and Bev do not speak. He has learned by now, from her, to concentrate all his attention on the animal they are killing, giving it what he no longer has difficulty calling by its proper name: love" (*Disgrace*, 219). It is in the treatment of animals, finally, that we get a glimpse of empathy and compassion. Their suffering educates us, pushes us towards a sentimental awakening. In this, they are Christlike: offered up as sacrificial lambs, they redeem us (so that we, in turn, might redeem them).

That animals are not only worthy of love but can teach us the true meaning of love, namely selflessness, is something also explored in *Elizabeth Costello*. Costello is the perfect Coetzee character, and the book that bears her name is the perfect distillation of Coetzee's preoccupations. In a series of "lessons," we follow Costello as she leads the rather humdrum life of the academic: traveling, attending conferences, delivering lectures. At various points, her lectures, which constitute the bulk of the novel, address issues ranging from Eurocentrism and the ethics of literature to animal rights. The latter has gained the most critical attention, but it is worth remembering that Costello's defense of the rights of animals is part and parcel of a larger critique of Western rationalism itself.[54] Reason, the faculty that distinguishes us from animals, that anoints us *rational animals*, may be no more, Costello suggests, than a specialized jargon:

> Might it not be that the phenomenon we are examining here is, rather than the flowering of a faculty that allows access to the secrets of the universe, the specialism of a rather narrow self-regenerating intellectual tradition whose forte is reasoning, in the same way that the forte of chess players is playing chess, which for its own motives it tries to install at the centre of the universe?
> (*Elizabeth Costello*, 69)

Like Rorty, Costello asks her audiences to abandon the dream of reason as a mirror of nature, to see it as no more than a specialized language game. More important than mastering the game is coming to know the lessons of the heart, for "the heart is the seat of a faculty, *sympathy*, that allows us to share at times the being of another" (*Elizabeth Costello*, 79). Sympathy includes, whereas reason excludes. It is for this reason alone that Rorty thinks we should busy ourselves with "sentimental education" instead of moral reasoning. "Sad and sentimental stories," he argues, have done, will do, more moral good than another distillation of Kantian universal laws. More important than knowing the right thing to do, in other words, is feeling the wrong, which is precisely why we have to imagine ourselves "in the shoes of the despised and oppressed."[55] With this Costello would agree. No doubt Coetzee would, too.[56]

Literature is particularly well suited for the task of putting us in the shoes of the other, and indeed, for expanding our notions of who—or what—even qualifies as "the other." Elizabeth Costello, as a writer, knows this. After all, this is what writers do, what she does. "If I can think my way into the existence of a being who has never existed," she explains, "then I can think my way into the existence of a bat or a chimpanzee or an oyster, any being with whom I share the substrate of life" (*Elizabeth Costello*, 80). The only boundaries to our sympathies are the boundaries of our imagination. In fact, what the narrator of *Diary of a Bad Year* at one point calls "moral meanness" is really no more than the inability to imagine, if not feel, the plight of others (*Diary of a Bad Year*, 4). The more we can imagine the more good we can do. So in order to be good, perhaps we should emulate not the philosophers but the novelists.[57]

THE LESSONS OF LOVE

With Coetzee's corpus in view, we can return to the question of literature's proper relationship to philosophy. Could it be that Coetzee's later work, rather than simply condemning the missteps of Enlightenment rationalism and its ties to imperial brutality, is, in its own fashion, rescuing a lost strand of the Enlightenment, the strand that made the education of moral sentiments as important a task—if not more important—as the pursuit of the mirror of nature? If this is true, we might not need to see literature and philosophy as entirely antagonistic. Instead, we can focus our attention on rescuing a certain kind of reason from the oblivion of forgetfulness. Perhaps he fits into Nussbaum's neo-Aristotelian program. Or maybe, in the fashion of Diamond and Crary, he forces us to expand our narrow conception of rationality. We might even go so far as to suggest an overlap with Habermas's attempt to rescue communicative rationality (the reason of the public sphere) from the logic of calculative rationality (the reason of the system and the machine). From any of these perspectives, perhaps Coetzee's work can be seen as ameliorative rather than accusatory. This seems possible, but it shortchanges the worried tenor of the novels. It glosses over the desperation that they chronicle, the desperation that marks life at the edges of the Western tradition, far from the easy comfort of its many achievements and much closer to its many failures.

What Coetzee's novels do not do is tell us how to live. They give us stories and vocabularies that might help us to expand the boundaries of our sympathies. They might even foster in their readers what Rick Anthony Furtak calls "an emotional orientation or attunement toward the world."[58] But they do not pose, let alone answer, timeless, transcendental questions. They do not seek an external, unshakable foundation for moral discourse. Coetzee consciously chooses ethics over science in this regard: "Whatever one thinks of the psychological origins of love or charity may be," he has written, "one must still act with love and charity" (*Doubling the Point*, 244).[59] For him, moral life is less about conclusive arguments or revelatory discoveries than it is the small actions of everyday existence. Here the novelist's ability to effectively create—or even recreate—the tightly woven fabric of an individual life is indispensible. Such work may not solve our most pressing moral dilemmas, but it will help us to envision acting with love and charity and compassion; at the very least, it might help us to recognize, as Robert Pippin suggests in his study of Henry James, that "the key issue of morality may not be the rational justifiability with which I treat others, but the proper acknowledgement of, and enactment of, a dependence on others without which the process of any justification (any invocation of common normative criteria at all) could not begin."[60]

When all is said and done, the novelist is simply more humble than the philosopher; the scale of his or her work is smaller and more intimate than the philosopher's. Indeed, in his Nobel Lecture, "He and His Man," Coetzee does not offer a necessarily exalted portrait of the modern novelist. Writers, he suggests, indirectly, are rather like lowly seaman—"they are deckhands, toiling in the rigging." Busy with the tasks of their various voyages, they have little time to acknowledge even one another: "their eyes lashed by the spray, their hands burned by the cordage, they pass each other by, too busy even to wave." But where are they headed, these task men, so busy with the chores and duties at hand that they cannot even acknowledge their fellow laborers? From where do they eventually return, and with what news?

If it is the novelist who extends our sympathies, who sensitizes us to suffering, then it is news of suffering that these sailors must bring back across the high seas. Like Robinson Crusoe, they must return from faraway lands, bringing news from the edges of civilization itself.[61] But "what species of man can it be who will dash so busily hither and thither across the kingdom, from one spectacle of death to another (clubbings, beheadings), sending in report after report?" (*The Nobel Lecture*, 19, 8) A species of man like Coetzee, we are forced to conclude. It is he who, like so many of his characters, has traveled to the edges of empire; he who has reported of suffering there; he who has told us "sad and sentimental" stories; he who has exhibited empathy. Why? Not for prizes, not for glory, certainly; deckhands are never afforded such things. Maybe it is only to convince us to pull more people, more animals—more creatures, finally—onto the ship. Otherwise, too many of us will live our lives with "neither loving hands nor a loving heart." And if that is the case then we, like Paul Rayment, will have been "lost in a choppy sea off a strange coast" for far too long (*Slow Man*, 261, 237).[62]

Notes

1. The press release is available online at http://nobelprize.org/nobel_prizes/literature/laureates/2003/press.html.
2. Ibid.
3. L. Wittgenstein, *On Certainty*, ed. G. E. M. Anscombe and G. H. von Wright, trans. D. Paul and G. E. M. Anscombe (1969; New York: Harper, 1972), 61e. On Wittgenstein's sometimes eccentric behavior, see R. Monk, *Ludwig Wittgenstein: The Duty of Genius* (New York: Penguin, 1990).
4. S. Bellow, *Herzog* (1964; New York: Penguin, 1976), 271.
5. F. O'Connor, "Good Country People," in *Collected Works* (New York: Library of America, 1988), 268.
6. I discuss the Heideggerian overtones of O'Connor's short story at greater length in the third chapter of my dissertation, "Being Here: Heidegger in America" (Ph.D. diss., City University of New York, 2006).
7. "Good Country People" first appeared in the June 1955 issue of *Harper's Bazaar*.
8. I. Murdoch, "The Idea of Perfection," in *The Sovereignty of Good* (London: Routledge and Kegan Paul, 1970), 34.
9. Ibid., 44.
10. C. Diamond, "Having a Rough Story About What Moral Philosophy Is," in *The Realistic Spirit: Wittgenstein, Philosophy, and the Mind* (Cambridge, Mass.: MIT Press, 1991), 374.
11. A. Crary, *Beyond Moral Judgment* (Cambridge, Mass.: Harvard University Press, 2007), 45. For Crary's specific comments regarding literature and philosophy, see especially chapter 4, "Moral Thought Beyond Moral Judgment: The Case of Literature."
12. M. C. Nussbaum, *Love's Knowledge: Essays on Philosophy and Literature* (New York: Oxford University Press, 1990), 24, 27.
13. Ibid., 44.
14. R. Rorty, "Philosophy as a Transitional Genre," in *Philosophy as Cultural Politics: Philosophical Papers*, vol. 4 (Cambridge: Cambridge University Press, 2007), 91.
15. Ibid., 95.
16. Ibid., 102.
17. N. Gross, *Richard Rorty: The Making of an American Philosopher* (Chicago: University of Chicago Press, 2008).

18. R. Rorty, *Philosophy and the Mirror of Nature* (Princeton: Princeton University Press, 1979), 394.
19. Ibid. It is interesting to note that Rorty thought of himself for quite some time as a "therapeutic positivist," as somebody who sought to remedy rather than overthrow philosophical positivism. See N. Gross, *Richard Rorty: The Making of an American Philosopher* (Chicago: University of Chicago Press, 2008), 197.
20. R. Rorty, *Contingency, Irony, Solidarity* (New York: Cambridge University Press, 1989), xvi.
21. R. Rorty, "Pragmatism and Romanticism," in *Philosophy as Cultural Politics: Philosophical Papers*, vol. 4 (Cambridge: Cambridge University Press, 2007), 115.
22. Ibid.
23. R. Rorty, "Kant vs. Dewey: The Current Situation of Moral Philosophy," in *Philosophy as Cultural Politics: Philosophical Papers*, vol. 4 (Cambridge: Cambridge University Press, 2007), 201.
24. Here Rorty is channeling the influence of Annette Baier's readings of Hume. In "Kant vs. Dewey," Rorty describes Baier as his "favorite contemporary moral philosopher" (187).
25. L. Kołakowski, *Metaphysical Horror*, rev. ed., ed. A. Kołakowska (Chicago: Chicago University Press, 2001), 7-8.
26. To take two examples (from different periods), see M. Heidegger, "The End of Philosophy and the Task of Thinking," in *On Time and Being*, trans. J. Stambaugh (New York: Harper Torchbooks, 1972), 55-73; and "Why Poets?" in *Off the Beaten Track*, ed. and trans. J. Young and K. Haynes (Cambridge: Cambridge University Press, 2002), 200-241.
27. See, for example, the essays collected in the second volume of Rorty's collected papers, *Essays on Heidegger and Others* (Cambridge: Cambridge University Press, 1991).
28. M. Kundera, *The Curtain: An Essay in Seven Parts*, trans. L. Asher (New York: Harper Collins, 2007), 71.
29. Ibid.
30. I am not the first, nor will I be the last, to see in Coetzee's fictional works an attempt to transcend the ethical limitations of philosophy. According to Derek Attridge, Coetzee's work demonstrates that "the impulses and acts that shape our lives as ethical beings—impulses and acts of respect, of love, of trust, of generosity—cannot be adequately represented in the discourses of philosophy, politics, or theology, but are in their natural element in literature" (D. Attridge, *J. M. Coetzee and the Ethics of Reading: Literature in the Event* [Chicago: University of Chicago Press, 2004], xi).
31. See Rorty, "Kant vs. Dewey," 201.
32. See H. Arendt, *Eichmann in Jerusalem: A Report on the Banality of Evil* (1963; New York: Penguin, 1994).
33. Ibid., 49.

34. See Agamben, *Homo Sacer: Sovereign Power and Bare Life*, trans. D. Heller-Roazen (Stanford, Calif.: Stanford University Press, 1998), part 3.
35. Much has been written about the rhetoric of empire. For a clear and concise case study, see A. L. Conklin, *A Mission to Civilize: The Republican Idea of Empire in France and West Africa, 1895–1930* (Stanford, Calif.: Stanford University Press, 1997). It should also be pointed out that Coetzee is a critic not just of historical imperialism but neo-imperialism as well. He has also spoken of the "colonising process" of neoliberalism, "of the new world order." "It passes my comprehension," he has said, "that we academic intellectuals in Africa and of Africa should want to spend our time tracking down the residual ghosts of the nineteenth-century British Empire, when it is clearly more urgent to recognise and confront the new global imperialism" ("Critic and Citizen," 111).
36. M. Horkheimer and T. W. Adorno, *Dialectic of Enlightenment*, trans. J. Cumming (New York: Continuum, 1972).
37. Ibid., xi.
38. Later on, the Magistrate even refers to himself as "old-fashioned" and worries that, insofar as he is beginning to criticize the course of imperial policy, he has become "unsound" (52). The implication of this, of course, is that civilized persons who oppose brutality are irrational or unstable. It is worth pointing out that that Coetzee borrowed the phrase "the black flower of civilization" from Nathaniel Hawthorne. See Siddhartha Deb, "Señor Year," *Bookforum* (December/January 2008), 24.
39. Joseph Slaughter, "A Question of Narration: The Voice in International Human Rights Law," *Human Rights Quarterly* 19, no. 2 (1997): 427.
40. E. Scarry, *The Body in Pain: The Making and Unmaking of the World* (New York: Oxford University Press, 1985).
41. While not specifically admitting to Beckett's influence on these works, Coetzee has explained that his spirit is nonetheless present in them: "It is unlikely that Beckett would have gripped me if there hadn't been in him that unbroken concern with rationality, that string leading men savagely or crazily pushing reason beyond its limits" (*Doubling the Point*, 26).
42. On Heidegger and the idea of "being-towards-death," see *Being and Time*, trans. J. Macquarrie and E. Robinson (San Francisco: Harper & Row, 1962), paragraphs 50–53.
43. J. Seigel, *The Idea of the Self: Thought and Experience in Western Europe Since the Seventeenth Century* (Cambridge: Cambridge University Press, 2005), 160.
44. L. Hunt, *Inventing Human Rights: A History* (New York: Norton, 2007), 38. Although he studies the bildungsroman rather than the epistolary novel and remains somewhat more sanguine about the hegemonic role of Western literary culture in the world today, Joseph Slaughter similarly suggests that the "novelistic wing of human rights" has done as much—if not more—to "naturalize" the notion of rights as official legal and political

45. Horkheimer and Adorno, *Dialectic of Enlightenment*, 91. For a different assessment of Enlightenment sentimentality, see J. A. Steintrager, *Cruel Delight: Enlightenment Culture and the Inhuman* (Bloomington: Indiana University Press, 2004).
46. R. C. Solomon, *In Defense of Sentimentality* (Oxford: Oxford University Press, 2004), 9.
47. In his Jerusalem Prize Speech from 1987, Coetzee suggested, tellingly, that "at the heart of the unfreedom of the hereditary masters of South Africa is a failure of love" (*Doubling the Point*, 97).
48. Horkheimer and Adorno, *Dialectic of Enlightenment*, 116.
49. M. Nussbaum, "Under Pressure," *Times Literary Supplement*, October 19, 2007, 5. Here Nussbaum is drawing upon the work of the social psychologist Daniel Batson.
50. J. G. Gray, *The Promise of Wisdom: An Introduction to the Philosophy of Education* (Philadelphia: Lippincott, 1968), 80.
51. G. Agamben, *The Open: Man and Animal*, trans. K. Attell (Stanford, Calif.: Stanford University Press, 2004). See also E. L. Santner, *On Creaturely Life: Rilke, Benjamin, Sebald* (Chicago: University of Chicago Press, 2006).
52. E. Mendieta, "Zoopoetics: Coetzee's Animals and Philosophy," unpublished manuscript, 2007. Mendieta goes a step further and argues that our relationship to animals, at least as portrayed by Coetzee, in fact pushes us to, and beyond, the limits of an anthropocentric view of the world. I do not have the space to do this argument justice here, but I think Coetzee's use of animals is less instrumental than this.
53. Iris Murdoch, "The Sublime and the Good," in *Existentialists and Mystics: Writings on the Philosophy and Literature*, ed. Peter Conradi, intro. George Steiner (New York: Penguin, 1998), 215.
54. See, for example, C. Bailey, "On the Backs of Animals: The Valorization of Reason in Contemporary Animal Ethics," *Ethics and the Environment* 10, no. 1 (Spring 2005): 1–17.
55. R. Rorty, "Human Rights, Rationality, and Sentimentality," in *Truth and Progress: Philosophical Papers*, vol. 3 (Cambridge: Cambridge University Press, 1998), 176, 185, 179.
56. In fact, Coetzee has commented on the importance of fiction's role in getting us to think from another's perspective. Fiction works not because it tells but because it acts in this way, it forces us into the minds, the worlds of others. See Coetzee, "Fictional Beings," 133–34.
57. In any case, there is a direct correlation between literacy and social engagement. A 2004 report by the National Endowment for the arts suggested that a decline in reading across the United States has gone hand in hand with a decline in volunteer and charity work. See E. Mendieta, "Introduction: 'Take Care of Freedom and Truth Will Take Care of

Itself': Toward a Postphilosophical Politics," in *Take Care of Freedom and Truth Will Take Care of Itself: Interviews with Richard Rorty*, ed. and intro. E. Mendieta (Stanford, Calif.: Stanford University Press, 2006), xv n. 6.

58. R. A. Furtak, "Skepticism and Perceptual Faith: Henry David Thoreau and Stanley Cavell on Seeing and Believing," *Transactions of the Charles S. Peirce Society* 43, no. 3 (2007): 545.

59. In this regard, Coetzee's novels go beyond Iris Murdoch's plea for a return of the "concept of love" to moral philosophy. Simply gaining conceptual or terminological clarity is not enough. See Murdoch, "On 'God' and 'Good,'" in *The Sovereignty of Good* (London: Routledge & Kegan Paul, 1970), 46. As Terry Eagleton has put it, "The meaning of life is not a solution to a problem, but a matter of living in a certain way" (*The Meaning of Life* [Oxford: Oxford University Press, 2007], 164). It should also be noted that the way of living Eagleton recommends is also, as with Coetzee's novels, the way of love.

60. R. B. Pippin, *Henry James and Modern Moral Life* (Cambridge: Cambridge University Press, 2000), 10-11.

61. The allusion here is of course to Coetzee's novel *Foe*.

62. For conversations, suggestions, and/or judicious comments on earlier versions of this essay, I would like to thank the following individuals: Sarah Burns, Marlene Clark, Rick Furtak, Anton Leist, Kevin McCabe, Roy Scranton, and Peter Singer. A special thanks goes to Eduardo Mendieta, who not only introduced me to Coetzee's novels but also encouraged (and challenged) my evolving analysis of them.

References

Coetzee, J. M. *Age of Iron*. 1990. New York: Penguin, 1998.

———. "Critic and Citizen: A Response." *Pretexts: Literary and Cultural Studies* 9, no. 1 (2000): 109-11.

———. *Diary of a Bad Year*. London: Harvill Secker, 2007.

———. *Disgrace*. New York: Viking, 2005.

———. *Doubling the Point: Essays and Interviews*. Ed. D. Attwell. Cambridge, Mass.: Harvard University Press, 1992.

———. *Dusklands*. 1974. New York: Penguin, 1982.

———. *Elizabeth Costello*. New York: Viking, 2003.

———. "Fictional Beings." *Philosophy, Psychiatry, and Psychology* 10, no. 2 (June 2003): 133-34.

———. *Foe*. New York: Viking, 1987.

———. *Inner Workings: Literary Essays, 2000-2005*. Intro. D. Attridge. New York: Viking, 2007.

———. *Life and Times of Michael K*. New York: Penguin, 1985.

———. *The Nobel Lecture in Literature, 2003*. New York: Penguin, 2004.
———. *Slow Man*. New York: Viking, 2005.
———. "Truth in Autobiography." University of Cape Town Inaugural Lecture, October 3, 1984.
———. *Waiting for the Barbarians*. New York: Penguin, 1982.
———. *White Writing: On the Culture of Letters in South Africa*. New Haven, Conn. : Yale University Press, 1988.

11

J. M. Coetzee, Moral Thinker

Alice Crary

> What great authors are masters of is authority. What is the source of authority...? If authority could be achieved simply by tricks of rhetoric, then Plato was surely justified in expelling the poets from his ideal republic. But what if authority can be attained only by opening the poet-self to some higher force, by ceasing to be oneself and beginning to speak vatically?
> —Señor C, in J. M. Coetzee, *Diary of a Bad Year*

While varying significantly in their narrative forms, settings, and relations to formal realism, the novels of J. M. Coetzee produce an impression of moral intensity that is decidedly constant. In this chapter, I explore sources of the novels' moral power. I argue that one thing we need to see, if we are to understand this power, is that some of the novels are designed to invite rational moral thought through their narrative structures. General claims about the possibility of this sort of necessary cooperation between literary form and (rational) ethical content are a familiar feature of recent conversations about the relationship between moral philosophy and literature, and here I begin by following up on a strand of thought from these conversations, suggesting that a successful defense of a thesis about the inseparability of literary form and ethical content needs to be understood as having philosophically significant implications for how we understand the nature of moral thought. I then turn to Coetzee's novels—and to *Disgrace* in particular—with an eye to showing that this elaboration of themes from ongoing debates about moral philosophy and literature helps to illuminate the novels' ethical interest. I close with a few remarks about how things I say about Coetzee's literary writing find support in his essays and interviews.

SOME QUESTIONS ABOUT THE RELATIONSHIP BETWEEN MORAL PHILOSOPHY AND LITERATURE

These words, as you read them, if you read them, enter you and draw breath again.
—Mrs. Curren, in a letter to her daughter, in J. M. Coetzee, *Age of Iron*

The particular strand of thought in recent discussions about ethics and literature that interests me starts from a disagreement about how to construe the notion of rationality. For the purposes of this chapter, this disagreement can be sketched as follows.

Suppose we speak of the *concept* of rationality, in a philosophically familiar manner, both in reference to our concept of truth-preserving or valid inferences and in reference to our concept of capacities necessary for making such inferences. Suppose we also speak of different *conceptions* of rationality in reference to different specifications of what falls under these two intimately related concepts. Armed with these terms, we can say that recent work in ethics by and large takes for granted a conception of rationality on which any stretch of thought capable of making a contribution to rational understanding must be recognizable as such apart from any tendency to engage a person's feelings, and on which a person's ability to grasp a rational bit of discourse therefore must in principle be independent of her possession of any particular affective endowments. This conception of rationality represents rational tutelage as the prerogative of *arguments*, if we understand "an argument" as a judgment or set of judgments (i.e., a premise or set of premises) that allows an additional concluding judgment (i.e., a conclusion) to be inferred in a manner that does not depend on any propensity of the initial judgment or judgments to engage our sensibilities. Philosophers sometimes speak of argument in a less restrictive manner, but it is argument in this sense that is the trademark of rationality on the conception that now prevails in moral philosophy.

The question of the credentials of this conception is at the heart of recent debates about whether literature as such informs moral philosophy. When combined with the observation that engaging us emotionally is one of literature's hallmarks, the conception appears to support the view that the distinctively literary features of texts cannot possess rational interest or directly contribute to moral philosophy's efforts to promote rational moral understanding. This view, while only reasonably well represented in conversations about ethics and literature,[1] is enormously influential in philosophy. It derives its larger significance from ways in which it creeps into the work of moral philosophers who do not take an explicit interest in the question of how literature can contribute to moral philosophy, shaping the manner in which they bring literary material to bear on their ethical arguments. Moreover, it is important to recognize that restrictions the view places on the philosophical value of literature are consistent with the thought that there are significant respects in which literature can inform moral philosophy. Moral philosophers who actively defend the view frequently stress that literary works may contain arguments of the sort used in moral philosophy, or fragments of such arguments, and that such works may be sources of rich and vivid illustrations of ideas developed within the sorts of arguments that get used in moral philosophy.[2] Anyone steeped in Anglophone ethics will recognize this basic account of the philosophical interest of literature as one that tacitly informs the way in which literary texts for the most part get used within moral philosophy. And if we think of those elements of a work of literature that are designed to address readers' feelings as its "literary" elements, we can ask whether the moral philosophers who adhere strictly to this familiar practice are right to assume, as they effectively do, that it is in principle possible to strip any rationally respectable features of a literary work away from its specifically literary features and that only the former features are directly pertinent to the core tasks of moral philosophy.

Some of the most interesting attempts to expand on this arguably cramped view of literature's significance for moral philosophy turn on reservations about the conception of rationality in which it is grounded.[3] There are, as philosophers with more expansive ambitions sometimes suggest, significant philosophical precedents for thinking that a stretch of thought that shapes our sensitivities in various ways may have rational powers insofar as it does so.[4] Taking "argument" in the restrictive sense that I introduced a moment ago, we might describe the conception of rationality that comes into play here as one on which the realm of the rational is wider than the realm of argument.[5] What gives this *wider* conception of rationality interest in this context is that it opposes constraints that a philosophically more traditional—*narrower*—conception imposes on how literature can contribute to moral philosophy. The wider conception accommodates the possibility that a bit of discourse that appeals to our heart can as such contribute to rational understanding. By the same token, it makes room for the possibility that literature, regarded as literature, can traffic in the kind of rational moral instruction that is of primary interest to moral philosophy. For instance, a novel can lead us to empathize with different characters, to look at specific events from a variety of perspectives, to find ambiguity in a gesture or mode of speech, to adopt a more or less lighthearted attitude toward actions and to see pathos in certain of a character's life passages. The idea here is that, in doing these things, a novel can refine readers' grasp of what things are or are not interesting and important and thereby elicit rational moral thought.

Although I think more light can yet be shed on the grounds for the conclusion that literary works may as such contribute to rational moral understanding, I am not here concerned with this project. My immediate object is to suggest that arguments for this conclusion have more substantial implications for ethics than is frequently supposed. I want to present the outline of a case for showing that, when grounded in the wider conception of rationality, these arguments bring into question deeply engrained assumptions about what moral thinking is like and thus, among other things, make way for a more attractive view of what it comes to to allow that literature as such can elicit such thinking.

A good place to start is with the recognition that the wider conception of rationality necessarily presupposes that certain sensitivities or propensities are internal to all rational capacities. This point is not trivial. There are philosophers who attempt to lay claim to the wider conception, arguing that it is impossible to make the connections constitutive of some (say, ethical) lines of thought apart from the possession of certain sensitivities, while also maintaining that it is in principle possible to register the contents of other (say, natural-scientific) lines of thought apart from the possession of any particular sensitivities. Such philosophers are aptly described as trying to balance attachment to the wider conception of rationality with the narrowly rational idea that genuine features of the world are in principle available to thought apart from any necessary reliance on sensibility. But there is good reason to think that this balancing act is doomed to failure.

Consider in this connection the work of Bernard Williams. Williams signals his interest in what I am calling the wider conception of rationality when he declares that ethical concepts are for the most part "thick" in the sense that there can be no question of grasping what speaks for their applications apart from possession of sensitivities characteristic of participants in practices with the concepts.[6] At the same time, Williams signals his partial retention of the narrower conception of rationality when he insists that it is in theory possible to assimilate the content of sound natural-scientific reflections in the absence of any particular sensitivities.[7] What deserves emphasis is that, in making this gesture toward the narrower conception, Williams commits himself to the idea of a standpoint, free from any contribution from sensibility, from which it is possible to discern not only that any sensitivities required to follow ethical lines of thought must have a tendency to distort our grasp of how things really are but, moreover, that, to the extent that a given ethical line of thought in fact depends for its apparent soundness on the perspective afforded by certain sensitivities, it needs to be seen as containing distortions that undermine its status as rational. Interestingly, Williams himself acknowledges that his preferred, narrowly rational understanding of natural-scientific discourse commits him to denying that ethical discourse, understood along the widely rational lines he favors, qualifies as rational in a full-blooded sense.[8] Without delving further into Williams's writing, we can say that it presents an illustration of how a thinker's willingness to represent some rational, discursive capacities as lacking necessary input from sensibility interferes with her ability to represent the wider conception of rationality as a conception of bona fide rationality. Or, in other terms, we can say that his writing effectively shows that, in order be understood as a conception of genuine rationality, the wider conception needs to be understood as tied to the view that certain sensitivities inform all rational discursive capacities.

Let me now briefly comment on implications of this view for how we conceive moral thought. For this purpose, it is helpful to say something about consequences of our willingness to embrace the idea, distinctive of the view, that the mastery of any genuine concept is inseparable from the possession of certain sensitivities, say, sensitivities to the importance of similarities and differences among the concept's uses. Now it appears that there can be no question of describing the form that conceptual mastery must take, apart from an effort to develop the relevant sensitivities. Moreover, although mastery of a concept may well be taken to require a sense of the significance of ties among certain of its specific applications, it appears that, without regard to which concept is at issue, an individual's sense of significance may invariably grow or deepen, opening her eyes to new, rationally authoritative uses. Finally, it appears that two individuals who are both masters of a given concept may nevertheless have different senses of the importance of the links among some of its uses. Combining the general picture of conceptual competence in question here with an observation about how individual speakers of a given natural language learn and use different concepts, we might say that learning a natural language is essentially a matter of acquiring an array of interpersonally variable sensitivities or, in other words, essentially a matter of acquiring a complex individual sense of what things are and what things are not important. This view of linguistic competence lays the groundwork for thinking of a person's growth into a language-user in ethical terms. If we help ourselves to an understanding of an individual's ethical outlook as her sense of what things are and are not important in the world, it can be seen as inviting us to regard learning a natural language as inseparable from the acquisition of an ethical outlook.

Although moral philosophers sometimes disagree about which of our concepts are rightly counted as moral ones, they nevertheless by and large agree in assuming that moral thinking is a matter of making moral judgments, where "moral judgments" are understood as judgments that apply specifically moral concepts. Moral thought is generally treated as the exclusive concern of one region of our discourse, namely, the region demarcated by the use of moral concepts. So it is noteworthy that there is a sense in which the view of linguistic competence I have been sketching speaks against the equation of moral thinking with moral judgment making. This view suggests both that certain sensitivities are internal to all of an individual's rational, discursive capacities and that, without regard to whether they are associated with her use of specifically moral concepts, these sensitivities play a role in constituting her ethical outlook. The view thus leaves open the possibility that we may draw on or develop sensitivities internal to our ethical outlooks when thinking about any subject matter and that our thought may therefore play the kind of role in expressing our ethical outlooks that establishes it as moral even when we make no use of moral concepts.

The point of the line of reasoning I just sketched is to suggest that the wider conception of rationality—the conception that permits us to say that literary works are as such capable of contributing to rational, moral understanding—is conceptually connected to a construal of moral thought as including more than moral judgments. If this is right, it means that our willingness to offer a widely rational account of the ethical significance of literature is consistent with an attractively expansive conception of how literary works can as such contribute to rational moral understanding. Our willingness here opens us to the prospect that literary works can as such contribute in ways that, far from being reducible to collections of moral judgments, involve the refinement of ostensibly non-moral ways of thinking and speaking. Or, in other words, it opens us to the prospect that literary works can as such contribute in ways that involve nothing more tangible or less significant than the enrichment of our larger visions of the world.

My goal in the remainder of this chapter is to show that this prospect is directly relevant to grasping the moral force of some of J. M. Coetzee's novels. I am going to represent the moral interest of some of the novels as traceable partly to narrative strategies that take for granted the wider conception of rationality, and I am going to do so without suggesting that the sole or even primary point of these narrative strategies is to open readers' eyes to the justice of a set of moral judgments. I am aware that philosophers and theorists skeptical about the very idea of a wider conception of rationality of the sort that will inform my remarks about Coetzee are unlikely to be won over by any readings of his novels. It is open to such readers to allow that a reading of a work of literature may establish that it is overwhelmingly natural to regard it as inviting sound moral thought through its strategy of emotional engagement—and yet not concede that we may be justified in representing it as actually inviting such thought. Although I believe that a gesture of wholesale repudiation of the possibility that literature as literature can possess rational moral power is unwarranted, I do not argue for this. My ambition in what follows is not to make a move in a philosophical argument about the authority of the wider conception of rationality and the unorthodox view of moral thought it funds but rather to make a plausible case for thinking that we need to avail ourselves of the kind of openness about what moral thinking is like that comes with the wider conception of rationality if we are to do justice to the moral ambition of some of Coetzee's novels.[9]

A READING OF *DISGRACE*

Do I have to change?
—David Lurie, in J. M. Coetzee, *Disgrace*

J. M. Coetzee's novels are for the most part set in societies riven by forms of insitutionalized discrimination with deep historical roots (e.g., Apartheid and immediately post-Apartheid South Africa; Australia; and other actual, historical, and allegorical colonial and postcolonial societies). Many of the novels foreground characters whose social privileges are marks of complicity with society's injustices and who, even if they to some extent try to free themselves from biased and unjust ways of thinking, fail to arrive at the sort of undistorted understanding of their lives that could underwrite just modes of conduct. These characters are often portrayed as unwilling or unable to trust or explore their responses to people with whom they come into contact, and a recurring theme of the novels is that their failures of moral understanding are direct functions of these affective limitations. Indeed, a motif about how certain sensitivities are essential to moral understanding figures significantly even in those of the novels, such as *The Life and Times of Michael K*, whose central characters are not socially or politically well situated.

This motif, which depends for its intelligibility on what I am calling the wider conception of rationality, finds expression not only in the terms in which Coetzee presents his characters and tells his stories but also in the novels' narrative structures. For instance, some of the novels—and here I have in mind, above all, *Waiting for the Barbarians*, *Age of Iron*, *Disgrace*, and *Slow Man*—unfold narratively in ways that to a great extent eliminate traces of an authorial standpoint, inviting readers to view their (often violent and disturbing) fictional worlds from the perspectives of morally compromised major characters. Through the kinds of qualified identifications that the novels thus invite, they call on us as readers simultaneously to respond to and think about features of these worlds in particular ways, and, in doing so, they position us to better understand the features in question. Qua works of literature these works are thus preoccupied with the idea that a certain emotional responsiveness is internal to moral understanding in ways that go beyond treating it as an element of a story. They are, as novels, designed to get us to follow up ourselves on lines of thought that take for granted this idea's cogency.

Consider in this connection Coetzee's *Disgrace*. The events of this novel are presented from the perspective of its central character, David Lurie, a fifty-two-year-old, divorced, non-Afrikaans, white academic in Capetown in newly post-Apartheid South Africa. While even David's surname—a traditionally Jewish one that is sometimes taken to be a sign of distinguished heritage[10]—tells us something about his social circumstances, he himself is in significant respects ignorant about these circumstances. It is not that David is unaware of political changes afoot in the country. Having been demoted from a professor of modern languages to an adjunct professor of communications as a result of nationwide restructuring of universities, he is at some level knowledgeable about and accepting of the new political order. Nevertheless, despite being reasonably well informed, David fails to register the extent to which social privileges he continues to enjoy are products of persistent inequalities. This failure is especially apparent in his sex life: David doesn't recognize that his ability to secure certain kinds of sexual attention is little more than a reflection of social privileges he enjoys as a result of the deep-seated forms of gender and racial bias.[11]

Within the novel, David's benightedness is traced to emotional and imaginative limitations he manages to hide from himself. He is the author of three books—on Boito's operatic interpretation of the Faust legend, on the mystical theology of Richard of St. Victor and on Wordsworth's poetry (4)—and he sees himself as sharing with his favorite thinkers and artists a doctrine about how personal development is inseparable from the growth of feelings and a sense for the comic. Indeed, he sometimes flatters himself that he has realized this doctrine in his life. But, although capable of biting irony, he is strikingly without a sense of humor, and although willing to nurture sexual desire, he is devoid of any real passion. What in fact gets expressed in David's conduct is not so much openness to new experiences and modes of response as a refusal to repress sexual (or other) desires. David is emboldened in this refusal by his sense that he is too old to change. He frequently tells himself that his temperament is fixed beyond alteration and that there can be no question of improving himself or learning new lessons (2, 49, 66, 72, 77, 172, 209, and 216). Admittedly, David's commitment to what he calls "the rights of desire" (89) is not without its appealing aspects. Among other things, it frees him from the tendency, well represented among his Capetown university colleagues, to automatically censor departures from received standards of conduct. But David's insistence on being guided by desire saves him from judgmentalism without deepening his insight into his own character or personal circumstances, and one suggestion that emerges from the portrait we are given of him is that the emotional responsiveness he extols without practicing in anything but a debased form is necessary for the growth of moral understanding.

This suggestion is developed in the novel's main storyline, which centers on two key events in David's life. The first involves a sexual harassment suit that is brought against him for a sexual relationship with a young colored woman in one of his classes, a theater student named Melanie Isaacs, and that ends with his dismissal from his job at the university. The second, which takes place in a house his grown lesbian daughter, Lucy, has on a small plot of land on the Eastern Cape, involves a violent assault by two black men and a boy, an assault in which he himself is badly burned and Lucy is raped and impregnated. In neither case is David able to arrive at a good understanding of what has happened. Although he recognizes that he is violating the trust invested in him as Melanie's teacher and taking advantage of her inexperience, his self-righteous impatience with his colleagues' moralism—with their refusal to register ways in which desire or feeling can lead us into conflict with social and institutional strictures—keeps him from undertaking the kind of self-examination that would enable him to see that what he is doing is truly exploitative (12, 18, and 37). Similarly, although David recognizes that the attack on him and Lucy is conditioned by specific political and historical injustices, and although he has little sympathy for those of Lucy's settler neighbors who overlook their enjoyment of spoils of past brutalities and arm themselves to meet violence with violence, he is too involved in his own fears as Lucy's father to see Lucy clearly. He cannot process her reasons for resisting his efforts to get her to terminate her pregnancy and flee the social world to which her small parcel of land connects her (111–12, 119, 133–34, 160–61, and 203–5).

Disgrace is no bildungsroman, and David is portrayed as making little progress in overcoming the limitations of his emotional repertoire that underlie his obtuseness about these matters. At the story's end, he is still preoccupied with thoughts of Melanie, and he has managed, through his refusal or inability to understand Lucy's wishes, to produce something like a rift with his daughter. Nevertheless, David is portrayed as now for the first time willing to admit that his attachment to a fixed set of desires may be a mark of limitation and to open himself to new experiences (218). One emblem of this shift is his absorption in an opera he is writing about Byron's last mistress. David has long believed that language is essentially an outgrowth of the expressiveness of song (3–4), and, even before he left the university, he hoped to work this theme into a modest operatic work. But it is only later, in his state of disgrace, that he begins to develop the kinds of receptive and responsive capacities required to explore his own expressive impulses in the work's composition (160–62, 180–81, 192, 209, and 213).[12] Now David begins to listen for a voice or sentiment capable of transporting him beyond the intellectual and moral order that he has hitherto accepted. If, following up on a proposal of Derek Attridge's, we think of the kind of responsiveness that David now allows himself as an openness to *grace*, we might say that Coetzee's novel suggests a play on the (conceptually only loosely linked) notions of grace and disgrace, bringing out a sense in which grace can be a condition of emergence from disgrace.[13] In plainer terms, the idea is simply that the novel invites us to connect David's new responsiveness with a glimmering of what better self-understanding will demand. Bearing this in mind, we might say that the novel's treatment of David takes for granted the value and legitimacy of modes of moral thought that depend for their cogency on the wider conception of rationality.

The novel's concern with these modes of moral thought is not limited to its storyline. It also brings out their value by means of a narrative strategy designed to guide readers' thought by guiding their responses. The structure of the narrative encourages significant if partial forms of identification with David. Proceeding almost wholly from his perspective, it invites us to enter into his experience. We are encouraged to take things in through his eyes both during his double ordeal and afterward when, having lost his job and undergone the trauma of the assault on Lucy, his manner of interacting with the world begins to change and he starts to catch a glimpse, however limited, of the kind of effort that might allow him to surmount his cognitive shortcomings. By calling on us to imaginatively participate in David's trials and their aftermath, the novel aims to equip us to see things that are lost on David and that he is, at the novel's end, at best starting to position himself to discern. *Disgrace* in this way reinforces the case it makes for the cognitive value of emotional responsiveness at the level of its story by engaging readers in ways intended to produce insight.

For a more detailed account of these matters, we might start by considering the novel's treatment of David's relationship with Bev Shaw. Bev, a friend of Lucy's in Salem, is a middle-aged woman who, out of concern for the welfare of animals, provides crude veterinary care in a local clinic. Upon meeting Bev for the first time, David focuses on her physical appearance, her cultural niche, and ways in which her social concerns get expressed in her personal hygiene and domestic arrangements. He describes Bev to himself as a "dumpy, bustling little woman with black freckled, close-cropped, wiry hair, and no neck" who is "full of New Age mumbo jumbo" (72, 84). At Lucy's urging, he agrees to help Bev with her clinic work, but in Bev's presence he is both impatient and brusque. When Bev urges David to "think comforting thoughts" because, as she puts it, animals "can smell what you are thinking," David internally dismisses her advice as "nonsense" (81). And when, on his first day at the clinic, he watches Bev calm a goat that is injured and in pain, what strikes him is the fact Bev lacks the training for a sophisticated veterinary intervention, and he accordingly feels more disdain than admiration (83–84).

David's relationship with Bev changes after he and Lucy are attacked. The attackers pour methylated spirits on David and set him on fire, badly burning his scalp and one ear (96). Reduced to a state of physical and emotional frailty, he begins to take comfort in social gestures he once disparaged and to notice aspects of people and situations he previously overlooked. Together with Lucy, David spends the night after the assault at Bev's house, and, before he and Lucy leave the next day, Bev changes his bandages, putting him in the position of the goat he earlier saw her treat. David now no longer focuses on Bev's appearance or the primitiveness of her methods. He is soothed by the delicacy with which she touches him, the quiet manner in which she works and the calm she produces. These are the things that now impress him about Bev, and he finds himself wondering whether the goat "felt the same peacefulness" (106). And, insofar as the novel presents David's ordeal from his perspective, inviting us to imaginatively participate in his devastation, it calls on us to respond to and think about Bev in ways that position us to recognize her sensible solicitousness.

For a second example of how *Disgrace* presents its readers with moral instruction through of its literary features, we might turn to the way in which the novel portrays David's relationship to animals. Early in the novel, David is inclined to treat animals as beings of a different order that, while meriting humane treatment, shouldn't be regarded as individuals deserving special forms of care and attention (73-74). He tells Lucy that he thinks of people like Bev who concern themselves with animal welfare as well-intentioned but misguided do-gooders, and when Bev asks him whether he likes animals he replies sarcastically: "I eat them, so I suppose I must like them, some parts of them" (81).

David's manner of dealing with nonhuman creatures is very different after he and Lucy are attacked. The shift is not a simply byproduct of the change in his relationship to Bev and her animals. It is also partly a function of David's attempt to cope with the slaughter of the half dozen watchdogs that Lucy boards on her property. David and Lucy's assailants also target these dogs. Before leaving, one of them systematically shoots all of them in their cages. This act of brutality is by no means politically incomprehensible, given that South Africa is "a country where," as David at one point tells himself, "dogs are bred to snarl at the mere smell of a black man" (110). Yet at the beginning of his stay in Salem, David betrays insensitivity to this interplay between race relations and dogs. When he first meets Petrus, the black man in his forties who lives near Lucy and who is both her assistant and coproprietor, David struggles for a way to start a conversation and then observes: "You look after the dogs" (64).

This is the background against which to understand changes in David's relationship to animals. The most striking changes come when David begins to identify with animals like the goat in Bev's clinic in their physical vulnerability and need for comfort. David's identifications encode an image of animals as individuals. When David looks at animals, he now sees beings whose individual reactions to physical threats are salient and significant. This new vision of animals gets expressed, for instance, as an unprecedented interest in vegetarianism. After the attack, David finds himself sympathizing with two sheep that Petrus tethers on the property and plans to slaughter to feed to guests at an upcoming party. Although David has always been a meat eater, he considers staying home from Petrus's celebration (which he has other motives to skip) partly to avoid eating the sheep (123–27). And David's new vision of animals also gets expressed in his attachment to the dogs at Bev's clinic. Looking at the unwanted dogs that are to be euthanized, David now sees individuals awaiting their mortal fates (143). He brings the dogs' corpses to the dump several days after they have been euthanized to arrange for their incineration and spare them what it now strikes him as appropriate to describe as the "dishonor" of being left with "waste from the hospital wards, carrion scooped up at the roadside, malodorous refuse from the tannery" (144). These points are significant because, by presenting its fictional world from David's perspective, *Disgrace* calls on us as readers to respond to and think about animals in certain ways. We are encouraged to sympathize with the feelings of vulnerability that lead David to identify with animals and at the same time to acknowledge these identifications as just and appropriate.

It seems clear that some of the different—simultaneously affective and cognitive—responses that Coetzee's narrative thus elicits are intended to bring within reach a better grasp of David's life and social circumstances than he himself possesses. To respond in relevant ways is, among other things, to see respects in which (human and nonhuman) individuals are submitted to natural and political forces beyond their control as significant for efforts to understand them, and this image equips us to bring the novel's world more clearly into focus than David himself ever brings it. Now it appears that there is in itself nothing distinctive about Lucy's subjection to political events she cannot control and that there is therefore a straightforward sense in which her decision to stay in her home after being attacked is reasonable. Further, it appears that, to the extent that Melanie's and Lucy's vulnerability to unwanted or violent sexual contact is the product of their positions within larger historical and political settings, there is a direct connection between what David did to Melanie and what happened to Lucy. And, finally, it appears that the novel's different human characters resemble animals in being subject to forces beyond their control and that animals are our fellow creatures.

Having described how the narrative strategy of *Disgrace* is designed partly with an eye to eliciting lines of thought that shed light on its social world, let me add that I am not suggesting that the novel aims somehow to render this world transparent to understanding. To the extent that Coetzee's novel is preoccupied, at the level of its narrative structure as well as at the level of its story, with the idea that we may require new sensitivities in order to further develop our moral understanding, it is aptly characterized as containing a distinctive lesson about the difficulty of moral thought, and the novel invites us to take seriously the possibility that we may need to grapple with this kind of difficulty in our efforts to make sense of the sort of situations of great misery that it describes and explores but does not pretend to fully illuminate. The post-Apartheid South African social environment that David confronts is characterized by great suffering on the part of human beings and nonhuman animals, and there is no suggestion in the novel of any miraculous key to tracing the deepest sources of and addressing this suffering. Through the identifications it seeks to produce with David in his different trials, *Disgrace* exposes us to human and animal affliction in ways that are designed both to bring us to the recognition that our reactions to it can overwhelm us and to get us to ask ourselves whether, like David, we are at risk of refusing to investigate our reactions, evading whatever pain and confusion they induce, and thereby shutting our eyes to new avenues of simultaneously intellectual and moral growth.

One virtue of the account of the moral power of *Disgrace* I just offered is that it lays the groundwork for a response to some of the political charges that have been leveled against the novel. When it first appeared in 1999, *Disgrace* attracted fierce criticism from a number of prominent South Africans and was attacked in the ANC's submission to the African Human Rights Commission's inquiry into racism in the media. Many of the criticisms began from the thought that the novel is rightly thought of as painting an irresponsibly negative picture of post-Apartheid South Africa. Some critics argued that the novel's portrayal of black-on-white rape is especially egregious and that such a portrayal cannot help but contain an antiblack racist message. To some extent, critics who argued along these lines seemed to be concerned with empirical questions about the kind of social response the novel was likely to produce, and it seems to me that these kinds of concerns have a legitimate place in the reception of literary works and other works of art. But in developing their arguments many of *Disgrace*'s critics implicitly presupposed that the novel can, without distortion, be regarded as an instrument for depicting particular political circumstances and that its literary devices are irrelevant to questions about its moral and political character. This presupposition is untenable. The novel's moral and political import is inseparable from its distinctively literary qualities. There is no such thing as appreciating the significance of its portrayal of the rape of a white woman by three black assailants apart from an appreciation of how this portrayal aims not only to open our eyes to features of the political landscape in which such an act might occur (features that include, e.g., an brutal and persistent history of antiblack racist violence) but also to impress on us the difficulty of bringing such a landscape clearly into focus.[14]

This brings to a close my discussion of *Disgrace*—a discussion that traces the moral interest of the novel in part to strategies for engaging readers that take for granted the logic of the wider conception of rationality. In the remainder of this chapter, I set aside reservations some philosophers and theorists have about the standing of this conception of rationality and consider an objection to things I have been saying about Coetzee's work that, while it may in fact appeal only to those who oppose the very idea of a wider conception of rationality, derives its original impetus not from philosophical resistance to this idea but from a study of his work.

FURTHER REFLECTIONS ON COETZEE AND ETHICS

Why should I bow to reason this afternoon and content myself with embroidering on the discourse of the old philosophers?
—The novelist Elizabeth Costello, in J. M. Coetzee, *Elizabeth Costello*

The objection that interests me is driven by an understanding of Coetzee that differs from the one I have been developing in that now Coetzee is seen not as presenting a picture of ethical life free from the constraints of the narrower conception of rationality but rather as repudiating the very notion of moral rationality. At the heart of the objection is the thought that, when in his novels Coetzee represents certain emotional capacities as internal to moral development, he is intimating not, as I have been arguing, that we should allow the wider conception of rationality to shape our image of moral thought and action but rather that we should situate moral concerns outside the domain of rationality altogether.[15]

At first blush it might seem possible to find good evidence for this image of Coetzee. In his essays and in interviews, he clearly expresses skepticism about efforts to bring our ethical commitments wholly within, as he once put it, "the project of rationality" (Coetzee, *Giving Offense*, 4), and it might seem as though we are justified in concluding from this that he thinks that morality needs to be understood as at least partly independent of rational constraints. Further, an initially plausible case can be made for representing at least some of the novels as supporting the same conclusion. Thus we might point to a passage late in *Disgrace* in which David is attempting to convince Lucy, now for the third or fourth time, that she should move away from Salem. David ends his case with the plea "Can't the two of us talk about it rationally?" In response, Lucy shakes her head and says: "I can't talk any more, David. I just can't . . . I know I am not being clear. I wish I could explain. But I can't. Because of who you are and who I am. I can't" (155). Given that *Disgrace* represents David as hampered in his relationship to Lucy by limitations of emotional responsiveness, and given that this passage indicates that he differs from Lucy in relying on certain "rational" methods, it might seem reasonable to read the novel as suggesting that David needs to grow emotionally and morally in ways that transcend the rational.

A similar conclusion might be drawn from a passage in *Elizabeth Costello* in which the eponymous character, an aging novelist, is giving a lecture on things human beings do to animals. Costello suggests that we need to rely on modes of speech that are capable of containing passion if we are to bring our lives with animals clearly into focus, and she adds that refusing to rely on such modes of speech is tantamount to wrongly "bow[ing] to reason" (67). If we assume that Costello is implying that speech intended to produce a passionate response operates on us in a manner at odds with the constraints of reason insofar as it does so, and if we also assume that the novel is recommending this position, then it will seem appropriate to represent the novel as urging us to situate moral reflection outside the realm of reason.

Rationality and truth are cognate concepts (viz., insofar as exercises of rationality aspire to the preservation of truth), and it might seem reasonable to try to promote an account of Coetzee as a fan of a nonrational morality by mentioning passages in his novels that deal with the concept of truth in moral contexts. In several novels as well as in several interviews, Coetzee seems to associate demands for "truth" with coercion and the abuse of power. Thus, for instance, in *Waiting for the Barbarians*, Colonel Joll, a military man who has been dispatched to an outpost of a decaying empire to report back on the workings of its institutions, freely tortures prisons to get at what he describes as the "truth" (3 and passim), and it is emphasized in the novel that the "truths" Joll uncovers are as epistemically unreliable as they are morally debased. Similarly, in interviews, Coetzee himself sometimes talks about "truth" as the counterpart to coercive methods of interrogation (*Doubling the Point*, 65). Given the conceptual tie between the concepts of truth and rationality, it might appear as though we are justified in taking these moments in Coetzee's thought to speak for an understanding of him as hostile to the very idea of a rational morality.

However plausible it initially seems, this understanding of Coetzee is flawed. It turns for its appeal on a failure to register the complexity of Coetzee's different treatments of the notions of rationality and truth. A careful study of his essays and interviews, for instance, makes it clear that when he disparages the idea that the moral life is a wholly "rational" endeavor, he is talking about the rational in reference to argument in something like the restrictive sense in which I speak of argument at the opening of this chapter. He is denying that it is possible to reflect responsibly on whether individuals are justified in insisting on the rational correctness of their deepest convictions when they treat argument as rationality's solitary touchstone, but he is not denying the possibility of using our minds, broadly construed, to authoritatively survey and assess matters of conviction. His thought is, rather, that, if we are to put ourselves in a position to examine our beliefs in an intellectually and morally responsible manner, we need to go beyond argument and allow ourselves to explore modes of thought that only a willingness to follow up on new responses to life brings within reach.[16]

Coetzee's genius lies partly in the way he uses this thought to animate his novels. Consider again the scene in *Disgrace* in which David asks Lucy whether they can discuss her situation "rationally." When David speaks of rational discussion here, he means discussion that comes in the form of argument in my restrictive sense. Given that David is for the most part incapable of engaging with others in ways that demand a flexible emotional response, we have every reason to take him to be fixated on such argument as a method of responsible, conversational exchange. At the same time, it seems clear that we miss the point of this interaction between David and Lucy if we fail to question this fixation on argument. For when Lucy rejects David's attempt to "rationally" discuss what happened to her, she intimates not that there is nothing there for him to get his mind around but rather that nothing short of a transformation of David's person would bring what she wants to say within his mental reach. ("I wish I could explain. But I can't. Because of who you are and who I am, I can't.") Moreover, the novel as a whole positions us to recognize Lucy as in the right in this instance. So, far from supporting an understanding of *Disgrace* as repudiating the very idea of rational moral interchange, this scene between David and Lucy supports an understanding of the novel as suggesting that, if we are to participate responsibly in moral conversation, we need to reject constraints internal to the narrower conception of rationality and avail ourselves of a wider alternative.

A complementary claim can be made about the passage from *Elizabeth Costello* touched on a moment ago. Although early in her lecture on animals Costello disparages constraints of reason (67), the point she is making is more complex than this gesture may seem to suggest. A bit later Costello admits that it may seem as though the only alternative to reason-governed discourse is inchoate emoting (68), and soon after this she adds that this is because any utterance that counts as intelligible will by that token fall within reason's domain (70). (This last point is also made by Costello's daughter-in-law, a philosophy Ph.D. who is a sort of old-fashioned rationalist and who openly dislikes Costello [92–93].) The day after her lecture, Costello gives a seminar in which she reads a couple of poems about animals. She considers respects in which the poems aim to play on passions, and she tries to show that a stretch of discourse such as a poem can present us with intellectually respectable modes of thought because of how it directs our feelings (esp. 94–96). The portrait of Costello we are given is thus of a thinker who, far from opposing the very idea of a rational ethics, is committed to approaching certain questions of ethics—for example, questions about human treatment of animals—in a manner shaped by a conception of rationality capacious enough to include literary speech, taken as such, in its inventory of rational discursive forms. Costello is rightly regarded as holding that we need a conception of rationality that swings wide of argument in order to make sense of challenges of moral thought.[17]

There is, as I have tried to demonstrate, good reason to read both Coetzee's nonfictional and fictional writings as attacking the incursion into moral reflection of an overly restrictive—or, in my terms, overly narrow—construal of the concept of rationality. Despite any initial appearance to the contrary, this conclusion is strengthened by Coetzee's various treatments of "truth." While, on the one hand, Coetzee's novels ask us to regard certain strategies for pursuing "truth" as morally prejudicial, on the other, they ask us not only to place value on the search for truth conceived as a search for more accurate images of our lives but also to regard the pursuit of truth, thus conceived, as depending for its success on the possession of a refined sensibility. For instance, although *Waiting for the Barbarians* represents certain kinds of demands for "truth" as morally despicable, it also recommends, through its treatment of the Magistrate, the kind of pursuit of an accurate self-understanding that requires a willingness to work on and transform ourselves. We might accordingly say that Coetzee's novels—and something similar can be said about some of his interviews—lay claim to a wider conception of truth that is the counterpart of the wider conception rationality that Coetzee takes for granted in describing the moral life.[18]

CONCLUSION

The last thing I want to do is *defiantly* embrace the ethical as against the political.
—J. M. Coetzee, *Doubling the Point*

I have been claiming that if we are to arrive at a reasonable understanding of the moral force of some of Coetzee's novels, we need to see that they are colored by the thought that we require certain sensitivities in order to arrive at a just and accurate grasp of elements of our lives and surroundings. Having set aside the task of offering a philosophical defense of the wider conception of rationality needed to underwrite this thought, I focused on showing that Coetzee's *Disgrace* in particular develops the thought in its storyline as well as in its narrative structure. My suggestion was that, in these different ways, the novel shows us that our inability or unwillingness to probe new modes of response to life threatens to condemn us to the position of David Luries, unable for all of our education and intelligence to bring into focus important features of our social world. Further, after arguing that the novel invites us to see that we are in danger of incurring this moral cost if we allow ourselves to be governed by narrower presuppositions about what rationality is like, I brought out how we find support for this basic understanding of *Disgrace* in Coetzee's other novels as well as in his essays and interviews.

Given that, as I noted earlier, *Disgrace* has been criticized as politically irresponsible, it is worth stressing in closing that this novel—and I believe something similar could be said about other novels of Coetzee's—highlights political ramifications of the image of ethical life that it develops. Set in a place and time of great political upheaval, it is intended to persuade us that the moral hazard we court if we refuse to think about the world in ways opened up by a rich responsiveness to life is not only that of failing to make sense of our own lives but also that of thereby succumbing to forms of moral blindness that condemn us to perpetuate or deepen grave political injustices.[19]

Notes

1. For explicit defenses of the view, see D. D. Raphael, "Can Literature Be Moral Philosophy?" *New Literary History* 15 (1983): 1–12; O. O'Neill, "The Power of Example," in *Constructions of Reason: Explorations of Kant's Practical Philosophy* (Cambridge: Cambridge University Press, 1989), 165–86; P. Lamarque and S. H. Olsen, *Truth, Fiction, and Literature: A Philosophical Perspective* (Oxford: Clarendon Press, 1994); R. Posner, "Against Ethical Criticism," *Philosophy and Literature* 21, no. 1 (1997): 1–27; C. Vogler, "The Moral of the Story," *Critical Inquiry* 34, no. 1 (2007): 5–35; and J. Landy, "A Nation of Madame Bovarys: On the Possibility and Desirability of Moral Improvement Through Fiction," in *Art and Ethical Criticism*, ed. G. L. Hagberg (Oxford: Blackwell, 2008), 63–94.
2. See especially Raphael, "Can Literature be Moral Philosophy"; O'Neill, "The Power of Example"; and Posner, "Against Ethical Criticism."
3. See I. Murdoch, "Vision and Choice in Morality" (1956), reprinted in *Existentialists and Mystics: Writings on Philosophy and Literature* (London: Penguin, 1997), 76–98; S. Cavell, *The Claim of Reason: Wittgenstein, Skepticism, Morality, and Tragedy* (Oxford: Oxford University Press, 1979), esp. part 4; S. Cavell, *Disowning Knowledge in Seven Plays of Shakespeare* (Cambridge: Cambridge University Press, 1987); M. Nussbaum, *Love's Knowledge: Essays on Philosophy and Literature* (Oxford: Oxford University Press, 1990); C. Diamond, *The Realistic Spirit: Wittgenstein, Philosophy, and the Mind* (Cambridge, Mass.: MIT Press, 1991), esp. chaps. 11 and 12; C. Diamond, "Martha Nussbaum and the Need for Novels," *Philosophical Investigations* 16, no. 2 (1993): 128–53; M. Nussbaum, *Poetic Justice: The Literary Imagination and Public Life* (Boston:

Beacon Press, 1995); D. Brudney, "Lord Jim and Moral Judgment: Literature and Moral Philosophy," *Journal of Aesthetics and Art Criticism* 56, no. 3 (1998): 265-81; S. Mulhall, *The Wounded Animal: J. M. Coetzee and the Difficulty of Reality* (Princeton, N.J.: Princeton University Press, 2009).

4. Thus, e.g., Nussbaum, *Love's Knowledge*, draws largely on ancient Greeks sources; Cavell, *The Claim of Reason*, and Diamond, *The Realistic Spirit* and "Martha Nussbaum and the Need for Novels," take the later philosophy of Wittgenstein as a significant point of reference.

5. This terminology is optional. Someone inclined to think that the realm of the rational is by definition coextensive with the realm of argument might equally well describe what is at issue here as a conception of rationality that presupposes an unusually permissive understanding of "argument."

6. B. Williams, *Ethics and the Limits of Philosophy* (Cambridge, Mass.: Harvard University Press, 1985), 129 and 141-42.

7. Ibid., chap. 8.

8. Williams offers a pithy formulation of his thought that scientific reflection can undermine what may once have appeared to be genuine bodies of ethical knowledge when he declares: *"reflection can destroy knowledge"* (ibid., 148; stress in the original).

9. I am concerned with the larger philosophical project set aside here in A. Crary, *Beyond Moral Judgment* (Cambridge, Mass.: Harvard University Press, 2007), chaps. 1-3.

10. I owe this observation to Cora Diamond.

11. In this paragraph, as well as in the rest of the treatment of *Disgrace* that follows, I use terms of racial and ethnic classification (e.g., "white," "non-Afrikaans," "Jewish") that are almost absent from Coetzee's novel. My justification for doing so has to do both with the fact, just noted, that the novel unfolds from the perspective of its main character, David Lurie, and with the further fact that David's modes of thought and action reflect socially articulated racial and ethnic distinctions that he is conscious of but that he doesn't recognize as materially affecting his conduct. Since one of my main concerns in discussing *Disgrace* is underlining ways in which it asks readers to notice shortcomings of David's that are related to this particular form of social blindness, it is helpful for my purposes to use terms that the novel mostly does not. I am indebted to Sandra Laugier for suggesting the interest of this topic.

12. For another treatment in Coetzee's opus of the idea that language begins with song, see *Foe*, 96-97.

13. See D. Attridge, "Age of Bronze, State of Grace," in *J. M. Coetzee and the Ethics of Reading* (Chicago: University of Chicago Press, 2004), 162-91, esp. 177-79.

14. For a helpful overview of the political controversy surrounding *Disgrace*, see the issue of *Interventions: An International Journal of Postcolonial Studies* that is devoted to a discussion of Coetzee's novel. The opening piece, D. Attridge, "J. M. Coetzee's *Disgrace*:

Introduction," *Interventions: An International Journal of Postcolonial Studies* 4, no. 3 (2002): 315-20, is especially helpful. The question of Coetzee and the political is taken up in a more general way in *J. M. Coetzee and the Idea of the Public Intellectual*, ed. J. Poyner (Athens: Ohio University Press, 2006). Poyner touches on *Disgrace* in particular in her introduction (see 11-12).

15. This objection was suggested to me by the two editors of this volume, Anton Leist and Peter Singer.

16. For a forceful treatment of these themes, see Coetzee, *Giving Offense*, 3-6.

17. In a recent paper, Cora Diamond ("The Difficulty of Reality and the Difficulty of Philosophy", in *Reading Cavell*, ed. A. Crary and S. Shieh [London: Routledge, 2006], 98-118) develops a congenial portrait of Costello in the course of offering an account of the portion of *Elizabeth Costello* that was originally published as "The Lives of Animals." S. Cavell, "Companionable Thinking," in *Wittgenstein and the Moral Life: Essays in Honor of Cora Diamond*, ed. A. Crary (Cambridge, Mass.: MIT Press, 2007), further develops some of Diamond's claims. Both articles are reprinted in S. Cavell et al., *Philosophy and Animal Life* (New York: Columbia University Press, 2008). For an insightful commentary on this conversation between Diamond and Cavell, see Mulhall, *The Wounded Animal*.

18. For Coetzee's own treatments of this alternative, "wider" conception of truth, see Coetzee, *Doubling the Point*, 60, 65, and 243-44.

19. I am grateful to Cora Diamond, Nathaniel Hupert, Anton Leist, Angus Ross, and Peter Singer for constructive criticisms of earlier drafts of this chapter. I presented versions of the chapter at the University of East Anglia, Cambridge University, New York University, and University of Rome, Sapienza, and also at a seminar of Michael Fried's and Ruth Leys's at the Humanities Center at Johns Hopkins University. I would especially like to thank, for their helpful comments on these occasions, Jay Bernstein, Simon Blackburn, Arnold Davidson, Piergiorgio Donatelli, Michael Fried, Gary Hagberg, Ruth Leys, Stephen Mulhall, Cathy Osborne, Rupert Read, and Cara Weber. I owe a particular debt to Sandra Laugier for an insightful commentary on my reading of *Disgrace*.

References

Coetzee, J. M. *Disgrace*. New York: Viking, 2005.
———. *Elizabeth Costello*. New York: Viking, 2003.
———. *Giving Offense: Essays on Censorship*. Chicago: University of Chicago Press, 1996.
———. *Doubling the Point: Essays and Interviews*. Ed. D. Attwell. Cambridge, Mass.: Harvard University Press, 1992.
———. *Waiting for the Barbarians*. New York: Penguin, 1982.

12

Being True to Fact
COETZEE'S PROSE OF THE WORLD
Pieter Vermeulen

FROM PHILOSOPHY TO PAIN

At least since he won his first Booker Prize in 1983, J. M. Coetzee's novels have generated a volume of critical work the size of which is virtually unique for a contemporary literary author. One explanation for this immense critical output is certainly the remarkable fit between, on the one hand, the formal and thematic concerns of Coetzee's novels and, on the other, the issues and paradigms that have governed the study of literature in the past twenty-five years. As the study of literature has increasingly occupied itself with questions about postcolonial identity, the determining force of history, and the discursive construction of subjectivity, Coetzee has explicitly touched on these questions in his fiction. His novels are overtly informed by postcolonial, postmodern, and poststructuralist themes, and it has proven to be a productive intellectual exercise to try to identify and explain these informing concerns in the form of critical articles and monographs. Indeed, it would seem that, as two critics have remarked, "academe would have invented J. M. Coetzee had he not already existed."[1] The result of this productive fit is that especially the first five novels (*Dusklands*, *In the Heart of the Country*, *Waiting for the Barbarians*, *Life and Times of Michael K*, and *Foe*) are, by critical consensus, approached as theoretically sophisticated works of "metafiction" that bring contemporary critical concerns into play and that are meticulously aware of the discursive and historical conditions of their own production.[2] The guiding assumption that the novels are first of all intensely self-reflexive and overtly theoretical rather than realist and mimetic works has often led to the political criticism that they are insufficiently engaged with historical reality, thus the often-heard judgment that Coetzee's work is politically impotent, or even irresponsibly escapist, because it allegedly loses itself "in self-defeating discourse that fails to confront the particularity of the political conditions of oppression in South Africa."[3]

While this prevalent understanding of Coetzee's work undoubtedly adequately captures many of the central aspects of what we may call his early "high-theory" novels, readers of Coetzee's later work will appreciate that it is manifestly insufficient as an account of much of the work after *Foe*. While *Age of Iron*, *The Master of Petersburg*, and *Disgrace* are still in an important sense *about* other literary works (the classics, Dostoevsky, and English romantic poetry, respectively), and therefore present themselves as a reflection on their own literary status, they also foreground a more realist dimension. It is especially with the most recent works, such as *The Lives of Animals*, *Elizabeth Costello*, *Youth*, *Slow Man*, and *Diary of a Bad Year*, that the limitations of the earlier critical consensus make themselves felt. While the more recent works should not be denied the theoretical sophistication that was central to the earlier novels, their concerns can no longer be translated into the familiar terms of critical discourse in any obvious way. Something very different is going on in these novels.

I don't believe that we must locate a radical break in Coetzee's work after, say, the first five novels. Instead, it is more accurate to say that the later work more explicitly (that is, more successfully) emphasizes an element that was already present in the early work but that was to some extent obscured by theoretical and metafictional concerns. The element that has increasingly found articulation in Coetzee's writing is, as I show in this chapter, the *undeniable fact of bodily suffering*. In Coetzee's more recent work, acknowledging the simple fact that human and nonhuman bodies suffer becomes more important than any theoretical analysis of the historical conditions and the power relations through which such suffering comes about. Of course, this is not to deny that the mutilated, tortured, or suffering body was already an important element in Coetzee's early work: think of the tortured girl in *Waiting for the Barbarians*, the tongueless Friday in *Foe*, or the regime of medical supervision undergone by Michael K. Still, these earlier bodies could easily be understood within the terms of gender inequality, racism, and colonial violence—the terms, that is, in which the ethical and political import of the early work has generally been described. Bodily suffering signaled the disastrous effects of the violence inflicted by patriarchal and colonial power regimes. As I argue at length below, such an understanding is deliberately complicated by, for instance, the amputation of Paul Rayment's leg in *Slow Man*, by the pain that David Lurie and his daughter, Lucy, suffer during the attack on Lucy's farm in *Disgrace*, or by the problems of old age of Coetzee's most recent protagonists. Something different from power relations is at stake here, and this different aspect has increasingly moved to the foreground in Coetzee's later work.

My claim in this chapter is double: first, I want to demonstrate that Coetzee's ethical investment in bodily suffering is more successfully foregrounded in his later work while the reception of his earlier work mainly emphasized his reflections on power and authority; second, I argue that this development is enabled by a gradual shift in Coetzee's conception of the relation between fiction and the truth—and therefore also between literature and philosophy. While the conception of the truth that guides Coetzee's more overtly self-reflexive, metafictional literary work is that of a nonpropositional, "higher" truth that consists in more than a mere correspondence between representation and reality (*Doubling the Point*, 17), the emphasis later moves from this revelatory conception of the truth to a more minimal demand to address and to acknowledge—to be true to—the fact of suffering. This ethical demand was sidelined somewhat in Coetzee's early conception of the truth, and this can be explained if we appreciate that this early conception relied on an intertext that it shared with the literary-critical reception of this early work: Coetzee's work is mediated by the phenomenon of "French theory," which in its turn relied heavily on Alexandre Kojève's influential reading of Hegel's *Phenomenology of Spirit*. Coetzee initially deployed Kojève's conception of history as a struggle for recognition between master and slave, as well as the privileged role that Kojève's scheme leaves open for literature. Still, as I explain in the next section of this chapter, this scheme is structurally incapable of responding to the undeniable fact of suffering; an adequate response to this fact will come to require a different literary practice, which I discuss in the third section, before showing how this ethical practice is embodied in Coetzee's recent work.

RECOGNITION AND GRACE (KOJÈVE, BLANCHOT)

Coetzee expounds the relation to philosophy and to the truth that supported his early work in the interviews with David Attwell in the 1992 collection *Doubling the Point*. This book collects much of Coetzee's nonfictional work up to that time and frames it with interviews between David Attwell and the writer. Both the first and the last interview mainly deal with the question of truth. In the last interview, Coetzee comments on his essay "Confession and Double Thoughts" (written in 1982–1983), an interpretation of Tolstoy, Rousseau, and Dostoevsky that demonstrates how these writers confront the structural interminability of secular confession, an impasse that can, for these writers, only be resolved by divine absolution, by the intervention of grace in the world (*Doubling the Point*, 249). Coetzee comments that he considers this essay "a submerged dialogue between two persons" who both hold to a different position about the "truth in autobiography," and, as "all writing is autobiography" (391), also about the very possibility of articulating the truth in language. The first of these two positions evinces a "secular skepticism about truth" (243) and holds that writing is "self-interested in every sense," and therefore "there is no ultimate truth about onself . . . what we call the truth is only a shifting self-reappraisal whose function is to make one feel good" (391–92). The debate in the essay is then "between cynicism and grace. Cynicism: the denial of any ultimate basis for values. Grace: a condition in which the truth can be told clearly, without blindness" (392).

Such a position of cynicism, or of "endless skepticism," corresponds to the familiar suspicion that human language can never attain the truth but is rather always and inescapably a partisan and perspectival instrument of power. Yet it is important to realize that Coetzee does not simply identify with this skeptical condition. While he cannot, like Dostoevsky, believe in the possibility of divine grace, neither does he think that an insight in the truth is simply inaccessible to man, or to human language. At the end of *Doubling the Point*, Coetzee calls his earlier attempt (in "Confession and Double Thoughts") to confront the impasse of endless skepticism and to negotiate the possibility of an undistorted access to the truth "the beginning of a more broadly philosophical engagement with a situation in the world" (394). In another interview, Coetzee takes great care to distinguish his "philosophical" practice from the work of philosophers: he insists that he is "not a trained philosopher," that he lacks "the philosophical equipment." The domain where his philosophical engagement with the truth is played out is then not that of philosophy, but rather that of the novel: "I am concerned to write the kind of novel—to work in the kind of novel form—in which one is not unduly handicapped (compared with the philosopher) when one plays (or works) with ideas" (246).

What makes this literary activity philosophical is, as Coetzee make clear, its manifest interest in the truth, that is, its ambition to transcend the conviction that all truth claims can be seen as a cover for power interests. Coetzee remarks that this philosophical concern should be read side by side with his novel *Waiting for the Barbarians*:

> The novel asks the question: Why does one choose the side of justice when it is in no one's material interest to do so? The Magistrate [the novel's main character] gives the rather Platonic answer: because we are born with the idea of justice. ["Confession and

Double Thoughts"], if only implicitly, asks the question: Why should I be interested in the truth about myself when the truth may not be in my interest? To which, I suppose I continue to give a Platonic answer: because we are born with the idea of the truth. (394-95)

While it may not be possible to represent reality in an undistorted way, fiction writing is at least propelled by the ideas of truth and justice. If we take his own word for it, Coetzee's writing is motivated by a desire to move beyond the skeptical denial of the possibility of truth, and this interest in the truth, which he himself identifies as philosophical, is also a matter of justice.

This complex relation to the truth can explain Coetzee's ambiguous political position in South Africa. His awareness of the relation between truth claims and power interests, and of his own inescapable complicity with the privileged white majority in South Africa, led him to renounce the supposedly neutral position of an uninvolved, totally uninterested outsider. At the same time, his suspicion that truth claims are often a mere cover for power interests, or are at least often perceived as such, can explain the fact that his work never simply identified with only one position in the struggle for power in South Africa, not even the position of the victims of Apartheid. Coetzee's early work did not naïvely participate in the South African power struggle, nor did it believe that it could simply transcend it. Rather than a formulation of clear and unambiguous denunciations and judgments, Coetzee's literary dedication to justice and truth took the complex literary form of what has been called "a strategy of paradox," in which every statement is "undermined even as it is articulated."[4]

But, we may well ask, how can such a self-subverting literary strategy lead to the truth? How does a strategy of paradox lead to the truth about the work of power that it refuses to condemn unequivocally, lest it be itself considered as just one more covert expression of the desire for power? We find a clue in the first interview in *Doubling the Point*, where Coetzee again comments on the relation between truth and writing. He distinguishes two kinds of truths, the first of which is "truth to fact, the second something beyond that" (17). This second, "'higher' truth" only emerges in the process of writing. Coetzee carefully describes this process as follows:

> It is naive to think that writing is a simple two-stage process: first you decide what you want to say, then you say it. On the contrary, as all of us know, you write because you do not know what you want to say. Writing reveals to you what you wanted to say in the first place.... That is the sense in which one can say that writing writes us. Writing shows or creates (and we are not always sure we can tell one from the other) what our desire was, a moment ago.

Writing, then, involves an interplay between the push into the future that takes you to the blank page in the first place, and a resistance.... Out of that interplay there emerges, if you are lucky, what you recognize or hope to recognize as the true....

Truth is something that comes in the process of writing, or comes from the process of writing.

(18)

Unlike the truth to fact, then, which consists in the correspondence of a representation to the world as it is, the truth of writing entails the creation of a new worldly reality, a new fact that can, "if you are lucky," be recognized as the true. Writing produces a new reality that cannot be understood as the result of the intention to produce that reality; only after the fact does it allow us to recognize what our initial intention appears to have been. It should be clear that a quite peculiar conception of human action is at work here. We need to understand this structure of human action and the related conception of the truth in order to gauge the philosophy of Coetzee's early work and the limits that this philosophy imposes on the ethics of the early novels.

While the paradoxical temporal structure in which a result reveals the desire that gave rise to it may not correspond to what we ordinarily think of as the intentional structure of human action, it is the very structure of action and historical change that we encounter in an important (even if indirect) source text for both Coetzee and many of his literary-critical interpreters, that is, Alexandre Kojève's lectures on Hegel's *Phenomenology of Spirit*, delivered in Paris between 1933 and 1939. Kojève famously interprets the Hegelian dialectic as an anthropological schema in which man makes history by creating a series of human worlds that are essentially different from the natural world with which man is initially confronted.[5] The essential difference between the natural (and biological) world and human history consists in man's unique status as "negating desire," that is, his properly human desire to transform the given and to create "a new being by destroying the given being."[6] Kojève explains that this human desire is essentially different from animal desire, which also raises itself above natural givens (if only by eating them) but is immediately satisfied upon consumption and soon returns to the same state it was in before the desire manifested itself. Animal desire, unlike human desire, ultimately does not transcend its given self. Human desire *does* transcend its given being, precisely because it does *not* desire another given being that can fulfill its desire but instead desires a *non*being. And because desire is itself the absence of being (it is "an *emptiness* greedy for content"), human desire is directed toward another desire, toward "another greedy emptiness."[7] Desire thus needs another desire that will recognize its superiority, that will recognize the first desire's "*exclusive* right to satisfaction" by renouncing its own right to recognition.[8] Now, because there is always more than one desire that desires this exclusive recognition, this situation inevitably leads to a fight of life and death, which ends when one party ultimately renounces its properly human desire for recognition and subjects itself to its opponent. This party prefers to become a slave rather than give up its biological, given condition. By deciding to hold on to its life rather than to the prospect of exclusive recognition, it cancels its distinctive humanity. This is the famous dialectic of master and slave, which for Kojève is what *makes* human history, and which is a crucial intertext for understanding what goes on between the characters in Coetzee's first five novels.[9]

Importantly, for Kojève, it follows from the conception of man as negating desire that the slave, rather than the master, makes history.[10] While the slave has subjected himself to his (not properly human) fear of biological death, this fear also has a positive value: "He caught a glimpse of himself as nothingness,"[11] and therefore realizes that he has to transform himself into something (else). So whereas the master will forever remain what he already is, and is therefore properly excluded from the changes and progressions of human history, the slave has to change and make history through his work. Working means transforming the natural world and thereby also changing oneself: "It is only by rising above the given conditions through negation brought about in and by *Work* that Man remains in contact with the concrete, which varies with space and time. That is why he changes himself by transforming the World."[12] It is this new, unanticipated result that in retrospect reveals the slave's desire to become this new creation and gradually leave his condition of subjection behind.

We can begin to understand the structure of human action that underlies Coetzee's idea of writing in *Doubling the Point* when we note that for him, writing is one such nonintentional, transformative activity that creates new and unexpected realities for the self.[13] In the same way that, for Kojève, the slave is moved by the abstract idea of freedom, writing, for Coetzee, is moved by the "Platonic" "idea of the truth." Before I comment on the limitations that Coetzee's debt to this scheme imposes on the ethics of his early fiction, we may well ask how writing not only offers an *example* of transformative action but even appears to be the example par excellence that can reveal the *truth* of this scheme. In his 1949 essay "Literature and the Right to Death," Maurice Blanchot explored what Kojève's work on Hegel meant for literature, and it is here that we can find an explanation for the privilege of literature. Blanchot's interpretation was extremely influential in French intellectual circles, as were Kojève's lectures; in addition to the subterranean influence this had on Coetzee's work (via the work of, especially, Jacques Lacan, Roland Barthes, and Michel Foucault),[14] many of Blanchot's phrases resonate in Coetzee's remarks on the relation between truth and literature. Blanchot observes that someone only becomes a writer if he has actually written something but that he can only write if he has the talent to write, a talent that can in its turn only be discovered if he has actually sat down to write. He will therefore begin to write "starting from nothing and with nothing in mind."[15] In the light of Kojève's conception of human action, literature is then not just "a passive expression on the surface of the world" that must be opposed to actual work, to "a concrete initiative in the world"; instead, literature exemplifies the process in which a nothingness works on the world in order to change both itself and the world—the process, that is, that for Kojève defines history. Blanchot writes: "If we see work as the force of history, the force that transforms man while it transforms the world, then a writer's activity must be recognized as the highest form of work."[16] When a man writes, he does "everything a man does as he works, but to an outstanding degree."[17] As such, the process of writing reveals the true structure of every human action, which often remains hidden when action is thought of as a pregiven intention that produces a certain result. Literature *exemplifies* and *reveals* the fact that man is a negating desire and that he is, even if only unconsciously, motivated by a desire for recognition, and therefore ultimately for power. It is this peculiar relation between literature and truth that resonates in the remarks by Coetzee that I quoted above.

This intertext for Coetzee's conception of literary truth can explain, first, the privileged relation literature holds for him as the place where truth is revealed and, second, the fact that the truth it reveals is a truth about the nature of human relations: driven by a desire for power and by particular interests, excluding others or inflicting violence on them. This makes clear why Coetzee's early novels can be perceived as self-reflexive, meticulously controlled, and neatly self-contained metafictions that investigate such relations of power and are fully aware that they cannot escape their implication in these relations. *Dusklands* and *Waiting for the Barbarians* can then be understood as investigations of the workings of empire and colonial power (with an explicit awareness of the writer's own status as a white man with Afrikaner roots); *In the Heart of the Country*, as an investigation of race and gender relations; *Foe*, as a reflection on the authority and power connected to the activities of writing and narration themselves; and *Life and Times of Michael K*, as, among other things, an exploration of biopolitical issues.

At the same time, some of the attributes of this larger scheme compromise the ethical thrust of Coetzee's writing, which leads even his early work to attempt to move beyond the confines of this framework. I will name the four most important of these constraining characteristics here. First, the scheme is uncompromisingly *anthropocentric*: only man is a negating desire, capable of overcoming his biological limits, and therefore only man is properly implicated in the power relations that are the central object of Coetzee's writing. It is man's distinctive, more-than-biological desire that defines him as a subject fit for fictional treatment and attention. Second, this emphasis on a desire that is more than biological also excludes a consideration of the essential *embodiedness* of human existence. The body can only enter as the place where the master makes his power over the slave felt, or as one part of the available reality that must be transformed; our human being is not in any way essentially connected to our bodily being. Third, nonhuman others can only really enter this picture as realities to be *objectified* and transformed, as so many occasions for the subject to develop and enrich itself. In a sense, the human subject relies on this material if it wants to overcome its nonhuman origins. Fourth, this scheme considers the *confrontation with death* as, first of all, an occasion to learn about one's own distinctive nothingness and about the need to transform this nothingness and to develop one's own being. An awareness of death is, in short, merely a spur to action, and it does not inspire an awareness of our mortality, our limitations, and our finitude.

It should be clear that the different limitations of this anthropocentric framework in which Coetzee's search for literary truth operates also constitute so many constraints on our capacity to relate to nonhuman others: we cannot find a relation in the embodiedness that we share with animals, nor can we find common ground in an awareness of our finitude. It is then no surprise that animals will come to play such a central role in Coetzee's work once it begins to move beyond these limitations and to construct a different ethics. The central role of animals in Coetzee's later work thus indicates his attempt to move away from his earlier reliance on the framework that I have sketched and to make room for a more ethically attuned mode of writing.

ACKNOWLEDGMENT AND DISGRACE (CAVELL)

Already in an interview in *Doubling the Point*, the book in which Coetzee formulates the conception of the truth that has guided his work until then, he registers the limits of that conception in no uncertain terms:

> Let me add, *entirely* parenthetically, that I, as a person, as a personality, am overwhelmed, that my thinking is thrown into confusion and helplessness, by the fact of suffering in the world, and not only human suffering. These fictional constructions of mine are paltry, ludicrous defenses against that being-overwhelmed, and, to me, transparently so.
> (*Doubling the Point*, 248)

"The fact of suffering" is, as this passage makes clear, not only a challenge to Coetzee's thinking but also a factor that he may not have managed to integrate successfully into his fiction. Moreover, Coetzee insists that the imperative to attend to the fact of suffering concerns him "as a person," and moreover in a way that challenges his rationality. Bodily suffering does not engage him as a rational being; it crosses the limits of human rationality and therefore also of the philosophical framework that supported Coetzee's earlier conception of the truth, as is borne out by Coetzee's further comments: the body, he notes, "is not 'that which is not,' and the proof that it *is* is the pain it feels." This is all very different from Kojève's idea that human consciousness is "what it is not," an "emptiness greedy for content." The blunt fact of a body that suffers points to the limits of the philosophical framework that informed Coetzee's meticulously self-reflexive early novels. No measure of textual paradox, of the endlessly skeptical processes of textualization, can spirit away the fact of suffering. Coetzee writes: "In South Africa, it is not possible to deny the authority of suffering and therefore of the body ... the suffering body *takes* this authority: that is its power. To use other words: its power is undeniable" (248).

As Coetzee makes clear here, the fact of bodily suffering is something no proposition can deny; it is something that any ethically engaged writing project has to take into account and respond to. The fact of suffering is not one of the things that a project of endless skepticism or the infinite transformation of all given realities can cancel. For Coetzee, the analyses of the power relations that lead to suffering and pain in his early novels are "paltry, ludicrous defenses" that do not adequately respond to this suffering. Suffering is an element that does not require cognitive or practical denial or affirmation; it demands to be addressed in wholly other terms.

So how are we to understand the importance accorded here to the quasi-ineffable fact of suffering without turning to a mystical, even theological register? In his seminal paper on the refutation of the skeptical position on the privacy of pain (the position, that is, that we cannot *know* the other's pain), Stanley Cavell shows how the *fact* of skepticism about the possibility of knowing someone else's pain is itself an indication that pain is a problem in relation to which "certainty is not enough."[18] Being certain that the other is in pain does not seem to be a sufficient response to the *fact* of his suffering, and it is in the sense of this insufficiency that the skeptic's wariness originates. Even if we do not "know" the other's pain, the fundamental thing remains "*that* he has it,"[19] and this points, according to Cavell, to "a special concept of knowledge, or region of the concept of knowledge; one which is not a function of certainty."[20] Where the skeptic's doubt about the possibility of knowledge treats pain as the occasion of an "intellectual lack," of mere ignorance, he fails to come to terms with the fact that pain rather points to "a metaphysical finitude" that does not so much demand to be known but must rather be *acknowl-*

edged.[21] Acknowledging the other's pain means that I give voice to the fact that his suffering makes a *claim* upon me and also to the fact of my powerlessness, my incapacity to do more than acknowledge this pain.[22] The expression "I know you are in pain" is then not an expression of certainty but rather an expression of *sympathy* in response to the other exhibiting his pain.

For Cavell, such expressions of sympathy are not a matter of course but something that we can all too easily fail to bring off: once we have been addressed ("overwhelmed" is Coetzee's term in the passage I quoted) by the claim of another's pain, our failure to acknowledge it is "an indifference, a callousness, an exhaustion, a coldness."[23] Sympathy, in other words, is something we have to afford and something that we fail to deliver when we rely on rational argumentation as a way to "make unavailable to ourselves our own sense of what it is to be a living animal"[24] or, in Coetzee's terms, when we erect fictions as ludicrous defenses against the claim of suffering. By referring to his fictions as meager defenses, Coetzee's acknowledgment of this claim in *Doubling the Point* also recognizes the inadequacy of his fictional response to it. Coetzee's later work can then be understood as an attempt to acknowledge the claim of the irreducible fact of bodily suffering. This attempt to "be true to fact" must also recognize its own incapacity to do more than acknowledge the fact of suffering, its inability to actually intervene and change it. It must concede that pain and suffering are an irreducible limit to what Kojève saw as the unlimited human capacity for transformation. This recognition moves us, in the words of a recent commentator, from "the ironic, skeptical, tautly cerebral voice" that is dominant in parts of Coetzee's early work to "a voice that insists, with a more visceral urgency, on the direct, factual, and compelling reality of bodily suffering and death."[25]

This new demand to be "true to fact" also implies that the association between truth and justice that Coetzee sketched earlier no longer holds. While I have here mainly been concerned with the intrinsic limitations of this association that made it necessary for Coetzee to revise it, we should also note the effects of the Truth and Reconciliation Commission, which was active in South Africa in the aftermath of Apartheid from 1995 on. While this is not the place to discuss this institution at any length, I yet want to remark that the commission's explicit ambition was the promotion of national unity and reconciliation after the devastations and atrocities of Apartheid. As the name of the commission indicates, its crucial working assumptions were, first, that "the publication or voicing of truth will lead directly to reconciliation" and, second, that exposing the truth "brings not only reconciliation but also a sort of justice."[26] Still, in practice the desire to bring about reconciliation at any cost often meant that the perpetrators' simple willingness to confess their past misdeeds was sufficient to be granted amnesty. In spite of the commission's lofty ambitions, reconciliation became, in the words of one commentator, "a fetishized claim that both devalues and displaces the experience of those who were wronged."[27] The revelation of the factual truth, then, far from leading to justice, in fact ended up perpetuating the violence and injustices of Apartheid.[28] And while the TRC offers a particularly strong instance of the dissociation of the search for truth and the ambition to further justice, I think it is possible to see it as symptomatic of a broader set of ethically relevant phenomena in which the attempt to get something right, to learn the truth about something, can contribute little to the effort to promote justice. Whether it is true or not, to name only two widely mediatized instances, that the war in Iraq was initiated on false premises or that both Israel and the Palestinians have been less than fully dedicated to achieving lasting peace, the effort to find out the truth about these issues can hardly begin to address the real pain and suffering involved in the facts *about* which they attempt to discover the truth. Something more is required in order to address these phenomena in a way that is in the least adequate. Coetzee's emphasis on these facts and on the obligation to acknowledge them implies that by limiting ourselves to a search for truth and certainty, we also fail to be true to the undeniable claim that this suffering has on our attention.[29]

THE ETHICS OF COETZEE'S LATER WORK

In the last section of this chapter, I briefly try to show how Coetzee's later work sets out to overcome the limitations of the framework within which his earlier fiction operated, limitations that we can also consider as so many failures to be true to the undeniable fact of suffering. These failures derived from the exclusive definition of man as a negating desire, which, as I showed in the previous section, threatened to silence the claim of the body and of nonhuman others, as well as the possibility of confronting our finitude in the face of death (a confrontation that, as we will see, can itself provide an occasion to relate to the finitude of others). The movement from these restrictions to a more successful acknowledgment of suffering is perhaps best exemplified in the development of David Lurie, the protagonist of Coetzee's 1999 novel *Disgrace*. Lurie, a fifty-two-year-old professor of literature, is introduced as a man carrying a "desiring gaze" (*Disgrace*, 12), and he later in the novel emphatically invokes "the rights of desire" to justify his actions. (69, 90) The point of view of the desiring gaze[30] and his self-understanding as a creature of desire blind Lurie to the perspective of Melanie, one of his students, whom he forces into a sexual relation.

The novel's exposure of the interestedness of human action and of the violence it does to others is of course reminiscent of Coetzee's early novels. Yet the remarkable thing is that *Disgrace* does not just diagnose these power relations but instead follows up this diagnosis by tracing the development of Lurie's character when he is forced to abandon a domain organized by power and desire and moves to a place that can no longer be analyzed in these terms and thus requires a new approach. After his disgraceful dismissal from the university he moves to his daughter's farm, and here the central role of desire makes way for what the novel repeatedly calls "despair" (108). During an attack on the farm, Lurie is humiliated and set on fire by the attackers: "He throws himself about, hurling out shapeless bellows that have no words behind him, only fear. He tries to stand up and is forced down again" (96). It is no coincidence that it is two of the features that were often supposed to distinguish the human from the nonhuman—language and bipedalism—that begin to fail Lurie when he is suddenly confronted with his embodied state (that is to say, with a body that is more than a mere instrument to achieve sexual gratification).

In the rest of the novel, Lurie gradually comes to terms with the limitations of his mutilated, aging body and learns to accept "disgrace as [his] state of being" (172). This process goes hand in hand with the ever closer connection that he feels to the fate of the dogs he nurses on the farm and in the animal clinic where he helps out. While Lurie first notes that animals accept "their lot, waiting their turn" (85), and thus denies them a sense of anxiety in the face of death, he later feels that "they too feel the disgrace of dying" (143). It is then because he experiences and acknowledges that "suddenly and without reason, their lot has become important to him" (126) that he can ultimately accept disgrace as also *his* state of being. Death, then, is no longer, as in Kojève's framework, an occasion for human transformation, but it now instills an awareness of our mortality that forges a link to human and nonhuman others who are equally aware of their finitude.

The sense of mortality has the power to establish a connection to others, and near the end of the novel Lurie takes it upon himself to incinerate the dead dogs instead of just letting them be processed "unmarked, unmourned" (178), by men who "use shovels to beat corpses into a more convenient shape for processing" (146). Lurie takes care of the body parts of dead dogs that "can neither be sold nor eaten" (145) as his way of acknowledging an absolute limit to restless transformation. It is because animals, too, have "foreknowledge of impending death" that their lot becomes important for Lurie and demands his acknowledgment,[31] which involves a growing recognition of the body as the site of suffering and of death.

This anticlimactic scenario, in which the main character of the novel is evacuated from the realm of desire to a situation in which he or she must cope with the demand to acknowledge death, the body, and suffering, returns in all of Coetzee's novels written since *Disgrace*—in *Elizabeth Costello*, in the autobiographical novel *Youth*, in *Slow Man*, and in *Diary of a Bad Year*. As *Youth* is overtly modeled on the life of the young Coetzee himself, and as it describes the development of the ambitions of a young artist, the way the scenario takes shape here has a particular relevance for the question how we are to understand Coetzee's own artistic practice. At the beginning of the novel, the ethic of the young poet consists in his "readiness" to be "transformed," "to be rid of his own self and revealed in his new, true, passionate self" (*Youth*, 93, 111). Writing literature is then one way to "transfigure" reality—it is "a flame that consumes yet paradoxically renews all that it touches" (25, 30). Still, the confrontation with "all in life that is miserable, squalid, ignominious" does not leave the young poet "enriched and strengthened" (66), as this aesthetic ethic would lead him to believe, but rather brings him to the realization that this framework based on desire and transformation is no more than unconvincing sophistry (164). The insight that his ethic of progressive self-transformation is incompatible with the sobering facts of life ultimately makes him abandon poetry altogether and turn to prose, which, unlike the gratuitous and abstract embellishments of poetry, "seems naggingly to demand a specific setting" (63). This attention to the specifics of a particular situation, an attentiveness that gives these particulars their due and that does not immediately consider them as so many "given realities" to be transformed will henceforth inform the young artist's work. Where Coetzee, in *Doubling the Point*, characterized his early position as "a more broadly philosophical engagement with a situation in the world," the perspective that emerges in the course of *Youth* and that is embodied in Coetzee's later fiction can better be described as a dedication to "the prose of the world," to what Hegel described as "a world of finitude and mutability, of entanglement in the relative, of the pressure of necessity from which the individual is in no position to withdraw."[32] For Coetzee, the fact that these particulars do not contribute to the discovery of philosophical truth is no reason to devalue them; it is because they are senseless and worthless that they demand to be acknowledged in his prose.

The refusal to consider particular incidents and facts of suffering and loss as occasions for personal development and worldly transformation is also central in Coetzee's novel *Slow Man*. The main character, Paul Rayment, at the beginning of the book loses a leg after a traffic accident. But just as David Lurie in *Disgrace* directs his attention to the dogs who will otherwise "be tossed into the fire unmarked, unmourned" (*Disgrace*, 178), Paul Rayment refuses a prosthesis to replace the leg that has been "dropped in the refuge for someone to collect and *toss into the fire*" (*Slow Man*, 10, italics mine). And just as the processing of the dogs conjures the word "*Lösung*," meaning "sublimation . . . leaving no residue, no aftertaste" (*Disgrace*, 142), the word "*Prosthese*" suggests to Paul Rayment the restless completion of an unstoppable progression: "Thesis, antithesis, then prosthesis" (*Slow Man*, 62). Both Lurie and Rayment will dedicate their disgraced lives to symbolic gestures that resist the restless completion of the work of transformation. Instead of replacing the lost leg, Rayment will learn to accept that his body is incomplete, that "never is he going to be his old self again" (53), that he is "a man not wholly a man ... a half-man, an after-man" (33-34). He will learn to embrace himself as a figure "beyond anger and desire" (224) who has "entered the zone of humiliation" (61), where he will live out the remainder of his years.

The shift from self-reflexive form toward an outright acknowledgment of the fact of suffering is also central to Coetzee's 1999 book *The Lives of Animals*. While the book, which originated in Tanner lectures Coetzee presented at Princeton University, has been criticized for its refusal to present clear arguments and conclusions about the momentous topics it deals with, an awareness of Coetzee's relation to philosophy should warn us not to confuse this indirectness with a strategy of evasion. The book consists of two parts, the former entitled "The Philosophers and the Animals," the latter, "The Poets and the Animals," and both use fictional devices to register the insufficiency of either a philosophical or a "poetical" approach to animals (the latter is the approach that Elizabeth Costello, Coetzee's *porte-parole* in the book, advocates). In the first part of the book, Costello takes to task philosophy's failure to acknowledge "suffering animal bodies" (*Lives of Animals*, 40) because of its unqualified insistence on reason. Philosophy can only approach animals in its own image, and this attempt to "humanize" the animal forces it "toward the humbler reaches of practical reason" where it cannot but fall short of human standards (33, 37). Philosophical reason, for Costello, is a "system of totality" that takes itself to be the self-evident standard of thought and action and so ends up reasserting its power over the nonrational other (46). The one thing that reason cannot do is "dethrone itself"; "reasoning systems, as systems of totality, do not have that power" (30). Philosophy, in other, words, not only fails to acknowledge the suffering of animals but also fails to recognize its own limits, its own finitude, its incapacity to adequately address that suffering.

Against the philosophical attitude, Costello asserts the power of the sympathetic imagination, which is a faculty "that allows us to share at times the being of another" (48). According to Costello, we can counteract our indifference and our contempt for animals through the capacity to "think my way into the existence of a bat or a chimpanzee or an oyster, any being with whom I share the substrate of life" (49). For Costello, "there are no bounds to the sympathetic imagination" because fullness of being counts for more than a difference in form of being: "being fully a bat is like being fully human" (45-49). While this "fullness, embodiedness" reads like an explicit denial of the conception of man as "negating desire," and therefore may initially seem to correspond to Coetzee's own position (as is indeed often assumed), I want to argue that there are vital differences between Costello's firm assertion of the grandiose capacities of the sympathetic imagination and the more minor and humble ethics that takes shape in Coetzee's later fiction.

It is important to realize that Coetzee has surrounded Costello's argument with enough markers to raise doubts about her belief in the possibility of "the experience of full being" (45). First, Costello's vocation of sympathy is part of a story in which her relation with especially her daughter-in-law is marked by irritation and resentment. While these characters seem capable enough of imagining each other's point of view, this does not automatically manifest itself into a caring attitude, which suggests that more is at stake in ethics than the capacity to imagine ourselves in the place of another.[33] Second, take Costello's central argument that "if we are capable of thinking our own death, why on earth should we not be capable of thinking our way into the life of a bat?" (44). In the light of the rest of Coetzee's recent work, the conditional clause here seems to remain sadly unfulfilled: the confrontation with one's own death is, for Coetzee, not so much a moment of empowerment, of insight into our human capacity for transformation as it is rather a moment in which we are forced to acknowledge our finitude. For Coetzee, and following Cavell, acknowledging the pain of the other is precisely also the acknowledgment of a "sense of incapacity,"[34] a certain powerlessness, and *not* a boundless capacity to think our way into the other. Such a strong capacity precisely disowns the crucial fact of our fateful separateness from the other's suffering. Third, Costello's example of the bat is itself less straightforward than she seems to think. She recognizes that the capacity to feel one's way into another being is distinctively human; there is no sense in saying that a bat can know what it is like to be human. What we are asked to imagine, then, is a situation (the being of a bat) in which we are paradoxically incapable of imagining such a situation, that is, of imagining the situation we are in fact imagining. Considered in this way, Costello's example does not illustrate the unboundedness of the sympathetic imagination but rather formulates the demand to imagine an absolute *limit* to the imagination. In the light of Coetzee's contemporary production, I take it that this insistence on human limitation is closer to his own position.[35] As one critic has recently remarked, Coetzee's fiction is not the celebration of an unbounded imagination but instead consists in acts "of sympathetic imagination that continually encounter their own bounds."[36] Instead of relying on imaginative projection, Coetzee's ethics are grounded "in the acknowledgement of one's ignorance of the other, on the recognition of the other's fundamental alterity" (120). Instead of Costello's sympathetic imagination, then, Coetzee enacts "a singularly *un*imaginative sympathy" (130).[37]

Coetzee's critique of the sympathetic imagination can only be uncovered when we are willing to read his works (and especially *The Lives of Animals*) as works of fiction that do not aim to present a logically sound argument, say, for or against animal liberation. Every argument that is presented by Costello is in principle hers only, which does not mean that we can simply dismiss it—indeed, the point of presenting her statements in a fictional frame is that this makes them all the more *undeniable*. We are not asked to agree or disagree with her argument, but we must at least register it. In the words of one commentator, "Coetzee employs the power of fiction to suspend disapproval and disbelief: he compels us to regard the truth that obsesses [Costello]."[38] It is this obligation that the reader cannot resist, and this powerlessness is, I argue, the place where Coetzee's ethics makes itself felt.

In fact, there is one part of *The Lives of Animals* that is not filtered through a fictional screen: the notes that accompany the two parts of the book. Whereas Costello's speech is to be attributed to her rather than to Coetzee, there is no such reason to attribute the notes, which are not part of the speech she delivers, to anyone other than the author of the book, J. M. Coetzee. Most of the twenty-three notes contain only bibliographical references, but I want to close this chapter by turning to one footnote that stands out. The eighth note to the second part of the book, which is printed on the last page, refers to Michael Leahy's infamous antiliberation polemic *Against Liberation*. Coetzee's footnote goes as follows:

> Leahy elsewhere argues against a ban on the slaughtering of animals on the grounds that (a) it would bring about unemployment among abattoir workers, (b) it would entail an uncomfortable adjustment to our diet, and (c) the countryside would be less attractive without its customary flocks and herds fattening themselves as they wait to die.
> (125)

Coetzee does not choose to offer a refutation of Leahy's arguments, but the note of sarcasm and indignation in the dry enumeration of these arguments will not be lost on any careful reader. This is as explicit as Coetzee's ethics becomes, in *The Lives of Animals* or elsewhere. Even if Coetzee does not transmit this ethics in clear arguments and propositions, the claim that his fictions make on their readers is yet properly undeniable. Even if we do not recognize this as philosophy, its claim remains ours to acknowledge.

Notes

1. G. Huggan and S. Watson, introduction to *Critical Perspectives on J. M. Coetzee*, ed. Huggan and Watson (London: MacMillan, 1996), 6.
2. Perhaps the clearest example (and certainly one of the most impressive) is Teresa Dovey's monograph on these five novels (T. Dovey, *The Novels of J. M. Coetzee: Lacanian Allegories* [Craighall: Ad. Donker, 1988]). Dovey considers the development of

these different novels as so many allegories of the novels' own relation to (and critique of) different traditional subgenres of South African literature, such as the journal of exploration and the liberal humanist novel. This resolute emphasis on the novels' awareness that the story they tell also applies to their own status is typical of the line of reception I am sketching here. For other prominent examples of the "metafictional" line of reception, see G. Huggan and S. Watson, eds., *Critical Perspectives on J. M. Coetzee* (London: MacMillan, 1996).

3. S. Kossew, introduction to *Critical Essays on J. M. Coetzee*, ed. S. Kossew (New York: G. K. Hall, 1998), 3.

4. M. Marais, "Places of Pigs: The Tension Between Implication and Transcendence in J. M. Coetzee's *Age of Iron* and *The Master of Petersburg*," in *Critical Essays on J. M. Coetzee*, ed. S. Kossew (New York: G. K. Hall, 1998), 236.

5. A. Kojève, *Introduction to the Reading of Hegel*, ed. A. Bloom, trans. J. Nichols (Ithaca, N.Y.: Cornell University Press, 1969), 32.

6. Ibid., 37-38.

7. Ibid., 40.

8. Ibid., 40.

9. This was first noted by Menàn Du Plessis ("Towards a True Materialism," in *Critical Essays on J. M. Coetzee*, ed. S. Kossew [New York: G. K. Hall, 1998], 117-25) and has been extensively demonstrated by, among others, D. Penner, *Countries of the Mind: The Fiction of J. M. Coetzee*, (Westport, Conn.: Greenwood, 1989); S. Watson, "Colonialism and the Novels of J. M. Coetzee," in *Critical Perspectives on J. M. Coetzee*, ed. G. Huggan and S. Watson (London: MacMillan, 1996), 13-36; and T. Dovey, "J. M. Coetzee: Writing in the Middle Voice," in *Critical Essays on J. M. Coetzee*, ed. S. Kossew (New York: G. K. Hall, 1998), 18-28).

10. Kojève's claim to intellectual fame derives mainly from his emphasis on the theme of the end of history. In the terms of his own framework, the end of history also means the end of man proper and man's return to the status of an animal "of the species homo sapiens." It is an indication of Kojève's anthropocentrism (on which I comment below) that, in subsequent editions of his lectures, he takes great pains to resist the animalization of man. For this, see G. Agamben, *The Open: Man and Animal*, trans. K. Attell (Stanford: Stanford University Press, 2004), 5-12.

11. Kojève, *Introduction to the Reading of Hegel*, 47.

12. Ibid., 51-52.

13. Teresa Dovey refers to this as Coetzee's "middle voice," following Coetzee's own reflection on the relation between writing and the grammatical middle voice, which is different from both the passive and the active voice (see *Doubling the Point*, 94-95).

14. These influences are documented in *Doubling the Point*. See especially J. Butler, *Sub-

jects of Desire: Reflections of Hegel in Twentieth-Century France (New York: Columbia University Press, 1987); and J.-M. Rabaté, *The Future of Theory* (Oxford: Blackwell, 2002), especially chap. 1, for the afterlife of Hegel in French theory; and M. Roth, *Knowing and History: Appropriations of Hegel in Twentieth-Century France* (Ithaca: Cornell University Press, 1988) for the wider intellectual reception of Hegel in France, with special attention to Kojève's role as a mediator.

15. M. Blanchot, "Literature and the Right to Death," in *The Work of Fire* (1949), trans. C. Mandell (Stanford: Stanford University Press, 1995), 300–43, 304.
16. Ibid., 313.
17. Ibid., 314.
18. S. Cavell, "Knowing and Acknowledging," in *The Cavell Reader*, ed. S. Mulhall (Cambridge, Mass.: Blackwell, 1996), 64.
19. Ibid., 53.
20. Ibid., 64.
21. Ibid., 68 and 63.
22. Ibid., 68.
23. Ibid., 69.
24. C. Diamond, "The Difficulty of Reality and the Difficulty of Philosophy," in *Reading Cavell*, ed. A. Crary and S. Shieh (London: Routledge, 2006), 102.
25. L. Tremaine, "The Embodied Soul: Animal Being in the Work of J. M. Coetzee," *Contemporary Literature* 44, no. 4 (2003): 588.
26. T. Urquhart, "Truth, Reconciliation, and the Restoration of the State: Coetzee's *Waiting for the Barbarians*," *Twentieth-Century Literature* 52, no. 1 (2006): 1.
27. H. Grunebaum, "Talking to Ourselves 'Among the Innocent Dead': On Reconciliation, Forgiveness, and Mourning," *PMLA* 117, no. 2 (2002): 308.
28. For a discussion of *Disgrace*'s critique of the TRC, see my article, P. Vermeulen, "Dogged Silences: J. M. Coetzee's *Disgrace* and the Ethics of Non-Confession," *BELL New Series* 2 (2004): 185–97.
29. It is in the light of this insistence on the facts of suffering and injustice (at the expense of certainty and truth) that Coetzee's later work leaves us, in David Simpson's words, "with the sense of having been evacuated from the comfortable space in which we can turn to our writers to tell us how to live, but with a searing sense that some way must be found" (D. Simpson, "Neither Rushdie nor Nobody: J. M. Coetzee on Censorship and Offense," *Pretexts: Literary and Cultural Studies* 10, no. 1 [2001]: 126).
30. The figure of the gaze in Coetzee's work always indicates the position of empire, of power, a position with which the framework of desire as I sketched it is inescapably implicated. For the figure of the gaze in Coetzee, see M. Marais, "The Hermeneutics of Empire: Coetzee's Post-Colonial Metafiction," in *Critical Perspectives on J. M. Coetzee*, ed.

G. Huggan and S. Watson (London: MacMillan, 1996), 71; and Coetzee, *White Writing*, 163-67. See my article mentioned in note 28 for the development of the figure of the gaze in *Disgrace*.

31. Tremaine, "The Embodied Soul," 595.
32. This quotation is used as the motto of M. P. Ginsburg and L. N. Nandrea, "The Prose of the World," in *The Novel*, vol. 2: *Forms and Themes*, ed. F. Moretti (Princeton: Princeton University Press, 2006), 244-73, which outlines the essential relations among prose, the novel, and the everyday in a way that is relevant for my discussion of Coetzee's literary ethics.
33. That there is a difference between being able to identify with someone and feeling (and acting) sympathetic toward them is also suggested when Costello says that "despite Thomas Nagel, who is probably a good man, despite Thomas Aquinas and René Descartes, *with whom I have more difficulty in sympathizing*, there is no limit to the extent to which we can think ourselves into the being of another" (48, italics mine).
34. Cavell, "Knowing and Acknowledging," 68.
35. We can compare this to J. Derrida, "The Animal That Therefore I Am (More to Follow)," trans. David Wills, *Critical Inquiry* 28, no. 2 (2002): 396, where he develops the question whether animals "can suffer": "[asking] 'Can they suffer?' amounts to asking 'can they *not be able*?'" For Derrida also, this inability, this vulnerability is a crucial moment in our relation to the animal. Cora Diamond, whose approach to *The Lives of Animals* parallels mine on more than one point, similarly foregrounds the importance of our "exposure to the bodily sense of vulnerability to death, sheer animal vulnerability" (Diamond, "The Difficulty of Reality", 111-12). While Diamond sees the sympathetic imagination (105) as conducive to this exposure, I want to insist that Coetzee's work also warns us that the capacity for sympathetic identification, as Costello conceives it, can disown the sense of limitedness that this vulnerability implies.
36. S. Durrant, "J. M. Coetzee, Elizabeth Costello, and the Limits of the Sympathetic Imagination," in *J. M. Coetzee and the Idea of the Public Intellectual*, ed. J. Poyner (Athens: Ohio University Press, 2006), 119.
37. For Coetzee's critique of the sympathetic imagination as Costello conceives it, see also O. De Graef, "Suffering, Sympathy, Circulation: Smith, Wordsworth, Coetzee (But There's a Dog)," *EJES* 7, no. 3 (2003): 311-31; and Laura Wright, *Writing "Out of All the Camps": J.M. Coetzee's Narratives of Displacement* (London: Routledge, 2006). And for a good discussion of the paradoxes generated by Costello's opposition to reason, see D. Head, "A Belief in Frogs: J. M. Coetzee's Enduring Faith in Fiction," in *J. M. Coetzee and the Idea of the Public Intellectual*, ed. J. Poyner (Athens: Ohio University Press, 2006), 110-14.
38. G. Hartman, "Trauma Within the Limits of Literature", *EJES* 7, no. 3 (2003): 273.

References

Coetzee, J. M. *Disgrace*. London: Vintage, 2000.

———. *Doubling the Point: Essays and Interviews*. Ed. D. Attridge. Cambridge, Mass.: Harvard University Press, 1992.

———. *The Lives of Animals*. London: Profile Books, 2000.

———. *Slow Man*. London: Secker & Warburg, 2005.

———. *White Writing: On the Culture of Letters in South Africa*. New Haven, Conn.: Yale University Press, 1988.

———. *Youth: Scenes from Provincial Life II*. New York: Viking, 2002.

Part Four

Literature, Literary Style, and Philosophy

13

Truth and Love Together at Last
STYLE, FORM, AND MORAL VISION IN *AGE OF IRON*
Samantha Vice

It is plausible to think that the spare style and distinctive form of J. M. Coetzee's writing has some close connection to the content and quality of his moral vision. In this paper, I explore this connection against the backdrop of a debate in moral philosophy, the debate about whether morality, or the "moral point of view," is essentially *impartial*. Here I will explore the moral point of view of Coetzee's 1990 novel, *Age of Iron*, though much of what I say applies to his other novels, too. In particular, I ask how Coetzee reconciles the demands of love with the demands of truth. Intuitively, the demands of love, whether moral or not, seem *partial* and *personal*, while the demands of truth, at least in one way it is presented in *Age of Iron* and in the philosophical tradition, require from us what Coetzee's protagonist, Elizabeth Curren, calls a "cold eye"—the kind of detached impartiality with which the moral point of view is often identified. It is one of the concerns of the novel to achieve a balance between truthful perception and the ethical demands of love. Mrs. Curren's dying hope, expressed in the long letter to her daughter that makes up the narrative, is that in her writing she can bring the two requirements together: "In this letter from elsewhere (so long a letter!), truth and love together at last" (*Age of Iron*, 129). To accomplish this synthesis is, Mrs. Curren realizes, the task of the moral life, and Coetzee's novel suggests that it is also the task of narrative art, which is worked out through the relation between the style, content, and particular form in which the narrative comes to us.

We might ultimately reject Coetzee's stringent ethics here and in all his novels. I aim neither to argue in its favor, nor to criticize it, but instead to suggest that his novel reminds us of neglected possibilities in the debate about partiality and impartiality.

PARTIALITY, IMPARTIALITY, AND THE COLD EYE

Impartiality is the absence of bias or favoritism toward oneself or one's own, whether one's own projects, loved ones, or just those related to one in some way felt to be significant. Insofar as morality has something to do with the equal consideration of everyone's well-being, to be partial is then prima facie at odds with morality. From the moral point of view, everyone counts equally, so one's moral judgments should not be affected by sentiment or loyalty toward loved ones or, at the limit, one's self. Partiality toward particular people and the love that is its ally has been regarded by some philosophers as extraneous or even inimical to morality. William Godwin's famous dismissal of partial relationships in favor of impartial moral principles—"what magic is there in the pronoun 'my' to overturn the decisions of everlasting truth?"[1]— is extreme, perhaps, but brings to the fore the commitments lying behind the modern moral tradition: that morality is essentially impartial and that the demands of love and self constitute a competing realm of value. Paul Taylor, for instance, lists impartiality as one of the necessary conditions for a rule or principle to "belong to the category of morality."[2] And R. M. Hare's "Archangel," Roderick Firth's "Ideal Observer," and the "point of view of the universe," in Sidgewick's words, provide vivid images of the kind of detached supermen thought to provide true moral exemplars.[3]

Adopting these exemplars' point of view as far as possible is therefore, on this view, ethically required. The images assume, too, that partiality is also epistemically required. Favoritism, bias, considering some things more worthy of attention or protection than others: all these habits of thought and feeling are obstacles in the way to truth. In order to see clearly and attain knowledge it is best to achieve some distance from the self and its loves, to "step back," as we say, in order to ensure the objectivity that comes from surveying one's own self as one would any other. So both in the realm of knowledge and in the ethical realm, we have strong reason to take up the impartial point of view. While more contemporary accounts of impartial theories are less stark than this and find ways of justifying from the impartial point of view some partiality on the ground,[4] the basic images recur, as Margaret Urban Walker notes:

> God's eye, the ideal observer, the third-person spectator, the disinterested judge. Such pictures are a familiar part of the prevailing *rhetoric* of impartiality—the way the concept is 'deployed' in standard tropes, repeated images or common patterns of description by philosophers.[5]

If the moral point of view in this conception reveals any love at all, it is *agape*—a universal love or concern for humankind, rather than love for the particular person one's fancy or instinct inexplicably lights on. And it is perhaps also worth noting here that *agape* or *caritas* belong properly in a theistic context. Probably only God, or some elect saints, can achieve this universal love. What we are asked to do, however, if as moral agents we also desire to love, is to aspire to God's benevolence. And here utilitarianism, that most resolutely secular of moral theories, oddly comes closest to articulating a version of this religious vision.

However appealing the vision of impartiality—and any moral theory must contain the prohibition against unfairness that is central to worries about partiality—the truth remains that ethical reality contains partial elements, and rightly so.[6] Most of us strive for particular love, not *agape*. Most of us would think that Iris Murdoch is on the right track when she says that "love is knowledge of the individual."[7] We favor certain people when there is no objective reason for picking them out as special. We know that each one of us matters no more than any other, and yet in the face of this knowledge we persist in pursuing our projects because they are our own and in favoring certain people because they stand in some significant relation to us. While we can, as Thomas Nagel rightly reminds us, naturally take up what he calls the impersonal point of view, we cannot, it seems, live comfortably and extensively *from* it.[8] And yet, at the same time, the demands of impartial truth cannot be ignored, and the cool objectivity and perspective that come from stepping back from oneself are often both morally and prudentially required.[9]

It is apparent already that allied to the notions of partiality and impartiality are others that have some more or less close conceptual connection. "Disinterestedness," "impersonality," "objectivity," and "abstraction" are often used interchangeably or in conjunction with "impartial," for example. However, this conflation of terms is unfortunate, and the worries generated on both sides of the debate are often a result of confusion here. We can, for instance, be impartial without being impersonal or abstracted, as Adrian Piper reminds us.[10] I will argue that the union of truth and love for which Mrs. Curren strives is then a union in which a true and unbiased vision is allied to a deep *interest in* particular individuals.

There is, however, a striking passage in *Age of Iron* that seems to accept the dichotomy between love and impartiality. An interest in loved ones apparently undermines truth, and the novel at this point demands that we be impartial if we are to see truthfully and know how best to respond. The novel's narrator, Mrs. Curren, is describing in a letter to her daughter her shattering journey into a South African township in the dying days of Apartheid and the terrible sight of her domestic worker's son, Bheki, lying dead from a gunshot wound. Then she stops her narrative of events and addresses her daughter directly. I quote the passage in full:

> I tell you the story of this morning mindful that the story-teller, from her office, claims the place of right. It is through my eyes that you see; the voice that speaks in your head is mine. Through me alone do you find yourself here on these desolate flats, smell the smoke in the air, see the bodies of the dead, hear the weeping, shiver in the rain. It is my thoughts that you think, my despair that you feel, and also the first stirrings of welcome for whatever will put an end to thought: sleep, death. To me your sympathies flow; your heart beats with mine. Now, my child, flesh of my flesh, my best self, I ask you to draw back. I tell you this story not so that you will feel for me but so you will learn how things are. It would be easier for you, I know, if the story came from someone else, if it were a stranger's voice sounding in your ear. But the fact is, there is no one else. I am the only one. I am the one writing: I, I. So I ask you: attend to the writing, not to me. If lies and pleas and excuses weave among the words, listen for them. Do not pass them over, do not forgive them easily. Read all, even this adjuration, with a cold eye.
>
> (*Age of Iron*, 103–4)

Mrs. Curren takes it for granted that her daughter's sympathy will align her to her mother's distress. Love makes us far more attuned to the distress of those we love than to those far away or to vague humanity in the abstract. Furthermore, the activity of narration itself and so of literature typically requires imaginative engagement with at least some characters, usually the protagonists and those to whom they are attached. Entering into the narration in the first place requires that the reader set aside some impartiality, that she be prepared to follow the characters, that she care for their fate. Mrs. Curren's letter requires sympathy from her daughter and concern for what she narrates if the act of writing is to have any force and if the significance of the terrible events are to be conveyed. We—her daughter and the reader of the novel—see the situation through her eyes, an instance of the characteristic work of the narrator or focalizer generally: "It is through my eyes that you see; the voice that speaks in your head is mine." Imaginative engagement gives rise to emotional responses, and also requires some sympathy to begin with if it is to work at all. The heart, in short, must be engaged if the literary act is to be successful.

And yet, just as her daughter and we are reminded of this, we are called back from our sympathies: We must "attend to the writing," not the writer, attend, that is, to *what is being depicted*, not to the person describing it. Imaginative engagement with the writer, so essential to the writing process, also brings with it the possibility of error—"lies and pleas and excuses"—which must not be passed over or forgiven. "Do not read in sympathy with me. Let your heart not beat with mine," she insists a little later (104). It is so easy for her daughter's sympathy with her mother's illness and her distressed reaction to the events in the township to cloud what is really morally important: the death of a child—and many children—and the injustice of Apartheid that makes these deaths a cause of terrible comradeship and pride. From this objective point of view, the suffering of her mother, a white woman accidentally caught up in events in which she feels complicit but to which she is really extraneous, are lower down the scale of moral significance than the sufferings of black people in a racist police state. Partiality toward her mother too easily obscures this, and it is, after all, her mother who is the "only one" speaking. Mrs. Curren, says Sam Durrant, "must find a way of writing that does not invite the traditional movement of identification.... A writing, then, at odds with itself, that writes against its own eliciting of the sympathetic imagination."[11] If we are to "learn how things are," the conclusion here is, we must "read everything" with "a cold eye"; this is the only way, insofar as there is a way, to truth and a mature ethical response. In an age of iron, at least, only the cold eye can be trusted.

Despite Mrs. Curren's warning to her daughter, she is aware that the ethical task is that of finding some accommodation between cold truth and love. As she says, her hope is that her letter will bring about some reconciliation: "truth and love, together at last," with the implication that, at least in her life, they have been divorced. A good life for any morally sensitive person requires such a balance or risks losing many of the goods that distinguish human life. Achieving this might require that we rethink the opposition with which we began. Truth and love are both more complex than the stark terms of the debate allow. The love Mrs. Curren feels for her daughter comes easily, for instance, but there is also another, more difficult love to strive for. What happens when both the heart and the clear eye meet the impenetrable other—those in *Age of Iron* like Vercueil or Bheki's friend, John, who reappear so often in Coetzee's novels; those who resist understanding and interpretation, and to whom the heart finds it hard to incline in warmth? Vercueil, John, the barbarian girl, Michael K, Friday, the Namaquas in *Dusklands*, the Russian Nechaev, and the dogs that populate Coetzee's novels all represent the limits of understanding and sympathy and therefore the astonishing difficulty of meeting ethical demands. There is a love that is not knowledge of the individual but an acceptance of the unknowable, and it is here, where sympathy and trust seem utterly unearned and gratuitous, and where knowing seems impossible, that the task to bring love and truth together is most difficult and most exigent.

As many commentators have pointed out, Coetzee's work here can be instructively read through the notion of the Other.[12] For Levinas, for example, ethics is essentially about the encounter between the self and the Other for whom the self finds itself responsible. In this light, the terms at play are not just those of, on the one hand, love of the particular person who is special because he stands in some relation to me and, on the other hand, universal impartial benevolence. What is at stake is also the highly particular love for someone beyond one's epistemic grasp—and achieving this is the true ethical task. Here, the information that might be revealed to the impersonal, abstracted point of view (at least to God's) is not available for the subject. And if every person can be the Other to someone, then this situation is the norm; it *is* the ethical situation.

Rather than investigating the often frustratingly protean notion of the Other, I want to pursue a more modest line of thought: I want to suggest that some accommodation between the impartial viewpoint and the demands of love is achieved in the novel in the interplay between Coetzee's style, the act of writing and the form it takes here, and the encounter with the elusive Other. Seeing this at work in the novel might make us more inclined to follow Walker's call for different, more earthly images of impartiality.

STYLE

Coetzee's instantly recognizable style in *Age of Iron* and in all his work to date is a good starting point because it brings into relief what is at stake in the conflict between the demands of sympathy, or love, and those of impersonal truth. Derek Attridge stands for many when he describes Coetzee's style as "chiseled" and marked by "economy and efficiency."[13] One of the most notable features of Coetzee's fictions has always been its austerity, spareness and the "slight self-consciousness" that makes his writing "forever on its guard against itself."[14] The paucity of ornament or flourish gives the texts an air of robust truthfulness—or less ambitiously, sincerity—and their very lack of adornment adds to the novels' intense effect on the reader. The impression is that truth is not hidden behind rhetorical tricks; the worst is depicted without any obvious "fashioning," even though the effect is the result of much stylistic work and discipline. If we could imagine the writing style of the Ideal Observer or the Archangel, if it made sense to talk of the "style of the universe" or of God, this might be the style we would imagine. Regardless of the content, there is some intuitive connection between an absence of rhetorical flourish, emotional excess, or ornament, and the kind of vision of the world attained by the impartial point of view.

However, allied to this sparse purity is the absence of any authorial intrusion, and this undermines the impression of impartiality toward which the style naturally seems to incline. As Attridge writes, the narratives are conveyed through the characters' consciousness, which, "whether they are represented in the first or third person, occupy the entire affective and axiological space of the fiction."[15] Even in a third-person narrative like *The Life and Times of Michael K* everything comes to the reader through the consciousness of the protagonist, K.

There is, therefore, on the face of it a rather strange cohabitation between the elements of Coetzee's style: On the one hand, there is the scrupulous, unadorned recording of events and mental states, which rewards the reader with a sense of impartiality. On the other hand, the channeling of events and meaning through one consciousness is just as much a feature of Coetzee's style. The particular socially and historically embedded consciousness is precisely what is supposed to be the cause of distortion, partiality, and moral blindness. Both these modes—detached recording and the filtering of events through one consciousness—carry their moral dangers.

For instance, there is the risk that the accurate, thorough, and impartial gaze will become detached or pitiless. Why, after all, should the Ideal Observer or the Archangel or especially "the point of view of the universe" attend with valuing or sympathy rather than utter disinterest or, given our apparently inexhaustible capacity for evil, even intense *dislike*?[16] Even when directed toward the self, why should the cold eye care? This is what those suspicious of the impartial gaze fear, and Mrs. Curren writes: "With every day I add to it the letter seems to grow more abstract, more abstracted, the kind of letter one writes from the stars, from the farther void, disembodied, crystalline, bloodless. Is that to be the fate of my love?" (*Age of Iron*, 137). That love will be lost to abstraction is the danger which the impartial eye must avoid.

On the other hand, the familiar and much discussed device of restricting the reader's access to events by the use of the focalizing consciousness has its own complexities. That some integrity and exculpation is earned by the *mere fact* of scrupulous and thorough honesty toward the self is a somewhat dubious idea, but one with roots, at least, in that romantic ur-text, Rousseau's *Confessions*. He begins, recall: "I am commencing an undertaking, hitherto without precedent, and which will never find an imitator. I desire to set before my fellows the likeness of a man in all the truth of nature, and that man myself."[17] Rousseau takes his sincerity, both here and throughout his life, to justify whatever was less than admirable; merely being true to himself and thus to the world is enough to exculpate him before God:

> I have shown myself as I was: mean and contemptible, good, high-minded and sublime, according as I was one or the other. I have unveiled my inmost self even as Thou has seen it, O Eternal Being. Gather round me the countless host of my fellow-men; let them hear my confessions. Lament for my unworthiness, and blush for my imperfec-

tions. Then let each of them in turn reveal, with the same frankness, the secrets of his heart at the foot of the Throne, and say, if he dare, 'I was better than that man!'[18]

Rousseau was, of course, confessing his own life, but the idea that sincere depiction carries some merit in itself is not restricted to autobiography. While sometimes less self-absorbed than those of Rousseau, the struggles of the conscience in Coetzee's fictions are somewhat soothed by the recording of principles, ambivalence, despair, disgust, and anger. One is at least knowledgeable enough about one's self to realize one's own shortcomings and to feel some degree of shame, guilt, or just discomfort about them. And if not immediately so, the novels follow the progression towards such self-knowledge or self-acceptance. More positively, the act of writing this progression can be the act of constituting the self,[19] or keeping it from dissolution in the face of threats. One is constituted and known—by the self and others—by what one stands for, as the Magistrate (*Waiting for the Barbarians*), Mrs. Curren, and David Lurie (*Disgrace*) realize. Writing then can be a way of saying, "Here I stand; this is who I—morally—am," even if later we come to see the limits of our commitment. In this way, writing the self can have significance beyond exculpation to the formation and maintenance of moral identity and integrity.

We can sometimes gain epistemically and morally from this kind of self-assessment, but there are undoubtedly risks. Returning to fiction, one risk is that while characters may achieve some scrupulous and anatomical self-scrutiny, they may also meticulously record an enclosed and self-justifying vision. Notoriously, Rousseau revealed his own fantasies, and many narrators in Coetzee's fictions are unreliable in the same way. With no authorial presence to keep check, error, bias, and distortion too easily creep in. From even her limited perspective, this is the error that Mrs. Curren is aware of and warns her daughter against, and her intervention in the quoted passage is reminiscent of the explicit intrusions of the omniscient author in much nineteenth-century fiction. She steers herself and her audience to a more correct reading of reality.

A second danger attending the device of the focalizing consciousness is that other equally vivid, equally valid sites of consciousness will be ignored. At the limit, this risks the extreme biases of solipsism or madness. I am reminded of that beautiful moment in *Middlemarch*, a world away from Coetzee, when George Eliot reorients the reader's sympathy. The chapter begins:

> One morning, some weeks after her arrival at Lowick, Dorothea—but why always Dorothea? Was her point of view the only possible one with regard to this marriage? I protest against all our interest, all our effort at understanding being given to the young skins that look blooming in spite of trouble; for these too will get faded, and will

know the older and more eating griefs which we are helping to neglect.... Mr Casaubon had an intense consciousness within him, and was spiritually a-hungered like the rest of us.[20]

The reader is recalled to other sites of consciousness just as intense as the heroine's, Casaubon's "blinking eyes and white moles" notwithstanding.[21] And Mrs. Curren does try to imagine other lives: An extended example occurs when she drops off Florence at her husband's place of work and, aghast at seeing him among the blood and feathers of chicken carcasses, imagines their evening together: "While I was driving back to this empty house, William took Florence and the children back to the living quarters. He washed; she cooked a supper of chicken and rice on the paraffin stove, then fed the baby" (42). And so she continues, describing as if she were there, as if it were a fact, the weekend of her domestic worker and her family. "All of this happened. All of this must have happened" (43). A later crucial instance occurs when she imagines John's death, and I shall return to this below. In *Waiting for the Barbarians*, the Magistrate tries to imagine the world of the torturer; in *Foe*, Susan Barton tries to enter Friday's consciousness. These attempts meet with more or less success, but there is something salutary in the attempt. As I shall explore below, there is also ethical significance in the failure.

How, then, can we understand the relation between Coetzee's austere style, which reminds us of the impartial point of view, and the absence of an impartial authorial presence? One possibility is that it is the device of the focalizing consciousness that prevents the spare style from becoming abstract or pitiless. What is filtered through a particular consciousness is scrupulously noted down, but what is recorded is, for the most part, the states of that particular consciousness. The writing is thus anchored by the focalizer, a device that gives us the moral identity and distinctive perspective of someone personally invested in the events. In this way, the writing cannot become entirely abstracted or impersonal, even if the purity of the style may contain an inherent tendency toward this. And this then suggests that the impartial eye need not also be impersonal or abstracted. At its core, as Adrian Piper notes, "impartiality" is fairness and lack of prejudice, while "impersonality," quoting from the *OED*, is "'having no personal reference or connection.' ... the view of oneself and others *sub specie aeternitatis*."[22] Impartiality and impersonality can thus come apart, and the relation between impartiality and personal involvement thus becomes more complex. In the context of the debate between partialists and impartialists in the moral realm, Piper argues that one may be *personally* invested in *impartial* moral principles, which inform one's public and private life, or one might be *impersonally* attached to *particular* people as, for instance, occasions for one to do the most good. If we worry that taking up the impartial point of view will necessarily also mean losing interest in particular people, the worry is unfounded. And so, to return to Coetzee, the style that eschews ornamentation and emotional excess in the service of truth needn't also eschew a deep interest in particular people.

This helps us with the question of how to reconcile the different responsibilities that both moral philosophy and Coetzee's novel note: the responsibility of escaping distortion and limiting sympathy by attending with a cold eye, while at the same time avoiding pitilessness or abstraction. However, it is not obvious that there can be any final resolution in these terms. Instead, what we are given is a different kind of truth and a different kind of seeing, with the suggestion that these are alternatives to that stark contrast. The formal device of the letter shows this alternative working, as Mrs. Curren tells her daughter the story of her physical disintegration and, perhaps, the tentative birth of her soul. The address to the second person, the intimate encounter between an "I" and a beloved "you," also shows how alternative images of unbiased thought and feeling might get a grip in the ethical realm. Marilyn Friedman argues that a public dialogue "with people of competing interests" might be a way of avoiding bias and unfairness and that "dialogue" provides a more practical model of *impartiality* than familiar devices like the veil of ignorance or universalization.[23] Walker, drawing on Friedman, argues that the central images of impartiality "are largely preoccupied with themes of detachment: one is to observe rather than engage, cogitate rather than converse, dispose of moral cases rather than situate them coherently in a continuing history of responsibilities, evaluations, and relationships."[24] And she responds that

> one methodological corrective is vigorous emphasis on facing up to the particular reality of each person and case and on refinement of perception, acuity of communication, flexibility of perspectives, and use of a range of moral categories closer, in variety and nuance, to our full nonmoral resources of interpersonal description and expression.[25]

It is not my aim here to assess these views, and what Friedman and Walker call for is clearly not sufficient to guarantee the elimination of bias. However, their views are useful because they make us aware of the assumptions underlying the traditional debate and open up the possibility of a fair, objective, yet *engaged* relation to others. My suggestion is that the second-person address of the intimate letter is yet one more device for anchoring clear vision to the particular, for achieving an undistorted yet still *interested* vision of the world. Again, this by no means guarantees moral knowledge and just outcomes, but then no model can. And it is not meant to be an answer to the debate between impartialists and partialists but an attempt to refigure the debate in a more fruitful direction. I want now to explore how this is worked out in the novel, beginning with a look at the two realms of duty suggested in *Age of Iron*: the ethical and the political.

POLITICS AND ETHICS: THE LAW AND THE EXCEPTION

Coetzee has noted in an interview with David Attwell that the "contest of interpretations" between the political and ethical is "played out again and again in my novels" (*Doubling the Point*, 338). The political realm is associated with violence and death and the ethical with the refusal of "retributive violence" (337). In a rare moment of autobiography, he calls the ethical the realm in which "my craving for privacy . . . distaste for crowds, for slogans . . . my almost physical revulsion against obeying orders" can be accommodated (337). Implicit in most of Coetzee's work, as he notes, the tension between these realms is obvious in *Age of Iron*. In this novel, the ethical also requires the sensitive discernment and appreciation of the significant features of each situation. The political, on the other hand, requires the singleness of purpose demonstrated by Bheki, John, and their comrades, and the natural condition for this, they think, is that abstraction from particularity with which the impartial point of view is often associated. Too much involvement with the particular is apt to muddy the moral waters just at a time when clarity and certainty are required if anything is to be achieved. In fact, however, the real conflict in the novel is not between impartiality per se and partiality. There is, after all, a fierce kind of partial loyalty within Bheki's pure political interpretation of the world—Florence's cousin, Mr. Thabane, insists that Mrs. Curren "doesn't understand very much about comradeship" (*Age of Iron*, 149). Rather, the conflict is between a movement of *abstraction* that notices only generalities, on the one hand, and an insistence on detail and particularity, on the other. As already suggested, however, this abstraction is not an essential constituent of impartiality per se. We can retain the virtues of impartiality without lapsing into abstraction, and, I shall argue further, we can pay attention to the details of situations without losing the fair and undistorted vision of reality that impartiality in its purest form strives for. The "cold" eye, while impartial, need not also be abstracted.

The conflict between abstraction and particularity is nicely illustrated in Mrs. Curren's words to John when she visits him in the hospital (it is hardly a conversation, for John remains sullen and unresponsive throughout):

Thucydides wrote of people who made rules and followed them.
    Going by rule they killed entire classes of enemies without exception. Most of those who died felt, I am sure, that a terrible mistake was being made, that, whatever the rule

was, it could not be meant for them. 'I!—': that was their last word as their throats were cut. A word of protest: I, the exception.

Were they exceptions? The truth is, given time to speak, we would all claim to be exceptions. For each of us there is a case to be made. We all deserve the benefit of the doubt.

But there are times when there is no time for all that close listening, all those exceptions, all that mercy. There is no time, so we fall back on the rule. And that is a great pity, the greatest pity. . . . It is a great pity when we find ourselves entering upon times like those. We should enter upon them with a sinking heart. They are by no means to be welcomed.

(*Age of Iron*, 80–81)

Here, Mrs. Curren admits that the times can demand that we live inflexibly by rules in order to achieve political ends, but she insists that this is nevertheless at great personal and moral loss. The Apartheid years are such a time. The death-bound comradeship of the youthful activists, their refusal to admit shades of ambiguities and complexities into their responses to the world—all these are natural consequences and probably prudential necessities of acting. As she comes to realize in her interaction with Mr. Thabane, Bheki, and John and in her journey into the township to discover young Bheki's dead body, their comradeship has its own terrible beauty and logic: "What I had not calculated on was that more might be called for than to be good. For there are plenty of good people in this country. . . . What the times call for is quite different from goodness. The times call for heroism" (165). And heroism requires, it seems, inflexible vision and action—it is, after all, in an age of iron that goodness is not enough. However, she insists, too, that this alone cannot be the foundation of a better and just society and that it comes with a terrible price: the inversion of natural relationships between parent and child—"there are no more mothers and fathers," Florence says (39)—the neglect of individual dignity and inevitable exceptions to the rules, the hardening of the heart so that *it* is cold and so that the love that recognizes the unrepresentable essence of another person becomes impossible. As she says, "For each of us there is a case to be made"; each of us is an "exception" to every rule precisely because no person is in every respect relevantly alike and because every person, however unlovable, can be the recipient of love. If rules are tailored for similarities and generalities, then significant differences among cases may be lost.[26] The ethical is the realm of the individual, the particular, and, we may suppose, though it is never put in these terms, the web of partial connections and interests that attach individuals to one another and upon which our flourishing so largely depends.

This view of the ethical is, Derek Attridge argues, *performed through* Coetzee's fiction, which "opens the possibility of an ethics of unique acts, rooted always in the here and now, yet acknowledging a deep responsibility to the otherness of elsewhere, of the past, and of the future."[27] I now want to explore the way the novel achieves this ethical vision while still allowing impartiality its proper place. One of the aims of ethical living is to prevent the abstraction that is inimical to a proper engagement with others. At the same time, however, the virtues of impartiality, separated from its inessential abstraction, need also to be retained. In order to see how these two aims are "performed" in the novel, I shall concentrate on the epistolary form and the encounter with the Other.

THE LETTER AND THE ENCOUNTER WITH THE OTHER

My suggestion is that the novel's epistolary form, along with its particular content, show this ethical ideal at work. The address to the second person, the very intimate encounter between an "I" and a beloved "you," shows how images and practices of unbiased thought and feeling might get a grip in the ethical realm. In *Age of Iron*, the reconciliation (of sorts) that is performed through the device of the letter concerns the ethical demands of love, and this connection is not accidental: it is through the letter to a distant but nevertheless beloved daughter that reconciliation between truth and love is worked through.

The particularized demands of the ethical are played out and meet their limits in Mrs. Curren's relationships with John, Bheki, and the vagrant, Vercueil. The most unlikely relationship is with Vercueil, who is outside the demands of conventional morality, decency, and obligations and yet to whom Mrs. Curren finds herself oddly drawn. Her letter to her daughter—and thus the novel—begins on the day she learns that her cancer is terminal, and it is also the day she discovers Vercueil in her yard: "A visitor, visiting himself on me on this of all days" (4). An unlikely messenger or angel (168), she finds herself thinking; a "herald of death," as Coetzee puts it in an interview (*Doubling the Point*, 340). Much of the dialogue in the novel takes place between Mrs. Curren and her visitor, and her letter to her daughter is increasingly filled with Vercueil and their unexpected closeness.

That Mrs. Curren's growing intimacy with Vercueil is based on no rational grounds is central to *Age of Iron*, which enacts a form of love and engagement with another person that is ethical precisely because of this. "I look for him to care, and he does not. Because he is beyond caring. Beyond caring and beyond care" (*Age of Iron*, 22).[28] Despite his indifference—or because of it perhaps—Mrs. Curren cares for him without reason and without understanding and in the end relies on him, though Vercueil's intentions and emotions remain opaque in return. But to have her love returned is not part of the novel's ethical compact. She risks on him, with no certainty of success, the only significance her death will have—she asks him to post the letter that constitutes the novel to her daughter after her death; her daughter's only inheritance, "all she will accept, coming from this country" (31–32):

> What is the wager, then, that I am making with Vercueil, on Vercueil? It is a wager on trust.... If there is the slightest breath of trust, obligation, piety left behind when I am gone, he will surely take it. And if not? If not, there is no trust and we deserve no better, all of us, than to fall into a hole and vanish. Because I cannot trust Vercueil I must trust him. I am trying to keep a soul alive in times not hospitable to the soul.
> (130)

This wager on Vercueil is also Mrs. Curren's wager on humanity and on her own capacity to keep her soul alive even as her body is dying, not to be another "soulless doll," as she characterizes white South Africans (110–12). Not to trust is to be unable to imagine a world that is better than hers, and if this is true—if no such world is possible—then it is better that we all vanish. Her wager on Vercueil is a wager on the possibility of ethics itself.

It is clear that reasonless trust cannot be an imperative of the reasoning, impartial "cold eye." And further, allied to this reasonless trust, Mrs. Curren suspects, is reasonless love. She describes herself to her daughter as being in a "fog of error" (136), and her error is that she cannot love the sullen, unattractive John. There is some unlikely warmth between her and Vercueil that makes her gesture of absolute trust possible, if nonetheless inexplicable. The love for her daughter is the reasonlessness of nature, but there is no such affection between her and John: "I do not love this child, the child sleeping in Florence's bed. I love you but I do not love him. There is no ache in me toward him, not the slightest.... My heart does not accept him as mine: it is as simple as that" (136). And yet, "Not wanting to love him, how true is my love for you? For love is not like hunger. Love is never sated, stilled. When one loves, one loves more. The more I love you, the more I ought to love him. The less I love him, the less, perhaps, I love you" (137).

This is a "cruciform logic, which takes me where I do not want to go!" (137), a logic that is difficult not only for Mrs. Curren to accept. Love does not seem to be the kind of thing that can be commanded.[29] And how, in any case, can we insist that such personal and engaged love must "travel" to all others and that unless it does so, the original love is not "true"? Here we have a command that is assisted neither by instinct nor reason. The sentiment is not entirely alien to us, however; we have it in some interpretations of the Christian injunction to "love thy neighbor" and in its secular counterpart in universal benevolence.[30] As I said in the introduction, it is not my concern to defend the ethical commands of Coetzee's novels. It is, however, good to have the difficulty and rigor of certain ethical visions fully apparent and imaginatively worked out for us, especially for those attracted to it. I will return to this point in the conclusion.

In *Age of Iron* and other novels by Coetzee, the ethical test—the success of which will enable the soul to remain alive—is thus to love and trust in the face of opacity and indifference and against all reason, a test that still insists on its own "logic." I mentioned earlier that one of the dangers of narratives that are filtered through a character's consciousness is that other sites of consciousness, and thus sites of love, are ignored. However, as I also noted, Mrs. Curren does attempt to enter other people's consciousness and to understand them. Sometimes her efforts have plausibility. Sometimes we suspect they reveal, rather, simply her wish to "connect": listening to the Goldberg Variations, aware of Vercueil outside, she remarks: "At this moment, I thought, I know how he feels as surely as if he and I were making love" (30). And at other times she finds that she is unable to comprehend, despite her efforts; sometimes the searching gaze meets blankness and opacity.[31] John and, in a different way, Vercueil, both represent the limits of understanding; in the one case because she finds affection impossible, and in the other because the person is so utterly beyond normal mores and expectations. And at this point, something other than ordinary vision is required if we are still to respond ethically to the Other, and it is not provided by even the interested cold eye.

The radical love and trust upon which the soul depends are achieved, the novel suggests, through a different kind of vision and truth. The image of the cold eye is countered by complex images that track the working of this alternative. The images of sight remain, but not 'cold' sight, and often they turn to blindness and closed eyes, the sight of the imagination and heart.[32] The form of the letter to a loved one, which can only be personal and particular even while it strives to report accurately, allows Mrs. Curren to "follow where her heart leads" precisely because it is the recording of love—for her daughter, for the unlikely Vercueil, and, finally, for John and Bheki. There is some safety in her love, which allows her to say what is in her heart without fear of rejection or ridicule. But her love strives also for truthfulness toward reality: not to be indifferent to unfamiliar virtues, not to allow self-pity to overwhelm her duty toward others, not to attribute to Vercueil emotions or beliefs it is merely comforting to wish for. With a letter there is always a concrete addressee in mind, a potential respondent, someone to take one up on what one has written and who therefore ensures a measure of responsibility for what is written. However personal the record of a soul, and however unlikely a response, there is reason to portray oneself and what one sees truthfully when one's audience is someone both loved and admired.

Let us look at some of the alternative images that work in her letter, first, the vision of the imagination. There is a seemingly casual description that suggests the process:

> A fly settles on my cheek.... It walks across my eye, my open eye. I want to blink, I want to wave it away, but I cannot. Through an eye that is and is not mine, I stare at it.... There is nothing in those bulging organs that I can recognize as a face. But it is upon me, it is here: it struts across me, a creature from another world.
> (27)

While there is nothing in this passage about love, it is an instance of that familiar encounter between the protagonist and the alien Other that we find in most of Coetzee's novels. The ethical task is to imagine and love these creatures from another world—whether Vercueil's world of sufficiency and terrible innocence or Bheki and John's world of comradeship and narrow courage or, perhaps, even her daughter's safe life in America. And it becomes John who, despite her dislike, "is with me more clearly, more piercingly than Bheki has ever been" (175). Near the end, she imagines John's death, hovers with him as he crouches in Florence's room with the pistol "that was his and Bheki's great secret, that was going to make men of them" (175). Here, second, we have another image, this time of the searching *closed eye*: "His eyes are open and mine, though I write, are shut. My eyes are shut in order to see" (175). It is worth noting that she imagines him in his last—political—stand here. She takes a step outside herself to that heroism she earlier could not comprehend and she does this *as* she is writing, in the act of her extended address to her daughter.

In the end, however, she is closer to these dead children and to Vercueil than she is to her daughter: "Because he is here, beside me, now. Forgive me. Time is short, I must trust my heart and tell the truth. Sightless, ignorant, I follow where the truth takes me" (162). This third further complex image, of following the heart in blindness and ignorance, does important work in the novel. An obvious way of reading "the heart" would be as a representation of our emotional life and, if we assume a cognitive view of emotions, its judgments. The emotions have their logic, even if "cruciform." However, this logic is often hidden from us, so while we trust to it we can follow the heart only in ignorance.[33]

It is important that the truths of the heart are not necessarily welcome, that they might not be what one wants to hear. This shows that they are not merely wishes or self-deceiving comforts. The heart can discriminate; as Pascal famously insisted, it has reasons, not just whims.[34] Mrs. Curren is *following* truth where it leads; this is important if the heart is to be allied to the search for truth and not inimical to the lessons of the cold eye in its proper sphere. And this, again, happens through the format of the letter: in a nice echo of her other words, she says, "I wrote. I write. I follow the pen, going where it takes me. What else have I now?" (108). Following the heart and following the pen: committed writing to a loved one is the following of a heart toward ethical truth.

Just what these truths are is not entirely clear. Sometimes they are accurate descriptions of events, unclouded by sentiment; sometimes they seem to be what is discovered about the self and other through emotional honesty and trust; at other times they are that which demands love and response in another person. What is important throughout is the commitment to being *truthful*: being respectful of and open to a reality that is often obdurate or painful, and to the slow, faltering progress toward this reality.

Finally, sometimes the truth seems to be *revealed* or *unveiled*. Perhaps only in death is another person exposed in her ethically essential nature to the attentive gaze. However, it seems that this moment of insight is also earned and is not gratuitous. Thinking over Bheki's death, for example, Mrs. Curren sees him as a child from whom the age of iron demanded adult courage: "So why should I grieve for him? The answer is, I saw his face. When he died he was a child again. The mask must have dropped in sheer childish surprise when it broke upon him that last instant that the stone-throwing and shooting was not a game after all" (125). This moment is repeated with John. Despite his rejection of her, she finds herself whispering, "Poor child" (147), seeing him as he is despite his posturing. Here is a moment of clarity, of vision unimpeded by the self and its dislikes or difficulties; possibly it is a moment in which the soul is glimpsed, an unimpeded truth of the heart. It is perhaps terrible that such clarity is achieved in this novel only in the face of death, but it is nowhere suggested that this realization comes easily even then. In order to reach it, much emotional, moral, and intellectual work is necessary. Mrs. Curren must transcend her visceral dislike of John and her impatience with Bheki and see them as they are: as children, not men, demanding a parent's love, not the admonishment of adults. This deep change is revealed in her last words, the last lines of the novel. Vercueil joins her in bed, and "for the first time I smelled nothing" (198). This difficult ending at least suggests the emergence of a soul to a new perception, even if "there is no warmth to be had" (198) in the embrace of death—Vercueil's embrace. We do not know whether the "soul, neophyte, wet, blind, ignorant" (186), emerges to new life; we do not know what final insight, if any, Mrs. Curren has. The novel is not obviously to be read in any redemptive way. But what is notable is that, once again, instinctual reactions—here disgust for Vercueil's usual smell—vanish. If the soul is that which is loved and which loves, and if her letter has been the faithful recording of its birth, we can see here that such a birth is hard and requires that we shed much that is learned or instinctual or even deeply valued. The soul must undergo a *metanoia*; the ethical life is a "discipline," a "task."[35]

TRUTH AND LOVE TOGETHER AT LAST

Coetzee is, properly, seldom explicit about the content of the truths sought in the ethical realm. That individuals, even in their final opacity, should be loved is certainly one of them; that one's own preoccupations and sufferings should not obscure reality is another; that one has responsibilities to others that come from one's place in the social order rather than from any direct actions on one's part and that this order can corrupt our relations to one another is perhaps a further truth. These and others can be grasped by the intellect, the emotions, the imagination, or a mixture of these. While complete understanding of situations and people may elude our grasp, we can still strive to attend to them in the receptive and vulnerable way that Coetzee's fictions suggest is ethically required, where this "attending" is at once intellectual and emotional and changes the way we perceive the world. We come to "see" John and Bheki and their comrades as mere children, though forced into the role of adults. We see that Apartheid policies changed white South Africans into soulless "dolls"; we come to see unwashed, indifferent vagrants as messengers upon whom the life of the soul depends. They are "truths of the heart." It takes an interested and partial exploration into the details and moral potential of others, as far as is possible, to yield such truths.

The truths of the heart have a central place in Coetzee's ethical realm, but ethics is not complete without a dimension of impartiality. The imagination, the emotions, and even the intellect, when they have settled into habits, can fail us or distort reality or be simply inefficacious. Because they issue from an individual who is limited in knowledge and restricted in sympathy, they may cloud her vision of situations that are unfamiliar and risky or to which she is extraneous. It is here that one needs to step back from the self in order to see better, with a cold eye unclouded by sympathy or self-concern. This "stepping back" and the impartial point of view it yields can, however, be achieved without abstraction and a loss of particularity; in fact, an impartial view might require the recognition of particularity if a complete appreciation of the situation is to be achieved. When the stepping back occurs from a generous impulse or from the sincere wish to understand oneself and the world, along with the commitment to attend to the details of the situation, an impartial gaze can yet remain deeply interested and rooted in the particular. It is when the cold eye ignores detail and exceptions—often as a political necessity—that abstraction occurs and moral losses result, despite the possible short-term political gains. The "coldness" of the impartial eye therefore contrasts to the comforting warmth of self-love or emotional attachments that undoubtedly can be distorting. Mrs. Curren, for instance, must abjure the natural sympathy her story will arouse, and her natural desire to be cared for as she dies, in order to achieve the *interested* objectivity required, she thinks, to understand her place in the Apartheid regime and her responsibilities to others.

I have argued, with Friedman and Walker, that a useful model of this kind of *interested* impartiality is sincere and well-intentioned interpersonal engagement. In *Age of Iron*, a letter to a beloved yet distant child becomes in the end a letter about the nature of proper ethical engagement in general—how one can love and see clearly at the same time. The love that motivates the writing of a letter can have its own ways of seeing clearly, even if they are not those of the "cold eye." But this is not enough unless a sense of proportion, of relative significance, of justice and responsibility in themselves motivate and inform the kind of personal encounter that the letter performs. Mrs. Curren "follows the heart" out of a sense of justice, out of a desire to reach truth, and *this* end in turn anchors partial love to what is reasonable and right.

While the demands of impartiality and partial love can therefore in many cases be reconciled, this certainly cannot be guaranteed. Sometimes the one will preclude the other; sometimes choices have to be made and values sacrificed. The world, tragically, might be such that open-hearted attention to particulars and exceptions is simply luxurious in the face of overwhelming social, structural, and political injustice. This seems to be the suggestion in this novel: that in an age of iron, in which natural relations between parents and children are undermined or destroyed, in which love must for the sake of efficacy step aside, we cannot blame those who forget individuality and ignore the exceptions, *even while*, the novel insists, living ethically requires just these things. Sometimes, living ethically may be impossible.

The novel is morally helpful here, I think, for at least three reasons. First, we explore through the novel how the attempt to live as well as possible might play out in the world: when it might be appropriate to follow the heart and when, rather, to trust to the cold eye; how people could conceive of and carry through these tasks; and what it means for their lives and self-conceptions. It is significant that we learn this through the exploration of imaginatively realized lives. The knowledge of when to look coldly and when to follow the heart can only be context- and character-dependent, something we learn *through* a literary act that is similarly so. We learn, too, the novel suggests, that living ethically is living in relations of partiality to particular people; the abstractions of politics and general principles, while sometime regrettably necessary, cannot give us guidelines for living in a difficult world. This is a world of concrete individuals: Florence, Bheki, John, not "black people"; Vercueil, not "the homeless"; Elizabeth Curren and her daughter, not "white South Africans." We need not agree fully with William Blake that the "General Good is the plea of the scoundrel, hypocrite and flatterer," to nonetheless agree that "He who would do good to another must do it in Minute Particulars."[36]

Second, we learn through the emotional engagement that literature demands and brings to us that truths are not the exclusive possession of the cold eye. That the emotions can give us knowledge of value is a familiar view in philosophy today, but here we see, again, how this might play out in a life. And, moreover, we see the remaining possibility, which cannot be ruled out, of tension between the emotions and the impartial perspective. Sometimes the emotions can distort reality, and impartiality is required. Equally, however, the cold eye can also distort if it demands reasons for loving "all the way down." This is especially apposite for an ethical vision centered around love and trust for the unknowable Other.

Finally, perhaps the most crucial lesson in light of the content of this ethical vision, is that of realizing just how hard it might be to *live* it. The vision that Mrs. Curren—and Coetzee[37]—is drawn to requires a groundless love and trust that is astonishingly stringent, that makes the responsibility for others boundless, and that may very well require the abdication of deeply entrenched and even admirable habits and principles, the shrugging aside of dignity and the need to be loved oneself. It is both helpful and necessary for philosophers to have before them some subtly imagined world in which this is the goal, to see just what it entails and how difficult it is. Only by fully inhabiting such a world in intellect, emotion, and imagination can its resources or truthfulness be adequately assessed.

If, in conclusion, to be impartial is to judge justly and fairly, to see the world as it is, unclouded by love or self-interest, then a better image for this kind of vision might be, as Walker argued, a loving and *interested* interaction between people. The intimate letter, though not ideal, suggests how one particular and complex exploration might take place. By addressing another person who is trusted and to whom one feels the need to justify oneself, one can remain invested in the process, yet alert to bias. This is not yet ideal, because one would wish one's address to be reciprocated. Mrs. Curren has to make do with imagining her daughter's reactions, with apologizing in advance if she hurts her, or with talking—usually in vain—to Vercueil or John or Florence. The letter is not yet a conversation, but in an age of iron it might be the best we can get.

Notes

My thanks to Tom Martin and Anton Leist for helpful comments on earlier drafts.

1. W. Godwin, *Enquiry Concerning Political Justice and Its Influence on General Virtue and Happiness* (1793), ed. F. E. L. Priestly (Toronto: University of Toronto Press, 1946), 2.2.
2. P. Taylor, "On Taking the Moral Point of View," in *Studies in Ethical Theory: Midwest Studies in Philosophy*, vol. 3, ed. P. A. French, T. E. Uehling Jr., and H. K. Wettstein (Minneapolis: University of Minnesota Press, 1978), 37.
3. R. M. Hare, *Moral Thinking* (Oxford: Oxford University Press, 1981); R. Firth, "Ethical Absolutism and the Ideal Observer," *Philosophy and Phenomenological Research* 12, no. 3 (1952): 317-45; and Henry Sidgewick, *The Methods of Ethics*, 7th ed. (London: Macmillan, 1907), 382. Along with these images of the ideal moral agent, we also find images of the kind of epistemic status of the ideal agent, e.g., Rawls's notion of the "veil of ignorance" in *A Theory of Justice* (Oxford: Oxford University Press, 1973).
4. E.g., see M. Baron, "Impartiality and Friendship," *Ethics* 101, no. 4 (1991): 836-57; and P. Railton, "Alienation, Consequentialism, and the Demands of Morality," in *Consequentialism*, ed. S. Darwall (Oxford: Blackwell, 2003), 160-96 (originally published in *Philosophy and Public Affairs* 13, no. 2 [1984]); for, respectively, a Kantian and consequentialist response along these lines.
5. M. U. Walker, "Partial Consideration," *Ethics* 101, no. 4 (1991): 759-60.
6. John Cottingham has argued this in a series of papers: see, for example, "Partiality, Favouritism, and Morality," *The Philosophical Quarterly* 36, no. 144 (1986): 357-73; "The Ethical Credentials of Partiality," *Proceedings of the Aristotelian Society* 98 (1998): 1-21; and "The Ethics of Self-Concern," *Ethics* 101, no. 4 (1991): 798-817. I leave it open whether these partial elements are essentially partial—"all the way down"—or whether they are ultimately justified impartially.
7. I. Murdoch, "The Idea of Perfection," in *The Sovereignty of Good* (London: Routledge, 2000), 28.
8. For a discussion of this within the context of the impartiality debate, see T. Nagel, *Equality and Partiality* (New York: Oxford University Press, 1991).
9. As S. Conly argues in "The Objectivity of Morals and the Subjectivity of Persons," *American Philosophical Quarterly* 22, no. 4 (1985): 275-86.
10. See A. Piper, "Moral Theory and Moral Alienation," *The Journal of Philosophy* 84, no. 2 (1987): 102-18, sect. 2.
11. Sam Durrant, "J. M. Coetzee, Elizabeth Costello, and the Limits of the Sympathetic Imagination," in *J. M. Coetzee and the Idea of the Public Intellectual*, ed. J. Poyner (Athens: Ohio University Press, 2006), 126.
12. E.g., see M. Marais, " 'Little Enough, Less Than Little: Nothing': Ethics, Engagement, and

Change in the Fiction of J. M. Coetzee," *Modern Fiction Studies* 46, no. 1 (Spring 2000): 159–82; E. Jordaan, "A White South African Liberal as a Hostage to the Other: Reading J. M. Coetzee's *Age of Iron* through Levinas," *South African Journal of Philosophy* 24, no. 1 (2005): 22–32; and D. Attridge, *J. M. Coetzee and the Ethics of Reading* (Scottsville: University of KwaZulu-Natal Press; Chicago: University of Chicago Press, 2005).

13. Attridge, *J. M. Coetzee and the Ethics of Reading*, 74, 70.
14. Ibid., 74. With the phrase "forever on its guard against itself," Attridge is quoting Peter Strauss, "Coetzee's Idylls: The Ending of *In the Heart of the Country*," in *Momentum: On Recent South African Writing*, ed. M. J. Daymon, J. U. Jacobs, and Margaret Lenta (Pietermaritzburg: University of Natal Press, 1984).
15. Attridge, *J. M. Coetzee and the Ethics of Reading*, 138.
16. M. Friedman makes a similar point in "The Impracticality of Impartiality," *The Journal of Philosophy* 86, no. 11 (1989): 651–52; also see Walker, "Partial Consideration," sect. 3.
17. J.-J. Rousseau, *The Confessions* (1781), trans. anonymous (Ware: Wordsworth Editions Limited, 1996), 3.
18. Ibid., 3.
19. Montaigne's *Essays* are an extended example of this: M. Montaigne, *The Complete Essays* (1580), trans. and ed. M. A. Screech (Harmondsworth, U.K.: Penguin, 1991).
20. G. Eliot, *Middlemarch* (1874; Harmondsworth: Penguin, 1965), 312.
21. Ibid.
22. Piper, "Moral Theory and Moral Alienation," 104.
23. Friedman, "The Impracticality of Impartiality," 656.
24. Walker, "Partial Consideration," 771.
25. Ibid., 773.
26. Whether moral rules must be construed like this is, of course, a matter of debate. Barbara Harman, for example, does an admirable job of rescuing Kant from this charge (see *The Practice of Moral Judgment* [Cambridge, Mass.: Harvard University Press, 1993]). I am not endorsing the stark distinction between rules and a sensitive appreciation of particularity that seems to map the distinction between the ethical and the political in Coetzee's work, only noting it.
27. Attridge, *J. M. Coetzee and the Ethics of Reading*, 8.
28. That there is nothing lovable or even likable about some of the characters Mrs. Curren feels obligated to love separates this view of love from the more familiar tradition of groundless love. This tradition argues that contingent features of the beloved cannot ground constant love, as the lover would then be rational in "upgrading" to a person who possesses those features to a higher degree. This view insists, however, that there is something lovable or attractive that draws the lover in the first place.
29. See I. Kant, *Groundwork of the Metaphysics of Morals* (1785), trans. and ed. M. Gregor (Cambridge: Cambridge University Press, 1997), 4:399.

30. A helpful discussion of the Christian injunction to "love thy neighbor" is provided in D. S. Oderberg, "Self-Love, Love of Neighbour, and Impartiality," in *The Moral Life: Essays in Honour of John Cottingham*, ed. N. Athanassoulis and S. Vice (Houndmills: Palgrave Macmillan, 2008), 58–84.
31. On this, see Durrant, "J. M. Coetzee, Elizabeth Costello."
32. As Marais notes in "'Little Enough, Less Than Little: Nothing.'" Marais, it should be noted, tracks the images of blindness and closed eyes without making the contrast, as I do here, between this and the image of the "cold eye."
33. Allied to images of the heart, are those of the soul. The moral task involves "trying to keep a soul alive in times not hospitable to the soul" (130), and the soul is what loves and what love responds to. Near the end of her narrative, Mrs. Curren writes that her letter was meant to be, not a "story of a body, but of the soul it houses" (185–86).
34. B. Pascal, "The Heart Has Its Reasons Which Reason Knows Nothing," in *Pensées* (c. 1662), trans. A. J. Krailsheimer (Harmondsworth, U.K.: Penguin, 1966), 423.
35. See Murdoch, *The Sovereignty of Good*, e.g., 28, 38, and 91.
36. W. Blake, *Jerusalem*, f.55 l.54, quoted in Cottingham, "The Ethical Credentials of Partiality," 7.
37. While the need to keep distinct the narrator and the author is obvious, the fact that this vision recurs through Coetzee's fictions and that he has articulated at least some of it in the interviews with Attwell suggest that here he shares his vision with his creation.

References

Coetzee, J. M. *Age of Iron*. London: Penguin, 1990.

———. *Doubling the Point: Essays and Interviews*. Ed. D. Attwell. Cambridge, Mass.: Harvard University Press, 1992.

14

The Lives of Animals and the Form-Content Connection

Jennifer Flynn

Time was, when it came to moral philosophy, "metaethics" referred to moral philosophy's role in the overall philosophical project: to engage in metaethics was to engage in the analysis of moral concepts and language.[1] *Normative* ethics, then, was taken to be beyond the purview of moral philosophy. Today, it is generally accepted that normative ethics does indeed occupy a legitimate branch of moral philosophical study. Even so, moral philosophy has been criticized, from within and without, on the grounds that even the shift toward the normative failed to inject the discipline with the richness of personal perspectives the investigation of (ethical) life warrants. Recall Bernard Williams's relatively recent suggestion that "the theoretically unlimited demands of impartialist systems of morality elbow out much that gives meaning to life, including anything that could inspire us to take any moral goal seriously."[2] A response to this, to the challenge to the assumption that "philosophical ethics deals primarily with right conduct among strangers"[3] has been an interest in the literary text as a focus for the exploration of ethical issues.[4]

What special role, according to those who espouse its use in the study of ethics, does the literary text play in reflection about moral life? What can the literary text uniquely offer the study of ethics? Martha Nussbaum holds that style, or as she puts it, "literary form," is not separable from philosophical content, that form itself "expresses its own sense of what matters."[5] According to Nussbaum, there are some views (of the moral world, about human life) "that cannot be fully stated in the language of conventional philosophical prose"; form (literary or philosophical) is, in at least some sense, *part* of content. Nussbaum makes two specific claims here. First, she says that (with respect to any text "carefully written and fully imagined") certain thoughts and ideas "reach toward," or are especially well suited to, a certain shape and form of writing, writing that uses certain structures and terms. In the case of any such text, there is, as Nussbaum puts it, an "organic connection between its form and its content."[6] For example, what Nussbaum calls an "abstract theoretical style"—a style she connects with the "philosophical treatise," if not directly with contemporary moral philosophy—makes (like any other style does) a statement "about what is important and what is not, about what faculties of the reader are important for knowing and what are not."[7] Second, we have the more extreme claim that certain truths about human life can *only* be properly stated by the sort of writing characteristic of the "narrative artist" (or fiction writer); this is not just to say, notice, that the truths in question are simply *better* communicated to readers through narrative. It is to say that such truths can *only* be expressed in literary form. How is it, though, that form actually expresses content—or, to take a slightly different (more Wittgensteinian) angle,[8] how should we think of the importance of the literary or otherwise stylistic aspects of (philosophical) writing? How do formal structures *express* content?

In this chapter, I shall not argue for the claim that some philosophically relevant ideas can be articulated only in literary form. Rather, I want to probe the assumed connection between form and content; by virtue of *what* are certain ideas about the moral life best suited to literary forms of expression and communication? I urge that J. M. Coetzee's novella (a word I use out of convenience) *The Lives of Animals* shows that the form-content connection can be mediated through a certain mode of reflection upon moral life, a mode made possible not only by a nonphilosophical, literary form but by techniques particular to Coetzee and *Lives* itself. I use *Lives* not because it is stereotypical literature, literature of the sort referred to by those philosophers convinced of literature's importance; it is not. Rather, I use it because in *Lives*, Coetzee is deliberately testing the distinction between literature and philosophy: he is doing philosophy and literature through the writing of fiction.[9] As Marjorie Garber notes in her response to Coetzee, Coetzee is as much asking about the value of philosophy, or of literature, as he is probing our disvaluation of animals. Add to this the fact that Coetzee himself offers *The Lives of Animals* as the 1997-1998 Tanner Lectures at Princeton University—lectures that are generally philosophical essays—and we have a work rife with potential for discussion of academic disciplinarity and methodology, a work that challenges an assumption that philosophy "should not be confused with any other kind of study, and which needs no other kind of study in order to understand itself."[10]

THE LIVES OF ANIMALS AND FORM

The Lives of Animals is a novella published in 1999; its story features as its main character Elizabeth Costello, an aging fiction writer who has been invited to deliver a series of lectures on her choice of topic at a small American college (where, as it happens, her own son teaches). Her topic of choice (much to the surprise of those who invited her, as it is not a topic on which her reputation is based) is our treatment of animals, and the novella contains not only the story of her visit to Appleton College and her stay with her son and his young family but the actual lectures Costello delivers. If, when we speak of a work's form, we are generally referring to its style and structure, Coetzee's *Lives* pushes on our standard distinctions and categories. Starting with the basic distinction between (moral) philosophy and literature: as Read and Cook point out, Coetzee's story is "told in very plain prose": "superficially, it does not offer a uniquely or essentially literary language."[11] It is clearly not plainly philosophical; we have a story, of course, and *Lives* does not rely upon the reader making inferential moves of the sort required by standard philosophical argument. *Lives* does not exhibit the directness of form we associate with standard philosophical argument; no clear premises are set out in the novella, and the work ends with a sense of unresolvedness. Certainly, no tangible conclusion on the issue of the treatment of animals is put forth and defended. But neither is Coetzee's work highly literary, with its mixture of story and argument.

In addition to Coetzee's mixture of story and argument, there are points at which we are reminded of the story's fictionality, reminded of the presence of the author's hand, that our attentions are taken various places by an author using certain literary conventions. For example, there is the deliberateness of the arguments posed at the banquets: the progress of the plot takes a deliberate turn toward philosophy. Also, Elizabeth Costello, during one of her lectures, mentions her own novel, *The House on Eccles Street*, and she emphasizes that its main character, Marion Bloom, never existed (*The Lives of Animals*, 35). Costello's point has to do with the importance of thinking one's way into another being—an ability she seems to think is lacking in most of her fellow human beings—but we arguably also have an indirect reference to fictionality: it is also true that Elizabeth Costello never existed.

There are also the references to historical works of literature. (We have Franz Kafka's "Report to an Academy," Wolfgang Köhler's *The Mentality of Apes*, Rilke's "The Panther," Ted Hughes's two poems "The Jaguar" and "Second Glance at a Jaguar," and Swift's *Gulliver's Travels*.) Finally, the novel is not a work intended to be interpreted in just one way: unlike most philosophical argument, *Lives* lends itself to many different readings. This is an important difference between fiction in general (and *Lives* in particular) and standard moral philosophy: when it comes to most standard philosophy, the point of the presented argument is the intended interpretation. When we consider the form of *Lives*, then, we have much more than an attempt on Coetzee's part to make certain abstract, philosophical ideas and concepts lived and concrete by exemplifying them in a story.

THE LIVES OF ANIMALS AND CONTENT

In order to explore the form-content distinction, I need to look at the presumption that there is some message, some "content" that we can extract from the novella in the first place. It would be a mistake to assume that it is a straightforward matter to lay out what *Lives* is about, to assume that we can talk of any "primary message" of Coetzee's.[12] This is a point made by literary theorist Samuel Goldberg about fiction in general. He says that it is not at all easy to say what a novel is about and that it is wrong to assume that extracting content from a work of fiction is an easy matter, "even after we reach the state of mind to which the work finally brings us."[13] Especially if we take the Wittgensteinian impetus for the study of the literary text seriously, it is dangerous to rely heavily on the idea of content. After all, a large part of the rationale behind the Wittgensteinian turn to literature arises from a problematization of the notion of philosophical content.[14] Further, according to Derek Attridge, the very distinction between form and content is too simple.[15] While acknowledging the indispensability of the concept of form to literature—he makes the point that any discussion of literature's differences from other textual activities must "involve some version of it"—he urges that it is overly simple to oppose form with content or meaning.[16]

Another challenge to setting up a discussion in terms of form's impact on content is that fiction in general, and most certainly Coetzee's *Lives*, is open to many different readings, unlike philosophical argument (I have already made this point in discussing the form of *Lives*). If fiction in general, and *Lives* in particular, opens itself up to a number of different readings, then there is no one, unproblematic version of its "content."

There is a further issue: there are questions surrounding the extent to which we can take Costello's voice to be Coetzee's. I will not attempt to sort out that question here, though without doing that we can still see that the idea of content is made more problematic the less we assume one character to be the mouthpiece for the author of the relevant work. Hacking writes that he did not deliberate about whether Coetzee believes what Costello says: "I imagine that Coetzee feels the force of almost all the ideas and emotions that his characters express."[17] We can contrast

Hacking's thinking here with a thought set out in Peter Singer's response to Coetzee in *The Lives of Animals*. Singer's narrator does suggest that the main function of the form of Coetzee's argument is to allow Coetzee to distance himself from what he presents, allowing him to avoid taking responsibility for the position put forth by his characters. Singer's narrator urges that "Coetzee's fictional device" allows Coetzee to avoid committing himself to claims put forth in the novella (*The Lives of Animals*, 93). Attridge discusses this "avoidance of responsibility" response to Coetzee's (related) novel *Elizabeth Costello*.[18]

All of this might suggest that any investigation of a form-content connection is misguided. Even if we cannot in any straightforward way speak of the "content" of *Lives*, the particularities of its formal features do work to take our thought about our treatment of animals in certain directions: I shall suggest two such directions.

Primacy Not Given to Philosophical Concepts

First, *Lives* is not primarily concerned with moral concepts and ideas with which we are familiar from philosophy. This basic idea is Samuel Goldberg's—he draws a distinction between texts that give primacy to familiar ideas and those that do not—and in discussing the relation between moral philosophy and literature, he argues that it is a mistake to read literature as exemplifying or instantiating ideas and principles that we already know, on other, "philosophical" grounds, to be "true" or "correct." As Goldberg puts the general point, it is not as though literature is just a storehouse of "philosophical" ideas (though many philosophers, he argues, treat it as such).[19] He writes that it is commonly (and wrongly) assumed that the themes of a literary work are just abstract moral truths that literature gives us to see.[20] There are strong indications that Costello, at least, wants to undermine so-called philosophical approaches to the issue, steering her audience's thoughts (and ours) away from traditionally philosophical questions and concepts. During her first lecture, she tells her audience that she will resort, for a while, to "philosophical language" (implying that it is constrained and limited: she is *resorting* to it) (*The Lives of Animals*, 32). Further, at various points during that first lecture, Costello contrasts reason with "unreason"—philosophy with poetry?—deriding the assumption that the realm of "reason" exhausts the valuable domain of human thought.

Granted, the idea of animals having rights—an idea with which we are familiar from philosophical debate—comes up in *Lives*, as does the question of the (moral) relevance of the fact that an animal does not appreciate whether its life is being spared or not. Thomas O'Hearne, a philosophy professor, suggests to Costello that animals cannot enjoy legal rights because they are not persons (or potential persons) (62). Dean Arendt, at supper after Costello's first lecture, raises this issue of beneficiaries not being aware that they are being benefited: "You can't explain to a steer that its life is going to be spared" (44). We are, though, invited to think beyond the sorts of issues raised here; such ideas might signal the *limits* of most discussion about our treatment of animals.[21]

A Focus Upon "Life-Morality"

I shall make use of another of Goldberg's distinctions, between "conduct-morality" and "life-morality." Goldberg sees moral philosophy as being concerned primarily with the realm of right *action*. Conduct-morality has as its primary object the "voluntary intentional actions of a moral agent" and "usually presents itself to the agent as an impersonal, regulative claim or imperative." Life-morality is also concerned with voluntary intentional action, but as Goldberg puts it, "now it is conduct seen as part of the whole range of a person's active existence."[22] Something Goldberg brings out in his book is how literature is especially well-suited to exploring, as he puts it, not just actions but whole lives. Literature, he says, thinks about people in a "double way," as voluntary agents (as philosophy does) but also as "lives":[23] this "double treatment" allows literature to attend to those aspects of characters' lives that cannot be called voluntary actions. So in addition to the distinction between conduct-morality and life-morality is the distinction between the voluntary and the involuntary when it comes to our moral lives. Seen from the conduct-morality point of view—from, as Goldberg has it, the standard moral-philosophical point of view—the moral agent "is seen as *voluntarily* forming the content of intentions, projects, deeds and habits."[24]

In suggesting that moral philosophy focuses far too heavily upon action, Goldberg writes that he agrees with Diamond when she says that most moral philosophers confine the sphere of the "moral" too narrowly to actions.[25] Along similar lines, in urging that Aristotle is much more of a conduct-moralist than he is made out to be by most moral philosophers, Goldberg asserts that even the virtuous men described by Aristotle are only specific types of "character": they are not individual lives or souls. As Goldberg puts it, they are abstractions "characteristic of that generalizing, 'philosophical' cast of mind: that type of mind which cannot apprehend and value human lives except as examples or instances of types or universals."[26] Indeed, one of Goldberg's criticisms of Martha Nussbaum is what he sees as her tendency toward mere conduct-morality.[27]

Literature, on the other hand, embodies the supposition that "'dispositions of character' extend, in incalculable ways, beyond consciousness and will"; it acknowledges the "involuntary" nature of our moral lives.[28] According to Goldberg, literature recognizes something that moral philosophy does not, that much of what takes place in our moral lives cannot be faithfully depicted as involving *choosing* to act in certain ways. This relates to the distinction between conduct-morality and life-morality in a fairly direct way: moral reflection that focuses on life-morality, as literature does—moral reflection that does not concern itself primarily with action—is reflection that recognizes that much of moral life involves modes of activity that are not, strictly speaking, "voluntary." (While it is true that the debate over whether humans are free or determined beings and its implications for moral responsibility is a part of standard moral philosophy, the conversation tends to be about whether certain *actions* are determined. Our focus, as philosophers engaging in the debate, is directed toward conduct.)

We can see how these distinctions—between conduct-morality and life-morality and between the voluntary and the involuntary—play themselves out in *Lives*, without attention, at least while the narrative focuses on Costello, directed toward life-morality. For example, we can think of how Elizabeth, in some sense, wishes she was different than she is: she *wants* to be able to be free of her preoccupation with our treatment of animals (*The Lives of Animals*, 69). There is a sense in which what is central to Elizabeth's struggle is the way in which she *has* to be who she is, that she is condemned to be plagued by our treatment of animals. (It is not a voluntary move, on her part, to simply take up this issue.) For instance, Elizabeth tells President Gerard that rather than being the result of moral conviction, her vegetarianism comes out of a desire "to save her soul" (43). The issue has to do with how one sees the world, we can picture Costello saying, not with discrete decisions and instances of deliberation. Or again, consider the ending of the story: on her way back to the airport, Costello says to her son: "Calm down, I tell myself, you are making a mountain out of a molehill. This is life. Everyone else comes to terms with it, why can't you? *Why can't you?*"(69). Costello is, in some sense, trying to convince herself not to be concerned with something she seems compelled to be concerned with, a "life"-focused (as opposed to a "conduct"-focused) struggle. We see the same dynamic—a playing off against each other of the philosophical and the nonphilosophical—in the question from the bearded man in the audience of her first lecture. He presses her on action choices: "Are you saying we should close down the factory farms? Are you saying we should stop eating meat?" (36). Costello rejects the assumption that it is incumbent upon her to "enunciate principles" and proscriptions. "I was hoping not to have to enunciate principles," Costello says. "If principles are what you want to take away from this talk, I would have to respond, open your heart and listen to what your heart says" (37).

Costello's responses to various challenges divert not just from the typical philosophical response,[29] but from a focus upon what the "right" (voluntary) action is.

(Costello emphasizes, as I have mentioned, the importance of the possibility of thinking one's way into the body of an animal, as opposed to emphasizing how one should decide to behave toward animals.) Attridge makes a point, in discussing "At the Gate" in *Elizabeth Costello*, that helps us to see that this maneuvering of our attention toward life rather than conduct is working on another level as well. Attridge does not put his point in the terms in which I am speaking here, but he says that "At the Gate" "does not present us with an argument about the place of belief in fiction, but enables us to participate in Elizabeth Costello's believing about believing."[30] The same could be said with respect to Costello in *Lives*: Costello does not present us with an argument about the proper treatment of animals, but asks us to participate in her struggle with the issue. In inviting us to think in terms beyond conduct morality, Costello does not give us instructions about how exactly she thinks we ought to behave.

There is much more to be said about the direction in which Coetzee pushes our thought; I have not aimed to definitively set out these directions. Let us, though, take these two directions of thought and move on to the question: What is the relation between taking up these directions of thought and the form of the invitation to do so?

HOW WE THINK: THE RELATION AMONG FORM, REFLECTION, AND CONTENT

How, for what reasons, are the "ideas" expressed in *Lives* suited to a certain shape and form of writing? What is the connection here between form and content? There are, I want to suggest, three modes of reflection set in motion by form, modes of reflection that make the mind receptive to the invitations of thought offered by *Lives*. Coetzee's *Lives* shows the relevance of form, shows how it is related to the expression of content. Mode of reflection, then, acts as a conceptual middleman; Coetzee's *Lives* shows us that form influences *how* we think. I shall identify each of these modes of reflection, and set out the connections between mode of reflection, form, and content.

Reflecting with More Than the "Capacities of the Head"

Coetzee's *Lives* places demands on its reader very different from the sorts called for by standard moral philosophy. As Goldberg writes, as readers of fiction we have to be willing to go where literature can take us. Not only is good literature geared toward the responsive reader, but literature can bring the reader to a "fuller mode of life" provided that "the reader's moral being can open itself up to that of the work."[31]

A similar idea is articulated by Diamond, with reference to Stephen Clark's book *The Moral Status of Animals* and Clark's placement of a poem, without any attending comment, at the end of one of the book's discussions.[32] One of Diamond's points about the placement of that poem is that if we read with an eye only for assertion and argument (as most philosophers, it is implied, are trained to do) we will miss the thought that is shown and asked for by the placement of the poem. Clark's use of the poem demands something of his reader that goes beyond what standard philosophical argument calls for. As Diamond puts it, Clark calls upon more than "the capacities of the head"; in inviting his reader to take up the view of animals he offers up, Clark demands that his readers use their imaginations, sensibilities, and intelligence.[33]

Taking these two points together, engaging with literature or certain nonstandard kinds of philosophizing requires that we willingly bring more to the text than is required by standard contemporary moral philosophy. In order to undergo the change in attitude and awareness offered by a good novel (a change discussed by Goldberg), the reader must bring his or her full being to the table, rather than just his or her rational mind. As well, as Diamond discusses, a work such as Clark's demands that we use our imaginations, that we look for more than the sort of argument trained philosophers are accustomed to dealing with. Coetzee's *Lives* is demanding in this way, demanding in a way that standard philosophical argument—a philosophical piece on the topic of the treatment of animals—is not (even if philosophical argument relies on such things as experience in reading human situations). As is obvious, a standard philosophical argument is not presented in *Lives*. We are forced to reflect in a way that involves our emotions and an engagement with characters.

This mode of reflection is set in motion by the novella's form, or so I want to suggest. Earlier, I made the point, referring to Read and Cook, that *Lives* is neither highly literary nor highly philosophical. In making that point, I mentioned that while *Lives* contains various arguments, it does not assume an argumentative *form*. That this is the case—that *Lives* does not involve the presentation of a standard argument—leads us to have to reflect in ways that involve more than the ability to scrutinize the strength of argumentative moves and the cogency of an argument as a whole.

That we are presented not with an argument but instead with various positions requires of us that we do more than evaluate. If Coetzee is asking us to feel the power of the various articulated positions on the issue, to experience confusion rather than to (just) exercise reason, his reader meets these demands through a mode of reflection that is agile and imaginative. What, though, to make of the relation between content, the direction in which our thought is being taken, and this mode of reflection? That we must do more than evaluate a standard philosophical argument is connected to the fact that we are invited to push past familiar philosophical concepts. (This was the first of the two directions of thought set out during our earlier discussion of content.) That *Lives* is not probing the issue in terms with which we are familiar—it does not simply showcase a discussion about the relevance of animal rights, for example, within a fictional framework—requires a kind of thinking on the part of the reader, a thinking that involves an engagement with the characters of the story. This sort of engagement would not be necessary if new formulations of well-worn philosophical concepts were the crux of the intended message of the novella. The suggestion that the lines along which the topic is discussed (by many philosophers, at least) are limiting—a suggestion that Coetzee, or at least Elizabeth Costello, is concerned to make—is particularly suited to the kind of reflection that follows from the structure of the text. Our primary task as readers is not to evaluate the power of one concept over another; we are not given the task of deciding whether an infringement of rights is occurring here but not there. The power and importance of philosophical argument are challenged on at least two levels: first, at the level of the form of *Lives*—while we are in some sense encountering philosophy, we do not confront philosophical argument—and second, on the level of the story. These points are substantive *and* metaphilosophical: they deal with animals and us, and with philosophy.

In discussing form, I earlier brought up how Coetzee refers to various literary works throughout *Lives*. The points that are made through the use of such references invite us to think beyond philosophical concepts. Consider, for instance, Costello's discussion of Köhler's *The Mentality of Apes*. Costello takes us (her audience, Coetzee's readers) through what she thinks, at least, must have gone through the ape Sultan's mind while deprived of food in his pen during the ape experiments Köhler catalogues in his book. We are given a description of the experimenter hanging the bananas three meters above his pen, of his introducing the crates, of his filling the crates with rocks, of his introducing the stick. More importantly, we are given a running list of the responses to these varying situations that go through Sultan's head, responses that take the form of questions; from the experimenter's point of view, though, they are the wrong questions. (Rather than Sultan asking of the experimenter, "Why has he stopped liking me?" he ought to ask, "How does one use the crates to reach the bananas?") As Costello puts it, the series of experiments drives Sultan, at every turn, to think the less interesting thought. But what sort of point is Costello (at least) trying to make here, and what is unique about this sort of historical-literary reference that helps her make it? On the face of it, Costello is making a point about what she takes to be the difference between poets and men like Köhler (namely that a poet would have shown some sort of feel for the apes' experience, or at least an interest in having that sort of feel, where Köhler demonstrated, at least as Costello has it, major limitations on this front).[34]

This point in itself is, naturally, nicely made with this reference: it might have been much less effective for Costello to have simply spelled out to her audience the importance of having a feel for an ape's experience (or the experience of animals in general). But beyond this, we have (arguably) a subtextual point subtly made about philosophical investigation and the sorts of questions it provokes, or, at the very least, we have some comment about certain modes of enquiry leading one (Sultan, in this case) "*away* from ethics and metaphysics toward the humbler reaches of practical reason" (*The Lives of Animals*, 29).

Encountering Personalized Insights

There are two senses in which *Lives* involves "personalized insights," or at least insights distinct in nature from the so-called depersonalized insights often attributed to standard moral philosophy; there are at least two ways in which *Lives* invites us to connect with a person in a way that moral philosophy does not. This connection shapes the reflection encouraged by the text in ways that set that reflection apart from the sort encouraged by standard moral philosophy.

The first sense in which *Lives* (or any fictional work) demonstrates personalized insights has to do with how it presents a sense of what sort of person the author is. Quite a lot has been made of this difference between literature and standard philosophy, this difference between writing that gives us a sense of the writer as a person and writing that does not. For instance, Nussbaum discusses what she sees as the tendency on the part of philosophers who, under the pressure of the convention of contemporary professional philosophy (along with some pressure from the notion that scientific enquiry is, or should be, paradigmatic) write philosophy without a recognition of its possibility as an "expressive creation," revealing of a "human personality with a particular sense of life."[35] Instead, most moral philosophy is done in the style of natural science in the sense that we do not, and are not meant to, get much of a sense of the person behind the writing.[36]

Nussbaum is critical not only of the complacency with which it is assumed that this style is uniformly appropriate for the study of ethics but of the way in which such imitation of science limits the possibilities of ethical inquiry. (It is true that not all moral philosophy is written in this style; think, for instance, of Iris Murdoch's *Metaphysics as a Guide to Morals*.)

The second and most important sense in which we, as readers of *Lives*, are invited to connect with a person can be provided by a text that presents individual characters and allows readers to imagine how those characters see and think about the world. Rather than proceed by standard argument, at least in the sense of setting out a formal argument with premises and a conclusion, Coetzee involves us in the life of Costello and (to a somewhat lesser extent) the lives of his other characters. This stands in obvious contrast to the way in which standard philosophy proceeds. As Goldberg puts it—what he says here is consistent with what he says about literature—drama does not hold before us depersonalized insights. Rather, it holds before us "a particular mode of life in the very way it imagines the lives and insights of particular individuals; and a drama holds particular individuals before us (in the sense of depicting them) rather than just the formulable views they express and 'represent.'"[37] Relatedly, Nussbaum tells us that reading stories places us in a position *unlike* the position we normally occupy in life: involved with the characters yet also free of the distortions and distractions that often preoccupy us.[38] When I say that Coetzee invites us to connect with Costello, I mean that Costello's perspective is the one the reader is likely to most closely engage with. It is also true, though, that we are given external perspectives on Costello, through the eyes of various other characters and their modes of response to Costello. The presence of these external perspectives might suggest that the reader is meant to be able to maintain some critical distance from Costello. In particular, one might take the entire story to be mediated through son John's unsympathetic perspective.

How does this way of thinking, which involves a connection with characters, relate to formal aspects of Coetzee's *Lives*? There is the obvious point that the presentation of a standard argument would not give the reader the opportunity to see things as Costello sees them, insights that promote our grasp of Coetzee's—or at the very least Costello's—view of the issue of our treatment of animals. Neither the writing of natural science nor the writing of standard moral philosophy involves personalized insights in either of the two senses just discussed.

Here again, our thought is steered in a particular direction—toward a focus on life-morality as opposed to deliberation about discrete action—by form and the sort of reflection it encourages. Costello's responses to the arguments others present to her do not follow the argumentative form that the challenges to her position take.[39] Those responses show, as Diamond writes, that Costello does not take seriously the conventions of argumentation, and through engaged with Costello's perspective, readers are encouraged to reflect on the possible limits of such conventions. It is important that the kind of argumentation Costello calls into question tends to address itself to issues of conduct: on what sort of grounds can I justify this action choice? Elizabeth's perspective works against the supposition that the treatment of animals is an issue to be taken up within the conventions of a certain discipline of thought.

In identifying with Costello's perspective, we are discouraged from viewing the issue (the treatment of animals) as "ethical" as such, one that belongs only to the realm of a departmentalized or philosophical academic discussion.[40] Now we might not, in the end, identify with Costello's perspective. Nonetheless, while showing that one *can* indeed argue about the treatment of animals, the book suggests the possibility (through Costello) that philosophical argument elicits the more narrow and les interesting thoughts on the subject of our treatment of animals. Elizabeth takes the issue to relate to her personal life; it relates, for example, to life with her grandchildren (witness the tension around mealtime at her son's house). Elizabeth, then, explicitly connects the issue to her lived life, in a way that stands in opposition to her interlocutors' handling of it. Finally, in another push past conduct-morality, Costello herself is critical of the limits of philosophizing, pointing out how it does not allow us to inhabit the body of the animals (which she seems to think is necessary for a deep engagement with animals' plight).[41] Elizabeth Costello is an animal for *us* to inhabit, with her flabby flesh, her old flesh (*The Lives of Animals*, 15, 69). *Lives* is an invitation to engage with Costello, rather than merely to take up her ideas (which seems to parallel Costello's view of the power of Hughes' jaguar poems).

Literature and Enactive Thinking

Goldberg describes what, on his view, the kind of (moral) thinking encouraged by literature is like. He writes that there is a certain kind of ethical reflection, or moral thinking, that is prompted by literary works—"thinking of a kind, particular, metaphorical and enactive, necessitated by the very nature of the moral sphere, and not readily available to us except in works of literature."[42] Along similar lines, Goldberg talks about how something about literature, which he calls its "dramatic action," brings the reader from one state to another with respect to awareness and attitudes.

A way of thinking about this shift in awareness and attitude is to think of our moral sensibilities being fine-tuned by literature, of our moral perceptions being sharpened by fiction. This is not to say that standard philosophizing does not aim to sharpen a reader's moral sensibilities. It is, though, to point out that the shift in perspective encouraged by literature is much less specific in nature as compared with the specificity of claims that are supported by standard philosophical argument. As Hacking puts it with respect to Coetzee's novel *Boyhood*, the intellect is bypassed.[43] Within the context of *Lives* this is not entirely the case, but the story enhances our capacities of moral perception and response by virtue of being a story (or, at least as some might be inclined to say, part story, part discursive argument).[44] We also have, in a sense, work to do: there is no argument with (to use a phrase of Nussbaum's) a "cooked" result.[45]

Could standard philosophical writing push our thought in the directions I suggest *Lives* does? Why could not a philosopher simply state that we should not be so concerned with "conduct" and more concerned with questions regarding the living of a good life? What is the importance of the fact that it is done through fiction here? How is this mode of reflection set in motion by form? That *Lives* is open to many different readings—an aspect of form I mentioned earlier—forces the reader to do more than evaluate an argument. And as Attridge puts it, reading fiction means that we are reading events rather than arguments, we participate in characters' believing rather than being presented with justified beliefs.[46] There is a difference, then, between this so-called enactive thinking and the thinking encouraged by standard moral-philosophical argument. That *Lives* is open to many different readings facilitates this difference; there is not one intended argument to evaluate. That *Lives* is not highly literary, yet not highly philosophical—another formal feature of the book—adds to the challenge faced by the readers: the power of the variously presented arguments must be set against Costello's more open-ended appeals.

The points at which we are reminded of the books constructedness and fictionality further contribute to this enactive thinking insofar as the reader is brought to realize that while his or her attentiveness is being manipulated, there is not one particular message—political or moral or otherwise—that is being conveyed. When we encounter, for example, the various argumentative sections, it is not just our job to evaluate those arguments: we are invited to reflect upon the power of argument itself in this domain.

There is a parallel between the push toward thinking in life-morality terms and the encouragement of enactive thinking. This is in contrast to the sort of case in which we are reading (and evaluating) a standard philosophical argument; there, we read something that supports a certain point of view (which might deal with which sorts of considerations might be relevant to a certain topic or with whether a particular action is morally permissible). An emphasis on life-morality and the involuntary is less amenable to discussion that uses standard argument, at least partly because that sort of discussion involves the putting forth of a specific claim that is in need of support. Action-centered discussion is much more suitable to the putting forth of discrete claims than is discussion that aims to divert attention away from action choices (should I refrain from eating this animal, because it has certain rights that I should respect?) and toward broader and in some ways more elusive matters (how should I think about the fact that this cow and I are each mortal beings?). To absorb the lessons of *Lives*, then—or at least the lessons Costello has for us—we ought to be engaged in a thinking that does not primarily concern itself with the evaluation of arguments.

TWO FURTHER THOUGHTS

First, there are connections to be made here to certain conversations within the philosophy of science. According to some, each style of scientific inquiry introduces its own objects for study.[47] If what I suggest about form's connection to reflection holds true, then it might be that a literary approach to the investigation of (moral) life makes certain questions salient rather than others, that moral philosophy and literature effectively introduce their own "objects of study." To pursue this parallel fully would require bringing into view a distinction that I have not discussed, between method's (or style's) relation to the *expression* of ideas (which is something I indirectly address in this chapter) and method's connection to the *encountering* of, or *formulation* of, ideas.

Second, though I note that I do not aim to argue for the claim that some philosophically relevant ideas can be articulated only in literary form, it seems as though, given that what I say Coetzee shows us about the relevance of form, I am committed to something in the neighborhood of that claim. And to this, one might say: we need more *evidence* for the thesis that such ideas can be set out only in literary form. A number of issues are introduced by this, ones I do not directly attend to in this paper. One has to do with the question: if it is the case that it is misguided to talk of literature's exemplifying (philosophical) ideas, how ought we to handle these requests for such justifications?[48]

Notes

1. D. Copp, "Metaethics," in *Encyclopedia of Ethics*, 2nd ed., ed. L. C. Becker and C. B. Becker (London: Routledge, 2001), 1080; K. Nielsen, "Ethics, Problems of," in *The Encyclopedia of Philosophy*, ed. P. Edwards (London: Collier MacMillan, 1967), 3:117–34, 3:118. Nielsen, writing around 1967, mentions that philosophers frequently claim that metaethical theories and metaethical statements are all normatively neutral (3:119).
2. This is discussed in Hilde Lindeman Nelson's introduction to her edited collection *Stories and Their Limits: Narrative Approaches to Bioethics* (New York: Routledge, 1997), viii. See B. Williams, "Persons, Character, and Morality," in *Moral Luck* (New York: Cambridge University Press, 1981), chap. 1.

3. M. Nussbaum, *Love's Knowledge: Essays on Philosophy and Literature* (New York: Oxford University Press, 1990), viii.
4. A similar challenge has been posed to bioethics—to a picture of bioethics according to which bioethics is "an endeavor to look at reasons and to determine what reasons should be credited by impartial, unprejudiced, nonculturally biased reasoners, whose only interests are in the consistency and force of rational argument"—by so-called "pathographies." The quotation is from T. Engelhardt, *Foundations of Bioethics* (New York: Oxford University Press, 1986), 10, as quoted in John Wiltshire's "The Patient Writes Back: Bioethics and the Illness Narrative," in *Renegotiating Ethics in Literature, Philosophy, and Theory*, ed. J. Adamson, R. Freadman, and D. Parker (Cambridge: Cambridge University Press, 1998), 181–98, 186. See Wiltshire's article for a sustained discussion of the challenge to mainstream bioethics posed by pathography.
5. Nussbaum, *Love's Knowledge*, 3.
6. Ibid., 4.
7. Ibid., 7. On pages 5–6, Nussbaum writes that only the style of a certain sort of narrative artist (which, she says, is decidedly not the style of the abstract theoretical treatise) can "adequately state certain important truths about the world, embodying them 'in its shape' and setting up in the reader the activities that are appropriate for grasping them."
8. For a discussion of the Wittgensteinian conception of philosophy according to which philosophy has no "positive content," see R. Read and J. Cook, "Recent Work: The Philosophy of Literature," *Philosophical Books* 43, no. 2 (2001): 118–31.
9. See Read and Cook, "Recent Work," 130: they put what Coetzee is doing in *The Lives of Animals* in these terms.
10. This quotation is from Bernard Williams; in the relevant passage, Williams sets out how this assumption has, in his view, prevented some of the "deepest insights of modern philosophy" from being developed. See his "Philosophy as a Humanistic Discipline," *Philosophy* 75 (2000): 477–96, 478.
11. See Read and Cook, "Recent Work," 130.
12. I. Hacking makes this point in "Our Fellow Animals," *New York Review of Books* 47 (2000): 20–26, 20. "Sympathy *between* (not for) may be the primary message of his recent book *The Lives of Animals*. Not that it makes much sense to talk of a primary message from such a many-messaged multilayered messenger."
13. S. Goldberg, *Agents and Lives: Moral Thinking in Literature* (Cambridge: Cambridge University Press, 1993), 306. Cora Diamond, in discussing the work of Austen and James, notes that there is an issue regarding whether the idea of extractable content makes sense; she says it probably makes some sense. See C. Diamond, "Anything But Argument?" in *The Realistic Spirit: Wittgenstein, Philosophy, and the Mind* (Cambridge, Mass.: MIT Press, 1991), 291–308, 300.
14. Ibid., 300n. 9.

15. Derek Attridge, *J. M. Coetzee and the Ethics of Reading: Literature in the Event* (Chicago: University of Chicago Press, 2004), 8.
16. Ibid., 8.
17. I. Hacking, *Historical Ontology* (Cambridge, Mass.: Harvard University Press, 2002), 20.
18. Attridge, *J. M. Coetzee and the Ethics of Reading*, 197.
19. Goldberg writes that Nussbaum rightly insists that literature is not merely a storehouse of examples for use in traditional philosophical discourse (Goldberg, *Agents and Lives*, 289). However, he goes on to criticize her, saying that Nussbaum makes her points in a general or theoretical way (rather than by employing cogent accounts of particular literary works) (294). It is as though, Goldberg continues, she is mining the work for a set of propositional claims. Further, she talks about a novel providing a persuasive argument for a claim, revealing her tendency, and the philosopher's tendency in general, to give priority to ideas (303).
20. Ibid., 306. Goldberg tells us that Nussbaum's approach to literature is too expressly cognitive: literature, as she handles it, is "about" recognizable moral problems, and it holds up before us cases of "practical wisdom" (291). In criticizing Alasdair MacIntyre's handling of literature, Goldberg says that MacIntyre exhibits a perennial weakness of philosophers, "giving priority to recognizable ideas over the unclassifiable" (278).
21. Hacking refers to Coetzee's *Boyhood: Scenes from Provincial Life*, remarking that it is devoid of rights talk and that this lack is "refreshingly unintellectual" (*Historical Ontology*, 20). *The Lives of Animals*, by contrast, sets rights talk against (for example) Ted Hughes's jaguar poem: philosophy and poetry confront each other.
22. See Goldberg, *Agents and Lives*, 38–39, for his discussion of this distinction.
23. Ibid., xv.
24. Ibid., 79, my emphasis.
25. Ibid., 254.
26. Ibid., 272.
27. Ibid., 286.
28. Ibid., 277.
29. Norma points this out to John while listening to Elizabeth's first lecture. "She's ranting," Norma says. "She has lost her thread" (*The Lives of Animals*, 31).
30. Attridge, *J. M. Coetzee and the Ethics of Reading*, 205.
31. Goldberg, *Agents and Lives*, 293. On that page, Goldberg continues: "It hardly needs saying that literature does not necessarily make the reader a better moral agent or improve his or her life, any more than moral philosophy does. In both cases, there are also other conditions to be met." Here, Goldberg is criticizing Martha Nussbaum, saying that she gives too little attention to those features of literature than can bring the reader to "a fuller mode of life itself."
32. Diamond, "Anything But Argument?" 303. Diamond surmises that Clark's book is

33. "demanding of a reader in quite different ways from those of standard contemporary moral philosophy." And also, "We are familiar enough with the kind of critical attention invited by philosophical argument, the kind of work demanded by it of the reader; but critical attention to the character and quality of thought in a work may be asked of a reader in many other ways as well" (303).

33. Diamond writes, "If Clark's aim is that his readers acknowledge something in themselves which habits of thought and response overlay and keep hidden, it is essential that he invites us to set our imagination and sensibility and intelligence to work; only that exercise can put us in a position properly to judge the view of animals he invites us to take up. Like any judgments worth bothering with, it will call on more than just the capacities of the head" ("Anything But Argument?" 303-4).

34. See *The Lives of Animals*, 30 for this discussion; see pages 27-30 for the discussion of Sultan and Köhler's book.

35. Nussbaum, *Love's Knowledge*, 20.

36. Nussbaum describes this as "a style correct, scientific, abstract, hygienically pallid, a style that seem[s] to be regarded as a kind of all-purpose solvent in which philosophical issues of any kind at all [are] efficiently disentangled, any and all conclusions neatly disengaged" (ibid., 19). With respect to the issue of the sense of a writer's personality that may or may not come through in fiction writing, the literary critic John Bayley makes a distinction between what he calls the minor fiction writer and the major one. He says that in the work of minor novelists (Philip Larkin is his example), there is a felt sense of the personality of the writer in the writer's work. The greater the novelist, he says, the more the reader feels the novelist's personality is not present in the work. His example of a great writer is Dostoevsky, and he says that the novels of his wife, Iris Murdoch, are similar to Dostoevsky's in this regard. See Richard Todd, "Discussions from Encounters with Iris Murdoch, 1988," in *From a Tiny Corner in the House of Fiction*, ed. G. Dooley (Columbia: University of South Carolina Press, 2003), 171.

37. Goldberg, *Agents and Lives*, 296. Goldberg is discussing Nussbaum's responses to particular dramas, but, as I note, what he writes here is consistent with what he writes about literature. Goldberg actually criticizes Nussbaum for imposing too "philosophical" a picture upon the novel, suggesting, as he says she does, that literature holds before us correct insights, ascertained wisdom—in short, the very depersonalized insights she herself admonishes standard philosophy for dealing with.

38. Nussbaum, *Love's Knowledge*, 48.

39. See C. Diamond, "The Difficulty of Reality and the Difficulty of Philosophy," in *Philosophy and Animal Life*, by Stanley Cavell et al. (New York: Columbia University Press, 2008), 43-90. Diamond uses as an example Costello's discussion of Camus' writing on the guillotine in response to the point that animals cannot claim rights for themselves as we can. See 62-3 of *The Lives of Animals* for that reference to Camus.

40. See I. Murdoch, *Metaphysics as a Guide to Morals* (London: Penguin Books, 1993), for a related discussion of whether the questions usually referred to as "ethical" should be taken up within an academic discipline dedicated especially to them. Murdoch criticizes moral philosophy for what she takes to be its overly rigid conception of itself as a subdiscipline of philosophy, a subdiscipline that is able to conduct itself in isolation not only from other areas of philosophy proper but from other disciplines of the humanities and social sciences more generally. Her view is tied to her argument against separating fact and value; in brief, moral philosophies that envisage a strict distinction between fact and value, at least according to Murdoch, are incompatible with the notion that thought in general is inherently moral (221-24). Murdoch's position on this "departmentalization" of morality can also be found in her article "Vision and Choice in Morality," *Proceedings of the Aristotelian Society Supplement* 30 (1956): 32-58.
41. For example, she tells us that the knowledge of what it is to be a corpse is not abstract (or "philosophical") but embodied (*The Lives of Animals*, 32); she talks about (in connection with Kohler's writing on his experiments with apes) how a poet would have zeroed in on an ape's experience (30). She describes Kafka has having seen himself as part (embodied) animal, as a monstrous thinking device mounted on a "suffering animal bod[y]" (30). She also uses Ted Hughes' poetry as an example of a kind of thinking that takes us into an animal's (a jaguar's) being, as an example of thinking that inhabits another's body (as opposed to inhabiting another's mind) (51).
42. Goldberg, *Agents and Lives*, 290.
43. Hacking, *Historical Ontology*, 20.
44. For a discussion of the idea that novel and other works of fiction enhance our capacities in this way, see J. M. Fisher, "Stories," *Midwest Studies in Philosophy* 20 (1996): 1-14, esp. 8.
45. Nussbaum, *Love's Knowledge*, 47.
46. Attridge, *J. M. Coetzee and the Ethics of Reading*, 198.
47. For example, see Hacking, *Historical Ontology*, chaps. 11 and 12.
48. I am grateful to Cora Diamond for comments on the dissertation chapter from which this chapter came. Thanks are also due to the Social Sciences and Humanities Research Council of Canada for doctoral-fellowship funding during the time the initial work on this paper was started and to my audience at the May 2007 Canadian Philosophical Association meeting at the University of Saskatchewan.

References

Coetzee, J. M. *Boyhood: Scenes from Provincial Life*. New York: Vintage, 1998.

———. *The Lives of Animals*. Princeton, N.J.: Princeton University Press, 1999.

15

Irony and Belief in *Elizabeth Costello*

Michael Funk Deckard and Ralph Palm

> In fact, now that she thinks of it, she lives, in a certain sense, by belief. . . . She lives by belief, she works by belief, she is a creature of belief. What a relief!
>
> —J. M. Coetzee, *Elizabeth Costello*

From the very beginning of *Elizabeth Costello*, J. M. Coetzee plays with his presentation of his protagonist's philosophical positions. As the narrative progresses through its eight "lessons," the reader is increasingly left to wonder whether Costello's positions are to be taken literally or ironically. In other words, are the opinions articulated by Elizabeth Costello a direct expression of J. M. Coetzee's own beliefs, or, through the manner of their presentation, does the author take some sort of distance from them? By the end of the novel, there remains a question not only as to Coetzee's particular beliefs but also what he considers to be the nature, and even the possibility, of belief itself.

In this article, we will ask three basic questions. First, in what sense are Costello's beliefs presented ironically? And given the manner in which they are presented, how are we to interpret the beliefs Costello expresses throughout the book? Second, we will explore the nature of belief in general, as discussed by Coetzee himself elsewhere, and in contrast to alternative possible views. Third, we return to the text and analyze the explicit discussion of belief as such found in *Elizabeth Costello*, especially in lesson 8, "At the Gate." In this way, we hope to show how the form of *Elizabeth Costello* shapes its content.[1]

IRONY?

We begin with the first question: Is *Elizabeth Costello* to be understood ironically? And if so, in what way and to what extent? There are simple, prima facie reasons for taking the lectures in *Elizabeth Costello* literally, that is, as direct expressions of Coetzee's own beliefs. First and foremost, there are the passages in which ironic readings are explicitly rejected. For example, during two of her lectures, Costello begins by comparing herself to Red Peter, the talking ape from Kafka's "Report to an Academy" (*Elizabeth Costello*, 18, 62). On the second occasion, she remarks: "I want to say at the outset that that was not how my remark—the remark that I feel like Red Peter—was intended. I did not intend it *ironically*. It means what it says. I say what I mean. I am an old woman. I do not have the time any longer to say things I do not mean" (62, emphasis added). At another point, she goes as far as to reject the "orthodox reading" of Swift's "A Modest Proposal," which is "stuffed down the throats of young readers" that Swift (otherwise considered one of the most famous examples of irony in all of English literature) "does not mean what he says, or seems to say" (101). This rejection of irony is also found in Costello's son John's characterization of her: speaking to Susan Moebius, John says, "If there is parody in her ... I confess it is too subtle for me to pick up" (23). Speaking to his wife, Norma, John defends his mother, insisting, "She's perfectly sincere" (113).

In addition, there are other, less direct but no less substantial, reasons for taking the content of Costello's lectures at face value. Of course, most of the "lessons" of *Elizabeth Costello* have been previously published by Coetzee elsewhere, as noted in the acknowledgments (233). It is important to note, for the sake of the casual reader, that it is not simply the *lectures* that have appeared elsewhere, but the *lessons* themselves—that is, the chapters, the lectures in their broader narrative context, presented in the form of a story. Moreover, these narrative lessons were delivered by Coetzee himself as public lectures.[2]

This has led some to treat *Elizabeth Costello* as merely a vehicle for Coetzee's presentation of his own views. In this reading, the narrative form is treated, at best, as if it served a merely defensive function. Coetzee is taken to be exploiting the voice of his character Costello as a way to avoid criticism for expressing controversial positions. There is a limited degree of truth to this charge. For example, on the occasion of at least one lecture, Coetzee responded to questions by interposing Costello between himself and his audience: "I think what Elizabeth Costello would say is that ... "[3] However, our purpose in analyzing the intent of the author is to come to a better understanding of the meaning of the text, not to speculate regarding Coetzee's personal motives in and of themselves.[4] So, while the presentation of the lectures in narrative form may serve a defensive function, this can hardly be considered its *only* function. Reducing the narrative of *Elizabeth Costello* to a sort of ideological roman à clef would be an oversimplification. Treating the presentation of the lectures of Costello in narrative form as *simply* a vehicle for the expression of Coetzee's own positions ignores the *complexity* of the manner in which Costello's views are presented.

First of all, there is the opposition between the way Costello presents her views and the way she is characterized. Coetzee introduces her physical appearance as frail. "After the long flight, she is looking her age. She has never taken care of her appearance; she used to be able to get away with it; now it shows. Old and tired" (*Elizabeth Costello*, 3). Her son John treats her with pity (e.g., 27). He feels the need to protect her (e.g., 30). His wife, Norma, characterizes her positions as "jejune and sentimental" (61), "rambling" (75), and "confused" (81). John does not try to defend her positions but excuses them on account of her frailty. "She's old, she's my mother. Please!" (81). The descriptions of physical frailty parallel suggestions of a sort of emotional and mental frailty as well. Costello even, at one point, suggests this "emotional frailty" herself: "Calm down, I tell myself, you are making a mountain out of a molehill. This is life. Everyone else comes to terms with it, why can't you? Why can't you?" John can give her only comfort:

> She turns on him a tearful face. What does she want, he thinks? Does she want me to answer her question for her? They are not yet on the expressway. He pulls the car over, switches off the engine, takes her mother in his arms. He inhales the smell of cold cream, of old flesh. 'There, there,' he whispers in her ear. 'There, there. It will soon be over.' (115)

If Costello's purpose is solely to voice Coetzee's own views, then it is quite strange that she would be characterized as so pitiful and (more significantly) so confused. If Coetzee's purpose was solely didactic, then one might expect more self-assurance from his spokesperson. Instead, these sorts of characterizations would seem to undermine rather than reinforce the content.

Second, there are a number of cues that the content of the lectures should *not* be taken at face value. There are, for instance, certain counterarguments posed by other characters. Norma repeatedly and forcefully rejects her mother-in-law's claims. "It's naive, John. It's the kind of easy, shallow relativism that impresses freshmen" (91); "there is no position outside of reason where you can stand and lecture about reason and pass judgment on reason" (93).[5] An even stronger criticism is voiced by Abraham Stern, the poet who protests her comparison of the slaughter of animals for food with the Holocaust. In a note explaining his absence, Stern writes:

> You took over for your own purposes the familiar comparison between the murdered Jews of Europe and slaughtered cattle. The Jews died like cattle, therefore cattle die like

Jews, you say. That is a trick with words which I will not accept. You misunderstand the nature of likenesses; I would even say you misunderstand willfully, to the point of blasphemy. Man is made in the likeness of God but God does not have the likeness of man. If Jews were treated like cattle, it does not follow that cattle are treated like Jews. The inversion insults the memory of the dead. It also trades on the horrors of the camps in a cheap way.[6]

(94)

Costello reads the letter and simply sighs. If Coetzee was solely interested in the unambiguous presentation of a set of principles, then one would expect Costello to make some sort of response to these criticisms.[7] If Coetzee was simply writing an anthology of essays on particular issues, in the form of a philosophical dialogue, then it would be very odd for his "Socrates" to be left speechless. A lack of direct response on these points presents a further ambiguity in Costello's positions. It presents an opposition to the reader between Coetzee, who expresses the counterarguments offered by other characters quite forcefully, and Costello, who can manage little or no response.

Such oppositions put the aforementioned protestations against irony in a new light. While Costello is "perfectly sincere" (113), Coetzee's presentation of her is not. Of course, the irony of the text is not *verbal irony*, that is, not an opposition between the literal and the figurative. It is only a reading in terms of verbal irony that the text explicitly rejects.[8] On the other hand, the opposition between the beliefs held (by Costello) and the way these beliefs are expressed (by Coetzee) strongly suggests the presence of irony. But, if not verbal irony, then what kind?

The first possible alternative is *Socratic irony*, or the opposition between a speaker's expressed and actual knowledge. This sort of "feigned ignorance" is the classical definition of the Greek *eironeia*. As is well known, Socrates is frequently portrayed using this sort of irony as a technique in discussion with his interlocutors. At the most basic level, the possibility of Socratic irony as a legitimate reading is excluded for the same reason that verbal irony is: Costello herself is "perfectly sincere." While her positions may be seem "irrational" to other characters (e.g., Nora), she is never portrayed with either ignorance or pretense.

However, the suggestion that the character-author opposition of the text represents a sort of Socratic irony is not completely absurd. At a more general level, one could suggest that, like Socratic irony, the opposition serves a sort of pedagogical or rhetorical function. From this point of view, Costello's expressions of self-doubt would make her appear less didactic and more sympathetic. And if one interprets *Elizabeth Costello* as a straightwardly ideological or didactic text (i.e., a direct presentation of Coetzee's own views), then these doubts combined with the doubts expressed by Coetzee, through other characters and contexts, serve that same rhetorical, sympathetic function. Rather than an opposition between expressed and actual knowledge, the opposition would be between expressed and real certainty. According to this reading, Coetzee would be "feigning doubt" through Costello, who expresses a lack of certainty he himself does not possess.

While not completely absurd, such a reading is not entirely fruitful either. It is both reductive and biographical. This interpretation simplifies *Elizabeth Costello*'s formal complexities into mere techniques for the expression of ideas. However, if the text is *simply* a vehicle for the expression of Coetzee's views, then why does it take the form of a novel in the first place? Why wasn't it written as a collection of essays? These questions are not simply biographical ("Why didn't Coetzee choose to write a book of essays instead?") but also textual. Without a source of information outside of the text, one must read the text as if this difference in form has some significance, that the narrative presentation of the ideas is an essential, rather than contingent, aspect of them. Otherwise, one has simply focused on one part of the text and ignored the whole. Or, in other words, form matters.

A second possible interpretation is that *Elizabeth Costello* expresses its views in the manner of a "liberal ironist," in Richard Rorty's sense of the term.[9] Rorty uses a broad definition of "liberal," as one who thinks that cruelty is the worst thing we can do.[10] This definition would seem to include Coetzee quite well.[11] As for the term "ironist," Rorty gives a more complex definition, in three parts:

> 1) She has radical and continuing doubt about the final vocabulary she currently uses....
>
> 2) She realizes that argument phrased in her present vocabulary can neither underwrite nor dissolve these doubts;
>
> 3) insofar as she philosophizes about her situation, she does not think that her vocabulary is closer to reality than others, that it is in touch with a power not herself.[12]

Parts 1 and 2 of the definition also seem to fit the views expressed in *Elizabeth Costello*. We have seen this a bit already, but one passage in particular highlights the relationship between the two:

> "*I don't know what I think*," says Elizabeth Costello. "*I often wonder what thinking is*, what understanding is. Do we really understand the universe better than animals do? Understanding a thing often looks to me like playing with one of those Rubik cubes. Once you have made all the little bricks snap into place, hey presto, you understand. It makes sense if you live inside a Rubik cube, but if you don't..."
> (90, emphasis added)

Here, Costello expresses both her own self-doubt ("what I think") and her doubts about rationality as such ("what thinking is"). This skepticism of rationality is a leitmotif of lesson 3. However, at that point, she seems unable to fully escape the urge to express herself in rational terms. For example, take these two lines: "For, seen from the outside, from a being who is alien to it, reason is simply a vast *tautology*" (70, emphasis added) and "I am alive inside the *contradiction*, dead and alive at the same time" (77, emphasis added). In both cases, her rejection of reason is expressed using the vocabulary of reason itself (e.g., "tautology" and "contradiction"). From the point of view of the literal, rational observer, this is absurd.[13] However, if interpreted in Rortian terms, these sorts of oppositions (between what Costello holds dear and what she is able to express) capture her ambivalence about reason as a final vocabulary. She repeatedly and explicitly rejects reason, yet she has difficulty escaping its terminology. She attempts to rely on another "final vocabulary," poetry, but this, too, fails.[14] She is both aware of the limitations of the "philosophical" and "poetic" vocabularies and, at the same time, unable to overcome them. Thus, according to the first two parts of Rorty's definition, Costello is a liberal ironist.

However, according to the third criterion, she is not. For Rorty, the recognition of the ironic opposition within one's vocabulary allows one to reject *all* vocabularies as final. No vocabulary is "closer to reality" than any other; there is no longer any need for a "power greater than oneself."[15] The ironist recognizes her own vocabulary as contingent. For Rorty, this recognition of contingency is a liberation that makes possible a liberal, public (and utopian) solidarity with others, freeing us from conflicts revolving around differences among private views. For Costello, on the other hand, this recognition of contingency is not a liberation but a tragedy.

This best expression of the tragedy of Costello can be seen in her love of animals. Costello does not see, cannot even imagine, her feelings toward animals as something contingent. For example, vegetarianism is not simply a matter of her own private choice but something she is compelled to speak publicly about[16] not only for ethical reasons but from a deep-seated spiritual necessity.[17] She feels compelled to speak, and yet she cannot communicate the nature of this necessity to anyone. All the other characters in *Elizabeth Costello* are static. None of them are changed or convinced by anything she says. At best, they remark that she has given them "much food for thought" (90). Her lectures convince no one. For a writer, for one whose feelings run so deep, what could be more tragic?

This is where the formal aspects of Coetzee's work become significant. While the characters in the novel may remain unchanged, the reader might not. What Costello cannot say, Coetzee might be able to manage. Coetzee not only expresses the content of Costello's views but also expresses those views in a certain *form*. Through the portrayal of her contradictory manner of expression and the responses of other characters (e.g., pity, doubt, indifference), through the descriptions of her desire to have an effect and the repeated frustrations of that desire, *Elizabeth Costello* the novel says something that Elizabeth Costello the character cannot.

The novel accomplishes this through irony. This irony is not essentially verbal, Socratic, or Rortian. The fundamental opposition, between the beliefs held and the way these beliefs are expressed, suggests the presence of a form of *romantic irony*: an "ironic attitude" or, more precisely, an irony toward attitudes. Naturally, this irony has nothing to do with a lack of seriousness. An ironic attitude imposes a distance between belief and its expression not for the purpose of simple evasiveness but rather for self-awareness of a special sort. Paul de Man, in a discussion of traditional romantics, provides a good description of this purpose:

> What they were against, predominantly, was reason and the enlightenment restriction of reason to a universal human norm. At the same time, they were aware of the paradoxes of a critique of reason. In order to argue against or challenge reason one needed to speak, but such speech would seem to demand understanding and would therefore rely on the very norms of reason it set out to delimit. The only possible response to this predicament would be irony: a speech which at once made a claim to be heard, but which also signaled or gestured to its own limits and incomprehension.[18]

Strikingly, De Man's description of romantic irony seems to conform almost perfectly to *Elizabeth Costello*. Costello rejects reason. Coetzee (through the voices of other characters, Costello's feelings of self doubt, and so on) is clearly aware of the paradoxes involved in such a critique. *Elizabeth Costello* expresses positions on a number of issues but expresses them in such a way as to call attention to their limitations. In terms of form, there is an opposition in the novel between its title character and its author. This opposition is ironic, in the romantic sense, because through the portrayal of both Costello's efforts and their frustration, Coetzee is able to express both these particular views while at the same time taking his distance from them, stepping outside them. As in romantic irony, the purpose of this opposition, this distance, is not evasiveness or self-concealment but a more honest self-awareness. The purpose is to examine one's attitudes from new angles, other perspectives, not for the purpose of relativizing or abandoning them[19] but in order to gesture to something greater, to attempt to express, indirectly, the ineffable.[20]

Once one takes into account this irony, the oppositions expressed in the form of its presentation, *Elizabeth Costello* can no longer be considered exclusively in terms of its particular content, its expression of this or that particular belief. A complete interpretation, one that takes the text as a whole, must address what the text says about the nature of belief as such.

BELIEF AS SUCH

Before exploring the question of belief in *Elizabeth Costello*, it is first necessary to examine the nature of belief from a broader perspective. To begin with, we can take the following as a general philosophical definition of belief: "A mental state, representational in character, taking a proposition (either true or false) as its content and involved, together with motivational factors, in the direction and control of voluntary behaviour."[21] Such a textbook definition is adequate but not complete. It is incomplete because it does not address how beliefs "stick" or become anchored in our minds or souls or how belief might relate to sentiment (except in the phrase "together with motivational factors," which may include a factor such as sentiment). Every day, we believe, in this limited sense, many things. For example, I believe that if I were to turn this door handle the door will open. I also believe that if I look outside when I get up in the morning and if there are clouds in the sky, a state of mind will exist in which I believe it may rain today. This leads me to an "action tendency" in which I bring an umbrella with me when I leave my house. At this basic level, it seems that it would be impossible for a human being to exist without any beliefs at all, as claimed by Elizabeth Costello (199–200).

There are two further analyses of belief that will help us to understand *Elizabeth Costello* better. On the one hand, there is an analysis of belief that is closely tied to knowledge, where "belief" is the same thing as "judgment." According to this view, if a belief is justified by reason, then it becomes knowledge. The founder of this view, Plato, uses the voices of Socrates and his interlocutors in a way similar to the way Coetzee uses Costello and the other characters.[22] Of course, we do not wish to claim that Coetzee is Platonic[23] but rather that in order to analyze Coetzee's view of belief, it is useful to have points of comparison. For the sake of simplicity, we will call this first account of belief B1.

A second analysis of belief (which we will call B2) is one in which knowledge is not the main concern, but probability. In *Elizabeth Costello*, there is no simply "black and white" view of belief in which one must either have a true or false belief concerning *x*, as found in the textbook definition above. Instead, the differing views of belief that we will examine here leave us in an *aporia* but, at the same time, provide a broader perspective regarding belief in general.

Belief as knowledge (B1), according to one definition, "is just as good a guide as knowledge, when it comes to guaranteeing correctness of action."[24] In this case, belief must both be true and useful insofar as it serves as a guide to knowledge and action. But is it necessary to have knowledge in order to take action? An interesting claim regarding B1 concerns how belief becomes anchored in our minds.[25] There is no doubt that human beings—even fictional ones like Elizabeth Costello—have true beliefs, at least at some level, that remain anchored. The problem then, which the text addresses indirectly, lies in how one anchors these true beliefs, thus bringing them to the level of knowledge. But Costello does not feel the need to develop rational grounds for why she believes what she believes. She only requires enough confidence to make her statement "at the gate."[26]

However, there is another view of belief, in terms of probability (B2).[27] B2 is closer to Coetzee's own view than B1.[28] Since most people are *too credulous*, believing everything that they hear, the question lies, "*Wherein consists the difference betwixt incredulity and belief?*"[29] The best that B2 can manage is a steady and habitual feeling. Regarding this point, David Hume writes,

> An opinion or belief is nothing but an idea, that is different from a fiction, not in the nature, or the order of its parts, but in the *manner* of its being conceived. But when I would explain this *manner*, I scarce find any word that fully answers the case, but am obliged to have recourse to every one's feeling, in order to give him a perfect notion of this operation of the mind. An idea assented to *feels* different from a fictitious idea, that the fancy alone presents to us: And this different feeling I endeavour to explain by calling it a superior *force*, or *vivacity*, or *solidity*, or *firmness*, or *steadiness*.[30]

Whereas the treatment of belief in terms of B1 relies on tying beliefs down with reasons in order to become pieces of knowledge, B2 requires nothing other than a firm or steady feeling, and this steadiness "gives them [beliefs] a superior influence on the passions and imagination." The only thing philosophy does, then, is enable one to distinguish "something *felt* by the mind, which distinguishes the ideas of the judgment from the fictions of the imagination. It gives them more force and influence; makes them appear of greater importance; infixes them in the mind; and renders them the governing principles of all our actions."[31]

This distinction between belief as knowledge (B1) and belief as probability (B2) helps us better understand Costello. While she becomes entangled in what it takes to have "foundational"[32] beliefs (that is, either true or false beliefs concerning x, e.g., the killing of animals), there may be degrees of truth and falsity behind or within the nature of belief as such. Keeping in mind this distinction between B1 and B2, we can proceed to discuss Costello and Coetzee's understanding of belief. Regarding Coetzee, Derek Attridge writes:

> The issue of belief is, of course, what has been at stake in all these fictional representations of positions held and debated. Does Coetzee, does the reader, *believe in* what Elizabeth Costello, or Emmanuel Egudu, or Sister Bridget have to say about the treatment of animals, the fictional representations of evil, the oral novel, the value of humanities?[23]

It is precisely this mental state of belief that Coetzee places into question in *Elizabeth Costello*, despite his overt awareness of the epistemological, ethical, and religious issues at stake. Coetzee writes at the beginning of lesson 8, "At the Gate":

> 'Before I can pass through I must make a statement,' she repeats. 'A statement of what?'
> 'Belief. What you believe.'
> 'Belief. Is that all? Not a statement of faith? What if I do not believe? What if I am not a believer?'
> The man shrugs. For the first time he looks directly at her. 'We all believe. We are not cattle. For each of us there is something we believe. Write it down, what you believe. Put it in the statement.'
> (*Elizabeth Costello*, 194)

What is important here is the quality of human belief as opposed to the seemingly "bovine" lack of belief. Cattle need not believe in anything, whether the grass is green or whether God exists. But for humans, according to our initial definition, there is a more elaborate version of belief, that is, a form of belief which takes a proposition as either true or false, and thus is linked to knowledge. The demand of the tribunal "at the gate" is for belief in the first sense (B1), requiring a statement, a *logos*, or an explanation. But what is also important in the "textbook definition," and underlying a more complete discussion of belief are the "motivational factors" or sentiments behind all (particular) beliefs. The assumption behind B2 is that humans will never act from reason alone. We require passions to move us. Since Costello cannot say that she believes or she doesn't, she tries to "suspend judgment until she hears it from his own lips" (167) and is thus left standing at the gate. Costello is forced into an *either* (believe) *or* (not believe) decision, a fixed alternative she attempts to reject. However, what she rejects is not belief as such but only belief as expressed in terms of knowledge (B1). Another sense of belief (B2) remains a possibility.

In an interview some years ago, Coetzee pointed out that he avoids "the structures of opposition, of Either-Or, which I take it as my task to evade." Along with Costello, he seems to suggest the possibility of a strangely disconnected meaning of belief, a state of mind somehow able to disengage from any form of belief whatsoever. He continues:

> Let me simply say that I am not enamored of the Either-Or. I hope that I don't simply evade the Either-Or whenever I am confronted with it. I hope that I at least try to work out what 'underlies' it in each case (if I can use that foundationalist metaphor); and that this response of working-out on the Either-Or isn't read simply as evasion. (If it is, I have been wasting my time.) . . . I try to talk about the Either-Or and about vagueness or slipperiness or other stances (or non-stances) toward the Either-Or in a more philosophical way. A more philosophical way which . . . must also be an appropriately foolish way.[34]

What could this "philosophical way" be? Why is it an "appropriately foolish way"? Coetzee claims to want to "work out" what underlies the opposition of the Either-Or while at the same time rejecting both evasion and resolution of it. The "structures of opposition" he rejects here is the false alternative of the Either-Or, not opposition as such. In fact, the purpose is to explore this opposition more deeply, not to escape it but to dwell within it.

The purpose of this exploration is not a resolution or set of answers (i.e., a statement of particular beliefs, a manifesto) but a better understanding of the question (i.e., "What does it mean to believe?"), thereby achieving greater self-awareness. What is important for Coetzee is not some didactic point in which we are exhorted to believe this or that principle, but rather his continual plea for consciousness of what is at stake. This plea is described, as one article puts it, in terms of the not forgetting of the past.[35] It is not merely animal rights or the history of South Africa or colonialism that is at stake here but a "movement *through* ignorance to attentiveness."[36] Put another way, the universal message of his work thus need not be taken only allegorically.[37]

COETZEE AT THE GATE

Having discussed belief in general terms, we can now return to a greater focus on the text at hand. In this section, we will examine more closely lesson 8, "At the Gate," where *Elizabeth Costello* explicitly discusses belief as such, in which, "as befits someone on the threshold between life and death, Costello finds herself compelled to give an account, or a moral justification, of her life *as a writer*."[38] As in Coetzee's earlier *Age of Iron*,[39] Costello "finds herself in some indefinite limbo between life and death."[40] Her inability to articulate such an account or justification for her belief makes her feel uneasy. There is an explicit tension at the heart of Costello's lack of decisiveness, since she is unable to believe (in terms of B1), let alone justify why or how she does not believe. She states clearly that it is not her profession to believe, just to write, which she says to the man at the gate, stating that she does imitations, "as Aristotle would have said" (194). She can even do imitations of beliefs yet doubts that is enough.

Looking back, we can see that Costello has attempted such justifications several times earlier in the novel. In lesson 3, she tries to use philosophy to support her position. There, she states: "I want to find a way of speaking to fellow human beings that will be cool rather than heated, philosophical rather than polemical, that will bring enlightenment rather than seeking to divide us into the righteous and the sinners, the saved and the damned, the sheep and the goats" (66). Yet for a writer who calls for sympathy, how can a conversation also be "cool rather than heated"? At the same time Costello appeals to the "cool" and the "philosophical," she rejects reason: "I could ask what St Thomas takes to be the being of God, to which he will reply that the being of God is reason. Likewise Plato, likewise Descartes, in their different ways. The universe is built upon reason. God is a God of reason" (67). Her "dilemma" is that she seems to want it both ways, both cool rationality and warm sympathy, a "cold sympathy" without any rational ground.[41]

Trying to work her way out of this dilemma, Costello, discussing Descartes, rejects the opposition of rational thought, on the one hand, and "fullness, embodiedness, the sensation of being . . . a heavily affective sensation" (78), on the other. In place of this dualism, she appeals to the heart, that "seat of a faculty, *sympathy*, that allows us to share at times the being of another" (79). This sympathy is what allows one to "get inside" others, to feel what they feel, to suffer with them. For Costello, this sympathy is, at least potentially, limitless: "Despite Thomas Nagel, who is probably a good man, despite Thomas Aquinas and René Descartes, with whom I have more difficulty in sympathizing, there is no limit to the extent to which we can think ourselves into the being of another. There are no bounds to the sympathetic imagination" (79–80). This "sympathetic imagination" is described as being both opposed to reason (insofar as it is a feeling), and at the same time beyond the opposition.

In lesson 3, Costello extols her audience to "open your heart and listen to what your heart says" (82). When Dean Arendt debates at the dinner table, "I will accept that underlying [your dietary taboos] are genuine moral concerns. But at the same time one must say that our whole superstructure of concern and belief is a closed book to animals themselves," (89) Costello (at this point) accepts the premise but rejects the consequences: "They have no consciousness *therefore*. Therefore what? Therefore we are free to use them for our own ends? Therefore we are free to kill them?" (90). But the premise itself is a problem. If animals have "no consciousness we would recognize as consciousness," that is, if they lack our (human) consciousness, how are we supposed to be able to sympathize with them? If we assume animals do have the same sort of consciousness as humans, then how would we be able to distinguish our sympathetic imagination from a mere projection, a substitution of our experience for theirs?

To where, we might ask, does Costello's strong sympathy for animals disappear by the time we reach lesson 8? When asked for a statement of belief, shouldn't she tell them, "I believe in animal rights"? By this point, it seems as if her convictions have been abandoned or at least forgotten. Whereas earlier Costello stated her positions with some confidence, now, after her failures and frustrations, she searches for "fixed beliefs," beliefs that "stick." In her first statement, she writes,

> I maintain beliefs only provisionally: fixed beliefs would stand in my way. I change beliefs as I change my habitation or my clothes, according to my needs. On these grounds—professional, vocational—I request exemption from a rule of which I now hear for the first time, namely that every petitioner at the gate should hold to one or more beliefs.
>
> (195)

This statement is, as she expects, rejected. What is at stake in this statement, however, are the grounds on which she supports her claim for why she cannot state her beliefs.

Costello claims, as writer, that she is a "disbeliever" (201). It is not simply that she lacks certain required beliefs, but that she is incapable of belief itself. Even when she asks for a glimpse of the other side of the gate, she wonders, "What has she seen? Despite her unbelief, she had expected that what lay beyond this door fashioned of teak and brass but also no doubt of the tissue of allegory would be unimaginable: a light so blinding that earthly senses would be stunned by it. But the light is not unimaginable at all" (196).

Costello's statement—in effect, her grounds—is not sufficient to get her through the gate. Why is this the case? In her second statement, she writes:

> I am a writer, and what I write is what I hear. I am a secretary of the invisible, one of many secretaries over the ages. That is my calling.... Before I can pass on I am required

to state my beliefs... I reply: a good secretary should have no beliefs. It is inappropriate to the function. A secretary should merely be in readiness, waiting for the call.... In my work a belief is a resistance, an obstacle. I try to empty myself of resistances. (199–200)

Yet at the same time, Costello is aware of the fact that, even as a writer, she cannot withhold all particular beliefs. She is aware of the unavoidability, the sheer humanness, of belief. In response to the judge who states twice, "Without beliefs we are not human," she answers,

Of course, gentlemen, I do not claim to be bereft of all belief. I have what I think of as opinions and prejudices, no different in kind from what are commonly called beliefs. When I claim to be a secretary clean of belief I refer to my ideal self, a self capable of holding opinions and prejudices at bay while the word which it is her function to conduct passes through her. (200)

In place of specific beliefs, she offers a meta-reflection on belief as such, an expression of her awareness of how belief works in itself. It is only as an "ideal self" that she can doubt everything.[42] Here, she returns to the dualism she rejected in Descartes, but in another form. For Costello, the dualism is transposed from (real, articulated) beliefs into (ideal, ineffable) heart. It is this dichotomy that allows her to claim, "I have beliefs but I do not believe in them. They are not important enough to believe in. My heart is not in them. My heart and my sense of duty" (200). This attempt to have it both ways, through division between the certainty of the heart and the uncertainty of belief is, from a rational perspective, tenuous and unsatisfying at best.

There is nevertheless a certain level of humility in this distinction. She maintains a provisional cynicism, not taking herself too seriously. Yet at the same time, she retains an (ineffable) attachment to that which she is reluctant to embrace. She cannot formulate any credo, as, when she responds to the question "You are not an unbeliever then" with the following: "No. Unbelief is a belief. A disbeliever, if you will accept the distinction, though sometimes I feel disbelief becomes a credo too" (201). She nevertheless follows her rejection of belief with a more positive conclusion: "Let me add, for your edification: beliefs are not the only ethical supports we have. We can rely on our *hearts* as well. That is all. I have nothing more to say" (203, emphasis added). This view is both unsustainable and unnecessary. It is possible, as we suggest earlier, to reject B1 without rejecting belief as such, without relying on dubious, artificial, and ineffable distinctions. B2 remains a possibility. We can have B2, which enables us to act in the world, without necessarily needing to have B1. Here, Coetzee falls back into the same sort of false alternative Either-Or which he elsewhere claimed to reject, an *aporia* that strongly resembles an inarticulate skepticism.[43] But this is not Costello's last word. She does have more to say, in particular, on the notion of heart, with which she continues to struggle, particularly when asked if she believes in God. This is the question to which, one way or another, all questions of belief appear to ultimately lead. The following pointed passage touches on the very essence of belief:

> 'And these voices that summon you,' says the pudgy man: 'you do not ask where they come from?'
>
> 'No. Not as long as they speak the truth.'
>
> 'And you—you, consulting only your heart, are judge of that truth?'
>
> She nods impatiently. Like the interrogation of Joan of Arc, she thinks. *How do you know where your voices come from?* She cannot stand the literariness of it all. Have they not the wit to come up with something new?
>
> A silence has fallen. 'Go on,' the man says encouragingly.
>
> 'That is all,' she says, 'You asked, I answered.'
>
> 'Do you believe the voices come from God? Do you believe in God?'
>
> Does she believe in God? A question she prefers to keep a wary distance from. Why, even assuming that God exists—whatever *exists* means—should His missive, monarchical slumber be disturbed from below by a clamour of *believes* and *don't believes*, like a plebiscite?
>
> 'That is too intimate... I have nothing to say.'
>
> (204-5)

Costello herself seems desperately to *want* to believe in something. She admits this, for the most part, only to herself, when she is not in front of the judges. "*I believe in the irrepressible human spirit*: that is what she should have told her judges.... *I believe that all humankind is one*" (207). She recalls the passions of her youth (e.g., art) but seems unable to hold on to even these. "Has she carried that childish faith into her late years, and beyond: faith in the artist and his truth?" (207). Later, she even poses a rather physiological option: does the flow of blood count as a belief? "Would they, the bench of judges, the panel of examiners, the tribunal that demands she bare her beliefs—would they be satisfied with this: *I believe that I am? I believe that what stands before you today is I?* Or would that be too much like philosophy, too much like the seminar room?" (210-11). She conjures up a vision of Odysseus in the underworld. She thinks this vision may be "the sum of her faith" (211). This theme is repeated continually in the last moments of the last lesson. When another woman asks, "What are you saying in your confession?" she answers,

"What I said before: that I cannot afford to believe. That in my line of work one has to suspend belief" (213). Even though she grasped at a stream of possibilities, every conviction fails to take hold. In response, another woman waiting at the gate states:

> Unbelief—entertaining all possibilities, floating between opposites—is the mark of a leisurely existence, a leisure existence.... They may say they demand belief, but in practice they will be satisfied with passion. Show them passion and they will let you through.... Who knows what we truly believe.... It is here, buried in our heart ... buried even from ourselves. It is not belief that the boards are after. The effect is enough, the effect of belief. Show them you feel and they will be satisfied.
> (213–14)

Costello moves "through ignorance to attentiveness,"[44] only to move back again to ignorance, albeit in another form. Durrant explains, "While ignorance may simply indicate a profound indifference to other lives, it can also indicate the wisdom of 'knowing not to know,' a state of humility or self-doubt that undoes the logic of self-certainty that founds the Cartesian tradition."[45] But of course, Coetzee casts a much broader net than this one tradition. More fundamentally than narrow reference to any particular thinker, *Elizabeth Costello* questions, through ironies and *aporias*, the nature of philosophical questioning throughout the whole of the Western philosophical tradition, all the way back to Socrates.

In the end, neither this line of questioning nor Elizabeth Costello's attempts at a "both-and" resolution are enough. She remains forever on one side of the gate, caught inarticulately in an opposition, unable to either articulate a belief in something or to abandon her attachment to the possibility of an abstract, ineffable alternative. She wants beliefs without belief, to convince others without reason, justification without grounds, a "heart" without blood. Ultimately, this unresolved conflict is the tragedy of *Elizabeth Costello*.[46]

Notes

1. All references are to J. M. Coetzee, *Elizabeth Costello* (New York: Viking Penguin, 2003).
2. See D. Attridge, *J. M. Coetzee and the Ethics of Reading* (Chicago: University of Chicago Press, 2004), epilogue.
3. Ibid., 193.
4. We are interested here in literary criticism, not biography. For the sake of ease of expression, any subsequent references to "Coetzee" should be understood in a limited sense as references to the author of the text *Elizabeth Costello*, rather than in the more general

sense of a kind of biographical or psychological claim about Coetzee as a person. Or, to put it another way, claims about the author's intent more properly refer to the text as a whole, with the form, content, author's intent, and reader's response each constituting parts of that whole. Thus, claims about "what Coetzee means" (for the purposes of this chapter, as that meaning is expressed in *Elizabeth Costello*) are included in what we mean by "text." On the other hand, claims about "what Coetzee thinks himself" are excluded from consideration.

5. For alternate discussion of the conflict between Elizabeth and Norma, see D. Head, "A Belief in Frogs: J.M. Coetzee's Enduring Faith in Fiction," in *J. M. Coetzee and the Public Intellectual*, ed. J. Poyner (Athens: Ohio University Press, 2006), 100–117, 110–11, where he argues that "Coetzee coaxes his readers to sympathize with Elizabeth rather than Norma, and so to experience the principle by which sympathy is privileged over reason."
6. This criticism is repeated, returning in lesson 6 (*Elizabeth Costello*, 156–57).
7. As found, for example, at the dinner at the end of lesson 3 (*Elizabeth Costello*, 84–90).
8. See, for examples, *Elizabeth Costello*, 23, 62, and 113.
9. R. Rorty, *Contingency, Irony, and Solidarity* (New York: Cambridge University Press, 1989).
10. Ibid., xv. Rorty cites this definition as originating with Judith Shklar.
11. If, of course, one keeps this general definition distinct from Rorty's later, more specifically humanist qualification. Rorty is concerned with human suffering, explicitly distinct from animal suffering (ibid., 36, 177)
12. Ibid., 73.
13. Elizabeth's last remark elicits "a little snort from Norma" (*Elizabeth Costello*, 77). How, for example, could a being alien to reason recognize a tautology? Norma's criticism expresses the point of view of the rationalist "philosopher": "There is no position outside of reason where you can stand and lecture about reason and pass judgment on reason" (93).
14. The end of lesson 4, "The Poets and The Animals," is the moment where Elizabeth breaks down crying in her son's arms (*Elizabeth Costello*, 115). See also her difficulties before the tribunal in lesson 8, discussed later in the chapter.
15. Rorty, *Contingency*, 73.
16. "John, I don't know what I want to do. I just don't want to sit silent" (*Elizabeth Costello*, 104).
17. When asked whether her vegetarianism is grounded in a moral conviction, Elizabeth responds "No, I don't think so. . . . It comes out of a desire to save my soul" (*Elizabeth Costello*, 89)
18. P. de Man, "Semiology and Rhetoric," in *The Norton Anthology of Theory and Criticism*, ed. V. B. Leitch et al. (New York: Norton, 2001), 1514–26, 1515.

19. As is the case for Rorty's "liberal ironist."
20. See this chapter, page 348.
21. Fred Dretske, "Belief," in *The Oxford Companion to Philosophy*, ed. T. Honderich (Oxford: Oxford University Press, 2005), 85.
22. Similarly, but not identically. See this chapter, pages 336–38.
23. The current fashion in Coetzee criticism is to speak of Coetzee as expressing the view of certain postmodern authors, such as Adorno (S. Durrant, "Bearing Witness to Apartheid: J. M. Coetzee's Inconsolable Works of Mourning," *Contemporary Literature* 40, no. 3 [1999]: 430–63), Agamben (S. C. Caton, "Coetzee, Agamben, and the Passion of Abu Ghraib," *American Anthropologist* 108, no. 1 [2006]: 114–23), Arendt (P. Ryan, "A Woman Thinking in Dark Times?: The Absent Presence of Hannah Arendt in J. M. Coetzee's 'Elizabeth Costello and The Problem of Evil,'" *The Journal of Literary Studies* 21, no. 3 [2005]: 277–95), Baudrillard (T. Carstensen, "Shattering the Word-Mirror in *Elizabeth Costello*," *Journal of Commonwealth Literature* 42, no. 1 [2007]: 79–96, 86–87.), Derrida (Attridge, *Coetzee and the Ethics of Reading*), Lyotard (B. Parry, "Speech and Silence in the Fictions of J. M. Coetzee," in *Critical Perspectives on J. M. Coetzee*, ed. G. Huggan and S. Watson [London: Macmillan, 1996], 37–65), Lacan (T. Dovey, *The Novels of J. M. Coetzee: Lacanian Allegories* [Craighall, South Africa: Ad. Donker, 1988]), Levinas (E. Jordaan, "A White South African Liberal as a Hostage to the Other: Reading J. M. Coetzee's *Age of Iron* Through Levinas," *South African Journal of Philosophy* 24, no. 1 [2005]: 22–32), or a combination of many of these (M. Canepari-Labib, *Old Myths–Modern Empires: Power, Language, and Identity in J. M. Coetzee's Work* [New York: Peter Lang, 2005]). We hope to avoid any sort of "projectionist" readings here. While we occasionally refer to the philosophy of belief in philosophical texts like Plato's *Meno* and Hume's *Treatise* as points of contrast, we do not want to run the risk of projecting other philosophers' views into the text at hand. Coetzee is a robust enough author to be understood on his own terms. For two texts that do an excellent job of discussing Coetzee with reference to Plato, see J. Lear, "The Ethical Thought of J. M. Coetzee," *Raritan* 28, no. 1 (2008): 68–97; S. Mulhall, *The Wounded Animal: J. M. Coetzee and the Difficulty of Reality in Literature and Philosophy* (Princeton, N.J.: Princeton University Press, 2009).
24. Plato, *Meno and other Dialogues*, trans. R. Waterfield (Oxford: Oxford University Press, 2005), 138 (97b7-8). In this dialogue, Plato describes the nature of inquiry itself, recollection, hypothesis, and the teachability of knowledge or virtue. For a recent discussion of how these work in the *Meno*, see D. Scott, *Plato's* Meno (Oxford: Oxford University Press, 2006).
25. For the problem of anchoring belief, see Plato: "There's as little point in paying a lot of money for an unrestrained statue of [Daedalus] as there is for a runaway slave: it doesn't stay put. But Daedalus' pieces are so beautiful that they're worth a great deal if they're

anchored. What am I getting at? I mean this to be an analogy for true beliefs. As long as they stay put, true beliefs too constitute a thing of beauty and do nothing but good. The problem is that they tend not to stay for long; they escape from the human soul and this reduces their value, unless they're anchored by working out the reason. And *this anchoring is recollection*, Meno, my friend. . . . When true beliefs are anchored, they become pieces of knowledge and they become stable" (*Meno*, 139 [97e-98a], emphasis added). For a discussion of this passage, see Gail Fine, "Knowledge and True Belief in the *Meno*," *Oxford Studies in Ancient Philosophy* 27 (2004), 41-81; Scott, *Plato's Meno*, 176-93.

26. See this chapter, pages 345-50.
27. For one origin of this view, see D. Hume, *A Treatise of Human Nature*, ed. D. Fate Norton and M. J. Norton (Oxford: Oxford University Press, 2000), chap. 1.3, "Of Knowledge and Probability."
28. See, for example, Coetzee, *Diary of a Bad Year* (London: Harvill Secker, 2007), 97-102.
29. Hume, *A Treatise of Human Nature*, 66 (emphasis in the original).
30. Ibid., 68 (spelling modernized).
31. Ibid.
32. In a different context, Coetzee discusses Descartes at *Elizabeth Costello*, 66-67, 79-80, 92, 106-7, and 112. It is interesting to point out then that, according to Descartes's foundationalism, there are three innate beliefs that foundationally "underlie" everything else: the belief that I exist and am thinking, the belief in God, and the belief in a world. These, for Descartes, are the beliefs that matter and thus become knowledge by means of their clarity and distinctness. See R. Descartes, *Meditations on First Philosophy*, ed. J. Cottingham (Cambridge: Cambridge University Press, 1996).
33. Attridge, *Coetzee and the Ethics of Reading*, 204, emphasis added.
34. "An Interview with J.M. Coetzee," *World Literature Today* 70 (1996): 107-10. See also the review of Coetzee by D. Novitz, *Philosophy and Literature* 21, no. 2 (1997): 482-84, where he writes, "For Coetzee turns out, in these essays, to be a theoretical fence-sitter of a kind that makes all intellectual effort redundant. He does have arguments but he seems whimsically to undermine them—so that in the end he lands up high and dry, deftly buggered by the fence post that he should have scaled" (482).
35. See L. Meskell and L. Weiss, "Coetzee on South Africa's Past: Remembering in the Time of Forgetting," *American Anthropologist* 108, no. 1 (2006): 88-99.
36. S. Durrant, "J. M. Coetzee, Elizabeth Costello, and the Limits of the Sympathetic Imagination," in *J. M. Coetzee and the Public Intellectual*, ed. J. Poyner (Athens: Ohio University Press, 2006), 118-34, 120.
37. See Attridge, *Coetzee and the Ethics of Reading*, chap. 2, for a nonallegorical reading of Coetzee. See also Mulhall's description of Coetzee as a "realist modernist" in chap. 9 of *The Wounded Animal*.

38. F. R. Ankersmit, "The Ethics of History: From the Double Binds of (Moral) Meaning to Experience," *History and Theory* 43, no. 4 (2004): 84–102, 94. See Mulhall, *The Wounded Animal*, 220–30.

39. In Coetzee's 1990 novel, *Age of Iron*, it is "via Elizabeth Curren, an ex-lecturer of Latin—which she describes as 'a dead language . . . a language spoken by the dead'—[that] Coetzee [describes] the discourse of liberal humanism, but . . . it is a discourse that is truly marginal, hovering as it is between life and death" (T. Dovey, "J. M. Coetzee: Writing in the Middle Voice," in *Critical Essays on J. M. Coetzee*, ed. S. Kossew [New York: G. K. Hall, 1998], 18–29, 26). In *Age of Iron*, Coetzee uses another female narrator, 'E.C.' to show the intransigent role of tying down belief. Dominic Head reads Coetzee's narratives as supporting a sentimental view of knowledge and morals, one in which "the risk of pathos and sentimentality is a risk that Coetzee deliberately courts, while simultaneously alerting us to its dangers" ("A Belief in Frogs," 108).

40. Ankersmit, "The Ethics of History," 94.

41. See D. Head, who writes, "Coetzee seeks to make his readers uneasy about the self-interest implicit in humanist reason and rationality, but, in another unsettling maneuver, he takes us beyond a straightforward rational and literal engagement with the arguments" ("A Belief in Frogs," 110).

42. This is also articulated well by Derek Attridge, who writes, "What we encounter are not these characters' beliefs, but their believings; we undergo their speeches and arguments as events, and we share, momentarily, the process of articulating feelings and ideas. . . . 'At the Gate' does not present us with an argument about the place of belief in fiction but enables us to participate in Elizabeth Costello's believing about believing" (Attridge, *Coetzee and the Ethics of Reading*, 205).

43. Hume had already well understood the problem of this sort of skepticism relative to belief when he wrote, "Nature breaks the force of all skeptical arguments in time, and keeps them from having any considerable influence on the understanding" (Hume, *Treatise*, 125).

44. Durrant, "J. M. Coetzee, Elizabeth Costello," 120.

45. Ibid., 120–21.

46. Many thanks to the Leuven Reading Group—Jo, Renée, Sarah, Heidi, Syd, and Julianne—for all the literary discussions over the years. This piece would not have been possible without their contributions.

16

Coetzee's Hidden Polemic with Nietzsche

Alena Dvorakova

This essay has been written on the double assumption that one does not have to be a philosopher to have something to say about Coetzee's fiction and its relationship to philosophy and that what one has to say on the subject may not be best expressed in the form of a philosophical argument. The first assumption is incidental: by training and practice I am a philologist. The second, however, relates to the topic of this essay. What is it that this essay cannot be? By a philosophical argument I understand roughly the kind of procedure where one argues from premises to conclusions and one does so in order to convince others, in as rational manner as one is capable of, of the truth of these conclusions. Implicit in this way of proceeding is the idea that reason is more or less commensurate with reality, that is, that reality (including manmade reality, such as novels) calls for rigorous systematization. Implicit in this way of proceeding is the idea that one may learn something entirely new from reading a philosophical argument, something one has not known before from experience. Also implicit in it is the idea that what one needs most is to know the truth and that the rest (good and justice) will follow.

It seems to me that both Nietzsche's and Coetzee's writings put obstacles in the way of a philosophical paraphrase of the above sort. It also seems to me that this resistance to philosophy is deliberate on the authors' part. What they seem to be questioning in their writings is the power of reason to be the ultimate judge of reality, the ruler of experience, the source of value in individual life and in politics. Nietzsche's objections to all three aspects of this specifically philosophical overvaluation of reason are well known and needn't be rehearsed here. Coetzee's ambivalence about philosophy is a less straightforward matter. First, Coetzee may be said to be a philosopher of a kind in that he is the author of literary-theoretical writings as well as of fiction. Second, his ambivalence about philosophy surfaces only occasionally, for example, in interviews, and therefore tends to be largely inferred from his fiction. This is problematical where the inference is from a literary character (such as Elizabeth Costello) to the author. But there is another of way of gauging his ambivalence. Coetzee is a writer of fiction that does not argue but attacks reason's supposed supremacy *indirectly*, from outside philosophy, by attempting to *subordinate* philosophical discourse to fictional discourse—for example, through parody or in a "hidden polemic," as I describe later. As if Coetzee shared Nietzsche's view of *the* task of the artist in relation to philosophy by enacting it.[1] This task is to reassess a systematically structured "scientific" response to the world by transforming it into an unstructured personal response;[2] to transform a discourse of truth into a discourse of the desire for truth; and, therefore, to use words not to convince by argument but to seduce by appealing to desires (the desire for truth being just one among many).

It is a crucial part of this strategy that the desire for truth be treated either as equivalent to other desires of a far less spiritual and noble kind (such as hunger or the sex drive or, at best, some kind of immoral aestheticism) or as actually being at bottom identical with some other desire similarly "base." And yet there is a kind of paradox involved in attacking philosophy in this way. What this strategy presupposes (what it needs in order to succeed) is precisely the kind of reader reluctant to give up his or her sense that truth is of absolute value, that it is irreducible to anything else. It seems to me that part of the experience of reading Coetzee is seeing that his works tend to presuppose (and to attract) a reader who is, at least initially, oriented above all by his or her desire for truth (rather than for, say, beauty or some other aesthetic value), and therefore a reader who tends to value truth above all else and who "reads for truth" as well. In other words, it is as if Coetzee as well as Nietzsche lay in wait for (*and depended on there being*) a philosopher for whom truth, even if redescribed as a desire for truth, remains a cut above the rest. Only such a truth seeker will be sufficiently alive to an attempt at subverting his or her valuation, to the double suggestion that one's own desire for truth may best be viewed as just one of many (not always appetizing) desires, and, moreover, that it may be the kind of desire whose fulfilment does not necessarily (or even as a rule) make life more just or more beautiful and hence worth living. The desire for truth is thus privileged even as it is disparaged. And this also means that the confrontation enacted by fiction can result neither in a victory over philosophy, nor in some lasting resolution of the conflict of values. Rather, its point is to seduce the truth seeker to another perspective and then to make him forever vacillate between two irreconcilable positions: between knowing the truth and needing (and therefore imagining) the truth to be different; between the believing something because it is true and the making something true by choosing to believe it.

But here it may be objected that inasmuch as this treatise is not a work of fiction, it must be philosophy. Is there no other way of writing that would take place from a critical distance, and yet make a common cause with fiction rather than philosophy? Once again it seems to me that both Coetzee and Nietzsche (and Coetzee in his "hidden polemic" with Nietzsche) point the way to such writing. This would take the awareness of the problem of the value of truth/reason as its starting point. It would pay as much attention to images and narratives as to truths, if not more: in Coetzee's case, to images and narratives of the body, and to the attempt to relegate the desire for truth to its place as one among a number of bodily desires. Experience would be accorded a greater weight than knowledge: that is, one's desire for exposure to experiences of the desirable kind (the beautiful, the good, the just) would be valued more highly than one's need to be convinced of what is beautiful, good, and just by a rational argument. Thus instead of arguing, such writing would primarily report on an experience of exposure—in this case, exposure to fiction, to narratives and images of desire. The form of an exegetical commentary would be more suitable for it than an argument. It follows that rather than trying to convince, such writing would testify (less like a religious believer and more like a recovered alcoholic in an AA meeting). It would testify to the power of a writer's word to reactivate one's desires, as well as to the critical process of sobering up and registering one's disenchantment. Needless to say, this writing could not escape the paradox mentioned above. Inasmuch as one of the desires reactivated by fiction (and perhaps *the* desire reactivated by Coetzee's and Nietzsche's writing) is the desire for truth, this writing, too, must vacillate between a close to absolute belief in truth, and a suspicion of the desire satisfied by this belief.

COETZEE AND NIETZSCHE

I ask in every instance, 'is it hunger or superabundance that has here become creative?'
—Nietzsche, *The Gay Science* V, 370

Hungering souls and overflowing bodies are at the center of "The Humanities in Africa," one of two chapters in *Elizabeth Costello* that I read here as the culmination of Coetzee's hidden polemic with Nietzsche.[3] (The other chapter is "Eros.") Something familiar and yet strange happens to the opposition between hunger and superabundance—for Nietzsche, *the* criterion of value in judging aesthetic (and all other)[4] matters—when Coetzee grasps it anew and reinscribes it into the stories of Elizabeth Costello's experience. Before discussing this and other similar transvaluations of distinctly Nietzschean images, motifs, slogans, and ideas in Coetzee's writing, a few words are needed on how the possibly misleading term "hidden polemic" is to be understood.

The Hidden Polemic

"Hidden polemic" was first used by Mikhail Bakhtin in his *Problemy tvorchestva Dostoevskogo* (Leningrad 1929),[5] to characterize one kind of so-called double-voiced discourses. It describes the uncanny effect, when reading, of two discourses unexpectedly clashing with each other, both in spite and because of their shared interest in a subject, the closeness of their approach to it, or the similarity of their assumptions about it. One of these discourses reads as if it were a more or less indirect attempt to set one's own views apart from the views of the other—without having to acknowledge either the closeness or one's polemical thrust.[6]

In claiming that Coetzee's writing is engaged in a hidden polemic with Nietzsche's, I am not concerned to make a statement about Coetzee's intentions, beliefs, or anxieties of influence. It seems clear from a number of Coetzee's works that their author is familiar with Nietzsche's writings to the point where he feels able to use easily and less easily identifiable Nietzschean "formulae"—such as the "pathos of distance"—to great effect (the effect usually being irony).[7] But Coetzee may be said to be equally familiar with the discourses of a great many writers other than Nietzsche, be they novelists, critics, or philosophers. So in speaking of his hidden polemic with Nietzsche, I voice a suspicion that Nietzsche is not just one of many "voices" that Coetzee as a novelist is free to exploit, in the sense that he could use Nietzschean ideas and turns of phrase for his own purposes (e.g., characterization) without contesting them—that is, without raising the question of belief.

Rather, in reading Coetzee's works one is repeatedly reminded—regardless of the author's intentions or unconscious propensities—of the existence of an other's discourse that needs to be contested even as it is evoked. (Sometimes one can hardly tell *how*.) It is a discourse close to Coetzee's own, in the manner described above, yet whose closeness has remained largely unacknowledged by Coetzee himself and most of his critics.[8] In what follows I try to show that in Coetzee's *Elizabeth Costello* this other, contested discourse is clearly that of Nietzsche's philosophy. The purpose of reading Coetzee from this perspective—*as* (or *as if*) engaged in a contest with Nietzsche—is double: first, it seems to offer an interpretive key to some of the more obscure passages in *Costello*; second, it seems to provide an illuminating perspective on a question often raised about Coetzee's fiction, namely, in what sense is it engaged in a dialogue or in a contest with philosophy?

Philosophy vs. Literature: Telling Truths, Creating Values

"What do ascetic ideals mean?" asks Nietzsche at the beginning of the third essay of *On the Genealogy of Morality*. His answer provides a way of distinguishing between artists on one hand, and scholars on the other.[9] Let us stay with the part of the answer that deals with artists, and therefore also with novelists: "With artists, [ascetic ideals mean] nothing, or too many different things."[10] Artists' first allegiance is neither to truth nor to justice (morality), however much they may protest that it is. This makes them likelier opponents of the ascetic ideal than philosophers or scientists.[11] For my purpose, the ascetic ideal can be defined as an absolute belief in truth, that is, a belief in truth as the highest authority.[12] Or, in an alternative formulation, it is "faith that truth can*not* be assessed or criticized,"[13] as a criterion either of what is most real or of the highest good. According to Nietzsche, it has been typical of scholars that they have not conceived of the value of truth as a problem (however much they may have disputed the nature of truth or the validity of various truths) and, therefore, that they have not appreciated either the extent or the significance of the abysses that open between truth and value in human life. It is art, "in which *lying* sanctifies itself and the *will to deception* has good conscience on its side,"[14] that is fundamentally opposed to philosophy and science, to scholarly resignation vis-à-vis facts, and to scholars' ongoing abstention from creating values.

In what sense does Nietzsche's notion of the ascetic ideal tell us anything about Coetzee's mode of writing, particularly in *Elizabeth Costello*? Let me start with an influential view of Coetzee's mode of engagement with philosophy, suggested, for example, by Peter Singer's response to *The Lives of Animals*.[15] In this view, Coetzee's use of fiction to present philosophical arguments amounts to a dubious stratagem. At best it allows the author to withhold his true beliefs from the reader; at worst it amounts to his hiding behind a fictive character in order to deflect straightforward criticism of his beliefs as candidates for the status of truths. This criticism closely mirrors some of the openly political-literary critiques of Coetzee's novels.[16] Coetzee writes fictions that at best undermine the notion of political commitment (in situations that demand the clarity of such commitment); at worst these fictions are written by the author in order to avoid the need to commit himself to a position, conceived as the truth about a political situation. What kind of *a lack* is it, these philosophical and political critics are asking, that makes Coetzee unable to commit to a belief—that is, to defend it as *the* truth?

In Todorov's review of Coetzee's *Giving Offense*, this lack of commitment to truth and truth telling (as opposed to storytelling) is ascribed directly to the influence on Coetzee of Nietzsche's thought:

> Coetzee's real inspiration . . . is Nietzsche. It was Nietzsche who declared that there are no transcendental values, only wills to power; and that life is the supreme value; and that right is but one force among others, and the law but a form of violence anterior to the others. It was Nietzsche, too, who concluded that truth does not exist, that there are no facts, there are only interpretations, which are more or less powerful. Coetzee agrees with all this.[17]

Todorov's critique comes closest to recognizing in Coetzee's mode of writing a sign of the author's engagement with the Nietzschean "problem of the value of truth." And yet it, too, refuses to see this engagement as a positive act of creation (rather than a nihilistic negation of truth telling): could something other than the arguing of truths be needed, if lives are to be changed for the better through writing? Neither is Todorov sensitive enough to the way in which Coetzee contests Nietzschean criteria of evaluation. In what follows I try to bring out both these aspects of Coetzee's polemic with Nietzsche.

Creating Creators of Values: Coetzee's Costello, Nietzsche's Zarathustra

Coetzee's Costello is best read as a response to Nietzsche's Zarathustra (of the first three parts of *Thus Spoke Zarathustra*). In *Elizabeth Costello* Coetzee has created an adept creator of values who undergoes a symbolic journey marked by strange metamorphoses, comprising a number of travels around the earth. Like Zarathustra, Costello grows from a teacher of virtue (to mostly unreceptive audiences) into a "learner" preoccupied with the redemption of no other than herself.[18]

Costello's travels are Coetzee's way of staging of the problem of truth, as well as his response to the problem, by stressing the role of creation. But little has been said so far about what could be called Coetzee's "geophilosophy."[19] The circumstances of Costello's travels are more than fictional "reality effects" or generic markers of the academic novel.[20] Heat and cold, land and sea, North and South, Europe and Africa; provincial towns in Italy and Australian swamps: these are at the same time places on earth and evaluative perspectives that upstage the territoriality and embodiedness of truths and values. (Some beliefs might make one unable to "bear the heat" of certain places. In some places, because of the heat, some truths might evaporate.) While Nietzsche in *Zarathustra* seems preoccupied with building up conceptions of the *Menschen-Erde* that would open up a space for a newly conceived humanity united by a single goal,[21] in *Costello* the emphasis is on the experience of displacement in a seemingly well globalized world (a world of standardized time zones, air travel, international conferences and prizes, globally recognized novelists, and English-speaking academics). For Nietzsche, the priority is leaving home and achieving, in Zarathustra, the kind of homelessness that is a precondition for the creation of new values. "Where is home and how do I get there?"—the question voiced by Costello on behalf of animals held in captivity finds embodiment in her own physical disorientation, accompanied by a lack of certainty in speech and thought. Costello revalues out of a drive opposite to Zarathustra's.

But one may object here: In what sense is Costello a creator of *new* values? Does she not affirm the desirability of the very *old* value of compassion, in a form parallel to *Zarathustra*'s but in direct contradiction of Zarathustra's final message in part 4 of the work? Given much of the critical reception of Coetzee's works, one would certainly expect that this is where his polemic with Nietzsche might reach its climax. One only needs to cast Nietzsche as the philosopher who categorically denies the value of all pity and compassion (and perhaps also as the philosopher who has no understanding at all of suffering and compassion, as distinct from pity).[22] And then one would go on to contrast Nietzsche's lack of feeling and understanding with the superabundance of figures and narrative events in Coetzee's fiction that confer the highest value on compassion, perhaps even elicit compassion as a readerly response. And yet this expectation of a head-on clash between Nietzsche and Coetzee deserves to be disappointed. It misrepresents both Nietzsche's position on compassion and the novelty of Costello's vision of how embodied beings might ideally relate to one another. As the latter is dealt with in the next part of this essay, let me just indicate how the matter is approached here.

It is part of Costello's predicament that in the world she inhabits the old values (the old gods) no longer seem *effective*, which is to say, they have lost their value. It is no longer enough to refer back to the narratives and arguments that once sufficed to reaffirm the general consensus and justified these values (regardless of whether they were Greek or Christian). These are now thought of as mere myths or religious dogmas, that is, lies. The old values need to be re-created, created anew, which is to say that one needs to find images and narratives with the power to make sense of, and to confer value on, certain evaluative complexes of feelings and thoughts that no longer seem to be necessary. And in this creation of values, it is science that has to be contended with anew, with its absolute demand for truth and truthfulness.

But Costello's predicament goes further. Why has compassion proved to be such a weak force in the modern world? (There never seems to be enough of it around to prevent evil, be it the Holocaust or the mass slaughter of animals.) Here Nietzsche's hints about the power of compassion might suggest an answer. Nietzsche refuses to grant compassion[23] the status of the highest value because it seems to him that it would turn suffering into the most significant fact about human existence and terminally poison the existence of the most fortunate (those who are both lucky and happy). Compassion has the power to deprive the fortunate of the confidence to enjoy their lives, and ultimately it poisons human existence. (Note that what is presupposed in Nietzsche's picture of compassion is both an excess of suffering in the world and an excess of feeling with those who suffer on the part of those who do not.) In the Nietzschean picture, compassion, if elevated into an absolute, works against life, understood as the best that human beings can become. Is it any wonder that people should actively close their eyes to suffering and their hearts to compassion? Even if we took the "message" of Coetzee's works to be the central significance of (human and animal) suffering and the need to respond to it so as not to increase it, it is not at all clear that an exhortation to compassion would be the best answer. Hence the nature of Costello's quest: What is to be the new, more powerful substitute for the old values, in a postreligious but also a postscientific age?

This is why an evaluative interpretation of the progress of Western civilization from its ancient "beginnings" to the present time forms the backdrop to Costello's progress, just as much as Nietzsche's critique of Western history plays this role in *Zarathustra*. From Costello's attack on modern science, her sister Blanche's attack on the humanities,[24] and Chandos's letter to Bacon there arises in Coetzee's book a doubly Nietzschean picture of modernity ruled by the ascetic ideal in the form of science and of the earth as the domain of the "last human," free of all "immortal longings" of the old kind (see *Elizabeth Costello*, 191): "Then the earth has become small, and on it hops the last human being, who makes everything small. His kind is ineradicable, like the flea beetle; the last human being lives longest."[25]

In this interpretation of Western history, a trajectory of learning is implied in the dialogue opened up between Chandos's letter and Costello's words. Chandos appeals to Bacon, a representative of science, to save her and her husband from unbearable revelations, by speaking the language of science that can be likened to a brick-laying exercise. But this is the kind of dismaying thought and speech that in a debased form has prevailed in Costello's world (see her remark on living inside a Rubik's cube: *Elizabeth Costello*, 90).[26] Chandos is in no doubt that her inability to bear the full weight of divine revelation is down to the "smallness" of human existence in the "time of fleas" (229). Costello appeals for a recognition of her plight from a complementary perspective at the other end of this trajectory. Here is someone who stands alone in recognizing the limitations of humanity for what they are, and who finds humanity's shameless embracing of those limitations (as if they were marks of superiority) hard to bear: "This is life. Everyone else comes to terms with it, why can't you? *Why can't you?*" (115). Coetzee's genealogy of our present-day morality is Nietzschean at bottom: we expected science, as born by the humanities, themselves as born by Christianity in its engagement with ancient Greece and Rome in the Renaissance, to become our savior. But the crown of our learning has turned out to be the opposite in Costello's experience—an obstacle to redemption.

Nietzsche and Coetzee come close in the diagnosis of the problem as well as in the method of "solving" it: God may be dead but gods (ideas and images of divinity) are alive in their accounts of value creation. However, the writers part ways in the proposed solutions. Instead of a Nietzschean affirmation of Dionysus (as against both Apollo and "the Crucified"), the best Coetzee can offer Costello is Blanche's half-joking suggestion of replacing Apollo with Orpheus (145)—the reforming priest of Dionysian worship (no meat eating) and the legendary poet able to "move" stones and animals in ways rather different from Bacon's "wall-building" and the scientific experiments of his heirs. But in what sense may Orpheus have provided (may yet provide?) a countercheck to Blanche's triumph? "To move stones, to turn animals into men—is that what you want from me? Oh, if you are still stones and animals, then better look for your Orpheus."[27] Nietzsche implies that expecting salvation from Orpheus is a sign of resignation of one's humanity (in its drive toward self-overcoming) and of a mistaken belief in art as magic. The Orphic magic works in the face of stonelike or animal-like determinacy and passivity. Earthly art is rather an active exercise of value creation. Coetzee's greater skepticism when it comes to the Dionysian art of value creation points to his ambivalence about the very value that art ends up placing above truth (and justice) and sanctifying as a higher authority: that value is desire.

In both Nietzsche and Coetzee it is our passions and desires that have psychological and ontological primacy in grounding our orientation in the world and giving life on earth its *Sinn*.[28] Our passions and desires are necessary to our sense making in a way that our convictions aren't: this is what enables art to lie with good conscience (*Elizabeth Costello*, 88–89). For both Nietzsche and Coetzee, desire is conceived not primarily as a spiritual lack (hunger) but as a superabundance of embodied force—as will to power in Nietzsche,[29] as something akin to gravity in Coetzee. Costello vacillates in her faith in art inasmuch as she sees opening between the real in art (desire) and the good the same gap that she earlier diagnosed between the good and the real in science (truth). She "has begun to wonder whether writing what one desires, any more than reading what one desires, is in itself a good thing" (160). She doubts that art is more than a form of moral adventurousness. Morally speaking, may not souls hungering for salvation be better creators than bodies overflowing with desire? (A question answered with a resounding "No" by Nietzsche.)

The terms of Coetzee's polemic with Nietzsche here help us understand where the otherwise peculiar lesson 1 fits in with the rest of *Elizabeth Costello*. The "simple bridging problem" of realism that Coetzee is trying to solve has little to do with literary form per se and everything to do with the problem of truth and value in art. How do we get from where we are (the world of ugly truths and necessities) to where we want to be (the world of desirable desires)? From where we are, how do we tell the truth without exposing ourselves to obscenities, if not to evil (see *Elizabeth Costello*, 1 and 32–33)? To get where we want to be, how do we create values without lying too much? Can one straddle the divide between the two and do both at the same time?

Nietzsche's hoped-for solution to this problem (at least at some point) was a synthesis of science and the art of value creation in a "philosophy of the future"; his answer to the question was affirmative, even if the affirmation was qualified by its very form (a prophecy). Coetzee seems to be much less sanguine about the future. The eternity Costello finds herself "married to" in the end differs from Zarathustra's in that it is a purgatory or hell rather than a paradise.[30] Instead of an unambiguous affirmation of the eternal return of the same, it represents the eternity of waiting for redemption. Does *Elizabeth Costello* go beyond Costello's predicament? Does it offer a way out of the impasse reached by Western culture at the moment when science has vanquished the humanities and art has lost the power to lead souls, that is, to be an alternative to religion? In *Elizabeth Costello* it is as if Coetzee engages in a similar project to Nietzsche's and yet also turns his back on it. In Costello he seems to embody at least two truths—one concerning the nature of living bodies, the other concerning the question of how one learns from art—that seem to be affirmative of a new ideal of desire and learning and that seem to reconcile fact and value, necessity and desire. And yet, at the same time, we are given forceful hints that this project—Costello's two truths—can be no more than another artist's (beautiful) lies.

DESIRE IN COETZEE AND NIETZSCHE

On How to Move Bodies and Souls

> *Haven't you read your Newton*, she would like to say to the people in the dating agency (would like to say to Nietzsche too if she could get in touch with him)? *Desire runs both ways: A pulls B because B pulls A, and vice versa: that is how you go about building a universe.* . . . The gods and ourselves, whirled helplessly around by the winds of chance, yet pulled equally towards each other, towards not only B and C and D but

towards X and Y and Z and Omega too. Not the least thing, not the last thing but is called to by love.[31]

(*Elizabeth Costello*, 192)

Playing the devil's advocate here, one might suggest that Nietzsche had known better than to stay with Newton: he had studied Roger Boscovich's *Theory of Natural Philosophy*.[32] Building on Newton and Leibniz, Boscovich (1711–1787) offered a new interpretation of the nature of the universe. He would deny there were atoms, extended, indivisible corpuscles completely filled with matter (i.e., plena), that persist through change and in which certain causal powers are located or inhere—namely the power to impart motion. He replaced the corpuscular theory of matter with a theory of force. Force was not to be understood as a relation between two substantial bodies. There were no substances in Boscovich's universe, only attractive and repulsive forces, modeled as "fields" of force surrounding extensionless points.

Nietzsche thought Boscovich's achievement groundbreaking, comparing it to the Copernican revolution. We can imagine his response to Costello's cosmology to be something like this: who can still hope, with Newton, to build a cosmology from atoms and those other small things with nonsense names? They are not things, after all, but the sum of effects of the action of a (probably finite) number of attractive and repulsive forces. We should try to think of such effects as effects of the action of "will upon will."[33] We should attempt to grasp that the existence of A and B, as well as the apparent mutual attraction between them, are summary effects of the will to power. I leave it to you to decide if you would still wish to call this constant process of devouring, of overcoming of force by force, "love."

More is at stake in Costello's quarrel with Nietzsche than the objective nature of the universe. Nietzsche believed Boscovich's theory to have confirmed that ontological concepts used to describe nature—such as "atom" or "substance"—tell us more about the human mind and its needs than about the nonhuman, indeed inhuman, universe. According to Nietzsche, these concepts had first been acquired by the human subject engaged in sensation and self-reflection and only then projected into nature.[34] The concept of the atom is thus a projection of unity derived from our psychical experience and a symptom of the human need to believe in one's own substantial unity;[35] that is, in one's persistence through change and one's causal powers or agency. Boscovich's overthrow of material atomism therefore had implications for our understanding of human subjectivity. Hence in the only overt reference to Boscovich in his published writings, Nietzsche claims him as his ally in the so-called war against "soul atomism."[36]

In what sense can Coetzee be said to show a concern for soul atomism? Perhaps the most influential modern tradition of thinking about the soul and the body that leads to soul atomism begins with Descartes's *Meditations*, on the possibility of knowing anything with certainty. The *res cogitans* is an example of the kind of first-person view of the self or the soul that might be called atomistic and in this context is attacked by Nietzsche as such.[37] It has been noted by a number of critics that in his first-person narratives (especially in *Dusklands*, *In the Heart of the Country*, and *Waiting for the Barbarians*) Coetzee engages in a critique of the Cartesian ego and especially of the way the Cartesian subject construes itself in relation to the world, positing the "I think" as the foundation of epistemic and existential certainty.[38] Coetzee's first-person narrators are constitutionally unable to arrive at any "immediate certainty" by self-reflection. Moreover, their discursive mania is linked with their propensity for various kinds of asceticism. Threatened with uncertainty at the core of their selves, they resort to ascertaining their selves' reality by subjecting their own and others' bodies to painful interrogations. It is the body that is granted if not an ontological, at least an affective primacy in the fictions.[39] This in turn leads to doubts about the power of written fiction—a Cartesian discourse par excellence—to touch on the body rather than just the mind, to move embodied creatures in the right direction.

Primacy of the Body

Coetzee himself has drawn attention to the kind of primacy given the body in his works:

> If I look back over my own fiction, I see a simple (simple-minded?) standard erected. That standard is the body. Whatever else, the body is not 'that which is not,' and the proof that it *is* is the pain it feels. The body with its pain becomes counter to the endless trials of doubt. (One can get away with such crudeness in fiction; one can't in philosophy, I'm sure.)
> (*Doubling the Point*, 248)

One of the questions repeatedly asked about Coetzee's treatment of the mind-body duality is whether any of his characters, for example, the Magistrate in *Waiting for the Barbarians*, arrive at a position at which the unbridgeable opposition between the mind and the body is dissolved (rather than confronted in the extreme or repolarized). No one seems to be picking up on Coetzee's hint quoted here. Granted that the disembodied self cannot be a source of any immediate certainty, in what sense is Coetzee's foregrounding of the body in pain as an immediate certainty more satisfactory? Why might it be indeed too crude—in philosophy? Nietzsche's war against atomism again provides us with a lead. Nietzsche, too, privileges the body as a source and standard of knowledge. But he sees the body as a social structure of impulses and emotions,[40] in effect a commonwealth of mortal souls to which the mind is not something foreign or even opposed but of which it is a tool—of communication and temporary unification that makes for effective action:

> And for us, even those smallest living beings which constitute our body (more correctly: for whose interaction the thing we call 'body' is the best simile—) are not soul-atoms, but rather something growing, struggling, reproducing and dying off again: so that their number alters unsteadily, and our living, like all living, is at once an incessant dying. There are thus in man as many 'consciousnesses' as—at every moment of his existence—there are beings which constitute his body.[41]

One consequence of the Nietzschean take on the body is that all so-called bodily processes of which we become conscious—thoughts and emotions, but also sensations produced by touch as well as by sight and such basic affects as pain and pleasure—are by no means immediately certain. They are *symptoms* of unconscious bodily activity: *signs to be interpreted*. They are abbreviations of the multiplicity of processes that have been thought, felt, and willed unconsciously by the body and evaluated for their overall effect on the forces struggling within its commonwealth, long before their translation into consciousness. Hence bodily pain, too, is "intellectual": dependent on the bodily judgment "harmful."[42]

Nietzsche and Coetzee share a point of departure—the privileging of the body over the mind—and jointly arrive at a point "where bodies are their own signs."[43] Once again they part ways over how to interpret this resistance of bodies to prima facie readability. And here by readability I mean the effacement of the body and its materiality in favor of pure mental contents—the thoughts and emotions experienced consciously by the mind.[44] The body in Nietzsche acts as a spur to interpretation but of a different kind than that practiced in traditional philosophy: the body does not give way to the mind because the mind is not something foreign to the body. It is its tool, in each of its activities, including the best and the worst, the most natural and the most antinatural of its dreams and fantasies. Thus the mind may be used by the body to inflict pain on the body itself: for there is a pleasure to be had from allying oneself with certain of one's own drives over others.[45] The result of such inflicted and self-inflicted cruelty practiced by men on a large scale throughout centuries, in complex ways and with some ingenuity, is culture. Culture, as the product of the mind, is thus not antithetical to nature.[46] The cruel disciplining of the body is inherent in any attempt at a deep understanding. Is there any reason why we should include science and philosophy under this rubric but exclude novels, or indeed any other mode of writing?

Unlike in Nietzsche, the body in Coetzee primarily puts a stop to interpretation. As Brian May has written,

> Coetzee's body is such that the bottom falls out of it—it expresses nothing more than the power to evade or frustrate the expressive metaphors by which we try to know it.... Here, then, bodies signify nothing but themselves. But what if a body that signifies nothing but itself signifies nothing?[47]

May argues that the body in Coetzee is not just a negative limit to the mind's powers. It can also wield creative powers: not just the powers of self-defense, self-repair, and self-delight but also the power of self-expression. According to May it is the texture of the body that "discloses, if nothing else, the possibility of disclosure, thereby stirring a distinctly ethical curiosity."[48] The preconditions for such ethical curiosity are said to be three: "the relaxation of the imperial will"; "the achievement of authentic openness to otherness"; and the possession of a substantial body by which "the approach to the substantial body of the other is mediated."[49] Thus in *Waiting for the Barbarians* the signifying power of the mind (especially in dream and vision) is rejected "except as a medium in which bodies, whether they speak or not, find a way to announce their presence, primacy, and power"[50] Here May has succeeded, even if he himself does not seem to be aware of it, in describing the return of the notion of a *substantial* body in Coetzee: an impenetrable plenum (full of matter, full of its *pull*) quite unlike the penetrable, impregnable, and divisible bodies full of holes and emptinesses omnipresent in Coetzee's fiction.

Coetzee has often described the self in ways that leave no doubt that he understands its supposed unity to be tenuous at best. May's analysis of the body brings us closer to understanding Costello's adherence to atomism in the bodily realm, believed and disbelieved by her author at the same time. This adherence has a political motivation. While the counterpart of the atom in the realm of personal experience is the first-person, self-reflexive subject, in the realm of communal existence, it is the indivisible individual. Such an individual substantial body seems the only conceivable bearer of rights to freedom from interference by external powers. Moreover, as Coetzee's Costello suggests, the individual, substantial body has a positive political function as well. It is the only conceivable seat of a causal power independent of belief, the only truly "given" reality: "I believe in what does not bother to believe in me" (*Elizabeth Costello*, 218). This power is love or, better, a desire of the irresistible and strictly reciprocal kind implied in Costello's cosmology. This desire is a power to impart motion without exercising cruelty, and it offers a tentative answer to tormented questions posed by the likes of Magda and the Magistrate, be they directed toward gods or human beings: "How can I move them?" (*In the Heart of the Country*, 145, par. 257); or "What do I have to do to move you?" (*Waiting for the Barbarians*, 47).

"To the extent that I am taken as a political novelist, it may be because I take it as given that people must be treated as fully responsible beings: psychology is no excuse. Politics, in its wise stupidity, is at one with religion here: one man, one soul: no half measures" (*Doubling the Point*, 249). We might wish to rephrase this dictum as follows: one substantial body, and therefore one soul: no half measures. And to add that art according to Coetzee seems to be at one here with politics and religion in their wise stupidity—is another name for this not *pia fraus*, a pious lie? To come back to Coetzee's engagement with the problem of truth: what is at stake when political commitment is seen as following upon knowing the truth and truth telling? The situation arrived at here is this: in order to promote the desirable in politics one might be forced to lie, for example, about the nature of the body and its desires—or more precisely, one may want to choose to believe in a lie as if it were the truth when the truth would be politically disastrous.

The reimagining of the body as substantial is the first step toward articulating what it means to be a creature longing for salvation, in the worlds envisioned by Costello and her earlier incarnation, Mrs. Curren: "There is no mind, there is no body, there is just I, a creature thrashing about, struggling for air, drowning" (*Age of Iron*, 132). Coetzee's novels hint at the possibility that such worlds might be no more than fictions held onto tooth and nail under the threat of terrifying torture and death—and perhaps for that very reason especially needful to the oppressed and to the old and dying. But they also suggest that only immortal beings—apathetic, curious monsters with no real body of learning (*Elizabeth Costello*, 188–89)—would be in a position to live free of such life-giving illusions.

The Problem With Desire in Elizabeth Costello: The Truth of the Oral

"'Show me what an oral poet can do.' And he laid her out, lay upon her, put his lips to her ears, opened them, breathed his breath into her, showed her" (*Elizabeth Costello*, 58). According to Costello, poetry is in a better position to move creatures than prose inasmuch as it is sense mingled with breath, a unity of mind and body, *Sinn* as both meaning and motion. Yet, by the same measure, poetry is in much greater danger than prose of erasing the difference between the real as truth and the real as desire. After all, the truth of the oral, as Costello calls it, is that the mouth has evolved to satisfy two brutal drives (hunger and the sexual urge) and only by accident gets also to be occasionally used for "singing" (54, see 34). Inasmuch as poets are oriented by hunger and desire in their mingling of sense and breath, the truth of the oral is that they, in Zarathustra's words, "lie too much."[51] Costello herself, although she recommends poetry for its power to move, also has doubts about its source (Emmanuel Egudu, the poet referred to in the above quotation, may be "freigebig" but he is also "kaum zu vertrauen" [57]).[52]

It is characteristic of Costello's "orientation" by desire that the argument on the humanities between her and her sister Blanche is to be decided by the "truth of the oral" revealed to us in the suppressed coda to Costello's letter to Blanche. Costello is said to be convinced that her performing fellatio on Mr. Phillips is an act of (Christian-like) charity: an action that ensues from the swelling (superabundance) of her heart. Thus her own particular experience supposedly testifies to the Christians' victory over the Greeks in opening to human intercourse (both bodily and verbal) a wider range of human experience. In Costello's words, the Christians paradoxically beat the Greeks at their own game: they are better at showing what humans are capable of being (see *Elizabeth Costello*, 139). But should we trust Costello to interpret the scene for us?

She does justice to the difference between her perspective and the perspective of outsiders who might incidentally witness the scene. Missing from her account, however, is any consideration for the presence, in Mr. Phillips, of another substantial body-and-soul that may not be moved by a corresponding desire for intercourse (mouth over eyes, "eating" over seeing). Is the pull of gravity between their bodies Newtonian? (See May's criteria for moving another without transgressing, especially the need to relax one's will.) Is Costello's act of charity not better described as an act of asymmetrical hunger? Her enactment of voracity suggests that will-to-power has once again been rechristened here, by a poet, love.

The fellatio scene shows the problem with Costello's argument on the imaginative writer's authority when speaking on behalf of another. Costello's "sole claim to . . . attention is to have written stories about made-up people" (66). She claims that this particular kind of making up involves a special kind of faculty and activity. The difficulty involved in exercising this skill is said to be the same whether the other exists only as a nonexistent fictive entity or a living, embodied being of a radically different kind from the one who does the thinking into and the making up (80). There is little sign in this account of the difference that an exposure of/to a living body makes: a difference displaced in writing where bodies are not their own signs. In what follows I suggest that Costello's authority as a speaker on behalf of others is actually put to the test in *Elizabeth Costello* where this crucial difference is foregrounded. This move on Coetzee's part has important implications for what kind of learning from fiction is presupposed in his writing.

LEARNING FROM STORYTELLING

Pressure of Desires, Degrees of Exposure

In "The Novel in Africa," Costello takes to the sea. She has decided to accept the offer to lecture on a cruise ship out of a curiosity that, on the face of it, has little to do with writing or with her other great preoccupation, the lives of animals: "She would like to visit Antarctica—not just to see with her own eyes those vast horizons, that barren waste, but to set foot on the seventh and last continent, feel what it is like to be a living, breathing creature in spaces of inhuman cold" (*Elizabeth Costello*, 35). And yet I would argue that, at this point of Costello's seeming disengagement from her two great concerns, we are best able to appreciate her place in the world she inhabits and with it the force of her intermingling discourses on animals and writing.

Costello "would like to feel what it is like to be a living, breathing creature in spaces of inhuman cold." As we go through the lessons in Coetzee's book we realize that her desire for exposure to otherness, to forces that in some way go beyond, exceed (if not transcend) the human, is not a one-off. Some such desire seems to mark her life from her youthful risk taking in love to her less risky but still uncomfortable exposures (of herself and others) in writing and later in classrooms and lecture rooms, all the way down to her willingness to bare her breasts to a dying man, to her "immortal longing" to expose herself to penetration by a god, and to her vision of a universe united by desire where humans are exposed to the pull of stellar gravity. Each lesson in *Elizabeth Costello* is a rendering of such a "fact" of exposure, both an event and an experience of it. (Here again Costello bears close comparison with Zarathustra, whose exposure to the elements—to the cold mountain air, the sea, the extreme heat of the desert—symbolically represents the grounding and testing of his truths.)

One might object that the fact of exposure should not be ascribed to Costello's desire as an effect following a cause (or even a symptom of an underlying pathology?). Is she not a reluctant participant in the events requiring that she expose herself? Does she not use various strategies to hide behind a mask, even as she seems to be exposing herself? ("She has come home with her true self safe, leaving behind an image, false, like all images" [30]). And does she not repeatedly deny or question the desirability of revealing all? (Costello's letter to Blanche remains unposted; cf.

her argument against Paul West in "The Problem of Evil" and her refusal to confess in front of the tribunal in "At the Gate.") In attributing to Costello a preference for exposure, has one willfully ignored what really motivates her, that is, the very different, wholly desirable desire to save her soul? One might bring in the "Postscript" and in Chandos's confession and plea read an allegory of Costello's plight. Chandos's exposure to otherness, unlike her husband's, is not a direct consequence of her longing for it. It comes to her through her love for her husband, who "would gaze like one bewitched at paintings of sirens and dryads, craving to enter their naked, glistening bodies" (227). As long as her heart remains open to her husband, she cannot help sharing his being, both its ecstasy and its madness.

I suggest we shouldn't let Costello interpret where the text that puts her through her motions provides a different perspective on what happens. In Costello, inasmuch as she is a creator of values, a poet is at work, a poet who cannot help but lie too much, especially on desire and love. (In "Eros," for example, a chapter concerned with the supposedly transcendent power of desire and lovemaking, Costello is on her own, free of the need to interact with anybody else. On love she only knows, and converses with, herself.) Another kind of poet is at work in the text that creates Costello, a poet who this time tries to be more truthful by foregrounding the necessity of artistic lies.[53] Costello can afford to keep certain matters unexposed only because Coetzee's text performs those undesirable exposures on her behalf: for example, the docker's violence is given a graphic expression in an otherwise gratuitous one-liner (166); Costello's (surely obscene?) intercourse with Mr. Phillips is described in detail; and so on. The truth about art is that it cannot but excite—expose rather than keep behind the scenes—transgressive desires if it is to achieve its effect. *As* a writer, and therefore as an authoritative speaker on behalf of animals, Costello is given direction by her desire for exposure, which is not absent but merely displaced into her creator's writing.

Understanding Another

Lesson after lesson in *Elizabeth Costello* ends on a note of disgust (1), disenchantment (2), discomfort (3), disharmony and distress bordering on despair (4, 5, Postscript), paralysis (6), or something close to damnation (8). Words fail Costello when she strives to communicate her dismay at her difference from others or even her desire to get to the bottom of that difference. What is it that prevents Costello from reaching her fellow humans; why do her embodied words (as opposed to her fictions) fail to move them? Can it really be just the others' stubborn obtuseness? And, further, how come we, as readers, seem to understand Costello so well (so *pain-*

lessly), whereas those "in touch" with her, even those closest to her, exposed not just to her words but to her living presence, fail? Shouldn't we in the first instance become suspicious of this better understanding we have of her; an understanding that fiction supposedly gives us?

Costello's own explanation of her failure to convince illuminates and misleads at the same time:

> If I do not convince you, that is because my words, here, lack the power to bring home to you the wholeness, the unabstracted unintellectual nature, of that animal being. That is why I urge you to read the poets who return the living, electric being to language; and if the poets do not move you, I urge you to walk, flank to flank, beside the beast that is prodded down the chute to his executioner.
>
> (111)

The passage implies a different way of learning about others (and hence speaking on their behalf with some authority) than the one defended earlier by Costello herself. *Elizabeth Costello* suggests that it is Costello's desire to "expose herself"—to move up and down a certain "ladder'" of love, from abstract discourse to poetry to bodily exposure and back—that provides the link between her authority as writer and her authority as a speaker on behalf of animals. This desire takes the place of, for example, some kind of more or less innate human capacity for thinking oneself into the being of an other while remaining physically absent, seated at a desk somewhere else (whether we want to call this capacity sympathetic imagination or negative capability).

The writer's ability to "share at times the being of another" (79) is the same that makes Costello able to "know what it is like to be a corpse": the kind of thought she thinks humans capable of "if we press ourselves or are pressed" (76–77). But what kind of a thought is this—and what is it that would press us into it? From Costello's first description of the process we get a hint that it is an activity of the body rather than of the mind: it has everything to do with feeling what something is like by literally transplanting oneself into an unfamiliar place, by making oneself inhabit it. Costello's aging body exposes her to the knowledge of what it is like to be a corpse;[54] her bodily exposure to violence gives her a privileged insight into evil; and her eventual exposure to the cold of the Antarctica gives her a knowledge of what it is like to be alive in inhuman spaces.

What presses one into a knowledge of the kind she advocates is desire operating in bodies that physically share a space. It is one's own desires, or the desires of others directed toward oneself—and whether or not one is in a position to act on these desires, to resist them—that have the power to bring this kind of embodied knowledge about. Whether the pressure is internal or external, one needs to be exposed to an embodied experience, "rammed into the face of it" (77), to "know" in the way that Costello advocates, in a way similar to which John, exposed to the sight of his sleeping mother's open mouth, is rammed into the realization that his mother's fleshy innards is where he comes from (34).[55]

Costello inhabits a world hostile not primarily to her words but to her changing body, the more so as she likes to let her body speak its mind. It is her desires and her willingness to act them out that place her in relationships to others that are at best uneasy, at worst hostile—whether those others are her closest kin or the people she is forced to associate with in the course of her travels and travails. Above all else, Costello seems to be a creature moved by desires not shared by others. Their pressure drives her into exposures that do not give direction (make sense) to other bodies. Understanding others in the sense of sharing their being is less about thinking oneself into them and more about moving in close proximity, breathing the same air and eating the same food, feeling the pressure of their bodily presence.

LITERARY REDEMPTION: FEEDING THE HUNGRY OR EXCITING DESIRE TO OVERFLOW?

Nietzsche noted that "no one can extract from things, books included, more than he already knows. What one has no access to through experience one has no ear for."[56] To know oneself, one must act first, reflect afterward, and then act again to validate reflection. And that means one cannot but make mistakes, perhaps bad ones, when one ends up acting on undesirable desires.

The high valuation accorded books of fiction sometimes seems to be based on the idea that learning to be good and just by reading fiction means that one can somehow avoid learning in person, that by exercising one's imagination or by reflection or contemplation one can learn to recognize and get to know *from afar* and *before the act* which desires lead to undesirable actions, and one can also avoid acting on those desires with no loss of learning. In other words, it is often believed that by reading fiction one could come to know what one has no access to through embodied experience. Costello's claim on behalf of books of fiction, their writers, and their readers could be interpreted in this way. Once again, it is as if Coetzee, in his hidden polemic with Nietzsche, were arbitrating between Nietzsche's and Costello's "truths," answering by implication the following questions: What is the relation of the activities of writing and reading fiction to desire? Can the gap between the real (desire) and the good be bridged? Can literature go beyond moral adventurousness and become a vehicle of redemption? Is the kind of exposure necessary to attain the embodied knowledge that Costello is after to be had from writing novels? From reading them?

Both "At the Gate" and the "Postscript" suggest that Costello embodies a perspective from which writing does in fact amount to at least potentially redemptive exposure. The writer's exposure is to the "powers beyond us" (*Elizabeth Costello*, 200). The practice of writerly exposure is described in terms of an embodied experience, an exposure to sounds and sights and other bodily sensations. One may expose oneself to evil in writing and be damaged by it in the exposure. The other danger inherent in such an exposure is enacted in the "Postscript": it is the dissolution of a "rush." (Chandos's experience of "rapture" seems to be reminiscent of the "fullness of being" described in "The Lives of Animals": "To be full of being is to live as a body-soul. One name for the experience of full being is *joy*" [78].) This disintegration, described so as to suggest the process of soul and body coming apart (falling through rotten boards, drowning, or being crawled through or pulled apart from the inside), goes hand in hand with submerging oneself in language that has lost all purchase on nonverbal reality (228–30).

And yet Costello's predicament "At the Gate" bears witness to Coetzee's skepticism about the power of words to do more than gesture toward whatever has been forever displaced in writing—that is, an encounter with a living body. Just as there are degrees of exposure to desire in living, there seem to be degrees of such displacement in writing. Thus in his lectures on *The Lives of Animals*, Coetzee seems to enact a polemical response to Nietzsche's following assertion:

> We should avoid the confusion to which the artist is only too prone, out of psychological contiguity, as the English say, of thinking he were identical with what he can portray, invent and express. In fact, if he really had that same identity he would simply not be able to portray, invent and express it; Homer would not have created Achilles and Goethe would not have created Faust, if Homer had been an Achilles and Goethe a Faust.[57]

Coetzee as the actual speaker of the lectures comes as close to being a Costello as it is possible to be between an embodied human and a fictive creation. He takes it on himself to enact one of Costello's experiences of exposure, foregrounding the similarity and the difference involved in understanding Costello/Coetzee. Thinking oneself into someone else's place is here linked to actually occupying her (kind of) place: bodily proximity, literal or analogical, is the key to this process. Inasmuch as we are willing to engage with the character of Costello as if she were just as embodied as Coetzee, we accede in the assertion of her (and Coetzee's) authority on this question of the power of words in relation to desire and to the kind of learning one can attain through them. But even if we concede that in special circumstances Coetzee as the author can be a Costello, can we as readers ever take their places?

As readers we do not make up people. We are not creators of creators of values that we dare send out into the world in the form of books. We read mostly alone, in private, and we are not moved by the most necessary of Costello's longings,[58] which is to say we do not expose ourselves to others in reading. But there's no replacing the need to expose oneself in acting on one's *own* desires if one is to learn. For the reader, the novel is a limited vehicle of learning if it makes him aware he harbors certain desires. But it is perhaps more important that it should attempt to intensify the pull of these desires, to excite them to overflowing. It seems the real effectiveness of art cannot be divorced from its moral adventurousness in amplifying desire, thus making it potentially transgressive. Learning from fiction seems inseparable from its immorality. The novel undoes the effect of such learning when it encourages us to believe that we learn by disembodiedly thinking ourselves into an other, without having to expose ourselves in bodily actions (i.e., in bodily proximity to an other) both before and after reading. Fictions lie too much if they feed the reader's hunger by fostering the illusion that readers can save their souls by reading—rather than by putting their book down and setting out to travel, in the manner of one Costello, or perhaps even one Don Quixote.

Notes

1. See Nietzsche, *Human, All Too Human*, WS123.
2. See S. L. Gilman, *Nietzschean Parody: An Introduction to Reading Nietzsche* (Bonn: Bouvier Verlag Herbert Grundmann 1976), 15-19.
3. In this section, as in this chapter's introduction, I draw on a paper I first gave at the J. M. Coetzee et les Classiques Conference at University of Limoges in June 2005, since published under the title "'Vous n'avez donc pas lu Newton?' La réponse de Coetzee à Nietzsche ou comment s'y prendre pour mettre un univers en place," in *J. M. Coetzee et la littérature européenne. Écrire contre la barbarie*, ed. Jean-Paul Engélibert (Rennes: Presses Universitaires de Rennes 2007), 73-85. The paper has been heavily revised and greatly extended here so that it now forms but a part of a new argument.
4. See "Points of view for my values: whether out of abundance or out of want?" (Nietzsche, *The Will to Power*, fragment 1009).
5. Bakhtin's theory was more widely disseminated following a new edition of the work under the title *Problemy poetiki Dostoevskogo* (*Problems of Dostoevsky's Poetics*) (Moscow, 1963).

6. "Unlike stylization and parody, each of which adapts another's words to its own intention, hidden polemic does not reproduce another's words with a new intention but rather, directing itself toward its own referential object, strikes a polemical blow at another's discourse on the same theme, the same referential object" (J. P. Zappen, "Mikhail Bakhtin," in *Twentieth-Century Rhetoric and Rhetoricians: Critical Studies and Sources*, ed. M. G. Moran and M. Ballif [Westport, Conn.: Greenwood Press 2000], 7–20).

7. One of the "divine" communications received by Magda in *In the Heart of the Country* paraphrases *On the Genealogy of Morality* 2.16. Nietzsche's ideas on the soul as a "manifold of subjectivity" and on the coexistence of different types of morality in one person (*Beyond Good and Evil*, 12 and 260) come to mind when Dawn in *Dusklands* remarks, "I speak to the broken halves of all our selves and tell them to embrace, loving the worst in us equally with the best" (*Dusklands*, 30). One is reminded of Nietzsche's analysis of the complexity of willing (*Beyond Good and Evil*, 19) when Dawn says, "Giving myself orders is a trick I often play on my habit of obedience" (*Dusklands*, 36). Nietzsche's remark that "fundamentally, 'way down below' in us, there is something unteachable, a bedrock of intellectual destiny, of predestined decision, of answers predestined, selected questions" (*Beyond Good and Evil*, 231) is echoed in *Waiting for the Barbarians* by the Magistrate's lament, "In all of us, deep down, there seems to be something granite and unteachable," which ends on a distinctly Nietzschean note: "And who am I to jeer at life-giving illusions?" (*Waiting for the Barbarians*, 157).

8. With the exception of P. Knox-Shaw's article ("Dusklands: A Metaphysics of Violence," *Commonwealth Novel in English* 2, no. 1 [1983]: 65–81) and Tzvetan Todorov's review of *Giving Offense* ("Tyranny's Last Word," *The New Republic* 18 [November 1996]: 30–34), Nietzsche surfaces in Coetzee criticism only in the form of name-dropping. See D. Attwell's allusions to Nietzsche and the "will to ignorance" in *J. M. Coetzee: South Africa and the Politics of Writing* (Berkeley: University of California Press 1993), 85 and 98–99; B. May's mention of the will to truth of the empire in "J. M. Coetzee and the Question of the Body," *Modern Fiction Studies* 47, no. 2 (Summer 2001): 391–420, 392; or B. Eckstein's reference to Zarathustra in "The Body, the Word, and the State: J. M. Coetzee's Waiting for the Barbarians," *Novel: A Forum of Fiction* 22, no. 2 (1989): 175–98, 194.

9. Nietzsche's term "scholar" is best understood as comprising both present-day academics in the humanities, including philosophers, and scientists.

10. Nietzsche, *On the Genealogy of Morality*, 3.1.

11. Ibid., 3.25.

12. Ibid., 3.24.

13. Ibid., 3.25.

14. Ibid., 3.25.

15. P. Singer, "Reflection," in *The Lives of Animals*, by J. M. Coetzee, ed. A. Gutmann (Princeton, N.J.: Princeton University Press, 2004), 85–91.
16. N. Gordimer's review of *Life and Times of Michael K*, "The Idea of Gardening," *New York Review of Books* 31, no. 1 (February 1984): 3 and 6.
17. Todorov, "Tyranny's Last Word," 31–32.
18. See L. Lampert, *Nietzsche's Teaching: An Interpretation of* Thus Spoke Zarathustra (New Haven, Conn.: Yale University Press, 1986), which stresses the narrative-fictional framework of the work and the necessity to interpret Zarathustra's and Nietzsche's teachings accordingly.
19. Nietzsche was first called the "inventor of geophilosophy" by G. Deleuze and F. Guattari, *What Is Philosophy?* (1991), trans. Hugh Tomlinson and Graham Burchill (London: Verso, 1994), chap. 4. I further rely on G. Shapiro, "Nietzsche on Geophilosophy and Geoaesthetics," in *A Companion to Nietzsche*, ed. K. Ansell-Pearson (Oxford: Blackwell Publishing, 2006), 477–94, concerning Nietzsche's project of constructing a geophilosophical map of thought.
20. M. Garber, "Reflection," in *The Lives of Animals*, by J. M. Coetzee, ed. A. Gutmann (Princeton, N.J.: Princeton University Press, 2004), 73–84.
21. Shapiro, "Nietzsche on Geophilosophy and Geoaesthetics," 480.
22. See M. Nussbaum, "Pity and Mercy: Nietzsche's Stoicism," in *Nietzsche, Genealogy, Morality*, ed. R. Schacht (Berkeley: University of California Press, 1994), 139–67, which argues that Nietzsche lacked an "inner understanding" of the contingency of suffering and its effects and therefore had no real appreciation of the value of compassion. G. von Tevenar, "Nietzsche's Objections to Pity and Compassion," in *Nietzsche and Ethics*, ed. G. von Tevenar (Oxford: Peter Lang, 2007), 263–82, takes issue with Nussbaum's view and argues, to my mind convincingly, that Nietzsche has a profound grasp of suffering and does distinguish between pity and compassion. In what follows I largely accept von Tevenar's conclusions.
23. I.e., the "great Mitleid" of the *Genealogy of Morality* as opposed to the Mitleid of most but not all of *Zarathustra*.
24. Blanche's humanities are none other than Nietzsche's own discipline, philology. The real target of her attack seems to be Nietzsche's high hopes for the future of philology (as a new kind of philosophy of value creation) rather than humanities as currently taught at Western universities, with their pragmatic emphasis on transferable skills and so on. Most of the exchanges between the sisters on the relative merits of the Greeks and the Christians are as if set up to refute Nietzsche's specific objections to Christianity (e.g., its "otherwordliness," see *Elizabeth Costello*, 141).
25. Nietzsche, *Thus Spoke Zarathustra*, 1.prologue.
26. "The philosopher Nietzsche knows where he stands: within a world of decayed Baconianism that has lost all memory of its origins in philosophy, in the rapidity, brevity, and

27. Nietzsche, *The Gay Science*, 4.286.
28. "Direction" as well as "meaning"; see Shapiro, "Nietzsche on Geophilosophy and Geoaesthetics," 481.
29. See especially Nietzsche, *Beyond Good and Evil*, 36.
30. Costello's story of the frogs in "At the Gate" is marked by a similar ambivalence. On one hand, there is the prima facie affirmation of the frogs' life cycle and their joyous singing on resurrection. On the other hand, the frogs bring to mind the chorus of frogs in Aristophanes and with it the specifically Orphic idea of the punishment meted out to souls of murderers, child molesters, and so on in Hades: they are buried in a sticky, filthy mud (see W. K. C. Guthrie, *Orpheus and Greek Religion* [Princeton, N.J.: Princeton University Press, 1993], 160).
31. Costello's interpretation of the third law of motion invites a misunderstanding. As gods are unlikely to be of the same mass as ourselves, we will be neither poised nor moved equally toward one another. There will be little equality between A and B in terms of effect. See I. B. Cohen, "Newton's Concepts of Force and Mass," in *The Cambridge Companion to Newton*, ed. I. B. Cohen (Cambridge: Cambridge University Press 2002), 57–84, 68.
32. The original title of Boscovich's work was *Theoria Philosophia Naturalis Redacta ad Unicam Legem Virium in Natura Existentium* (1758). I draw on accounts of Boscovich's influence on Nietzsche in K. Ansell-Pearson, "Nietzsche's Brave New World of Force," *Pli* 9 (2000): 6–35; P. Poellner, *Nietzsche and Metaphysics* (Oxford: Clarendon Press, 1995), 46–56 ("Atoms and Force"); and J. Hill, "Nietzsche and Boscovich: 'A War to the Knife' Against Soul Atomism," unpublished paper presented at the Nietzsche and Man conference, Charles University, Prague, Czech Republic, June 2–4, 2005.
33. Nietzsche, *Beyond Good and Evil*, 36.
34. Nietzsche, *The Will to Power*, 635–36.
35. Ibid., 632.
36. Nietzsche, *Beyond Good and Evil*, 12.
37. Ibid., 16.
38. See B. Eckstein, "The Body, the Word, and the State," 181. Attwell compares Coetzee's *Dusklands* to Beckett's parody of Cartesian rationality (*J. M. Coetzee*, 37–38). See S. VanZanten Gallagher, *A Story of South Africa: J. M. Coetzee's Fiction in Context* (Cambridge, Mass.: Harvard University Press, 1991), 61. May identifies Magda's self-creations in *In the Heart of the Country* as the only available equivalent of the Cartesian self ("J. M. Coetzee and the Question of the Body," 398).

39. Although Coetzee himself has pointed out that he "would not assert the ethical superiority of pain over pleasure" (*Doubling the Point*, 248), I agree with Brian May that his fiction "asserts its affective primacy" ("J. M. Coetzee and the Question of the Body," 404).
40. See Nietzsche, *Beyond Good and Evil*, 12.
41. Nietzsche, *Writings from the Late Notebooks*, 37 [4].
42. Ibid., 40 [42].
43. See Coetzee, *Foe*, 157.
44. For a detailed discussion of Nietzsche's positing of the body as a text and of every text as a work of the body, see E. Blondel, *Nietzsche: The Body and Culture. Philosophy as a Philological Genealogy* (London: The Athlone Press, 1991), esp. chap. 4, 22–41.
45. Nietzsche, *Beyond Good and Evil*, 229.
46. Blondel makes this point: "The gap that, within nature itself, contrasts culture with nature might precisely be that of desire. But what nature? Might this lack of nature in the self not be specified as the opposition between nature as desire and nature as necessity, which would produce the illusion of an opposition between nature and culture? Culture would then be the name given to the task undertaken by nature as desire to assimilate nature as necessity to itself or assimilate itself to it" (*Nietzsche: The Body and Culture*, 46–47).
47. May, "J. M. Coetzee and the Question of the Body", 410.
48. Ibid., 415.
49. Ibid., 414.
50. Ibid., 416. Nietzsche argues that the source of all mental activity, no matter how antibody or antinature in significance, is the body: a body in which a certain kind of will to power has gained momentary ascendancy over all other wills effective in the body and thus revealed "the physiological demands for preserving a certain type of life" (*Beyond Good and Evil*, par. 3).
51. Nietzsche, *Thus Spoke Zarathustra*, 2: On Poets.
52. The truth of the oral is at the center of *Foe*. Susan Barton's efforts to empower Friday founder on her confusion about whether Friday's tongueless mouth signifies primarily cannibalistic hunger, castrated sexuality, or the lack of his capacity for speech (a symptom of his lacking a soul).
53. Why did Coetzee choose the mask of a woman in Costello? "Because a 'woman' takes so little interest in truth, because in fact she barely even believes in it, the truth, as regards her, does not concern her in the least. It rather is the 'man' who has decided to believe that his discourse on woman or truth might possibly be of any concern to her." (J. Derrida, *Spurs: Nietzsche's Styles/Éperons. Les Styles de Nietzsche* [Chicago: University of Chicago Press, 1979], 63).
54. Is Costello's claim to know what it is like to be a corpse incoherent? One can think of at least two different responses to this objection. One is that an aging and dying body is not

entirely different from a corpse inasmuch as it already participates in death by sharing at least some defining attributes of a corpse (a certain kind of smell being the most prominent of these). Thus one may claim to know what it is like to be a corpse if one can smell the corpse off one's own body. The other response is to see the claim in the context of a challenge that fiction issues to a philosopher: you may know the truth (the impossibility of knowing the unknowable, of imagining the unimaginable), but your truth is useless if what you want is to understand another and share another's experience. What you need now is a different truth, one that you create by imagining what (philosophers say) cannot be known. Beckett's "imagination dead imagine" comes to mind as the ultimate negative expression of this drive that is given a positive form in Costello's experience.

55. In *Age of Iron* Coetzee implies a similar process of learning through exposure. Mrs. Curren's reading of Leo Tolstoy's short story "What Men Live By" suggests a "ladder" of love and learning that depends on differing degrees of exposure to embodiedness: from the highest degree, undergone by the angel Michael, redeemed by his direct embodied experience of mortality, to the lowest degree of learning (the greatest remoteness from embodied experience), ascribed to the reader of Tolstoy's story.

56. Nietzsche, *Ecce Homo*, Why I write such excellent books, 1.

57. Nietzsche, *On the Genealogy of Morality*, 3.4

58. Thus the move from *The Lives of Animals* to *Elizabeth Costello* may seem to lessen the work's potential to promote the desired kind of learning. In the absence of a body, language strains to undo the work of displacement: see Coetzee's overuse of similes that express human experience in animal terms in Costello. Barbara Smuts, "Reflection," in *The Lives of Animals*, by J. M. Coetzee, ed. A. Gutmann (Princeton, N.J.: Princeton University Press, 2004), 107–20, is partly a reaction to this displacement of the body always at work in writing. It is not just that literature is always too much "about animals" as opposed to being the record of an engagement with animals; it is too much about inhabiting another (human) mind rather than sharing a space with another (human and animal) body (see *Elizabeth Costello*, 96).

References

Coetzee, J. M. *Age of Iron*. Harmondsworth, U.K.: Penguin Books, 1998.
———. *Doubling the Point: Essays and Interviews*. Ed. D. Attwell. Cambridge, Mass.: Harvard University Press, 1992.
———. *Dusklands*. London: Secker & Warburg, 1982.
———. *Elizabeth Costello*. London: Secker & Warburg, 2003.
———. *Foe*. London: Penguin Books, 1986.
———. *In the Heart of the Country*. London: Vintage Books, 1999.

———. *The Lives of Animals*. Ed. A. Gutmann. Princeton, N.J.: Princeton University Press, 1999.

———. *Waiting for the Barbarians*. London: Vintage Books, 2004.

Nietzsche, F. *Beyond Good and Evil*. Ed. R.-P. Horstmann and J. Norman. Cambridge: Cambridge University Press, 2002.

———. *Ecce Homo*. Trans. R. J. Hollingdale. Harmondsworth, U.K.: Penguin Books, 1985.

———. *The Gay Science*. Trans. W. Kaufmann. New York: Vintage Books, 1974.

———. *Human, All Too Human*. Trans. R. J. Hollingdale. Cambridge: Cambridge University Press, 1996.

———. *On the Genealogy of Morality*. Ed. K. Ansell-Pearson, trans. C. Diethe. Cambridge: Cambridge University Press, 2004.

———. *Thus Spoke Zarathustra*. Ed. A. del Caro and R. Pippin. Cambridge: Cambridge University Press, 2006.

———. *The Will to Power*. Ed. W. Kaufmann, tran. W. Kaufmann and R. J. Hollingdale. New York: Vintage Books, 1968.

———. *Writings from the Late Notebooks*. Ed. R. Bittner. Cambridge: Cambridge University Press 2003.

Contributors

ELISA AALTOLA is a postdoctoral research fellow affiliated with Manchester Metropolitan University, the Oxford Centre for Animal Ethics, and University of Turku (Finland). Her research interests are in animal and environmental philosophy and the concept of "suffering." She has written numerous papers and two books on animal ethics (*Eläinten moraalinen arvo*, Vastapaino, 2004; *Animal Individuality: Cultural and Moral Categorisations*, University of Turku, 2006), and is currently working on a book on the concept of and meditations concerning animal suffering.

ALICE CRARY is associate professor of philosophy at the New School for Social Research in New York. Her main research and teaching interests are moral philosophy, philosophy and literature, and Wittgenstein. She is the author of *Beyond Moral Judgment* (Harvard, 2007), the editor of *Wittgenstein and the Moral Life: Essays in Honor of Cora Diamond* (MIT, 2007) and the coeditor of *Reading Cavell* (Routledge, 2006) and *The New Wittgenstein* (Routledge, 2000). She is currently working on a book on animals and ethics.

KAREN DAWN is a writer and animal advocate who has hosted talk shows on major radio stations and runs the media watch site DawnWatch.com. She is the author of *Thanking the Monkey: Rethinking the Way We Treat Animals*, which was chosen by the *Washington Post* as one of "Best Books of 2008."

MICHAEL FUNK DECKARD is assistant professor of philosophy at Lenoir-Rhyne University (North Carolina). He is coeditor of two books, *Philosophy Begins in Wonder* and *The Science of Sensibility*, as well as the author of articles on early-modern philosophy, aesthetics, and the relationship of religion, philosophy, and literature.

ALENA DVORAKOVA teaches at the School of Philosophy at University College Dublin in Ireland. Her main interests are literature and philosophy, comparative literature and translation, the nineteenth-century novel, and Nietzsche. She is the author of a number of articles on English fiction. Her most recent work is a study of the relationship between prose and poetry in Nietzsche's writing (forthcoming 2010).

JENNIFER FLYNN is academic fellow at the Joint Centre for Bioethics at the University of Toronto. Her interests are moral philosophy, bioethics, and philosophy and literature.

IDO GEIGER is associate professor of philosophy at Ben-Gurion University of the Negev in Israel. He works mainly on German idealism, especially on Kant and Hegel, and on the intersection of ethics and literature. He is the author of *The Founding Act of Modern Ethical Life: Hegel's Critique of Kant's Moral and Political Philosophy* (Stanford University Press, 2007).

ANDY LAMEY is a Ph.D. student in philosophy at the University of Western Australia. His essays have appeared in *The Journal of Social Philosophy*, *The New Republic*, and *The Times Literary Supplement*.

JONATHAN LEAR is John U. Nef Distinguished Service Professor, Committee on Social Thought/Department of Philosophy, University of Chicago. His other affiliations include faculty positions at the Chicago Institute of Psychoanalysis and the Western New England Institute for Psychoanalysis. His most recent book is *Radical Hope: Ethics in the Face of Cultural Devastation* (Harvard, 2006). He was to present the Tanner Lectures on Human Values at Harvard in the fall of 2009 under the title "Irony and Identity."

ANTON LEIST is professor of philosophy at the Ethics-Center of the University of Zurich. His interests concerning teaching and research include moral philosophy, pragmatism, and applied ethics. His most recent book is *Ethics of Social Relationships*.

JEFF MCMAHAN is professor of philosophy at Rutgers University. He is the author of *The Ethics of Killing: Problems at the Margins of Life* (Oxford, 2002) and *Killing in War* (Oxford, 2009).

RALPH PALM recently defended his dissertation, entitled "Hegel's Concept of Sublation: A Critical Interpretation" at the Katholieke Universiteit Leuven (Catholic University of Leuven). His main research interests are German idealism, political philosophy, and hermeneutics. He is currently working on an article developing the application of statistical methods to the study of philosophical texts.

ROBERT PIPPIN is the Evelyn Stefansson Nef Distinguished Service Professor in the John U. Nef Committee on Social Thought, the Department of Philosophy, and the College at the University of Chicago. He is the author of several books and articles on German idealism and later German philosophy, as well as a book on literature, *Henry James and Modern Moral Life*. His book on film, *Hollywood Westerns and American Myth: The Importance of Howard Hawks and John Ford for Political Philosophy*, will appear in early 2010, as will a new book on Nietzsche, *Nietzsche, Psychology, First Philosophy*. He was twice an Alexander von Humboldt fellow, is a winner of the Mellon Distinguished Achievement Award in the Humanities, was recently a fellow at the Wissenschaftskolleg zu Berlin, is a fellow of the American Academy of Arts and Sciences, and is a member of the American Philosophical Society.

PETER SINGER is Ira W. DeCamp Professor of Bioethics in the University Center for Human Values at Princeton University and Laureate Professor at the University of Melbourne. His books include *Animal Liberation*, *Practical Ethics*, *Rethinking Life and Death*, *One World*, and most recently, *The Life You Can Save*.

ADRIAAN VAN HEERDEN is member of King's College, Cambridge. Adriaan has previously published articles on Foucault and Kierkegaard in international journals, as well as an article on the science vs. religion debate for *Contemporary Review* (UK). He is currently working on an article exploring the idea of the "superman" in Nietzsche and Kierkegaard.

PIETER VERMEULEN is a postdoctoral research fellow at the University of Leuven, Belgium. He has published on the contemporary Anglophone novel and on critical theory. He is also the coeditor of two volumes on the relation between literature and cultural identity and of an issue of the journal *Phrasis* on the work of Adorno. His book on the work of Geoffrey Hartman, *Romanticism After the Holocaust*, is forthcoming in 2010.

SAMANTHA VICE is senior lecturer in the Department of Philosophy at Rhodes University. She is coeditor, with Nafsika Athanassoulis, of *The Moral Life: Essays in Honour of John Cottingham* (Palgrave, 2008) and, with Ward E. Jones, of *Ethics at the Cinema* (forthcoming). She has written articles on impartiality and partiality in ethics, on the concept of the Good, on the narrative self, and on the philosophy of Iris Murdoch.

MARTIN WOESSNER is assistant professor of history and society at the City College of New York's Center for Worker Education. He works primarily in the field of twentieth-century intellectual and cultural history. His reception study, *Heidegger in America*, is forthcoming.

Index

abstraction, particularity vs., 303–4
acknowledgment, disgrace and, 277–80
activism, 133–34
Adorno, T. W., 232–33
aesthetics, 5
Agamben, Giorgio, 232, 237
agency, 24, 35, 38n8
Age of Iron (Coetzee): "Bheki" in, 295, 297, 303–5, 307–10, 312; "Elizabeth Curren" in, 9, 234–37, 293, 295–97, 300–312, 314n28, 315n33, 356n39, 371, 383n55; as epistolary novel, 9, 236; location of, 23; love in, 295–97, 305–12, 314n28; moral point of view of, 293; realms of duty in, 303–5; style of, 298–303; "Vercueil" in, 9, 297, 305–10, 312
allegory, 7, 28, 184, 201–2
alternative animal ethics: critique of, 134–40; elements of, 119–22, 141; standard animal ethics vs., 120–24
amoralism, creativity and, 10–11
analytic animal ethics, 142n24
analytic philosophy, 3–4, 119, 197–98
animal ethics: analytic, 142n24; classical present view in, 221n24; Diamond on, 136–38; experientialism in, 119–20; identification in, 125–28, 140; interaction and, 140; in *The Lives of Animals*, 119–20, 124, 214–17; nature of morality and, 179; in philosophy, 119, 127; polemics of, 124; standard, 120–24, 135. *See also* alternative animal ethics
animals: activism and, 133–34; apes, 116, 121, 154–59, 162–63, 180–81, 213–14, 222n27, 326–27, 338; desire of, 274; in *Diary of a Bad Year*, 115; in *Disgrace*, 10, 52, 54–59, 110–11, 128–31, 134, 146, 148–50, 162, 238–39, 259–61, 281; disgrace and, 147; dog-Antigone and, 146, 148; dog-man and, 43, 54–59; domesticated, 127–28; "Elizabeth Costello" and, 10–13, 38n10, 56–57, 109–17, 120–26, 131–35, 138, 151–54, 178–79, 189, 214–17, 319–24, 327–29, 338–43, 348–49; ethics of sympathy and, 173–81, 186; Holocaust analogy and, 111, 115, 122–23, 131–35, 143nn25–26, 153, 172–74, 178, 181, 188, 339–40; humanity and, 127; killing of, 215; kindness to, 56; in *The Lives of Animals*, 109–10, 113–14, 116, 119–20, 124, 131–34, 146, 150–54, 214–17; in *The Master of Petersburg*, 56; mental abilities of, 134–35, 138; Nobel Prize and, 117; particularity of, 140; postmodernism and, 127; research on, 126; rights of, 321–22; scapegoating and, 172; suffering of, 175, 288n35; treatment

animals (*continued*)
　　of, 10–13, 38n10, 109; vegetarianism and, 110–15, 122, 175, 323; viewpoint of, 125–28; violence against, 150
"Anna K" (fictional character), 201
anthropocentrism, 120, 128, 132, 134, 136, 140, 214, 276–77, 285n10
anthropomorphism, 139–40
Antigone, 146, 148
antilinguist barrier, 206, 220n14
antirealism, 213
anti-reason, as joy, 211–17, 220n14, 221n26
"Anya" (fictional character), 67, 70, 72–75, 85–86
Apartheid: Coetzee during, 8, 187; end of, 43, 49, 54; legacy of, 60, 261; TRC and, 44, 49, 279–80
apes: Red Peter, 116, 121, 154–59, 162–63, 180–81, 213–14, 338; Sultan, 156–58, 163, 222n27, 326–27
archaic ethics, 216–17
archaic postmodernism, 205, 210, 218–19
Arendt, Hannah, 123, 192n27, 232
argument, 211–12, 250–52, 267n5, 325
Aristotle, 44, 46–47, 70, 227–28, 322
ascetic ideals, 361
atomism, 367–69
"At the Gate," in *Elizabeth Costello*, 337, 346–52, 377, 381n30
Attridge, Derek, 51–52, 57, 257, 298, 305, 321, 324, 356n42
Attwell, David, 271, 303, 315n37
authority, 33–34, 74

Bacon, Francis, 164–65, 364
Bakhtin, Mikhail, 360
barbarians: culture of, 211; fear of, 209. *See also Waiting for the Barbarians*
Bartley, Robert, 77
Barton, Susan, 382n52
Bayley, John, 334n36
Bekoff, Marc, 126

belief: in *Elizabeth Costello*, 344–52; as knowledge, 345; nature of, 344–47
Bellow, Saul, 224
Bentham, Jeremy, 175
"Bev Shaw" (fictional character), 55, 162, 179–80, 238–39, 258–60
"Bheki" (fictional character), 295, 297, 303–5, 307–10, 312
bioethics, 332n4
birth, 73
Blair, Bonnie, 94
Blanchot, Maurice, 275
body: "Elizabeth Costello" and, 370–71; in mind-body duality, 368; primacy of, 368–71; suffering of, 234–35, 270–71, 278
Boscovich, Roger, 367
Boyhood (Coetzee), 8–9, 168n17, 329, 333n21
branding, 87nn15–16, 88n21
Burkert, Walter, 182
Bush, George W., 78–79, 87n15, 93, 95, 101–2

calculative rationality, 240
Camus, Albert, 158, 168n17
Cartesian subject, 234, 368
Cavafy, Constantine, 205
Cavell, Stanley, 278
CIA, 82–83, 103–4
citizenship, 78, 84
clarity, 215
Clark, Stephen, 325, 333n32, 334n33
classical literature, 4–5
coercion, 20
Coetzee, John M.: in Apartheid era, 8, 187; authority of, 67–68; *Boyhood* by, 8–9, 168n17, 329, 333n21; characters treated by, 9; critical output regarding, 269; critique of reason and, 223–24; desire and, 365–73; *Doubling the Point* by, 271–73, 275, 277, 279, 282; as "Elizabeth Costello," 171–73, 189, 320, 337–43, 352n4, 377–78, 382n53; ethics of social

relationships and, 8; *Foe* by, 23, 171, 175, 179, 180, 301, 382n52; Girard and, 183, 187-88; *Giving Offense* by, 183, 362; "He and His Man" by, 241; hidden polemic of, 358-61, 377; as "JC," 66-67, 70; "Meat Country" by, 111-13, 115; metaphysics and, 11, 13; moral philosophy and, 249-55; moral psychology and, 43-44; Nietzsche and, 357-66, 376-77, 379n8; Nobel Prize won by, 117, 171, 223; paradoxical oeuvre of, 6-14; philosophers reading, 1, 198, 357; philosophical character of writing by, 6-14, 358-59, 361; political actuality of power and, 22-25; position of, in South Africa, 273; postmodernism of, 33-34, 40n23, 205, 210, 218-19; projectionist readings of, 354n23; *Slow Man* by, 154, 225-26, 282-83; style of, 6-7, 298-303; truth and, 263-65, 271-80; vegetarianism and, 110-15, 122; *Youth* by, 9, 226, 281-82. *See also Age of Iron*; *Diary of a Bad Year*; *Disgrace*; *Dusklands*; *Elizabeth Costello*; *In the Heart of the Country*; *The Life and Times of Michael K*; *The Lives of Animals*; *The Master of Petersburg*; *Waiting for the Barbarians*

cold eye, 295-98, 311
collective guilt, 90-91, 95-100, 102-4, 105n10
collective identity, 92-95
collective pride, 93-94
collective punishment, 98-99, 105n12
collective responsibility, basis for, 100-102
collective shame: avoidance of, 102-4; basis for, 100-102; collective as irreducible bearer of, 95-100; collective identity as basis of, 92-95; novelists and, 100; torture and, 89-90, 92, 103-4; in United States, 78-81, 83, 91-93, 100, 102-4
"Colonel Joll" (fictional character), 206, 263
colonialism, 20, 23, 30, 90

communicative rationality, 240
compassion, 237, 363-64
conceptualist strategy, 3
conduct-morality, 322-23
consciousness, focalized, 299-301
content: form and, 318, 324-31; *The Lives of Animals* and, 320-31; reflection and, 324-31
Contingency, Irony, Solidarity (Rorty), 228
contract theory, 176-78, 186
corpse, 382n54
Crary, Alice, 227, 230
creativity, amoralism and, 10-11
Crist, Eileen, 126
culture: of barbarians, 211; liberal public, 212; study of literature and, 226
cynicism, 272

"David Lurie" (fictional character): in *Disgrace*, 7, 47-59, 60, 62n40, 63n44, 128-31, 146-50, 159, 162-63, 181, 183-85, 238-39, 256, 262, 264, 267n11, 280-82, 300; as dog-man, 43, 54-59; love and, 238-39; mortality of, 280-81; social blindness of, 256, 267n11
death, 73, 235, 277, 281, 382n54
Defoe, Daniel, 171
De Man, Paul, 343
denial, 123, 128
dependence, 19, 21, 36
Derrida, Jacques, 136, 140, 288n35
Descartes, René, 348, 355n32, 368
desire: animal, 274; Coetzee and, 365-73; in *Disgrace*, 50-54, 60, 256-57, 281; "Elizabeth Costello" and, 371-73, 375-76; for exposure to other, 373-74; mimetic, 182; negating, 274-76; Nietzsche and, 365-73; politics of, 187-88; sense making and, 365; sexual, 51-53; writing and, 376-78
Detainee Treatment Act, 81

dialectic of responsibility, 70, 83

dialogue form, 68

Diamond, Cora, 110, 134–38, 168n17, 227, 268n17, 288n35, 322, 325, 328, 332n13, 333n32, 334n33, 334n39

Diary of a Bad Year (Coetzee): animals in, 115; "Anya" in, 67, 70, 72–75, 85–86; ethical thought and, 69–70, 75; guilt in, 78–80, 84; "JC" in, 66–67, 70–86, 91, 109–10, 225; metaphysical ache in, 71, 74, 85–86; moral meanness in, 240; shame in, 78–80, 83–85, 89–91; split pages of, 70, 91; *Strong Opinions* in, 67, 70–75, 85, 104; torture and, 66, 75–78, 80–84, 88n20, 89–91

Discipline and Punish (Foucault), 50

discrimination, institutionalized, 255

disgrace: acknowledgment and, 277–80; animals and, 147; conditions of, 59–60; in *Dusklands*, 44; morality and, 43; moral psychology and, 43, 59; new South Africa in, 52

Disgrace (Coetzee): animals in, 10, 52, 54–59, 110–11, 128–31, 134, 146, 148–50, 162, 238–39, 259–61, 281; "Bev Shaw" in, 55, 162, 179–80, 238–39, 258–60; "David Lurie" in, 7, 47–59, 60, 62n40, 63n44, 128–31, 146–50, 159, 162–63, 181, 183–85, 238–39, 256, 262, 264, 267n11, 280–82, 300; desire in, 50–54, 60, 256–57, 281; dog-man in, 43, 54–59; double open ending of, 163; embedded in *Elizabeth Costello*, 148–49, 158, 163; grace in, 9–10; guilt and, 43–44, 46–47; hope in, 43; identification in, 130, 258; location of, 23; "Lucy Lurie" in, 7, 49, 51–55, 57–59, 162, 184–85, 257–60, 262, 264; "Melanie Isaacs" in, 47–48, 51, 62n40, 147–50, 159, 181, 257, 260; moral philosophy and, 255–62; new South Africa in, 43, 47, 50–55, 58, 60; "Petrus" in, 54–57, 260;

poetics of, 128–31; political charges against, 261, 266; power relations in, 280; private sphere in, 48–50; romanticism in, 48; sacrifice in, 183; shame in, 47–48, 63n41; wellsprings of morality and, 179–80

disintegration, 24–25

dog-Antigone, 146, 148

dog-man, 43, 54–59

domesticated animals, 127–28

Donadio, Rachel, 67

Dostoevsky, Fyodor, 10–11, 56, 271

Doubling the Point (Coetzee), 271–73, 275, 277, 279, 282

dualism, 215

Dusklands (Coetzee): colonization and, 23; disgrace in, 44; "Eugene Dawn" in, 24, 26–29, 37n4, 230–32, 379n7; fantasy of power in, 25–30; pessimism of, 232; political actuality of power and, 23–24; power relations in, 276; reciprocity and, 24

"Duties Concerning Islands" (Midgley), 180

duty, 303–5

ego, 46, 61n17

Eichmann, Adolf, 232

Eliot, George, 299–300

Elizabeth Costello (Coetzee): anti-reason as joy in, 211–17, 220n14, 221n26; "At the Gate" in, 337, 346–52, 377, 381n30; belief in, 344–52; criticism of, 186; *Disgrace* embedded in, 148–49, 158, 163; Girard and, 185; humanities and, 47; irony in, 337–43; learning and, 383n58; love and, 239; motives and themes of, 199–200; "The Novel in Africa" in, 359, 373–76; "The Philosophers and the Animals" in, 152, 172, 283; "The Poets and the Animals" in, 152, 172, 283; postscript to, 164–66; "The Problem of Evil" in, 160–61,

163–64; "Realism" in, 156–57; scapegoating in, 183

"Elizabeth Costello" (fictional character): animals and, 10–13, 38n10, 56–57, 109–17, 120–26, 131–35, 138, 151–54, 178–79, 189, 214–17, 319–24, 327–29, 338–43, 348–49; attack on, 53; belief and, 345–52; body and, 370–71; Coetzee as, 171–73, 189, 320, 337–43, 352n4, 377–78, 382n53; corpse and, 382n54; desire and, 371–73, 375–76; Holocaust analogy of, 55, 111, 115, 122–23, 131–35, 143nn25–26, 153, 172–74, 178, 181, 188, 339–40; humanities and, 48; identification and, 175, 179, 186–87, 284; "John Bernard" and, 111–12, 114, 339; passion and, 263–65; philosophy and, 120–21, 329; Red Peter and, 116, 121, 154–59, 180–81, 338; senility of, 180; Stern's exchange with, 132, 152, 174–75, 178–79, 339–40; values and, 362–66, 374. *See also Elizabeth Costello; The Lives of Animals*

"Elizabeth Curren" (fictional character), 9, 234–37, 293, 295–97, 300–312, 314n28, 315n33, 356n39, 371, 383n55

embeddedness, 148–49, 158, 168n17

emotion, 124, 129, 312

empathy, 215, 217, 223, 230, 236–37, 240

enactive thinking, 329–31

Enlightenment, 2, 5, 27, 232, 235–36, 240

epistolary form, 9, 236, 305–10

ethical ache, 74

ethical thought: Americans and, 78; definition of, 65–66; in *Diary of a Bad Year*, 69–70, 75; ersatz, 66, 70, 75, 86; shame and, 86; writing and, 66–68

ethics: archaic, 216–17; bio-, 332n4; contextualization of, 131; liberation struggles and, 145–46; literature and, 13, 317–18; meta-, 317; of mutual advantage, 186; normative, 317; other and, 297–98;

particularity of, 304; personalized, 124; radical transformation of, 166n5; of social relationships, 8–9; starting point for, 136; virtue, 122–23, 130, 132, 141; writing and, 66–68, 163–66. *See also* animal ethics; sympathy, ethics of

ethnocentrism, 136

"Eugene Dawn" (fictional character), 24, 26–29, 37n4, 230–32, 379n7

existentialism, 225

Exodus, 184–85

experientialism, 119–20

experimental postmodernism, 199–200, 205, 217

externalist view, 126

fact, truth to, 273–74, 279

failed self, 30–35, 39n16

father voice, 231

Foe (Coetzee), 23, 171, 175, 179, 180, 301, 382n52

form: content and, 318, 324–31; dialogue, 68; epistolary, 9, 236, 305–10; *The Lives of Animals* and, 319–31; philosophy and, 317–18; reflection and, 324–31

Foucault, M., 50, 62n38, 221n21

freedom, 203

Fugard, Athol, 55

Furtak, Rick Anthony, 241

Gaita, Raimond, 126, 135–36

games, 198

Gauthier, David, 176, 186–87

gaze, 35, 83–85, 280, 287n30, 299

genealogy, 3–4

Gilbert, Margaret, 96–99

Girard, René, 172–73, 182–88

Giving Offense (Coetzee), 183, 362

God, 54–59, 72, 365

Godwin, William, 294

Goldberg, Samuel, 320–22, 324, 328–29, 333nn19–20, 334n37

393

INDEX

Gómez, Juan Carlos, 126–27
"Good Country People" (O'Connor), 224–25
Gordimer, Nadine, 187
grace, 9–10, 257–58, 271–77
Gray, J. Glenn, 237
Grice, G. R., 177
Gross, Neil, 228
Guantanamo Bay, 77, 84, 87n14
guilt: collective, 90–91, 95–100, 102–4, 105n10; in *Diary of a Bad Year*, 78–80, 84; in *Disgrace*, 43–44, 46–47; of meat eaters, 129; moral, 90; objective, 46–47; personal, 96–98, 105n10; shame and, 89–91; subjective, 46–47

Hacking, Ian, 137, 180–81, 329, 333n21
"He and His Man" (Coetzee), 241
Hegel, G., 22, 24, 32, 37n1, 145, 159, 271, 274
Heidegger, M., 224–25
Heider, Susan, 203, 219n9, 221n20
Herzog, Moses, 224
hierarchy, 20, 33
higher truth, 271–73
historicism, 2–3, 197–98
Hobbes, T., 8, 176–77, 186
Hofmannsthal, H. von, 164–66, 364, 377
Holocaust analogy, 55, 111, 115, 122–23, 131–35, 143nn25–26, 153, 172–74, 178, 181, 188, 339–40
Homo Necans (Burkert), 182
hope, 43
Horkheimer, M., 232–33
"Hulga Hopewell" (fictional character), 224–25
humanities, 47–48
humanity: animals and, 127; meaning of, 35–37, 44, 48, 86, 210; moral superiority of, 190n4; rediscovering, 58
human rights, 235
Hume, David, 186, 345, 356n43
Hunt, Lynn, 235–36

ideal ego, 46, 61n17
identification: in animal ethics, 125–28, 140; in *Disgrace*, 130, 258; "Elizabeth Costello" and, 175, 179, 186–87, 284; sympathetic, 175, 179, 187, 221n20, 283–84, 288n33, 288n35, 319
ideology, 22
imagination, 125, 129, 138–40, 175, 186, 228–30, 240, 283–84, 288n35, 296, 301
impartiality, 294–99, 301–3, 305–6, 310–12
imperialism, 244n35
imperial power, 28
imperial reason, 232
independence, 19, 21, 29, 35
individual: judgment of, 79; society vs., 44–45
institutionalized discrimination, 255
institutions, immoral, 101–2
instrumental thinking, 216
intellectuals, liberal, 76–77, 79–81, 83–84
interdependence, 45
In the Heart of the Country (Coetzee): colonization and, 23; failed self in, 30–35, 39n16; interdependence and, 45; political actuality of power and, 23–25; power relations in, 276; reciprocity and, 24; structure of, 32; suffering in, 31; time frame of, 38n8; unreliable narration in, 32–33
ironist, 341
irony, in *Elizabeth Costello*, 337–43
irrationality, 22
isolation, 32, 44, 209

Jamieson, Dale, 139
"JC" (fictional character): Coetzee as, 66–67, 70; in *Diary of a Bad Year*, 66–67, 70–86, 91, 109–10, 225; *Strong Opinions* by, 67, 70–74, 85, 104
Jesus Christ, 182–83
"John Bernard" (fictional character), 111–12, 114, 339

joy, anti-reason as, 211–17, 220n14, 221n26
"Joy Hopewell" (fictional character), 224–25
justice, 59, 62n28, 176, 221n19

Kafka, F., 84, 154–59, 162–63, 167n14, 180–81, 213–14, 338
Kahn, Herman, 25–26
Kant, I., 5, 176–78, 232
Kirkegaard, S., 68–69, 87n7, 226
knowledge: belief as, 345; Plato and, 1; postmodernism and, 3–4; self-, 28, 300; status of, 2
Köhler, Wolfgang, 156–57, 163, 216, 222n27, 326–27
Kojève, Alexandre, 20, 271, 274–76, 281, 285n10
Kundera, Milan, 228–29

Leahy, Michael, 285
legal morality, 58–59
"Letter of Lord Chandos" (Hofmannsthal), 164–66, 364, 377
liberal certainties, 207–8
liberal intellectuals, 76–77, 79–81, 83–84
liberal ironist, 341
liberalism of fear, 221n19
liberal public culture, 212
Life and Times of Michael K, The (Coetzee): allegory in, 201–2; animal killing in, 215; "Anna K" in, 201; colonization and, 23; history influencing, 205; medical officer in, 201–4; motives and themes of, 199–200, 255; pessimism of, 232; power relations in, 276. *See also* "Michael K"
life-morality, 322–24, 328, 330
linguistic competence, 253
literacy, 245n57
literary characters: as aesthetic constructs, 23; Coetzee's treatment of, 9; emotional deformations of, 226; extremity of, 8–9; intellectuals, 230; in philosophy, 68. *See also specific characters*

literary form. *See* form
literary redemption, 376–78
literature: classical, 4–5; emotional engagement with, 312; empathy and, 240; enactive thinking and, 329–31; ethics and, 13, 317–18; imagination and, 228–29; immorality of, 378; importance of, 226–28, 324–25; innovation in, 5; modern, 4–6, 11–12, 14, 25; moral philosophy and, 250–55, 321; origin of, 168n20; philosophy's relation to, 1–6, 13, 227–30, 240, 250–55, 318–20, 361–62; Plato and, 1, 14; postmodern, 4–5, 11–12; reality transfigured in, 282; on shame, 91; South African subgenres of, 285n2; study of, culture and, 226. *See also* style
"Literature and the Right to Death" (Blanchot), 275
Lives of Animals, The (Coetzee): animal ethics in, 119–20, 124, 214–17; animals in, 109–10, 113–14, 116, 119–20, 124, 131–34, 146, 150–54, 214–17; content and, 320–31; denial in, 128; Diamond on, 136–38; form and, 319–31; Gaita criticizing, 135; learning and, 383n58; lessons of, 163; opening self to others in, 150, 159; personalized insights in, 327–29; philosophy and, 150–51, 321–22; poetics of, 131–34, 152–53, 214–15; rhetoric of, 131; suffering in, 283–85
Lodge, David, 173
loneliness, 30–32
Lösung (final solution), 130, 149, 166n4, 181, 184, 282
love: in *Age of Iron*, 295–97, 305–12, 314n28; "David Lurie" and, 238–39; *Elizabeth Costello* and, 239; impartiality and, 295–97; lessons of, 240–42; moral philosophy and, 246n59; particular, 295; rape and, 150, 159, 162; truth and, 307–12

"Lucy Lurie" (fictional character), 7, 49, 51–55, 57–59, 162, 184–85, 257–60, 262, 264

"Magistrate" (fictional character), 33, 35–37, 37n3, 39n14, 44, 89, 205–10, 220nn14–15, 221n19, 233, 244n38, 300–301, 371
Marx, Elaine, 192n27
Marx, K., 20
master morality, 31
Master of Petersburg, The (Coetzee): animals in, 56; creativity and amoralism in, 10–11; Dostoevsky in, 10–11, 56; location of, 23
mastery, presumption of, 26
materialism, 2–3
May, Brian, 370
McConnell, John, 82
McDowell, John, 139
"Meat Country" (Coetzee), 111–13, 115
medical officer, in *The Life and Times of Michael K*, 201–4
"Melanie Isaacs" (fictional character), 47–48, 51, 62n40, 147–50, 159, 181, 257, 260
Mendieta, Eduardo, 237–38, 245n52
Mentality of Apes, The (Köhler), 156–57, 326
metaethics, 317
metafiction, 26, 269, 271, 276
metaphysical ache, 71, 74, 85–86
metaphysics, 11, 13, 29–30, 326
"Michael K" (fictional character): freedom of, 203; living outside society, 200–204, 219n5, 220n10, 220n14; nature and, 202
Middlemarch (Eliot), 299–300
Midgley, Mary, 172, 175, 177–78, 180–81, 186, 192n27
mimetic desire, 182
mind-body duality, 368
mindlessness, 133–34
modern literature, 4–6, 11–12, 14, 25
modern philosophy, 12
moral awakening, 223, 233

moral guilt, 90
moral improvement, 206, 210
moral instruction, from novels, 235, 311–12
morality: in *Age of Iron*, 293; authentic, 54; conduct-, 322–23; development of, 55; disgrace and, 43; impartiality of, 294–98; legal, 58–59; life-, 322–24, 328, 330; master, 31; nature of, 179; opinions on, 73; outside of rationality, 262–65; pseudo-, 50–51; spiritual, 58–59; theory of, 177; wellsprings of, 179–80
moral judgments, 253–54
moral philosophy, 227, 246n59, 335nn40–41; action in, 322; Coetzee and, 249–55; *Disgrace* and, 255–62; literature and, 250–55, 321; love and, 246n59; metaethics and, 317; personalized insights and, 327; reflection and, 325; responsibilities of, 302
moral psychology, 43–44, 59
Mukasey, Michael, 82
Murdoch, Iris, 226–27, 246n59, 295, 327, 335nn40–41

Nagel, Thomas, 125, 151, 187, 212, 214, 288n33, 295, 348
national shame, 78–81, 83, 92–93
naturalist strategy, 3
nature, 202, 382n46
neoliberalism, 244n35
neo-Puritanism, 50
Nietzsche, F., 3–4, 10, 20, 29, 35, 226, 380n22, 380n24; Coetzee and, 357–66, 376–77, 379n8; desire and, 365–73; *On the Genealogy of Morals* by, 31; *Thus Spoke Zarathustra* by, 362–66
Nobel Prize, 117, 171, 223
normative ethics, 317
novel: epistolary, 9, 236, 305–10; moral instruction from, 235, 311–12; truths in, 318

"Novel in Africa, The," in *Elizabeth Costello*, 359, 373–76
novelistic thinking, 229
novelists: collective shame and, 100; ethical thought and, 66–67; individual lives created by, 241; philosophers and, 224–30, 241
Nussbaum, Martha, 124, 227, 230, 237, 317–18, 322, 327, 332n7, 333nn19–20, 334nn36–37, 380n22

Oakeshott, Michael, 228
objective guilt, 46–47
objective shame, 79, 90
objective truth, 4
O'Connor, Flannery, 224–25
one-leggedness, 225–26, 282–83
On the Genealogy of Morals (Nietzsche), 31
ordinary people, 76–77, 81, 83
other: desire for exposure to, 373–74; epistolary form and, 305–10; ethics and, 297–98; metaphysics of, 11; modalities of, 40n24; opening self to, 150, 159; understanding of, 374–76
outsiders, 45

pain, body in, 234–35
paradoxical truth seeking, 7–8, 10
partiality, 295–98
particularity, 140, 295, 303–4, 314n26
passion, 263–65, 365
pathos of distance, 31, 33, 35
"Paul Rayment" (fictional character), 225–26, 282–83
perfectionism, 120, 141n6
personal guilt, 96–98, 105n10
personalized ethics, 124
personal responsibility, 122–23
personal shame, 96–97
personhood, 126–27
"Petrus" (fictional character), 54–57, 260

Phenomenology of Spirit (Hegel), 22, 32, 145, 271, 274
philosophers: Coetzee read by, 1, 198, 357; novelists and, 224–30, 241; peculiarities of, 224; postmodernist, 3–4, 6
"Philosophers and the Animals, The," in *Elizabeth Costello*, 152, 172, 283
philosophy: analytic, 3–4, 119, 197–98; animal ethics in, 119, 127; in Coetzee's writing, 6–14, 358–59, 361; current endeavors of, 3; "Elizabeth Costello" and, 120–21, 329; form and, 317–18; history of, 1–3; limitations of, 243n30, 329; literary characters in, 68; literature's relation to, 1–6, 13, 227–30, 240, 250–55, 318–20, 361–62; *The Lives of Animals* and, 150–51, 321–22; modern, 12; political, 19–22; reorientation of, 228; of science, 331; shame and, 44; style and, 317–18; as transitional genre, 227, 229; uses of, 71. *See also* moral philosophy
physical disintegration, 24
Piper, Adrian, 301
Plato, 1, 14, 68, 73, 354nn24–25
plural subject, 96
Plutarch, 114–15
poetics: communication with, 141; of *Disgrace*, 128–31; of *The Lives of Animals*, 131–34, 152–53, 214–15; passion and, 264–65; power of, 214, 371–72
"Poets and the Animals, The," in *Elizabeth Costello*, 152, 172, 283
polemics: of animal ethics, 124; hidden, 358–61, 377
political actuality: political philosophy and, 19–22; of power, 22–25
political life, 19–20
political philosophy, 19–22
political violence, 19–20, 184
politics: of desire, 187–88; legitimacy of, 20–21; power and, 19–25; societal arena of, 19

positivism, 243n19

postcolonialism, 20, 33, 269

postmodernism: analytic approach and, 119, 197; animals and, 127; archaic, 205, 210, 218–19; of Coetzee, 33–34, 40n23, 205, 210, 218–19; conceptual skepticism of, 198–99; experimental, 199–200, 205, 217; genealogy and, 3–4; knowledge and, 3–4; literature of, 4–6, 11–12; philosophers of, 3–4, 6; themes of, 25

power: agency and, 24; authority vs., 33; fantasy of, 25–30; imperial, 28; of poetry, 214, 371–72; political actuality of, 22–25; politics and, 19–25; relations, 276, 280

practical identities, 230

pragmatism, 3–4, 12, 205, 207, 218, 220n16

predatory subjectivity, 29–30

pregnancy, 73

pride, collective, 93–94

principles, virtues vs., 122–24

private sphere, 48–50, 221n21

"Problem of Evil, The," in *Elizabeth Costello*, 160–61, 163–64

propaganda, 26–28, 124

pseudo-morality, 50–51

pseudonyms, 68–70, 87n7

psychological disintegration, 24

punishment, collective, 98–99, 105n12

Puritanism, 50–52

racial stereotypes, 207

rape, 51–54, 147, 149–50, 159, 162, 257–59, 261

rationalism, 223, 232

rationality: arguments and, 250–52; calculative, 240; communicative, 240; doubts about, 342; modern, fragility of, 225–26; moral concerns outside of, 262–65; wider conception of, 252, 254–55

rationalization, 47, 80, 233

Rawls, John, 176

"Realism," in *Elizabeth Costello*, 156–57

reality: ache for, 86; literature transfiguring, 282

reason: emotion vs., 124, 129; imperial, 232; as language game, 239; limits of, 230–40; overdependence on, 225; understanding and, 211–12

reason, critique of: body in pain and, 234–35; Coetzee's novels united by, 223–24; fragility of modern rationality in, 225–26; imagination and, 228–30

rebellion, myth of, 27

reciprocity, 24–25, 31, 33

recognition, grace and, 271–77

redemption, literary, 376–78

Red Peter (ape), 116, 121, 154–59, 162–63, 180–81, 213–14, 338

reflection, mode of, 324–31

reflectivity, 6–8, 10

Regan, Tom, 173

relativism, 213

religion, 2, 227–28

"Report to an Academy" (Kafka), 154–59, 167n14, 181, 213–14, 338

responsibility: avoidance of, 321; collective, 100–102; dialectic of, 70, 83; of moral philosophy, 302; personal, 122–23

retribution, 98–99, 105n12

Rhetoric (Aristotle), 46–47

rights: animal, 321–22; basic, 237; human, 235

"Robinson Crusoe" (fictional character), 171, 175, 179, 180

romantic irony, 343

romanticism, 2–3, 48

Rorty, Richard, 3, 198, 221n19, 221n21, 224, 226–27, 230, 239, 243n19, 243n24, 341, 353n11

Rousseau, J. J., 218, 235, 271, 299–300

sacrifice: in *Disgrace*, 183; of Jesus, 182-83; scapegoating and, 181-85
scapegoating: animals and, 172; history of, 183; sacrifice and, 181-85
Scarry, Elaine, 234
Schnurer, Maxwell, 133
science, philosophy of, 331
Seigel, Jerrold, 235
self: dissolution of, 200-204; failed, 30-35, 39n16; opening of, to others, 150, 159
self-improvement: of "Magistrate," 205-10; from suffering, 210
self-knowledge, 28, 300
selflessness, 239
sexual desire, 51-53
shame: in *Diary of a Bad Year*, 78-80, 83-85, 89-91; in *Disgrace*, 47-48, 63n41; ethical thought and, 86; feeling of, 97; gaze and, 83-85; guilt and, 89-91; literatures on, 91; national, 78-81, 83, 92-93; objective, 79, 90; personal, 96-97; philosophy and, 44; subjective, 79. *See also* collective shame
Singer, Peter, 134, 137, 139, 190n4, 321, 361
Slaughter, Joseph, 234, 244n44
sleepiness, 220n15
Slow Man (Coetzee), 154, 225-26, 282-83
Smith, Adam, 186
social contract, 176-78, 186
social control, 45
social relationships, ethics of, 8-9
society: dissolution of self outside of, 200-204; engagement in, 245n57; harmony in, 45; individual vs., 44-45; living outside of, 200-204, 219n5, 220n10, 220n14; political arena of, 19; repressive structures of, 203-4
Socrates, 1, 4, 68, 70, 72-73, 224, 226, 340
Socratic irony, 340
Sophocles, 146

soul atomism, 367-69
South Africa: Coetzee's position in, 273; collective guilt in, 90-91; future civil war in, 200; literary subgenres of, 285n2; new, 43, 47, 50-55, 58, 60
spectacle of embedding, 70, 84
spiritual morality, 58-59
standard animal ethics, 120-24, 135
Stern, Abraham, 132, 152, 174-75, 178-79, 181, 185, 188-89, 218, 339-40
story-report, 155
storytelling, learning from, 373-76
Strong Opinions (JC), 67, 70-75, 85, 104
style: of *Age of Iron*, 298-303; of Coetzee, 6-7, 298-303; philosophy and, 317-18
subjective guilt, 46-47
subjective shame, 79
subjectivity, 29-30
substitutes, 198
suffering: of animals, 175, 288n35; bodily, 234-35, 270-71, 278; fact of, 277-78; in *In the Heart of the Country*, 31; in *The Lives of Animals*, 283-85; news of, 241; self-disintegrating, 25; self-improvement from, 210; thinking and, 217
suicide, 103
Sultan (ape), 156-58, 163, 222n27, 326-27
symbolic action, 102-3
sympathetic identification, 175, 179, 187, 221n20, 283-84, 288n33, 288n35, 319
sympathy, ethics of: animals and, 173-81, 186; appeal of, 187; vicariousness of, 186
systematic truth, 198

Tanner Lectures on Human Values. *See The Lives of Animals*
terrorists, 100, 102
Thus Spoke Zarathustra (Nietzsche), 362-66

torture: Bush and, 78–79, 87n15, 93, 95, 101–2; collective shame and, 89–90, 92, 103–4; in *Diary of a Bad Year*, 66, 75–78, 80–84, 88n20, 89–91; moral guilt and, 90; origin of literature and, 168n20; personal guilt and, 97–98; in *Waiting for the Barbarians*, 25, 35–37, 39n14, 89, 200, 205–11, 233–34; waterboarding, 81–82, 88n20

TRC. *See* Truth and Reconciliation Commission

trust, 9

truth: Coetzee and, 263–65, 271–80; cruelty and, 218; empire dictating, 209; to fact, 273–74, 279; higher, 271–73; love and, 307–12; novels expressing, 318; objective, 4; pursuit of, 263–65, 358; systematic, 198; *Waiting for the Barbarians* and, 272–73; women and, 382n53

Truth and Reconciliation Commission (TRC), 44, 49, 279–80

truth seeking, paradoxical, 7–8, 10

Tutu, Desmond, 43–45, 49

ubuntu, 43–45, 50, 55–56, 60

unbelief, 350, 352

United States: collective shame in, 78–81, 83, 91–93, 100, 102–4; ethical thought and, 78

unreliable narration, 32–33

values, 362–66, 374

vegetarianism, 110–15, 122, 175, 323

vengeance, 184–85

verbal irony, 340

"Vercueil" (fictional character), 9, 297, 305–10, 312

Vernant, J. P., 79, 93

Vietnam, 23–28, 38n7, 230–32

violence: against animals, 150; political, 19–20, 184; rape, 51–54, 147, 149–50, 159, 162, 257–59, 261

virtue ethics, 122–23, 130, 132, 141

Waiting for the Barbarians (Coetzee): animal killing in, 215; "Colonel Joll" in, 206, 263; colonization and, 23; internal critique of, 233; liberal certainties in, 207–8; "Magistrate" of, 33, 35–37, 37n3, 39n14, 44, 89, 205–10, 220nn14–15, 221n19, 233, 244n38, 300–301, 371; meaning of humanity and, 35–37; motives and themes of, 199–200; pessimism of, 232; political actuality of power and, 23, 25; power relations in, 276; reciprocity and, 24; torture in, 25, 35–37, 39n14, 89, 200, 205–11, 233–34; truth and, 272–73

Walker, Margaret Urban, 294, 298, 302, 311–12

waterboarding, 81–82, 88n20

West, Paul, 160

will, 28

Williams, Bernard, 252, 317, 332n10

Wittgenstein, L., 3, 125, 134, 136, 138–39, 144n43, 224, 320

Wolfe, Cary, 136

women, truth and, 382n53

work, 275–76

writing: Coetzee's, philosophical character of, 6–14, 358–59, 361; desire and, 376–78; ethical thought and, 66–68; ethics and, 66–68, 163–66; self-knowledge from, 300

Youth (Coetzee), 9, 226, 281–82

"Zarathustra" (fictional character), 362–66

Zionism, 185, 188–89, 192n27